Year Zero of the Arab-Israeli Conflict

The Schusterman Series in Israel Studies

Editors ➤ S. Ilan Troen ➤ Jehuda Reinharz ➤ Sylvia Fuks Fried

The Schusterman Series in Israel Studies publishes original scholarship of exceptional significance on the history of Zionism and the State of Israel. It draws on disciplines across the academy, from anthropology, sociology, political science, and international relations to the arts, history, and literature. It seeks to further an understanding of Israel within the context of the modern Middle East and the modern Jewish experience. There is special interest in developing publications that enrich the university curriculum and enlighten the public at large. The series is published under the auspices of the Schusterman Center for Israel Studies at Brandeis University.

For a complete list of books in this series, please see www.upne.com

ISRAEL INSTITUTE

*Published in
cooperation with the
Israel Institute*

YEAR ZERO OF THE ARAB-ISRAELI CONFLICT 1929

Hillel Cohen

Translated by Haim Watzman

Brandeis University Press ➤ Waltham, Massachusetts

Brandeis University Press

An imprint of University Press of New England

www.upne.com

© 2015 Brandeis University

Manufactured in the United States of America

Designed by Eric M. Brooks

Typeset in Minion by Passumpsic Publishing

Published in Hebrew as *TaRPa"T: shnat haefes basikhsukh
hayehudi-aravi* by Keter Jerusalem, 2013

Library of Congress Cataloging-in-Publication Data

Cohen, Hillel, author.

[Tarpat. English.]

Year Zero of the Arab-Israeli Conflict 1929 / Hillel Cohen;
translated by Haim Watzman.

    pages cm. — (The Schusterman series in Israel studies)

"Published in cooperation with the Israel Institute."

Includes bibliographical references.

ISBN 978-1-61168-810-8 (cloth: alk. paper) —

ISBN 978-1-61168-811-5 (pbk.: alk. paper) —

ISBN 978-1-61168-812-2 (ebook)

1. Arab-Israeli conflict — History. 2. Jewish-Arab relations.

3. Palestine — History — Arab riots, 1929. I. Title.

DS119.7.C6323413   2015

956.94'04—dc23   2015004536

10 9 8 7 6

Dedicated to the rescuers,
   Jews and Arabs,
and to the memory of my parents,
   Esther and Aharon

Contents

Introduction

Why 1929?

➤ Because it is impossible to understand Jewish-Arab relations in the Land of Israel–Palestine without understanding the events of 1929 (the year TaRPa"T, according to the Hebrew calendar).

➤ Because in August 1929 the fears and hopes of the Arabs of Palestine collided head-on with the aspirations and frustrations of the Jews. For the first time since the two nations encountered each other in this land, the clash left in its wake hundreds of mutilated and charred bodies. During the course of the riots, many — perhaps most — Jews and Arabs came to believe that they were caught in an unbearable, bloody conflict with each other, and this view became indelibly fixed in their minds.

➤ Because many people speak of the Israel-Arab conflict as if it began in 1967 and as if that year is the key to understanding it and finding a solution. Others maintain that it was the Nakba (the catastrophe that befell the Arabs of Palestine) and the establishment of the state of Israel in 1948 that should be taken as the baseline. I maintain that we need to go back farther, to 1929. Not because it is the real starting point of the conflict (I will devote part of the first chapter to the question of when it all began), but because it is the year in which relations between Jews and Arabs changed radically, the year that shaped the consciousness of both sides for decades thereafter.

➤ Because 1929 was very much in the minds of the Jewish forces fighting in 1948. In this book, you will meet soldiers and commanders who saw combat in 1948 but whose worldviews were shaped by their experiences in 1929.

➤ Because it was the attacks on Jewish communities in 1929 that forged the Yishuv — the Jewish community in Palestine under the British Mandate. Jews who had kept their distance from the Zionist movement drew closer to it, and Zionist institutions accelerated their work to bring the Jews of Middle Eastern and North African origin under the movement's wing.

➤ Because the victims of the 1929 massacres came largely from the ranks of the long-established Mizrahi, Maghrebi, and religious Jewish communities that predated the Zionist influx. The new Zionist settlements were largely able to repel the attackers with the help of the Haganah (the Yishuv's defense force), which demonstrated its effectiveness. This granted the Haganah great prestige in the non-Zionist communities, for which security now became a first priority that overshadowed whatever reservations they had about the Zionists. These communities thus came to accept Zionist leadership at least in the security realm, giving birth to the Zionist military ethos.

➤ Because 1929 is the starting point for a journey to the roots of Jewish life in the Land of Israel, of the long-time Arab experience in Palestine, and the causes of violence and bloodshed between the two.

➤ Because in Jewish historical memory the riots of 1929 became emblematic of Arab savagery, serving as ostensible proof that Arabs thirst for Jewish blood. At the same time, in the view of the Arabs, the disturbances were a legitimate national uprising. It is important to understand how two different publics can understand the same events in such different ways. While the broad strokes of the Jewish version of the story of 1929 are familiar to most readers of Hebrew, and to readers of English and other languages who have read Zionist and Israeli accounts of the riots, most people are ignorant of many details. Furthermore, the Palestinian understanding of the events is barely known to outsiders, and it includes elements that may well surprise readers of this book. Beyond its place and time and the Palestinian-Israeli context, the story of 1929 affords an opportunity to consider the larger issue of truth and fabrication in historical writing.

➤ Because, astonishingly, the events of 1929, the Yishuv's greatest trauma during the period of the Mandate, have not been the subject of a book by an Israeli author since 1930. True, the riots are addressed, briefly or extensively, in books on the Mandate period, and memorial books were written about the victims in Hebron and Safed. But no Israeli overview of the events, nor any overview of the events from both Jewish and Arab perspectives, has ever been written.

➤ Finally, I have visited Hebron many times. I have spoken at length with both Arabs and Jews in this city over which the memory of 1929 still hangs like a dark cloud. These conversations have impelled me to try to tell the story of the two peoples and their aspirations, hopes and crises, and their moments of transcendence and their moments of madness. My aim has been to understand, not to argue or justify or indict. I offer this attempt in full awareness of the limits of my ability to enter into the consciousness of a Jew who lived in Palestine in the 1920s, let alone the mind of a Palestinian Arab of the same period. But it is important to try.

The process of writing a book of history, and as a consequence, the creation of a larger historical corpus, has two aspects: inclusive and exclusive. Historians write what they want to present to their readers, while at the same time not writing everything else. Why don't they include everything? Well, in the first place, a written account of everything that happened on even a single day would take weeks or even months to write and to read. For this reason alone, historians must make choices about what to include and what to leave out. The basis for their choices is simple — they include in their books the things that seem significant to them, and they leave out everything that seems irrelevant. Bear in mind that decisions about the level of importance of each fact, idea, argument, or document are made by each individual historian, based on his or her understanding of history. But there are other reasons to exclude something. A history book might neglect significant events or details because they did not come to the attention of the historian, perhaps because they left no trace in the available sources, or because research did not turn them up. And a historian may shunt aside some matters despite their importance, simply because they do not touch directly on the question he or she chooses to study.

Furthermore, there are details, and processes as well, that historians simply do not notice because of the paradigms through which they think or because of their preconceptions. And, of course, it is hardly uncommon for books to be written with the primary purpose of covering up some events by writing about others. In such cases, historical writers tell a particular story from a particular point of view to confer exclusivity on that story, and in so doing to diminish the force of other events and other experiences in the same period.

I can understand those who present just one side of a historic conflict. In this book I quote many writers, both Jewish and Arab, who chose to do exactly that. But the goal of the present book is to paint a broad canvas showing as many points of view as possible. I do not seek to make the picture on either the Arab or Jewish side look pretty, but neither do I seek to sully it. In other words, both a reader who wants to read a book about 1929 to reinforce the picture he already has about Arab barbarity and a reader whose interest is to prove that the Jews are bloodthirsty are likely to be disappointed. I offer instead an unhurried and complex view of the past. I aim not to prove a preexisting thesis, but rather to get to the roots of different understandings of these events, and the different experiences of those who lived through the period.

This book's inclusive approach does not require it to stand above national history — that is, to be anational. I do not overlook national sentiment or disregard the power of national identities, nor do I affect neutrality. This book is inclusive because my purpose is not, at least not consciously, to reinforce or revile any national narrative. My goal is to encompass not only different national stories but also many that extend beyond national templates. I aim to present a picture of the past that is close to what the past was actually like at the time, when women and men of disparate ways of life, attitudes toward nationalism, life experiences, and aspirations all acted side by side. These people differed also in what made them cry or laugh, murder or save lives. I will try to offer an understanding of each character I encounter and to give each of them a voice, even when I do not believe them or do not seek to justify their actions.

Nevertheless, this book obviously does not include everything that occurred in Palestine in 1929. Among the incidents that make no appearance here are the attack on Mishmar HaEmek and the evacuation of the families living there; the attack on Migdal 'Eder (near today's Etzion Block Junction) and the rescue of its inhabitants by those of the Arab village of Bayt Ummar; the end of the Jewish community in Gaza; the dispute over what happened at Moshav Hittin in the Lower Galilee; the attacks on Be'er Tuvia, Hulda, Kfar Uriyah and the Sharon settlements; and the evacuation of Yesod HaMa'alah. In my case, the reason for the omissions is the very question that motivated the writing of the book. The riddle I wanted to crack when I set out on this project was how the Arabs of Palestine perceive the events of 1929. How do they relate to the horrifying massacres their parents or grandparents committed against the Jews? Over the course of many years I posed that question to Palestinians I met in Hebron and in other places. My assumption (a naïve one, it turned out) was that I had sufficient basic knowledge of and background about the massacres. I wanted to hear Palestinian responses, preferably an acknowledgment of guilt or regret. But, as I conducted my research, as I had more and more conversations with Palestinians, as I read Palestinian writings and testimonies from the time of the events themselves up to the present day, and as I delved into what Jews have written and said about those same events, I discovered how little I actually knew. I was astonished by how differently the events were understood by Jews and Arabs. In the process, my position changed from that of a Jewish Israeli historian placing Palestinians at the center of his work to a Jewish Israeli scholar examining both sides with the same tools and according to the same criteria (but always, inevitably, as a Jew and an Israeli). In the process, I again encountered that phenomenon that almost goes without saying—the extent to which both Jews and Arabs have difficulty facing up to crimes committed in their names, or even calling such acts crimes. It became clear to me that a focus on one side of the conflict was liable to distort the picture. For that reason I set out on a scholarly quest that sent me back and forth between Jews and Arabs. The major stops along my way were the places where I was able to locate accounts in both Jewish and Arab sources. This impelled me to set aside important events and figures worthy of mention. I hope that another writer can complete that work.

Some readers of this book's Hebrew edition have had trouble with my side-by-side presentation of Jewish and Arab deeds in 1929. They argue that writing in this way is tantamount to claiming that the two sides were equally culpable and that their actions were symmetrical. Israeli Jews note that the number of Jews murdered by Arabs in Hebron in 1929 was unprecedented in Palestine and that the number killed by Arabs throughout the country was on an order of magnitude higher than the number of Arabs killed by Jews. Palestinian readers, in contrast, argue that comparing the colonizers with the colonized creates a false symmetry. These arguments are important, and they are related to the essence of the book. Its idea is to try to achieve the almost impossible: to tell the story of both the murderers and the murdered, the colonizers (who might also be seen as refugees) and the colonized (who might also be seen as rebels or murderers). While doing so, the book seeks neither to judge nor to compare instances of injustice — this I leave to each reader who wishes to do so — but to understand historical events and to answer the following questions: How can it be that each side tells an entirely different story about what happened? How is it that different historians perusing the very same archives and examining exactly the same documents reach diametrically opposed conclusions about the processes that led up to the riots and about the people who led them? By presenting the deeds of all actors side by side (rather than obscuring the actions of one side, as is the usual practice), and the ways that each group related to the events in real time, I focus attention on the influence that each side's actions had on the other, as a way of beginning to answer these questions. My suggestion to readers is thus not to try to compare atrocities but to study the historical story in three dimensions: First, what happened (broadly, not just what did the Arabs do to the Jews or vice versa)? Second, how did different people perceive what happened when it happened? And third, how did entirely different versions of the past develop over the years that followed? In the process, readers will be rewarded with a deeper knowledge of the experiences, feelings, and political and religious views of the Jews and Arabs who lived in the Land of Israel–Palestine following World War I, during the period that shaped the conflict as we know it today.

The Structure of the Book

I have not constructed the book chronologically. Therefore, for the reader's convenience, I offer for reference a chronological overview of the riots and a table of the number of casualties by region following the introduction.

The Text

In the text I move back and forth over the years in an attempt to express the spirit of the time and to get into the heads of the actors in the story — murderers, survivors, and victims; believers and heretics; and Jews, Arabs, and British. My goal is to portray the ways in which their consciousness was shaped prior to the events, what they felt at the time, and what they did during those horrible hours.

The riots did not begin in Jaffa and Tel Aviv, the two adjoining coastal cities that served as the cultural and economic centers of the Arab and Jewish communities in Palestine, and those cities were not focal points in the crisis. The bloody clashes that took place there have nearly been forgotten. But by examining events in these two cities in 1929, chapter 1 offers an understanding of how the history of the riots was written — what was set down in writing, what was left out, and why. And of course who killed whom and why.

In chapter 2, I turn my attention to the religious feelings of Jews, Muslims, and Christians in the Holy City. It traces the intra-Jewish debate about the correct path to achieve messianic redemption, and the Muslim view of the actions of the Zionists. In the process, I offer an account of the increasing tensions between Jews and Arabs in the city leading up to the outbreak of violence, and I highlight the places where bloody clashes occurred.

In Hebron, Motza, and Safed, Arabs slaughtered their Jewish neighbors. In chapters 3, 4, and 5, I scrutinize some of the murderers and ask what made these atrocities possible. The chapters also portray relations between Jews and Arabs in these places prior to and following the massacres.

Finally, in chapter 6, I offer different perspectives of the riots after they came to an end. I touch on the fierce disagreements that the events aroused in the Jewish communities, and on the different approaches taken in the Arab communities. In this chapter I also take up (again) several of the wonderful cases in which people on one side were rescued by those on the other. I also consider the punishments meted out to the murderers and the execution of three of them.

References

References appear in shortened form in the text rather than as footnotes. They refer to the full bibliography that appears at the end of the book. References to documents in archives use the abbreviations listed in the bibliography.

A Note on Quotes

In a small number of cases, I was unable to locate the original English versions of trial transcripts, judgments, and other documents. In such cases, I quote from Hebrew or Arabic translations that I found in archives or that appeared in the press. In other words, these quotations are translations back into English and thus most likely not the precise wordings that appeared in the original documents.

Chronological Overview of the Events

This list includes events that are not discussed in this book.

Sep. 24, 1928: Yom Kippur in the Hebrew year of תרפ"ט (5689, or TaRPa"T, as the Hebrew letters denoting the number are read). Jews erect a divider in front of the Western Wall in Jerusalem, their most sacred prayer site, to separate men and women worshipers as is customary in synagogues. The British remove the divider. The conflict over Jewish prayer rights at the Wall begins.

Nov. 1, 1928: An Islamic conference chaired by Grand Mufti of Jerusalem Hajj Amin al-Hussayni and attended by clerics from throughout the Muslim world demands restrictions on Jewish activity at the Western Wall.

Dec. 17, 1928: The British issue a policy paper on the Western Wall, stating that Muslims own the site, but that the Jews have a right to pray there.

May 1929: The Muslim Council renovates buildings and opens an entrance to the al-Haram al-Sharif (the Temple Mount) adjacent to the Wall. Scuffles and fights between Jews and Arabs become routine at the site.

Aug. 11, 1929: The Zionist Congress in Zurich declares that the Jews have a right to pray at the Western Wall and decides to expand the Jewish Agency to include non-Zionist Jews in this body.

Aug. 15, 1929: The fast of the Ninth of Av (Tisha B'Av), commemorating the destruction of the Jewish Temples by the Babylonians and Romans. Jews stage a procession to the Western Wall. The Ashkenazi Chief Rabbi of Palestine, Avraham Yitzhak HaKohen Kook, is interviewed by the Hebrew newspaper *Do'ar Hayom* and calls for the evacuation of the Maghrebi quarter, the Arab neighborhood adjacent to the Western Wall.

Aug. 16, 1929: Friday, the birthday of the Prophet Mohammad. Arabs set out from al-Aqsa Mosque on al-Haram al-Sharif and head down to the Western Wall, where they desecrate Jewish holy books.

Aug. 17, 1929: Jews and Arabs clash on the boundary of Jerusalem's Bukharan neighborhood, outside the Old City. One Jew, Avraham Mizrahi, is killed. A number of Arabs are injured. Arab homes are torched by Jews.

Aug. 20, 1929: The funeral of Avraham Mizrahi. There are clashes between Jews and British police and, in the week that follows, several incidents of stone throwing by Jews and Arabs.

Aug. 22, 1929: The acting British high commissioner for Palestine brings Jews and Arabs together for the purpose of reconciliation, without success.

Aug. 23, 1929: Friday. The riots begin. There are lynchings of Arabs and Jews along the margins of the Old City, Arab attacks on Jewish neighborhoods, and many casualties.

Aug. 24, 1929: Saturday. In the morning, Arabs massacre Jews in Hebron and murder the Maklef family in Motza. In the evening, there is the first Arab attack on the Jewish neighborhood of Hadar HaKarmel in Haifa. The attacks in Haifa continue intermittently for two days.

Aug. 25, 1929: There are Arab attacks on Jews in Jaffa and Tel Aviv. Five Jews are killed, and the 'Abd al-Ghani 'Awn family are murdered. There are also Arab attacks on and destruction of the Jewish farming settlement of Hartuv in the Judean Hills and an attack on the Jewish settlement of Kfar Uriyah southwest of Jerusalem. The inhabitants are saved by the *mukhtar* of the adjoining Arab village of Bayt Far. The Jews living in the Arab city of Gaza on the southern Mediterranean coast are evacuated.

Aug. 26, 1929: Evacuation and rescue of the residents of the Jewish village of Migdal 'Eder in today's Etzion Block south of Jerusalem, with the aid of residents of a nearby Arab village, Bayt Ummar. There are attacks on the Jewish villages of Be'er Tuvia (southwest of Jerusalem), Gedera (south of Jaffa), and Mishmar HaEmek (in the western Jezreel valley, in the north). The Jews defend their homes and suffer casualties. Some of the settlements are evacuated.

Aug. 27–28, 1929: Attacks on Jewish neighborhoods in Haifa. Seven Jews and thirteen Arabs are killed. A British warship arrives.

Aug. 28, 1929: The attack on Hulda. Efrayim Chizick is killed defending the kibbutz.

Aug. 29, 1929: Jews are massacred in Safed and Ein Zeitim.

Sep. 1, 1929: The high commissioner issues a statement condemning the Arab rioters. There are furious Arab retaliations in the days that follow.

Sep. 1929–May 1930: Trials of those charged with crimes during the riots. The death penalty is handed down against twenty-six Arabs and two Jews. Most appeal and have their sentences commuted.

Oct. 24, 1929: The Commission on the Palestine Disturbances of August 1929 (the Shaw Commission) arrives in Palestine.

Mar. 1930: The Shaw Commission issues its report, pegging the Arabs as the assailants but clearing the mufti of having instigated the attacks. The report also states, however, that the larger context for the outbreak of violence is Jewish immigration.

June 13, 1930: The British forbid Ze'ev Jabotinsky to return to Palestine.

June 17, 1930: Red Tuesday — the three Arabs whose death sentences remained in force are executed.

Oct. 1930: Lord Passfield issues his White Paper. Its principal provision: limits on Jewish immigration.

Feb. 13, 1931: Following Zionist lobbying, Prime Minister Ramsay MacDonald declares that Jewish immigration will not be restricted.

May 1931: A few members of the Hebron Jewish community return to the city, but the community does not thrive and those who remained leave when further disturbances begin in 1936.

Casualties in the 1929 Riots

Region	Jews	Arabs
Jerusalem	31 killed, 119 wounded	50 killed (including 3 Christians), 56 wounded
Hebron	67 killed, 53 wounded	9 killed, 9 wounded
Jaffa	8 killed, 33 wounded	12 killed, 28 wounded (including 1 Christian)
Ramla	1 killed, 1 wounded	5 killed, 7 wounded (including 1 Christian)
Gaza	0	3 killed, 11 wounded
Majdal Ashkelon	0	9 killed, 1 wounded
Haifa	6 killed, 67 wounded (one fatally)	17 killed (including 1 Christian), 94 wounded (including 8 Christians)
Acre	3 wounded	0
Nazareth	1 wounded	1 killed, 1 wounded (a Christian)
Nablus	0	15 wounded (including 3 Christians)
Beisan	25 wounded	4 killed, 2 wounded
Safed	20 killed, 39 wounded	6 killed, 8 wounded

Source: The data are based on the annual report of the Palestine Police Force for the year 1929 (TNA CO 814/4: 22).

Note: Total fatalities: 133 Jews, 116 Arabs. Total injured: 241 Jews, 232 Arabs.

The British counted the casualties by religion (Muslim, Jew, Christian) rather than by nationality. The category "wounded" counts those who were hospitalized. Some historians believe the number of Arab dead was higher but that some were uncounted because the assailants managed to carry their dead away.

A large majority of the Jews slain were unarmed and were murdered in their homes by Arabs. Most of the Arab dead were killed as they attacked Jewish settlements or neighborhoods. Most of the Arabs were felled by bullets fired by the British armed forces; some were shot by members of the Haganah. As will be shown, about twenty of the Arabs killed were not involved in attacks on Jews. They were killed in lynchings and revenge attacks carried out by Jews, or by indiscriminate British gunfire.

Year Zero of the Arab-Israeli Conflict

JAFFA AND TEL AVIV

Sunday, August 25, 1929

> We will open with an account of what happened in Tel Aviv, Acre, and Jaffa in 1929 because these cities were on the margins of the disturbances. We will learn of the triangle of relations between Mizrahi Jews, Ashkenazi Jews, and Arabs and the way these relations were shaken, and we will meet, among others, Mustafa al-Dabbagh, Yosef Haim Brenner, Simha Hinkis, Nisim Elkayam, and Ahmad al-Shuqayri. One thing leads to another, and one person leads to another.

In the summer of 1929 the Jews provoked the Muslims: thousands of their young and old people gathered on the streets of Jerusalem with the Zionist flag, adorned with black ribbons, waving over their heads. They marched in an organized fashion to the Western Wall—al-Buraq—enthusiastically singing the Zionist anthem, "*Hatikvah.*" Their voices rang out: "The Western Wall is ours, beware all who sully our holy site." It was this provocation that led to the clashes that spread through the country in August 1929.

In Jaffa Jews, led by a Jewish policeman in the government service, attacked the home of Sheikh 'Abd al-Ghani 'Awn, the imam of the Abu Kabir neighborhood mosque, next to Tel Aviv. They killed him and all six members of his family and defiled the bodies criminally. They slashed open the father's belly and smashed the heads of his nephew and his wife and son, who was three years old at the time. (Dabbagh 2002, 4:265)

This description appears in the volume on Jaffa and its environs, of the ten-volume work titled *Biladuna Filastin* (Our land of Palestine) by Mustafa Murad al-Dabbagh (2002). It is not a work of history but rather a geographical encyclopedia, arranged by region. Neither does it offer in-depth analysis. Rather, it surveys all the cities and villages of Palestine, noting significant events that took place in each one. An important reference work, it is frequently consulted by readers of Arabic. Given its nature, it does not offer a comprehensive survey of the events of 1929. Yet it cites a significant event — unfamiliar to Israeli and foreign readers as well as to many Arabs — the murder of an Arab family and the mutilation of their bodies by Jews.

The picture is a harsh one. It is not easy to read about the smashing of children's skulls, the mutilation of bodies, and the slitting open of bellies. Furthermore, what connection is there between the riots of 1929 and the slaying of an Arab family by Jews? After all, the theme of the events of 1929 — at least as far as Jews are concerned — is Arab brutality. But this is what al-Dabbagh tells us about what happened in Jaffa and Tel Aviv in 1929. In short order we will examine the truth of the story, but in any case it is important to keep in mind that it was not the start of the 1929 riots.

Not the Start

The 1929 riots officially started not in Jaffa but in Jerusalem, two days earlier, on Friday, August 23. The climax came the following day, Saturday, when Arabs massacred Jews in Hebron (the events in those cities are recounted in the chapters that follow). Violence continued, in various forms, throughout the country in the days that followed. But the events of that Friday were not in fact the start. The disturbances of August 1929 grew out of the relations between Jews and Arabs in Palestine throughout the 1920s. And those relations were built on the foundation, and in cognizance, of hundreds of years of Jewish-Muslim and Jewish-Arab encounters preceding the advent of Zionism. These relations were not static; they varied over time and space. Competition and cooperation, animosity, discrimination, feelings of superiority and compassion and hatred, as well as a complex of other human emotions and behaviors, all played a role. The recent and distant past are parts of human consciousness, and they were part of the emotional and political substrate of what people experienced in 1929 and how they acted during the violence. The historical memory of the inhabitants of Tel Aviv and Jaffa included a previous round of riots in 1921, eight years previously; the Jews remembered the dozens of their compatriots who had been killed then. Among the victims was the seminal Hebrew writer Yosef Haim Brenner.

Yosef Haim Brenner

Brenner was a symbol, both in life and in death. An essayist and novelist, he arrived in Palestine as part of the Second Aliyah, that wave of Jewish Zionist immigration lasting from 1904 to 1914. Central among the newcomers were young Eastern European Jews of socialist ideology who believed in the importance of manual labor and the revival of the Hebrew language, and who established the first communal Zionist settlements. Brenner was a man of great contradictions.

He despaired and offered hope. He loved but suffered because of it. A tough critic of other people's work, but a nurturer of talents. One of the great figures in the revival of the Hebrew language. One of the Zionist labor movement's most prominent intellectuals. He often behaved, looked, and dressed oddly—some said like a prophet. For some he was the best and purest man in the Yishuv. He was killed, along with five companions, by Arabs from Jaffa on May 2, 1921, on the second day of that year's riots, not far from an isolated Jewish farmhouse where he had been living, a short way outside the city, near Abu Kabir. The story was that the other residents had urged him to leave for safety when the violence began, but he insisted on remaining with them.

Brenner was painfully aware of Arab hostility toward the Zionist enterprise; among Arabs he felt just like he had among the gentiles who inflicted pogroms against Jews in Eastern Europe. Unlike a number of his friends, he had a hard time believing that the Jews would be able to forge an alliance with Palestine's Arabs or with the Arab working class. Deep down, the Orient terrified him. He was certain that he would be killed by Arabs. About a year before his murder he wrote words that later seemed prophetic:

> Tomorrow, perhaps, the Jewish hand writing these words will be stabbed, some "sheikh" or "hajj" will stick his dagger in it in full sight of the English governor, as happened to the agronomist Shmuel Haramati, and it, this hand, will not be able to do a thing to the sheikh and the hajj, because it does not know how to wield a sword. Yet the remnants of the people of Israel will not be lost. The stock of Jesse [the Davidic line] will not be extinguished. He will tell of our enemies to his sons—it will be told to those who remain. It will be told that we are the victims of evil, victims of the malicious ambition to gain power and property, victims of imperialism. Not us. We had no imperialist aspirations. (Y. Brenner 1985, 4:1758)

And eulogizing Avraham Sher, who had been slain in the Upper Galilee in February 1920, Brenner wrote in the monthly journal *Ha'adamah*: "Our savage neighbors, as always, know not what they do, whom they murder: humanity's best" (1985, 4:1479). Many Jews felt the same way when Brenner was killed.

The Savages Know Not

The "savages" did not know who Brenner was, not before and not after they murdered him. Palestinian writing on the events of 1921 hardly mentions Brenner. When it does, it makes no reference to his important place in the life of the Yishuv or to how beloved he was. But there is another side to this story. Brenner himself knew nothing about his neighbors. His worst nightmare was Jewish integration into the Orient. Every bone in his body sensed the weakness of Zionism, the difficulty of living in the Land of Israel, and the horrors of the never-ending pogroms of Eastern and Central Europe. With all that in mind, he could not understand by what right the Arabs of Palestine opposed something that seemed to him so simple and clear and just: the desire of Jews from Romania, Lithuania, Russia, Ukraine, Poland, and everywhere else to save their lives and honor and to rebuild themselves as whole human beings, as a nation in the land of their fathers. Thus, the Arabs could only be savages, fighting against everything human and decent.

Humanity

Brenner arrived in Palestine in 1909. Between 1904 and 1911, Ibrahim al-Dabbagh of Jaffa published in Cairo a periodical called *al-Insaniyya* (Humanity), which was distributed in Jaffa as well. Brenner never read it, nor could he have read it had he wanted to. It presumably never occurred to him that there might be a periodical with such a name available in the port city where he disembarked. Neither did he know the extent to which the Arab press of the time identified with the persecuted Jews, and how furiously it condemned the pogroms in Eastern Europe — as shown by Shaul Sehayek in his PhD dissertation "Demut haYehudi beRe'i ha'Itonut ha'Aravit bein haShanim 1858–1908" (The image of the Jew in the Arabic press 1858–1908; 1991). So great was Brenner's terror of the Arabs and so potent his disappointment at the fact that in Palestine, too, the Jews were no more than a powerless minority that he could think of no solution other than insularity and isolation from the non-Jewish environment. Only in the last essay he wrote, just before he died, did he express a shred of regret for the path he had chosen. He related an encounter with an Arab youth who addressed him as he was walking along the edge of Jaffa: "He asked me something in a clear, somewhat strident voice, clearly accented and precisely pronounced. I am sorry to say that I did not know how to respond to him, because I never taught myself to speak the Arabic tongue . . . at that moment I castigated myself harshly for never having taught myself to speak the Arabic tongue" (Y. Brenner 1962, 212).

It is a rare confession on his part. His writing makes it clear how far he was from an understanding of Arab society or even from a desire to understand it. He saw his position clearly, but he was also willfully blind to its implications. The world, in his experience, was full of hatred of Jews, and to cope with it one had to fill oneself with hatred. So he wrote to his pacifist friend Rabbi Binyamin (the pen name of the journalist Yehoshua Radler-Feldmann): "What, R. Binyamin, we are supposed to talk about love for our neighbors, natives of this land, if we are sworn enemies, yes, enemies. . . . We must, then, be prepared here also for the results of hatred and to use all means available to our weak hands so that we can live here as well. Since becoming a nation we have been surrounded by hatred, and as a result are also full of hatred—and that is as it should be, cursed are the soft, the loving" (1985, 4:1038).

Unlike Jewish political leaders, Brenner saw no reason to conceal Jewish hatred of the gentiles, the joy of having the opportunity to kill and be killed for the Jewish homeland. He felt no compunctions about declaring that war and bloodshed could be salutary, inasmuch as they could help shape and forge the nation. Others also spoke of the joy of dying for one's homeland and the benefits of war, but it is difficult to find such clear-cut praise for hatred of the Arabs and gentiles in the works of other Zionist thinkers.

Uri, His Son

Uri Brenner was seven years old when his father was murdered. When violence broke out in Palestine in 1921, he was living in Berlin with his mother, Chaya Broide. By 1929 they had moved back to Tel Aviv, and Uri was a fatherless boy of fifteen. His uncle, Yeshayahu (Isaiah) Broide, was then serving as vice-chairman of the Zionist Executive in Palestine. Just prior to the riots Uri was tapped to enlist in the Haganah, the Yishuv's defense force, and he immediately agreed. Along with other teenagers, he served as a messenger between the organization's headquarters and outposts on the dividing line between Jewish and Arab neighborhoods, not far from the place where his father had been murdered. And not far from the home of the 'Awn family. Forty years later, Uri Brenner gave his testimony for the Haganah History Archives: "The subject of the Haganah is connected to my father, and his death in 1921 was a painful subject that was repressed, perhaps because it was not spoken of at home, and perhaps because of an urge for revenge. The offer [from a member of the Haganah to enlist] was for me a saving moment in a certain sense, because I was suspended between an aggressive, avenging spirit and a defensive one" (HHA, testimony 11/7).

Uri Brenner chose an aggressive defense. In 1937 he was one of the founders and defenders of Kibbutz Ma'oz Hayyim in the Beit She'an Valley, and a year later he joined the Special Night Squads organized by a British officer Orde Wingate, who taught that the best defense was an offense. In *HaKibbutz HaMe'uchad ba-Haganah* (The united kibbutz movement in the Haganah; 1980), Uri Brenner wrote of the squads' cruel and vengeful streak. In 1943 he enlisted in the Palmach, the Yishuv's elite strike force that was closely tied to the kibbutz movement, and in the 1948 war he served as its deputy commander. In a sense, he embodied what his father had written about: "Yet the remnants of the people of Israel will not be lost. The stock of Jesse will not be extinguished." But if Uri bore hatred of non-Jews in his heart; if he reveled at the opportunity to spill blood, as his father had; if he shared the complexities of his father's attitude to the Arabs and the culture of force, he did not say so in anything he wrote.

Keep in Mind

The riots of 1921 were just one memory in the minds of the people of Jaffa and Tel Aviv in 1929. That is, those involved in the riots—assailants, victims, horrified onlookers, provocateurs, journalists and readers, poultry merchants, thinkers, warriors, pacifists, Jews, Arabs, Britons, washers of hands, assumers of responsibility, criers for peace—all went into these disturbances with heavy historical baggage that played a role in how they understood and responded to events. In this respect, the genesis of the disturbances long preceded their actual beginning and even the births of their protagonists. The riots' roots reach deep into oral traditions and myths, stories of famous people; tales of real and imagined enemies told by grandparents; and legends from the Old and New Testaments and Qur'an that the people involved heard as children, in arguments their parents had with friends before the protagonists' bedtime, while they were trying to fall asleep in their homes in Eastern and Western Europe, in the Hebron highlands and the orange groves of Jaffa, in the glens of Scotland, in Baghdad, and everywhere else they came from—while they lay in beds in proper houses or slept on rags with their siblings in a hut. The events began in souls imprinted with stories and were shaped when children had their first encounters with strangers. Traditions and stories provided the templates, and experiences were the material that, melted together, was cast in these molds—except that sometimes what came out was not the shape imprinted there but its reverse, and at other times the figure that emerged was twice as sharp as the mold itself. But it did not end there—the templates themselves were melted down and recast at junctures in these people's lives, when they were at school or under the instruction of an Eastern European melamed or a local sheikh, when they helped their parents in the fields or served as cheap hired labor. That was when their political and nationalist consciousness awakened—or did not.

It would be best, then, to start in all those places at once, but that is not possible. A writer has no choice but to choose a starting point and to move forward and backward in time, keeping in mind always the gap between what he knows and what people knew at the time.

Knowledge Gaps

The participants in and observers of the events of 1929 knew their times better than anyone who did not live through them. However, we have knowledge of what happened in their future, which they obviously lacked at the time. We know what happened in Hebron and Motza and Jaffa and Safed and Hulda and Jerusalem and Acre and Migdal 'Eder and so on, while they, in real time, saw only what was happening before their eyes. We also know how events progressed after the riots, that animosity between Jews and Arabs did not end, and that there was a fateful war in 1948 in which the Arabs were defeated and during which the State of Israel was founded. We know that hundreds of thousands of Arabs became refugees and that the conflict continues. This knowledge makes it difficult for later generations to view events from the perspective of those who lived through them. Jews today have trouble really feeling the dread felt by Jews who lived as a persecuted minority (even if some observers believe that existential fear is the key to understanding Israel's actions in the present). Palestinians today have trouble imagining Palestine as it was at the end of the 1920s, part of a spacious Arab land from which one could travel unimpeded to neighboring Arab countries and within which were scattered, here and there, Jews who were trying to gain a foothold in the country and to take control of it.

But all that is connected to how the events played out and turned out. We are still at the beginning, in Jaffa in 1929, seeking to understand what happened in this city and what we can learn from what happened there regarding the 1929 riots as a whole. Before we investigate what occurred in the 'Awn family's house, let's take a look at the book in which their story appears: *Biladuna Filastin* (Our land of Palestine).

Our Land of Palestine

The first volume of the *Biladuna Filastin* encyclopedia was published in 1947. The set was completed in 1965. Al-Dabbagh relates in his introduction to the new complete edition: "When I issued the first volume of my book, I did not imagine that the Nakba would take place in the country within the year and disperse its inhabitants as a storm scatters the sand" (2002, 1:7). He goes on to describe how, at the height of the fighting, before Jaffa fell, his cousin arrived on a boat from Egypt and persuaded him to sail away, in so doing saving his life:

> I did not take anything on the trip except for a small suitcase containing the manuscript of more than 6,000 pages of my book on the history and geography of Palestine, my only book, the product of more than a decade of collecting material and writing. I blessed God for the fact that, a few days earlier, I had sent my wife and children to relatives in Beirut, and boarded the ship with my cousin and his friends, uprooted as we were.
>
> The sea was rough, the waves rolled and roared, a gale raged and a hard rain fell. Water began to enter the boat on all sides. The captain shouted that we should cast the cargo into the sea to lighten the boat, otherwise it would sink. I held my suitcase fast to my breast, but the arm of a tough sailor, aided by a wave that fell over the ship,

separated the suitcase from me and hurled it into the sea. So the book was lost to me and with it the labors of many years. (2002, 1:7)

Al-Dabbagh spent another fifteen years reconstructing his manuscript, and later in his introduction to the complete edition he offers the principal conclusion of his research: "The book shows that the Jews' claim of a historical right to the land is baseless. The claim is unsubstantiated in a manner without historical precedent, a bald fabrication. . . . The Jews have passed through our homeland, as have other nations that have vanished from the earth" (2002, 1:7).

Reading the Final Sentence Precisely

Three points in the last of al-Dabbagh's sentences quoted above are worthy of note. First, he acknowledges that the Jews were once present in Palestine. That is not to be taken lightly. It contradicts a popular Palestinian claim then and now that the Jews of today are not descendants of the Israelites of old but are rather, for example, Khazars. The second important point is the claim that the Jews' presence in the country in the past does not validate their claim to sovereignty in the present—they came to Palestine during their wanderings in the past, and now they are passing through once more. The third and central point is encompassed within the term "our homeland." For the Arabs of Palestine, the country is their homeland from before the Hebrews or Jews first reached it, and they continue to be its natural inhabitants and heirs. This is a fundamental Palestinian concept. The fact that Palestinian society is composed of families and tribes —some of which have roots in Palestine and others of which arrived in waves of immigration over the years, prior to Islam and afterward—does not, in this view, diminish this claim, because by its nature Palestine is a land that serves as a melting pot for its inhabitants and melds them into a single Palestinian people.

This Palestinian perception, which frequently sees the Jews who lived in Palestine prior to the inception of Zionism as part of the Arab Palestinian people, is profoundly opposed to the common Zionist Jewish view. First, Palestinian nationalism is based on the principle of *jus soli*—right of land. That is, it is the land that creates the nation, and the inhabitants of a country possess the right to it, no matter what their origin. The rival Jewish perception is based on the principle of *jus sanguinis*—right of blood. In this view, blood descent is the central component of nationhood, and the right to the Holy Land derives from its association with the Jewish people. The practical implications are, then, that the Palestinians see the land as their homeland and the Jews as foreigners (who can, under certain conditions, merge with the Palestinian people), while the Jews see it as the homeland of the Jewish people, no matter where they may be. But let's return to Jaffa in 1929 and search for further sources of that year's killings.

More Sources on the Murder in Jaffa

Further information on the 'Awn family's murder can be found in contemporary newspapers. They did not report the crime when it occurred, but they did cover the trial of Simha Hinkis, a Jewish policeman arrested by the British as a suspect in the crime. A large amount of material on the case can be found in the Central Zionist Archives in Jerusalem and in the National Archives of the United Kingdom, and the incident is also mentioned in *Sefer Toldot HaHaganah* (The Haganah history book; Dinur 1973), a history of the Yishuv's major military force, written in the 1950s.

The Haganah History Book

Sefer Toldot HaHaganah is considered a classic of the "old history"—that is, traditional Zionist historical writing—because it tells the story of the Yishuv and the Haganah from the point of view of the central current of Zionism at the time, the labor movement. The work was a collective undertaking, and the names of its authors make it tempting to view the book as having a manifestly political agenda. The principal writer was Yehuda Slutsky, a professional historian and writer; the editorial board's members included Shaul Avigur (whose previous assignments included being chief of the Haganah's intelligence service and one of the leaders of the illegal immigration operation that brought European Jews to Palestine in violation of British immigration restrictions), Yitzhak Ben-Zvi (a leader of the Second Aliyah, one of the founders of the Haganah, and later the second president of Israel), Elazar Galili (nicknamed Lasia, head of the Haganah's Culture Department, founder of *Ma'arakhot*, the official journal of the Israel Defense Forces, and a member of Kibbutz Afikim), and Yisrael Galili (whose posts included chief of the Haganah's national command in 1947–48, member of the Knesset, and member of the cabinet in 1966–77). The chief editor was Ben-Zion Dinur, a prolific historian of the Jewish people who served as Israel's education minister from 1951 to 1955. But the work was not just a megaphone for the political ideas of its writers and editors. Its thick volumes contain a trove of information, including about the "Hinkis incident" (a euphemism for the murder of the 'Awn family). The fact that the "incident" was included is just one of many examples that show that the authors and editors did not, as a general rule, seek to conceal problematic parts of the Zionist project in Palestine, but they present such incidents in soft focus. Here is what the work says about the murder: "A short time after this event [the killing of members of the Haganah in Abu Kabir], several Jews, among them the policeman Simha Hinkis, broke into one of the Arab homes in Abu Kabir that were adjacent to Tel Aviv. Four Arabs, among them a woman and a child, were killed. It was an act of retribution, the product of an emotional outburst, after news of the massacre in

Hebron reached Tel Aviv and after the murder of Jews who had set out to save human lives" (Dinur 1973, 2:327).

Note that *Sefer Toldot HaHaganah* gives a different figure for the number of dead than does al-Dabbagh. Was it four or seven? The indictment and judgment in Hinkis's trial will provide an answer.

And what about the event that, according to the Haganah history, preceded Hinkis's raid on the house? Who were the Jews who were murdered in Jaffa? The answer can be found in *Sefer Toldot HaHaganah*: On Sunday around noon, a day after the massacre in Hebron, a Haganah patrol set out to rescue Jews who had been trapped in an ethanol factory outside Abu Kabir that was being besieged by Arabs. The British ordered the patrol to return to Tel Aviv and sent a British unit to disperse the Arabs and evacuate the besieged Jews. The Haganah patrol headed toward Tel Aviv, and, according to the book, "on its way back the group of defenders encountered an Arab mob that was, apparently, guarding the entrances to its neighborhood, and it attacked the [patrol's] vehicle. Four Haganah men were killed" (Dinur 1973, 2:327).

Jaffa: A Historical-Literary Reader

The account in *Sefer Toldot HaHaganah* is pretty concise. A more comprehensive picture of the events can be found in *Yafo: Mikra'ah Historit Sifrutit* (Jaffa: a historical–literary reader), published in 1957 by the Education and Culture Department of the Tel Aviv–Jaffa municipality. The editor was Yosef Aricha, at the time an important and influential writer of Hebrew fiction. The book includes memoirs, poetry, and a history of the city from biblical times to Jaffa's surrender to Zionist forces in 1948, written by dozens of writers. One of its chapters is devoted to the 1929 riots in and around the city. Here is the general background the book offers:

> In Tel Aviv the riots began on Sunday, 19 Av 5689 [August 25, 1929], after an inflamed Arab mob emerged from the Hasan Beq Mosque south of Tel Aviv. The Arabs had long prepared for an attack on the city. The sheikhs and effendis incited the fellahs and poor people to stage a massacre of the Jewish Yishuv and promised them their wives and daughters. Each Arab who promised to take part in the attack was given a pack of cigarettes and a shilling. Thousands of inflamed Arabs, craving loot, gathered from the entire region and in the afternoon commenced their attack on Neveh Shalom and next to HaCarmel Street from the alleys across from Allenby Street. (Hinkis 1957, 229–30)

So Tel Aviv was also attacked in 1929. The street called HaCarmel then is today's King George Street, in the heart of Tel Aviv's downtown, and that is where the first act of the offensive took place. To be continued.

Hasan Beq Mosque, Jaffa (Matson Photograph Collection, Library of Congress).

An Inflamed Mob?

The term "inflamed mob" connotes that the mob lacked any ideological motivation or judgment of its own. It is derisive of the people in the mob, as they have been inflamed by someone and are following his or her exhortations rather than thinking for themselves. Inflamed mobs have three attributes: first, they operate outside any organized framework; second, they are irrational; and third, they are not acting of their own volition. The attackers in Jaffa, Hebron, and other places in 1929 meet the first criterion, as they were not part of a professional force on a mission and had not been trained as fighters. Rather, they were a large group of people who were driven to act after learning (or hearing rumors about) what had happened in Jerusalem. The other two criteria are more complicated, as they have to do with the attackers' logic and judgment and their motivation for acting. The author of the quoted part of *Yafo* maintains that their motive was a vile one — effendis (members of the new economic elite) and sheikhs (religious leaders) incited the masses and distributed measly gifts — and the masses, mostly poor people, went on the attack. They did not truly understand the significance of their actions and did not consider the moral implications. For them, human life was worth less than a pack of cigarettes.

Is that convincing? Were these Arabs really goaded into action by a pack of cigarettes and a shilling? By dreams of beautiful women — a motive frequently cited in Jewish accounts of the events in both Jaffa and Hebron? The explanation is attractive in its simplicity, but I am not certain that it is sufficiently comprehensive. The claim that the Arab masses of 1929 had no powers of judgment is unpersuasive for the simple reason that there were people who attacked and people who refrained from doing so. The explanation is also invalid for another reason—had these same people been offered a pack of cigarettes in exchange for murdering their own friends and families, would they have done so? If the answer is no—as presumably it would be—the only possible conclusion is that these attackers had stronger motives than just immediate gratification. We may also presume that the incitement encouraged an outbreak of already existing animosities, rather than creating new ones.

The concept of the "inflamed mob" has another flaw: implicit in the phrase, for many, is an assumption of the moral inferiority of the mob as opposed to organized forces. But this is not necessarily true. Just as organized forces can act with or without a moral compass, so can a seething (or "inflamed"—that is, responding to emotional appeals directed to it) mob. Jaffa's own history provides an example.

Napoleon in Jaffa

A memorable event in Jaffa's long history is its conquest by Napoleon Bonaparte in 1799. French forces had captured Egypt a year earlier, and at the beginning of 1799 they began moving overland toward Palestine, from El-Arish to Gaza and from there to Ramla. During the campaign the French took thousands of Ottoman prisoners, whom they took with them on their northward progress. On March 3, Napoleon's army reached Jaffa and besieged it. The city resisted for four days before falling. French soldiers looted Jaffa's homes and slaughtered many of its inhabitants. Two days later, the French led 3,000 prisoners southward on an organized march. Just outside the city limits, on the seashore, they were divided into small groups and shot dead by French soldiers. The executions lasted for hours. Those who were not killed by the bullets were stabbed to death with bayonets.

Napoleon and his men justified the massacre on the ground that they did not have enough troops both to guard the prisoners and defend their positions, adding that they also lacked food for the captives. They claimed too that the Ottomans had been the first to violate the customary laws of war—the Ottoman governor of Jaffa had had beheaded the messenger that Napoleon sent him. Even more critically, the Ottoman prisoners who had surrendered in the country's south and were subsequently released violated their pledge to stay away from the battlefield, instead joining the forces defending Jaffa. Of course, logical, political, and moral justifications have been offered for almost every massacre from the dawn of history to the present day.

So Muslims are not the only ones who can commit atrocities—European Christians are fully capable of doing so as well. And not just any Europeans —this was the army of the French Revolution, spreading the gospel of *liberté*, *egalité*, and *fraternité*. In *Napoleon: His Army and His Generals*, Jean Charles Dominique de Lacretelle wrote that the piles of bodies in time turned into pyramids of bones. These monuments to the dawn of modern cultural interaction between the West and the Levant long stood on Jaffa's beach (1854, 106).

The Modern Age

Napoleon's eastern campaign—the conquest of Egypt and capture of Jaffa (commemorated in several classic paintings)—is often seen as the beginning of the modern age in the Middle East. But it did not exactly put Western-style modernity's best foot forward. At a conference on religion and the state held at Bar-Ilan University in May 2011, the Indonesian historian Azyumardi Azra spoke of the far-reaching consequences of the event in another sense. He argued that Middle Eastern Islam developed in the direction of intolerance as a result of the siege mentality under which the Arab world lived after Napoleon's attack. It was this, he claimed, that impelled the Arabs to avoid interaction with the West and to turn toward sectarianism (Mandel 2011).

From Napoleon's Massacre to 1929

Napoleon's slaughter of his prisoners is an inevitable association when the subject is massacres in Jaffa. But there is another reason why I mention it here: to correct a historical distortion—or, rather, to cleanse that distortion from the minds of those who maintain that only an inflamed crowd or only Muslims are capable of committing a mass murder of innocent people. That claim is manifestly without foundation, yet the more it is shown to be so, the more some people seem to assert it. After the horrors of World War II nobody really needs to be reminded that Europeans are capable of mass murder. Nor did Jews need such a reminder in 1929. At the end of the nineteenth century and the beginning of the twentieth, pogroms were part of everyday life (and death) for Jewish communities in Eastern Europe (and less so in Central Europe), and by 1929 dark clouds were gathering over the entire continent.

We've cited Christian brutality and Muslim brutality. Now we need to examine the Jews and mass murder.

What about the Jews?

During the nineteenth century, in Palestine and throughout the world, Jewish involvement in massacres was very one-sided—they were always victims. One example is the Peasants' Revolt of 1834, a seminal event in the history of

Palestine. Some background: About thirty years after Napoleon's campaign, a dispute broke out between the Ottoman sultanate and Muhammad 'Ali, who ruled Egypt under nominal Ottoman suzerainty. The dispute was about the sphere of the Egyptian ruler's influence and the extent of his powers. Muhammad 'Ali took military action, sending forces northward that conquered large swaths of the Levant, up to the border of what is Turkey today. He controlled Palestine for about a decade (1831–40), during which time he instituted important changes in its administration, as well as in the social and legal sphere. Among other things, he introduced mandatory conscription and mandated legal equality for Jews and Christians, putting them on a par with Muslims. Keep in mind, however, that conferring equal rights on minorities is tantamount to depriving the majority of its privileges. That is one reason why majority communities throughout the world often oppose the concept of equal rights so vociferously and sometimes violently. The history of European Jewry during the nineteenth and twentieth centuries offers a notable instance of this. But there are even more recent examples.

In 1834 the Arabs of Palestine rose up against the Egyptian administration and its innovations. In *Palestinians: The Making of a People* (1993), Baruch Kimmerling and Joel Migdal present this revolt as marking the first glimmering of Arab nationalism in Palestine (many other scholars dispute this claim, for a variety of reasons). The rebels were led by the most powerful families in the region's rural areas. The revolt encompassed all of Palestine, from Gaza in the south to Safed in the Galilee. At the end of May the rebels attacked Jerusalem, and with the help of the city's Muslims they reached al-Haram al-Sharif, the Temple Mount. From there, masses of rebels and local Muslims marched toward Jaffa Gate, pushing back the Egyptian forces step by step. Muhammad 'Ali's troops retreated into a fortress near the gate, now known as David's Citadel; the rest of the city fell to the rebel villagers. The conquerors began to plunder the city. Muslim homes and establishments were not touched; their owners may well have joined the looters. Christians fled for their lives into fortified monasteries.

The city's Jews bore the brunt of the attack. In 1938 Asad Rustum of the American University of Beirut published Egyptian documents relating to the revolt. He cited this passage from a report on Jerusalem: "The homes of the Jews were demolished completely, leaving them without beds to sleep on. Many of them were slaughtered and their wives and daughters dishonored." In Safed the rebels broke into the Jewish quarter, "looting and violating the accepted bounds of decency and honor" (1938, 60). Despite Muhammad 'Ali's ostensible liberalism toward minority groups, the Jews in Hebron found that they could not depend on his protection when his forces defeated the rebels. The commander of the Egyptian troops gave his men a free hand to rape and plunder, "and boldness entered into their limbs and murder into their bones. They killed some with torches and some they slashed with swords. Many women were tortured and sullied," the members of the community wrote of the disaster after they rose from their period of mourning (Avisar 1970c, 56).

One Law for Jews, the Uncircumcised, and the Ishmaelites

Bloody events like these were not routine. While Jews did not enjoy equality under the Ottoman Empire, in Palestine and elsewhere, prior to the era of nationalism, it was one of the easiest places in the world for Jews to live. At the beginning of *Igrot Eretz Yisra'el* (Letters from the Land of Israel; 1943), Avraham Yaari quotes a number of letters penned at the beginning of the modern age that contain material relating to the condition of Palestine's Jews under Mamluk and Ottoman rule. The writers of the letters, he notes, emphasize

> that the regime does not discriminate against the Jews and that the Arab inhabitants harbor no special hatred of the Jews as Jews. The writers stress in particular that there was no contempt for the Jew and his faith, the kind of contempt that had become etched in their souls during their time living in Christian lands; they declare in astonishment that the Arabs honor Jewish holy sites and the tombs of Jewish saints.
>
> Rabbi Yitzhak Latif writes in his letter from the last quarter of the fifteenth century: "The Arabs are at peace with us. They will never strike us and never pillage." At about the same time, Rabbi Yosef da Montagna declared in his letter from Jerusalem: "On the way we were sometimes in the field among many Ishmaelites and I never heard a man open his mouth to speak evil." A few years later, in 1488, Rabbi Ovadiah of Bartenura wrote in his first letter from Jerusalem: "The Jews feel no sense of repression at all from the Ishmaelites in this place; I have traveled the length and breadth of the country and no one opens his mouth or jeers." A student of this same Rabbi Ovadiah of Barentura describes in a letter the punishments imposed by the authorities, remarking that "as a rule, there is a single law for the Jews and the uncircumcised [Christians] and the Ishmaelites, but they do not hate Jews and castigate and abuse them as in your country [Italy]. . . ." In the mid-eighteenth century, Rabbi Avraham Gershon of Kitov wrote from Hebron: "The gentiles here very much love the Jews. When there is a *brit milah* [circumcision ceremony] or any other celebration, their most important men come at night and rejoice with the Jews and clap hands and dance with the Jews, just like the Jews." (Yaari 1943, 18–19)

The letters include additional accounts of close interaction and cooperation between Jews and Muslims, certainly much beyond what was customary in Europe. The attack on the Jews in Jerusalem, Hebron, and Safed during the uprising of 1834 was thus an exception that proved the rule of generally placid, if not equal, relations between the Muslim majority and the Jewish minority. But they also marked the beginning of a change for the worse for the Jews. Here it is important to be precise: the assaults on Jews during the revolt indicate that anti-Jewish sentiment did not begin to increase solely as a reaction to organized Zionist activity in Palestine. In 1834, that had not yet begun. Rather, it seems to have been a response to Western attempts to gain political and economic control over Palestine and the Middle East as a whole. The role that the Jews played in this process — their increased immigration to Palestine during these years, and the support they enjoyed from European governments — aroused resentment against them.

Pre-Zionist Anti-Zionism

It can be put this way: European penetration of the Middle East heightened awareness of the difference between the Muslim majority community on the one hand and the minority Christian and Jewish communities on the other. Christians and Jews appealed to the European powers with the goal of improving their legal and economic status and gaining full equality, and in doing so were often seen as promoters of foreign interests and non-Muslim rule. So political enmity began. The Jewish and Christian alignment with Christian powers also had religious significance; the choice Jews (and Christians) made to prefer the protection of foreign powers was interpreted, understandably, as an act of renouncing their traditional status as wards of the Muslim sovereign. For Muslims, this was a watershed in their relations with these communities. Legally and theologically, from that point onward Muslims viewed themselves as absolved of the obligation to protect the Jews and Christians of the Holy Land and elsewhere in the Middle East. Furthermore, if the Jews wished to turn Palestine into their own land, as rumors began to say they did, the Muslims were bound to fight them. Political contention between the Jews and Muslims thus commenced prior to the dawn of organized Zionist settlement, even before the arrival of the proto-Zionist settlers of the Bilu and Hovevei Zion movements in the nineteenth century's latter decades.

Implications for Today

Arabs commonly viewed the Jews in Palestine as colonialists and emissaries of Western imperialism. This seems to have been the background against which many Arabs understood, and still understand, the Jewish-Arab conflict. The basis for the evolution of this view can be found in the 1830s. During that decade, under Muhammad 'Ali's rule, Jewish immigration to Palestine increased with the help of foreign powers, and this continued after the reassertion of Ottoman control over the country. The British consulate that opened in Jerusalem in 1839 took under its protection all Jews who were neither Ottoman citizens nor citizens of any other European power, and its staff was inspired in part by the belief that it was God's will that the Jews return to Zion (Schölch 1993). Palestine's Arabs were aware of the messianic Zionist outlook of many British officials, and this was a source of their perception (and inference) that the Jews and Europeans had concluded an anti-Islamic compact aimed at establishing a Jewish-Western territorial outpost in Palestine at the expense of its Arab inhabitants. While the Jews who came to Palestine at the time did not see themselves as agents of the European powers but rather as their wards, and their main goal was to live their lives free of the constant threats and discrimination they had endured in their countries of origin, the Arabs viewed their arrival as part of a deliberate project of dispossession. From the Arab perspective, all of the events of the decades that followed — the Balfour Declaration of 1917, the UN partition resolution of 1947, the Israeli, French, and British attack on Egypt in 1956, and European and American aid to Israel since its establishment — have confirmed their belief that Israel is a tool of the Western powers in the Middle East.

Back to Anticolonialism, Colonialism, and Murder

We can draw some interim conclusions from our comparative look at the conduct of Napoleon's army in Jaffa in 1799 and that of the Arab rebels in Jerusalem and Safed and of Muhammad 'Ali's army in Hebron in 1834. Clearly, an unorganized mob, an organized army of conquest, and a rebel force are no different in this respect: in all three cases, national and religious rivalries, combined with superior force and a measure of frustration, can make the forbidden (looting, murder, or rape) permissible. Studies of mass psychology show that there are deeds that we do not permit ourselves to commit as individuals, but that we may well commit when we become part of a collective action. We also know that what is perceived to be out of bounds in everyday life can, at times, be seen as acceptable in a crisis.

But it is still important to keep in mind that there are different kinds of violent mass actions and that each of them presents different moral issues. There is action against the authority of an exploitative ruler (for example, the storming of the Bastille or certain incidents in the Algerian war of liberation), action against a vulnerable minority (Ukrainians against Jews or lynchings of blacks in the American South), and contention between equal groups in which both sides conduct pogroms (episodes in the interethnic war in the former Yugoslavia).

Where Does 1929 Stand on the Scale?

This is one of the principal questions under dispute. To answer it, we need to try to determine the facts that everyone can agree on. It is a fact that the Jews were at that time a numerical minority in Palestine. It is a fact that most of them aspired to achieve Jewish sovereignty, even if they did not always use those words explicitly. It is a fact that their actions were detrimental to the national aspirations that the country's Arabs had begun to develop at the same time. It is a fact that a decisive majority of Jews had no intention of harming the country's Arabs, at least not directly. It is a fact that they did in fact do them harm at various levels. It is a fact that on other levels the country's Arabs benefited from the presence of the Jews. The upshot: The Arabs viewed the Jews as foreign usurpers. The Jews viewed themselves as members of a persecuted minority that returned to its homeland. Many Arabs perceived their struggle to be an anticolonialist one, even if, at the time, they used this terminology only sparingly. Many Jews viewed Zionism as a national liberation movement and the Arab uprisings as an extension of the pogroms they had experienced as a minority in Eastern Europe.

The question of whether the Arabs were conducting pogroms or fighting a war of liberation is, of course, linked to the question of whether Zionism has been a colonialist movement.

Has It Been Colonialism?

In addition to the British support for Zionist aspirations, the claim that Zionism is a colonialist movement is based on the following assertions: it is a movement that worked to transfer a European population to a region inhabited by a less technologically developed, and thus weaker, population (as in other colonialist movements); its members settled in that region without the consent of the local population (as with other colonialist movements); its members felt themselves to be fundamentally superior in culture to the native population (as in other colonialist movements).

Those who dispute the charge also offer serious arguments: the Zionist movement was not a great power; Zionist settlers did not have the support of a powerful country where they enjoyed full and equal citizenship, as most other European colonialists did; the Zionists did not intend to exploit the local population as cheap labor as other settler societies did; and the Zionists did not work to extract the resources of the land they settled and send those resources to another country, as colonialists generally do. Another argument is a historical one — the Jews were not in fact foreigners in the country but rather natives whose ancestors had been sent into exile generations previously. Thus Zionism, in the eyes of its adherents, is a national liberation movement that calls on Jews to return to their historic homeland. (Fundamentally, the debate over whether Zionism is colonialism is a political one; God is present only at its margins. There is a parallel polemic, a religious one, over the question of whom God gave the land to — which is the subject of the next chapter.)

This complex picture means that Zionism can be seen as a movement that combines nationalist and colonialist aspects. The Jews experience it primarily as a realization of their goal as a nation, while the Palestinian Arabs experience it as colonialist. That explains why Zionism did not view those fighting it as anti-colonialists but rather as an inflamed and ignorant mob that did not appreciate the benefits that Jewish settlement brought to the country and opposed the progressive values that Zionism promoted.

Ironically
Colonialists everywhere have viewed local inhabitants who opposed them as an inflamed and ignorant mob opposed to progress.

An Example from 1929
Maurice Samuel, a Jew born in Romania in 1895, moved as a child to England with his family, where he attended high school and the University of Manchester (in Manchester he met and became fond of Chaim Weizmann, the Zionist leader). He then emigrated to the United States, where he was conscripted and served in the army in World War I. After his discharge he served as an interpreter at the Versailles peace conference and on the Morgenthau Commission investigating the pogroms in Eastern Europe. Subsequently he joined the staff of the World Zionist Organization's New York office, and in the mid-1920s he published several books in which he wrestled with the question of the Jews' role in Western history and their relations with non-Jews. Samuel was in Tel Aviv when the 1929 riots broke out, and he volunteered to serve in one of the contingents that the Haganah organized to defend the city. Shortly after the riots he published a widely read book about them. In one passage, he recalls his own thoughts and those of other guardsmen at a lookout point:

> To complete the caricature, we could not help feeling that in this petty squabble (for such it was bound to appear to us) we did stand on the side of a principle. And the principle was symbolized for us there by the scene at our feet. On the one side lay Tel Aviv, a city which had sprung up in twenty years on empty and forbidding sands. A city that was modern in the least objectionable sense; peopled by men and women conscious of social and intellectual purposes. On the other side, Jaffa, a very ancient city, a city typical of the decayed East, with a few rich and many poor — and a poverty of that awful and indescribable type which can be found only in the East. . . . On the one side Tel Aviv with its poets and painters and thinkers. On the other, backward Jaffa, in which education is a fantastic luxury, and modern intellectuality — in a levantinized form at that — the possession of a handful. (1929, 75–76).

The author underscores, with an arsenal of literary techniques, the fact that he is rooted in Western culture, just like other Zionists, and in contrast with the backward Arab masses. He writes at length about the events of the day as a whole, but completely disregards a specific event that took place quite close to his guard post—the murder of the 'Awn family.

Perhaps mentioning it would have weakened the thesis of his book. He mentions a Jewish wagon driver, Baruch Rozin, who was murdered nearby, and the killing of the Haganah troops who went out to rescue the Jews who had been trapped in the ethanol factory. Those deaths were compatible with the image he wanted to foster.

The Murder of Rozin the Wagoner

On Sunday, the day of the attack on Tel Aviv, Baruch Rozin the wagoner was moving out of his home in Neveh Shalom into a new apartment in the center of town. Not far from the Hasan Beq mosque, as he and his sons Aharon and Leib made their third haul of his belongings, they ran into an Arab mob advancing from Jaffa toward Tel Aviv. Aharon was driving the wagon while Leib and his father walked alongside. The mob approached and they heard voices calling out "*Udrub* [beat them]!" A wave of Arabs surged forward and attacked them with poles and sticks. Leib managed to get away, running toward Tel Aviv; Aharon, slightly wounded, evaded the mob, and also fled northward. He almost collapsed a short while later, and a passing car rushed him to a hospital. Their elderly father was beaten again and again until he died. An autopsy found a bullet entry wound. Apparently someone shot him at short range. Binyamin Plastovsky, a police officer, was on duty nearby. He later testified that he saw, from a distance, a mob attacking Jews, but he was deterred from getting any closer because he was alone. When the mob dispersed, he approached and found Baruch Rozin's body (record of the trial of the attackers, October 10, 1929, CZA L59/58).

What Does Al-Dabbagh Say about That?

Al-Dabbagh does not mention the attack on the ethanol factory, the killing of the Haganah men in Jaffa, or the murder of the wagoner Baruch Rozin, all of which took place on the same day that the 'Awn family was slaughtered. He also has a nationalist outlook he seeks to promote and a set of images he uses to that end.

A possible inference: both sides engage in similar techniques of denial, repression, and cherry-picking the events they write about. In other words, they use like methods of constructing a national narrative. In this regard, there is no difference between Western and Levantine intellectuals. Another inference: each writer mentions the victims that he cares for, those who are closest to him.

Funeral of Tel Aviv victims, August 1929 (Central Zionist Archives).

The Seething Mob: A British View

In normal times, some of the British in Palestine were attracted by the vibrancy of Jaffa. Some of them took a romantic, Orientalist view of it. Others were put off by the city. One account of the beginning of the troubles comes from a British officer, S. C. Atkins:

> At about 1200 hours I received information that a mob was preparing to attack the Governorate. . . . [B]y this time some 2000 Moslems had collected in the Square and about 100 were already on the Governorate steps, although the mob was disorderly and excited, I do not think that there was any intention to attack the Governorate, furthermore any attempt would have been easily repulsed since I had a cordon of Police with batons at the entrance of the Governorate and an armed guard in reserve inside (out of sight). Seeing that this was the time for pacifying the mob, I cleared the Governorate steps using [as] little force as possible and then proceeded in amongst the crowd explaining what would happen if they did not clear, in a few minutes the square was clear. A little later, however, on the arrival of a wounded Moslem, a mob again began to collect shouting we want a "Turkish Government" (the Ringleader has since been arrested), the mob was dispersed in a manner similar to the former and the square was again clear. (Atkins 1929, 1)

Atkins's temperate mob control method turned out not to be effective when more Arab casualties were reported. The mob gathered again, he reported, and at this point he had no choice but to fire shots in the air.

A Reminder

When attacked by natives, an officer with military experience, serving an imperial power, experiences the incident differently than do the members of a civilian community attacked in their home city, even when they are targets of the same attack. What is the significance of this difference? And to what extent are the attackers aware of it? Hard to say.

Isma'il Tubasi, Incendiary No. 1

The term "inflamed mob" presupposes that someone has inflamed it. The British police in Jaffa identified two incendiaries prior to the outbreak of violence. In the district police log Officer Alfred Riggs (the policeman who repelled the attack on Tel Aviv and who arrested Hinkis) recorded what happened that morning. At 8:00 a.m., he wrote, a crowd gathered at the mosque. Orators spoke of the Western Wall, and Isma'il Tubasi gave a fiery speech. Some of the older sheikhs tried to cut him off, without success. He got so emotional that he fainted and had to be revived and carried away. His talk, Riggs said, had a very bad effect on the audience.

In his testimony before the commission of inquiry, Riggs offered a more detailed account of what Tubasi said. Riggs placed the event at a slightly later hour, but the substance was the same: "[At] about 10.00 hours he [Sheikh al-Muzaffar] addressed the people. He asked them to refrain from demonstrating and told them to be quiet. Ismail Tubassa [sic] rose and said: 'In the name of God, in the name of Mohammed and religion, we do not want protests; we are ten years protesting but without results. This protest will receive the same fate as the others, we must demonstrate, attack our enemies by ourselves, lose our lives for the country.' He was excited and made the assembly very excited" (Commission on the Palestine Disturbances of August 1929 [hereafter Commission] 1930, 2:997–98).

Tubasi, as his name indicates, came to Jaffa from the town of Tubas in northeastern Samaria. He had been born in 1907 and was twenty-two years old in 1929, having just completed his studies at the Islamic College in Jerusalem. Following the riots he was sentenced to imprisonment for incitement. After his release he served for several years as a leader of the Arab Scouts in Palestine, working also as a teacher and journalist. In the war of 1948 he joined the forces defending Jaffa. After the city's fall he returned to his hometown of Tubas, where he taught at the local high school. In 1979 he published in Amman a book titled

Kifah al-Sha'ab al-Filastini 1908–1965 (The struggle of the Palestinian people). His speech in Jaffa in 1929 was his first public appearance.

Stalin's Man in Jaffa

A second activist involved in the events in Jaffa—a provocateur, according to the police—was Hamdi Hussayni. He personified a different social and political phenomenon than Tubasi did. Born in Gaza in 1899 to one of the city's prominent Muslim families, he was sent to a church high school. At the end of World War I he went into journalism, eventually serving as editor of *al-Karmil* in Haifa, one of the most important Arabic periodicals in Palestine, and writing for other publications. At the beginning of the 1920s he served as a teacher in Ramla. About seventy years later, 'Abd al-Rahman Kayyali, who had been a student of his, related how proud he and his fellow students were when Hussayni refused to stand up in respect during a visit by the British high commissioner to the town (Shina'a 1993).

In 1927, Hussayni assumed the editorship of the Jaffa newspaper *Sawt al-Haqq* (Voice of truth) and served as an active member of the anti-British Young Muslim Association, in the latter capacity helping promote a manual laborers' union. As a result of this activity, the Palestinian Communist Party invited him to participate in an international conference of the League against Imperialism, organized by the Comintern in Germany in 1928. He seems to have made a very good impression on the participants (he was not just an analyst and organizer but also spoke several languages, among them Spanish, Italian, Hebrew, and Turkish). He was then invited to Moscow, where he met Joseph Stalin and other senior figures.

When Hussayni returned to Palestine, he was placed under surveillance by the British secret service. He was still being followed during the tense days of August 1929. British police officers who testified before the Commission on the Palestine Disturbances of August 1929 (the Shaw Commission) referred to him as a professional troublemaker. He tried to stir up the crowd politically, they said, but quickly realized that religious appeals were an easier way of influencing the masses. He thus adopted the claim—commonly voiced by the mufti of Jerusalem, Hajj Amin al-Hussayni—that the Jews were trying to take over al-Aqsa.

Communist sources depict Hamdi Hussayni in a different light. Leon Zahavi, an Israeli Communist activist and the Israeli Communist Party's representative in Moscow, refers to Hussayni as a "well-known nationalist revolutionary" and relates that Hussayni advocated directing the struggle against the British, not the Jews (Zahavi 2005, 155, 178), because the struggle should be anti-imperialist, not nationalist. The 1929 pogrom, Zahavi writes, occurred because the communists in Palestine did not succeed in taking charge of and organizing the struggle.

In any case, Hussayni received in his office in Jaffa a telegram from the Committee for the Defense of al-Buraq (the Western Wall) asking him to organize demonstrations in his city in response to the Jewish procession to the site. He does indeed seem to have been involved in organizing the demonstrations, but we do not know what he thought about the attack on Tel Aviv.

And One Who Did Not Incite

A third prominent figure in these events was Sheikh ʿAbd al-Qader al-Muzaffar, one of the leaders of the Palestinian national movement at the time and a man of great public influence. Al-Muzaffar was born in Jerusalem in 1892 to a family of *ʿulamaa* (Islamic scholars). He pursued advanced studies at al-Azhar Institute in Cairo, graduating in 1918. Al-Muzaffar spent the period following World War I in Damascus, along with other nationalists who gathered in the city in the hope of taking part in the establishment of a large and united Arab kingdom encompassing the entire Arab east (the territory that later became Iraq, Syria, Lebanon, Jordan, and Israel-Palestine) under the rule of Faisal ibn Hussayn of the Hashemite clan. While in Damascus, al-Muzaffar maintained friendly relations with another native of Jerusalem, Yosef Yoel Rivlin, then headmaster of the Hebrew school for girls in Damascus and later a translator of the Qur'an into Hebrew (and father of Israel's President Reuven Rivlin). Yosef Rivlin referred to al-Muzaffar as a leader of "the extremist anti-Zionist clique in Damascus" ("Beit-Hashem beMaʿarbolet," *Hed haMizrah*, March 17, 1950) But he also recalled that in the 1930s al-Muzaffar sent his nephew to study Qur'an exegesis under Rivlin at the Hebrew University, and that the sheikh, then living in Jaffa, took a great interest in the innovative interpretations that his nephew learned from Rivlin. In 1923, when the British announced elections for a legislative assembly in Palestine in which seats would be apportioned on a religious basis among Muslims, Christians, and Jews, al-Muzaffar was among the leaders of the campaign for a boycott of the elections. Only a few men declared their candidacies, and the voter turnout was extremely low. In the end the British decided not to establish the assembly. It was one of the most important of the (very few) successes of the Palestinian national movement during the Mandate period, but it had a negative impact in the long run.

Al-Muzaffar's public career later had ups and downs, as did his relations with the mainstream of the Palestinian national movement. The peak of his popularity came at the time of the mass demonstrations against the Mandate regime in 1933, when many of the protest leaders were arrested. All agreed to post bail except for al-Muzaffar, whom the Palestinian national poet of the time, Ibrahim Tuqan, memorialized in verse:

Palestine in flames, roars in fury
Step aside — you are not my men
The captive [al-Muzaffar] is he who has gained honor
And those who pursue office are his atonement. (Tuqan 1966, 48–49)

Al-Muzaffar shared a prison cell with Abba Ahimeir, chief of Brit HaBiryonim, a cell of radical Jewish nationalists. "As a Zionist of the Nordau-Jabotinsky school, the author of these memoirs had no interest in meeting with Arabs," Ahimeir wrote in an article he published at the time of al-Muzaffar's death (*Herut*, July 1, 1949). But the struggle against the British, even if pursued by both men separately, led them to the same prison cell in downtown Jerusalem's Russian Compound. "That time spent in the company of Muslim Arabs and Levantine Christians buttressed my negative view of the East," Ahimeir wrote. He called al-Muzaffar the leader and founder of Islamic extremism in Palestine.

Ahimeir's conduct in the period leading up to the 1929 riots will be examined below. But here we can see that Ahimeir's characterization of al-Muzaffar as "extremist" had no foundation. That same Sunday, when the riots began in Jaffa, al-Muzaffar had called on the crowd at the Hasan Beq Mosque not to head to the Jewish neighborhoods. It was the second speech, by Isma'il Tubasi, that ignited the crowd and persuaded it to take action. Perhaps Tubasi's collapse during his speech made his appeal more powerful. When he came to his senses, Tubasi repeated his call to attack the Jewish neighborhoods and set out to do so himself. In other words, two opposing views about attacking the Jews were voiced at the same time at the same mosque in Jaffa. Perhaps at that very moment the first sparks of resistance to the mufti's belligerent strategy appeared in al-Muzaffar's mind. During World War II, he opposed the mufti's alliance with Nazi Germany (H. Cohen 2008, 184–85).

Jaffa, Sunday, Early Afternoon

The crowd that had assembled at Hasan Beq set out after Tubasi. The first wave of the attack was repulsed by Officer Riggs and his men, who positioned a machine gun at the corner of HaCarmel Street and fired at the attackers. But they were not deterred, and the gunfire continued. The historical-literary reader put out by the Tel Aviv–Jaffa Municipality includes an account of the events written by a Jewish policeman who was positioned at the end of Herzl Street:

I made out two Arabs armed with rifles appearing from under the orange grove's barbed-wire fence and aiming their rifles to the right, toward our position. When I saw this I instantly aimed my rifle. A single shot and then another one and I saw one Arab fall. The second had also been hit but still had the strength to drag his friend by the feet into the grove.

I gathered up a group of courageous men and we set out on a counterattack. I was the only one with an English rifle and the few rounds that remained. The others—with pistols. The shooting from the side of the orange grove gradually fell silent. The Arabs must have suffered losses from our counterattack. We were able to advance to Herzl Hill, and I again heard lots of shooting at the hill. I raised my head up and saw, at a distance of 200 meters from me, a car with a group of Haganah members who had returned by this route, stuck in the middle of the Abu Kabir neighborhood's main road; a few of the passengers had jumped out and began running one by one in our direction. They were heading toward Tel Aviv, to Herzl Street. The first to arrive was Tula Gordon and he called for help. After him came the driver, Verobichek, badly wounded in the head. Not far from him was Feingold's son, wounded. After them a few others. The last was Binyamin Goldberg. When he was two meters from me a bullet hit his head. His white pith helmet was knocked aside and he fell bleeding into my hands, badly wounded in the head. I fired furiously at the advancing Arabs. . . .

At the same time I noticed that a ladder stood next to a one-story Arab house and that a group of armed Arabs was going up and down it between the grove and the yard of the house. I informed some of my comrades and asked them if they agreed to go there with me. They consented. We broke through the door into the yard with our weapons ready for any surprise. When I went into one of the rooms I heard the voices of people talking. I gave a sign to the guys and we broke into the room. The seven Arabs who were there were armed with pistols and sticks and were lying there surprised. Our desire for vengeance burned within us like fire and was satisfied. I checked the rest of the rooms but they were empty. We closed the door and went out. (Hinkis 1957, 231–32)

The author of this article in the book *Yafo* is Simha Hinkis.
The house in question was that of the ʿAwn family.
His version of the event: there were seven victims, all of them armed.
When he wrote the piece, he was an official of Tel Aviv municipal government.

Binyamin Goldberg and His Companions
Binyamin Zeʾev Goldberg, who fell bleeding into Hinkis's arms, was born in 1905. He was the youngest son of Yitzhak Leib Goldberg, a wealthy Zionist activist who had opposed Theodor Herzl's proposal to establish a temporary Jewish home in East Africa (called the Uganda Plan) and who had been one of the first donors to the Zionist land purchase organization, Keren Kayemet Le-Yisrael (Jewish National Fund). The senior Goldberg financed the purchase of land throughout Palestine, including an expanse on Mount Scopus, just east of

Jerusalem, that belonged to Sir John Gray Hill and on which the Hebrew University was built. He also purchased the land on which Hartuv, a farm village in the Judean Hills, was established; Hartuv was also attacked in 1929. Yitzhak Goldberg owned citrus groves in the area of Ramat Gan, just east of Tel Aviv, and was a cofounder of the daily newspaper *Ha'aretz* and the Carmel distillery. Hayim Nahman Bialik wrote a poem about him, beginning with the line "May my lot be with you, the humble of the earth, the silent souls" (Gershon Gera identified Goldberg as the subject of the poem in his biography of 1984, *HaNadiv HaLo Noda'* [The unknown philanthropist]). Yitzhak's brother was injured during the 1921 riots and died of his wounds; the brother's grandson, Dan Tolkovsky, who was eight years old in 1929, later became commander of the Israeli Air Force. Binyamin was twenty-four when he was killed. He had graduated from Tel Aviv's Herzliya Hebrew Gymnasium high school eight years previously and been sent by his father to study mechanical engineering in England. When he returned to Palestine in 1927 he went to work at Haroshet HaEmek, an underground arms factory established by the Zionist Labor Brigade on the western side of the Jezreel Valley that was camouflaged as a repair shop for agricultural machinery. But the factory did not last long, so Binyamin returned to Tel Aviv and joined the Haganah.

On Friday, when the disturbances began, Binyamin Goldberg rode to Jerusalem on his motorcycle to take part in defending Talpiot, an isolated Jewish neighborhood to the south of the Old City that was under attack. On Sunday morning he returned to Tel Aviv and immediately set out to evacuate the Jews trapped in the ethanol factory next to Abu Kabir. It later turned out that this mission had been superfluous, because the British had taken responsibility for rescuing the people in the factory. The residents of Abu Kabir thought that the Haganah contingent had come to kill them, so they took the offensive and killed their presumed assailants. Three other members of the Haganah force who had volunteered for the mission were also killed: Yosef Berkowitz, a customs clerk for the Mandate administration; Moshe Harari-Bloomberg, an actor and musician; and Isaac-Yehoshua Feingold, a founder of the Ariel cigarette factory. According to the page about him on the Defense Ministry's memorial website, Harari called out to the Arabs who were approaching them: "We mean no harm to you, let us pass." Goldberg's last words were: "But the Land of Israel will be ours no matter what" (Gera 1984, 218).

This is the Zionist story in miniature: The Jews arrive in Palestine to save their lives and those of their brethren. They speak to the Arabs in two voices: "We mean no harm to you, let us pass" and "But the Land of Israel will be ours no matter what."

The Police Version

The next morning, on August 26, at 8:15 a.m., an account of the discovery of the bodies in the 'Awn home was recorded in the log of the Lod District police headquarters (which was responsible for Tel Aviv and Jaffa as well). An Arab family consisting of three men, one woman, and one child were murdered by Jews and cut to pieces, the log entry states. Immediately afterward is another entry reporting that Be'er Tuvia had been attacked by 2,000 Arabs. The Jews had all taken refuge in a single house, and the entire village was on fire. Trucks needed to be sent to evacuate the inhabitants to Rehovot. Then comes another entry: all the Jewish families in Gaza have been brought to Tel Aviv.

Be'er Tuvia was burned down and later rebuilt. The Jewish community in Gaza was never reestablished. Several Jewish settlements were founded in the Gaza Strip after it was taken by Israel in 1967, but all were evacuated in 2005. That same year the fourth and perhaps fifth generation of Palestinian refugees who left Jaffa in 1948 was growing up, many of them in Gaza.

The members of the 'Awn family were buried after a medical examination of their remains; the doctors filled out death certificates with details about their wounds. Photocopies of the certificates are on file in the Central Zionist Archives.

The Investigation

The police assumed that the Jews murdered the 'Awn family. Haganah operatives in Tel Aviv reported the incident by telephone to their counterparts in Jerusalem: "It has not been proven that it was done by Jews. Arab robbers are on the loose and it could be that it was a provocative act by Arabs" (ISA P69776/2). That was the first response, and perhaps the hope, of the Haganah.

The police launched an investigation. Officers went to the site and collected bullet cartridges. Witnesses were questioned. They related that a Jewish policeman had arrived at the house at the head of a group of Jews. The investigation continued in an unambiguous direction. In an interview in the daily newspaper *Ma'ariv* some thirty years later, Hinkis recalled:

> The next morning the British officer Ricks [the journalist's misspelling of Riggs] came to me and instructed me to take my rifle and go to the Jaffa police station. There the rifle was taken from me and I was dismissed. I sensed that something was wrong and that the rifle had been taken from me as a court exhibit. Two days later I learned that the Arabs had informed the British that a Jewish policeman had killed the seven [victims found in the house]. A Jew also had a hand in informing about that. In the end they arrested me. For a month and a half I had no respite. Interrogations day and night. I denied everything. In the meantime they organized all the incriminat-

ing material against me. . . . The trial was conducted in Jaffa. The Jewish Agency and National Committee provided me with defense counsel. The late Drs. Eliash and Dunkelblum, as well as Olshan, Henigman, and Frankel, may they have long lives. (*Yamim VeLeilot* supplement, November 12, 1965)

Investigating Magistrate

Rules of procedure established in the wake of the riots called for the suspects to be brought before an investigating magistrate. If the magistrate was persuaded that there was sufficient evidence implicating them in manslaughter or murder, he would send the case to a panel of three British judges. On November 6, 1929, the investigating magistrate decided to indict Hinkis on five counts of murder, the victims being Sheikh 'Abd al-Gani 'Awn (about fifty years of age), Ibrahim Khalil 'Awn (forty), 'Abd al-Gani 'Ali Bahalul (fifty), Maryam (forty-five), and Halima (twenty-eight). Hinkis was also charged with the attempted murder of two other victims: a five-year-old boy and a two-month-old baby. They were wounded in the attack and taken to the hospital, where they recovered (the testimony heard by the investigating magistrate can be found in CZA L59/68, 61).

No Children Were Killed

Notwithstanding al-Dabbagh's account, the initial police report, and *Sefer Toldot HaHaganah*, no children were killed in the incident. The five-year-old was wounded when a bullet penetrated his left arm and exited from his ankle, damaging his internal organs. He spent forty-three days convalescing in the hospital and was released. The two-month-old baby spent ten days in the hospital. According to the medical report, he had suffered a blow from a blunt instrument to the left side of his head—on his ear, temple, and cheek. In other words, he was apparently beaten or struck, but his skull was not shattered. A third child, nine-year-old 'Ali, the sheikh's son, was found unhurt, lying under his mother's body.

Medical Reports

The public considers such reports to be extremely reliable. Courts generally view them that way as well. Why? Because it is both necessary and convenient to do so. After all, neither the readers of this book nor the judges were present at the site when the incident took place. No one knows for certain who did the killing. No one knows precisely what caused the victims' wounds. Medical reports imbue with authority the general picture of events that a court must construct in order to reach a judicial decision. The expertise that writing such a report requires and the professional language in which it is couched add to its gravity. In fact, courts often receive contradictory medical reports, one from the defense and another from the prosecution. That did not happen in the case at hand. The reports on the victims of the attack in Jaffa were written by the director of the city's government hospital, Fuad Dajjani.

Arab (and Jewish) Civil Servants

The fact that the medical reports were written by an Arab doctor does not in and of itself mean they were biased. Arab civil servants coped with conflicting pressures and reacted in different ways. During the riots, some Arab policemen took action against the Arab attackers and in some cases testified against them in police investigations. Other Arab policemen joined the attackers, as in Jaffa in 1921. In one well-known case from 1929, a British officer, Raymond Cafferata, shot an Arab policeman who was trying to rape a Jewish woman in Hebron. In general, the conduct of most Arab policemen can best be described as navigating between a rock and a hard place—they were not overly diligent in thwarting Arab attacks, choosing not to become the targets of ire from their own community, but they also sought to do their duty adequately enough to avoid reprimands from their superiors. The assumption here, which many Zionists disputed, was that the British administration sought to squelch the riots rather than encourage them.

The classic example of an Arab police officer who acted against the assailants was Halim Basta, a Copt from Egypt who served as an officer in the Jewish and Arab villages that fell under the purview of the Ramla police station. Basta sent his men to defend the Jewish settlements in the region. The Ben Shemen Youth Village's logbook praised him to the skies (as reported in *Davar*, September 5, 1929). Among other things, his men arrested the *mukhtar* of Hadid, a nearby Arab village, using him as a hostage to prevent an attack on the youth village. The newspaper recounts how Basta assembled the leaders of the surrounding Arab villages and warned them against attacking their Jewish neighbors. He later testified for the prosecution at the trials of the Arabs who attacked Be'er Tuvia and other settlements. For the Arabs, Basta crossed the line. At the beginning of November 1929 Arabs from Ramla wrote to the high commissioner demanding that he dismiss Basta for having treated "those who suffered damage in the riots" harshly. They meant that he had arrested Arabs who had been involved in attacks on Jewish settlements and who had been wounded in the process. *Davar*, the daily newspaper of the labor movement, reported this demand and interpreted it:

> What did this Arab police officer do? He did his duty properly. He did what every other officer in the country should have done during the riots. For days before [the riots] Halim Basta's car made the rounds of the area under his purview to warn, oversee, inspect. He visited many Arab villages during the riots, cautioning them

not to attack Jewish settlements, as they craved to do. He also threatened arrests and other punishments if any sort of public disturbance occurred on his beat. . . . And the fact that flourishing Jewish settlements remained safe despite everything rankles the provocateurs. . . . After the riots he searched the villages, found stolen items, and arrested the guilty. Can the Arabs of Ramla and the rebel villages pass over that in silence? "We demand the dismissal of Halim Basta." (*Davar*, November 12, 1929)

What Happened to Him?

Basta was not dismissed. He kept his position, serving for a while in Hebron, then in the northern valley district and afterward in Haifa. He excelled at his job as an investigation and intelligence officer. In 1933 he solved a horrifying murder in the Jezreel Valley, the killing of Yosef Ya'akobi of Nahalal and his nine-year-old son David in a bomb attack. Basta collected the nails that the bomb had sent flying; located the store in which they had been purchased; and traced them to the bombers, disciples of Sheikh 'Izz a-Din al-Qassam, a jihadist Haifa preacher. The suspects were tried and sentenced to death. Basta continued to monitor al-Qassam's adherents throughout the first year of the Arab Revolt of 1936–39, earning their indignation. In mid-April 1937, Basta and his bodyguard, an Arab policeman named Hanna Shehada, were walking near the Haifa courthouse when three gunmen overtook them and shot them to death at close range. Basta left a wife and a five-year-old daughter. The annual report of the Mandate police force for 1933 cited him for his work on the Ya'akobi case. The 1936 report praised him for his exceptional courage and devotion to his duties. The next annual report, that of 1937, stated that he had been posthumously awarded the king's medal for police work (Palestine Police Force, *Annual Administrative Report*, TNA: CO 814/8, 11, 12).

A Multifaceted Dilemma

Under British rule, many Jewish policemen also had to maneuver between their professional obligations and their national affiliation. Shlomo Schiff served as a police officer in Tel Aviv in the 1920s. During the 1929 riots he was Hinkis's commander. When he testified at his subordinate's trial, he seems to have done his best not to incriminate Hinkis. But Hinkis felt that his commander did not do enough to defend him (HHA testimony 37/17). In Tel Aviv Schiff was remembered favorably for his role in repelling the 1929 attacks. At the time he also warned a group of armed Jewish defenders that the British forces were searching for illicit Jewish arms (Dinur 1973, 2:367). Schiff continued to serve in the police force during the 1930s and the early 1940s. His nemesis was Lehi (which the British called the Stern Gang), a radical Jewish national guerrilla organization. During these years Lehi perpetrated a series of attacks against British targets.

Schiff's duties included counterinsurgency actions against the splinter group, which acted against the directives of the Jewish agency and the Yishuv's leadership. In January 1942 Lehi set an ambush for several senior police officers on Yael Street in Tel Aviv. Their primary target was Geoffrey Morton, head of the police force's plainclothes Criminal Investigations Division. They laid a trap involving three bombs—a small one intended to draw police officers to the chosen spot, and two larger ones that would detonate after the officers arrived. Schiff arrived after the first explosion, along with several other Jewish officers, and was killed in the second explosion; another Jewish officer, Nahum Goldmann, was wounded and died the following day. Morton survived. By some accounts, the assassin who was assigned to shoot him got cold feet. Others say he survived because the third charge never went off. Following the attack, Lehi issued a broadside declaring that Schiff had been sentenced to death by an underground court for having devoted himself to turning Jewish freedom fighters over to the British enemy (differing accounts of the event can be found in Weinshal 1956 and Heller 1989). Al-Qassam's disciples justified their attack on Basta in a similar way.

"The First of the Bloodbath"

About three weeks after the attack on the officers, on February 12, 1942, Morton's operatives burst into the hide-out of Lehi's commander, Avraham Stern, whose nom de guerre was Yair. Morton killed him on the spot. Some Jews cheered, but many mourned. One of the mourners was Yonatan Ratosh, a poet and a prominent figure in the Canaanite movement, a group that sought to create a Hebrew-Arab local culture on the basis of the country's pagan and biblical past. In his elegy to Stern he wrote:

> You are the first—like a dog put to death
> You are the first—on the single road
> Who steps on the altar alone
> Who digs his grave with his own hands.
> You are the first of the bloodbath
> You are the first of the dawn of days. (Ratosh 1974, 55–56)

On the Witness Stand

We have jumped a decade ahead—it's time to go back. In 1929 the Haganah was still the only Jewish defense organization. Etzel had not yet been formed, and Lehi had not yet broken away from Etzel. The Haganah's level of organization and operational capabilities were still very limited. Jewish policemen, some of whom were also members of the Haganah, had to decide first of all how to act against the Arabs, not whether to act against Jewish underground organizations. Hinkis, according to the prosecution at his trial, had not only made a decision that violated his duty as a policeman, but also one that violated the law and morality—he had used his personal weapon to kill innocent people. His trial began in a small courtroom on January 21, 1930. There was a bench for the prosecution, another one for the defense, and one more for newspaper reporters, both Jewish and Arab. Unlike at most trials, people who wished to enter had to undergo a search to ensure that none of them was bearing arms. Policemen and officers from the Tel Aviv and Jaffa forces were called as witnesses. So was Mahmoud Gohar, husband of Maryam, one of the victims. He told the court that he and his family had lived in the same building as the 'Awn family. He had been in the house when the incident took place. When the door was broken down by the Jews, he had climbed a ladder to the roof. He heard gunfire and hid under a pile of straw. When the attackers had gone, he went back down into the living room. His wife was wounded, could not speak, but was still breathing. His children were wounded. He saw the sheikh's wife dead and her son 'Ali under her, still alive. There were bullet cartridges between the pools of blood. He took the children with him to seek a hiding place and medical assistance. In the meantime his wife died. He testified that the shooter had been a Jewish policeman.

Mahmoud, Maryam's Husband

The Hebrew press covered the post-riot trials extensively. These newspapers frequently exhibited a cynical tone. They tended to be dismissive of Arab testimony and relatively uncritical of Jewish witnesses. "He has a cataract on his right eye and the other eye is shortsighted," *Davar* reported on February 5, regarding one of the prosecution witnesses. However, the same issue reported Mahmoud Gohar's testimony in a more objective way, perhaps out of respect for the loss he had suffered: "About 30 years old. Dressed in breeches, dark, like the other principal inhabitants of Abu Kabir, a settlement of immigrants from Egypt founded by Ibrahim Pasha in the middle of the previous century." This description is given offhandedly and does not include just one witness but makes a generalization: that most of the inhabitants of Abu Kabir had, just two or three generations previously, been Egyptian immigrants. They had arrived in Palestine about a century before, during the reign of Ibrahim Pasha, when Palestine was under Egyptian rule. Is this meant to imply that they are not truly natives of Palestine? That they are less indigenous to Palestine than the Jews? Perhaps. In any case, the writer does not claim that they were drawn to Palestine by the economic growth brought on by the Zionist influx—as, according to some writers, a large part of the Palestinian Arab population were. After all, the forebears of the inhabitants of Abu Kabir arrived prior to the inception of Zionism.

The Egyptian Immigration

Like many other facts, the Egyptian immigration to Palestine sometimes serves as a political weapon. In the debates over the problem of the refugees from the 1948 war and about the connection the Arabs have to the land, some point to the fact that many of the refugees from Jaffa and the southern coastal plain had actually lived in Palestine for only a single generation, or if not that, then their ancestors had been there for only a century. This claim is meant to prove that they have just a tenuous tie to the land, and therefore that the Palestinian tragedy is not all that tragic. Indeed, this attempt to define these people as Egyptians — that is, to claim that they retained stronger emotional and political ties to their forebears' country of origin than to Palestine — is tempting for Zionists but is not at all convincing. Had that been the case, they presumably would have fled to Egypt when they had to leave their homes in 1948. The evidence that I have been able to unearth indicates that very few of the refugees from this region did so. The vast majority of Palestinians of Egyptian descent found refuge in the Gaza Strip's refugee camps after the war; they constitute an integral part of the Palestinian nation. Furthermore, having been in a place only a generation or two did not make being uprooted any easier. Israeli families who lived in the Yamit salient in the Sinai Peninsula for two decades or in the Gaza Strip for a generation, where Israeli government decisions on withdrawal from territories forced Jews out of their homes, can testify to the agony displacement causes even after a much shorter stay.

Arab immigration to Palestine is a subject studied largely by Israeli researchers, and the question of who was here first, the Arabs or the Jews, always hovers in the background. As a rule, Arab historians do not share the fundamental assumption that determining priority will show whose claim to the land is stronger. They view migration within the larger Arab region as natural, including the movement of peoples from the Maghreb (North Africa) and the Mashriq (the Arab lands of Asia) into Palestine. They see no relationship between this and the strength or weakness of the Palestinian national claim. For example, Hasan Ibrahim Sa'id matter-of-factly notes the Egyptian and Maghrebi origins of many Jaffa families in his comprehensive book on Jaffa in the first half of the nineteenth century (Sa'id 2006). Why do they not see this as undermining the Palestinian claim of a continuous presence on the country's soil? The reason is that nation-states in the Middle East are a modern phenomenon created by the Western superpowers. That being the case, migration from one place to another within the Arab world, prior to World War I and even after it, is considered natural and unremarkable. Beyond that, Palestine, as a sacred land, had always been a special case. It had been a melting pot for Muslims who came there from all over the world, along with immigrants of other faiths. Hanna 'Issa Malak

(1993, 13) goes even further and reminds his readers that one of Jaffa's nicknames is Umm al-Gharib (mother of strangers), referring to its warm welcome of people from all over the world. Muslims fluent in the Hadith literature (the sayings of the Prophet) add that the Prophet Mohammad told his companions that it was specially virtuous to perform a *hijra* to — that is, leave one's home and go to live in — the land of the prophets. One of his companions, 'Abdallah ibn 'Omar, a major figure in the Hadith tradition, heard him say: "There will be a *hijra* after *hijra*, to the place that your father Ibrahim moved to" (Ibn Hanbal 1978, 2:84). This would be in preparation for the Day of Judgment.

Hinkis's Sentence: To Be Hanged until Dead

Immigrant or not, Maryam's husband gave the court his testimony. In their cross-examination, Hinkis's lawyers attempted to undermine the credibility of the prosecution's witnesses. But there was other testimony about the involvement of a policeman, and the forensic evidence confirmed this. An ammunition clip found at the site was of the type in police use, the bullets extracted from the bodies of the dead had been shot from Hinkis's gun, the door had been broken open with a rifle butt — and the forensic finding was that it had been the butt of Hinkis's rifle: "The British expert Dr. Becker proved black on white that I shot from my rifle, in such a clear way that Dr. Eliash and my other lawyers had no recourse. My position began to look very serious. I lost all hope. . . . The judgment was eighteen pages long, and concluded: the High Court for Serious Crimes has found you guilty and sentences you to death by hanging. You will be hung on a rope until your soul leaves you. The high commissioner will determine your place of burial and may God have mercy on you" (HHA Hinkis testimony 37/17).

Davar on the Conviction

Davar published an editorial the day after the sentencing. It was titled "No Confidence":

During the riots unforgivable crimes were committed in this country. Among the hundreds of cases in which Jewish blood was shed by Arabs, of robbery and arson against Jewish property, there were isolated cases of Arabs falling victim [to acts] that had no defensive justification. These cases must be greatly regretted, but they should not be judged with the same severity as attacks on Jews. No judgment can disregard the fact that these cases occurred after Jerusalem and Hebron, Hulda and Safed. But despite the bitter and indignant mood of those days, when it seemed that the government had forfeited the blood of the Jews and that they had no one on whom they could depend, the court had to do its job in these cases. We demand justice and will not contest it even when the arm of the law falls on a Jew. We demand only that the judges and the government take into account the unusual moments in which these incidents took place. But we will not say that such a crime is not a crime because it was committed by a Jew, even during those horrible August days.

That being the case, what is the source of the furor that overcame the Yishuv when it heard the death sentence against Hinkis? . . . [The reason is that] Hinkis's trial was preceded by the Maklef trial [of the murderers of the Maklef family of Motza, near Jerusalem; the defendants were not convicted, see below] and before and after that by less prominent and less horrifying cases, but with the same nature — a distortion of justice against the Jews. . . . It can only be that the legal investigation has been subverted. It can only be that a hidden hand is, it would seem, directing the courts to the detriment of the Jews. ("No Confidence," *Davar*, February 7, 1930)

On Revenge

When *Davar* emphasized its opposition to acts of revenge, it was not just speaking in platitudes. This was consistently the official position of the labor movement, and therefore of the Jewish communal institutions led by the labor movement, both preceding 1929 and during the Arab Revolt of 1936–39. The policy was known then as *havlaga* — self-restraint. While it was not pursued without exception, it was nevertheless the reason why a group of the policy's opponents within the Haganah broke away and formed Etzel. The ongoing debate over when and where resorting to arms was justified was a prominent feature of the public discourse of the Yishuv, as it continues to be in Israel today.

Contempt

On closer reading, *Davar*'s editorial shows itself to be carefully crafted, a jigsaw puzzle of arguments and counterarguments. It categorically condemns the murders, declares support for the courts, and proclaims the principle of equality before the law. But it also states that, despite this fundamental equality, the mind-set of the Jewish murderers should be understood. There is also a claim that Hinkis's conviction resulted from biases in the investigation of his case. The newspaper clearly states that revenge is unacceptable, yet it supports Hinkis. The sum total is a sort of interweaving of the dialectics of socialist Zionism with the tradition of Talmudic disputation.

The British charged *Davar* with contempt of court. On the defendant's bench sat Zalman Rubashov, the newspaper's deputy editor who later, after changing his last name to Shazar, served as Israel's third president. The attorney representing the newspaper was Moshe Smoira, who nineteen years later would be appointed Israel's first chief justice. In February 1930 he made every effort to explain the editorial's logic to the British judges. The paper did not accept

Hinkis's conviction, he said, not because it suspected that the judges had been partial, but because the police investigation had been biased. So the newspaper had criticized the police, not the judges. He also argued, and demonstrated, that British courts no longer handed down indictments for contempt of court.

The court did not accept Smoira's arguments and responded at length to the last claim. While it was true that England itself no longer tried people for contempt, the court, quoting a special commission on the court system in the West Indies, reached the conclusion that "in small colonies in which the population was composed largely of colored natives, charging locals with contempt of court could be useful and necessary." *Davar's* February 28 issue quoted from the judgment on its front page, making no effort to conceal that it saw this as an insult to the Yishuv. How could the Jewish community in Palestine be compared to colored peoples in the colonies? What about the common interests and values shared by Great Britain and the Zionist movement? The newspaper's chagrin was mollified by the reaction of the public, which donated money to cover the fine of eighty Palestinian pounds (roughly equivalent to the yearly salary of a clerk in the British administration in Palestine at the time), that the court had imposed on the newspaper.

Hinkis's Appeal

The day following his conviction, Hinkis was taken to Jerusalem and put in the central prison there: "When I arrived at the prison they removed the light chains and an Arab blacksmith restrained me with chains that were twice as heavy, on my hands and on my legs. They dressed me in a red uniform and a black hat—marking those sentenced to death [and gave me the number] 4171; then, after several days, they placed me in isolation. I spent 40 days in a cell measuring 1 by 1.8 meters. In the meantime my lawyers submitted my appeal to the High Court of Appeals" (HHA testimony 172/22).

The major claim of the defense had been that the charge of murder required the prosecutor to prove prior intent, which had not been accomplished. Hinkis had been frenzied, the defense argued, because just a short time previously he had encountered Jews who had been attacked, and one of them, Goldberg, had died in his arms. Hinkis had thus not set out in advance to commit a murder. The appeals court accepted this claim and commuted the charge to unpremeditated murder and the death sentence to fifteen years' imprisonment (Rotenberg 1935: 467). *Davar* reported that two of the three judges had commented in their opinions that "it is unfortunate that in Palestine the law does not permit imposition of a death sentence against a man who murders five people even if he did not do so with prior intent" (March 20, 1930).

The Appeal: A View from the Inside

What led the judges to overturn the lower court's judgment and find that the murder was not premeditated? Here is a firsthand account of what happened behind the scenes:

> Hinkis, who did what he did in reaction to Arab slaughters of Jews, was found to have been, by almost incontrovertible proofs, in a difficult condition, and the possibility of a severe judgment hung over his head. The Section [Haganah] commenced efforts to get him released, and when these were ineffective they began to plan his escape from jail. One of these attempts, which could almost certainly have succeeded, was planned for when Hinkis was taken to participate in a lineup in Abu Kabir. It was arranged with the policemen charged with guarding the site that they would make the escape easier for him and they agreed. But Hinkis did not flee. Afterward the policemen said that he refused to flee because it might be interpreted on the one hand as an admission [of guilt] and on the other as cowardice. . . .
>
> I went to Jerusalem and, with the help of a bottle of whiskey, I was able to visit him in jail. He was dressed in a red uniform, the uniform of those sentenced to death, bound in chains and in a low mood. I tried to encourage him and promised him that we would not abandon him and would make every effort to change the verdict. Using some connections, we managed to visit him every Saturday. At the same time we saw that the appeal was prepared.
>
> The appeal took place behind closed doors and I managed to be present at the hearing as the aide of the late defense attorney [Mordechai] Eliash. By bribing the general prosecutor, the lawyer managed to get the death sentence voided. During the appeal hearing the prosecutor was asked by Eliash whether he really believed that Hinkis had committed premeditated murder, and the prosecutor replied, as had been agreed on in advance, that he did not think so. This point determined the sentence, which was commuted from death to fifteen years in prison. ("The Hinkis Affair," in Yehuda Blumrosen testimony, HHA, testimony 7/39)

Oral History

Blumrosen was present at the hearing, but his account was not recorded until twenty-five years afterward. Such evidence has well-known pluses and minuses. One obvious plus is that it contains information that cannot be found in contemporary documents, because many of the actions taken by Jewish underground forces were not put into writing. One of the minuses is that time can alter memory. Subsequent events on occasion retroactively revise a witness's understanding of the events he saw and heard. Furthermore, witnesses might have a tendency to flatter certain people, aggrandize themselves, and underrate the part played by others. These issues are often raised in discussions of oral history and the reliability of such sources. Nevertheless, in many cases there is no sub-stitute for such testimonies.

In our case, Blumrosen told the staff member of the Haganah History Archives who interviewed him not only about the event he had witnessed but also about his attitude toward it. His basic position was one of support for Hinkis, but not necessarily for his actions. That support was a product of his assumption that Hinkis's killing of the 'Awn family was a response to the killing of Jews in Hebron and Jaffa. This was also the position taken by Yishuv institutions, which sought to help Hinkis; planned his escape; and in the end provided him with legal representation, both in the lower court and in the appeals court.

Behind Closed Doors, Continued

The appeal was heard, in part, behind closed doors. At the time it was understood that sometimes a courtroom's doors were shut not to prevent the revelation of state secrets, but to give the defendant a chance to bribe the judge or prosecutor. There was no difference between Arab and Jewish conduct in this regard, as can be seen in a book written by Bahjat Abu Gharbiyya, a participant in the Arab Revolt of 1936–39 and a commander of the Holy Jihad militia in Palestine in 1948. In this important memoir, he relates how Arab rebels were aided by the British practice of accepting bribes (Abu Gharbiyya 1993, 117). At the same time, all parties vilified the officials of the previous regime, the Ottomans, for doing the same.

In Hinkis's case, an illicit agreement was reached with the prosecutor that he would retract his charge of premeditated murder. The prosecutor kept his word. Instead of hanging, Hinkis was given a long prison sentence.

Scion of an Indigent Nation from Poland

The support offered to Hinkis was not limited to under-the-table contacts with the prosecutor. Emmanuel Harusi, a poet who had come to Palestine during the Third Aliyah, wrote a paean to Hinkis immediately after his death sentence was handed down. Myriad copies of the poem, printed on the back of a double postcard, were disseminated. On one side was Hinkis's picture; the poem was on the other side. The British police forbade its distribution and confiscated it from kiosks (*Davar*, August 29, 1930). The poem describes Hinkis conducting an internal dialogue with his mother, first speaking of the persecution of the Jews in Poland, which he had left for Palestine, and then addressing the riots and his arrest. Here are the final verses, with the mother's voice in italics:

Bullets flew like hail
Like bees circled on all sides

But my Jewish mother's voice
Crooned in each and every shot.

What is this fear I see
Why do you so bitterly cry
You were born a Jew
Hold your head high

My feet now smashed by stone
In my prison cell
I sit in bonds and chains
With killers and common thieves.

To my mother I wrote
Mother, I am weary
Long ago despaired
Of ever being free.

In my red shirt
I fall into an abyss
But to my dungeon mother sent
A message in these words:

What is this fear I see
Why do you so bitterly cry?
You were born a Jew
Hold your head high.

Harusi was a poet with his feet on the ground. He took part in the defense of Tel Aviv during the riots, while his wife was near the end of her pregnancy. The news of the arrival of his firstborn son came to him while he was manning his position. That came with another report: their friend, Police Sergeant Nahum Shalom Yudelevitz—nicknamed Nurka or Nuri, a gifted musician and outstanding soccer player—had been killed in Jerusalem's Beit HaKerem neighborhood. Emmanuel and his wife decided to name their new son after their friend, modifying Nahum's nickname, Nurka, into the Hebrew name Avner—from Av, being the name of the Hebrew month of both the riots and the baby's birth, and "ner," from Nurka. So Avner related when he was eighty years old (Harusi 2009).

Another Harusi Poem from 1929

The poem about Hinkis has sunk into oblivion, perhaps because of the commutation of his sentence. But Harusi wrote another poem about the riots that has been sung by generations of Hebrew-speaking children:

Sleep, child, sleep at peace
Do not weep and cry.
Next to you your mother sits
Safeguarding you from evil. . . .

In Tel Yosef a granary burns,
From Beit Alfa billows smoke
But cry no more my little son,
Slumber, lie and sleep.

Tonight, tonight the night's fire
Consuming straw and hay
Never, no, must you despair
We tomorrow begin anew. (Lampel 1954)

The familiar melody came from a song sung by Chabad Hasidim, adapted by
Shalom Haritonov. The song contrasts fire and destruction with construction,
working the land, and human warmth. The enemy who has set fire to the granary at Tel Yosef and at Beit Alfa is not named, and it sounds as if the struggle is
not against him but rather an inner battle against despair. Why does the enemy
not appear explicitly? There could be two reasons: either to avoid teaching children to hate or as a way of utterly ignoring the Arabs, to the point of not seeing
them. Both might well be true.

"From Beit Alfa Billows Smoke"—
and from the Tents of Ghazawiyya, Too

A few words on what happened at Beit Alfa. The kibbutz, located on the
boundary between the Jezreel and Beit She'an Valleys, at the foot of Mount Gil-
boa, was attacked five times during the disturbances. Hundreds of Bedouin descended on it, shot at it from the mountain, and set its fields afire. Three of these
attacks involved shooting from a distance, but twice the raiders tried to break
into the kibbutz and assault its inhabitants. A report that reached the Haganah
situation room in Jerusalem at 5:45 a.m. on August 26 stated: "Beit Alfa's situation is serious. The children were evacuated yesterday and today the people
of Beit Alfa are surrounded and they have no weapons" (ISA, P69/776). With
the aid of British forces (which included a contingent from Transjordan) and
two aircraft, the kibbutz defenders managed to repel the invaders. No Jews were
killed, but the Bedouin caused serious damage to kibbutz property—the granary was set on fire and 160,000 kilograms of silage went up in smoke, as did
6,000 kilograms of straw.

Following one of the volleys of gunfire, a British patrol car set out to the east to locate the source of the shooting but encountered no armed men. On the way back to the kibbutz the soldiers heard an explosion. They jumped from their vehicle, took cover, and began to shoot in the direction of a group of Bedouin they thought had attacked them. The Bedouin did not return fire. When the situation had calmed, the soldiers discovered that the explosion they heard had been from one of their tires blowing out, and that the Bedouin were local shepherds. A Bedouin boy, about seven years old, was killed in the incident. An elderly man was wounded, and about ten domestic animals were hit ("Report of the Commander of the Beisan Police," August 1929, ISA P987/16). The Bedouin, it emerged, were members of the Ghazawiyya tribe, one of the largest of the Beit She'an Valley, which owned land on both sides of the Jordan River. Beyond the human tragedy, the incident was a horrible error. The tribe, and in particular its emir (tribal chief), Mohammad Zeinati, had maintained close ties with the Jewish settlers in the region. A decade earlier he had warmly received Lord Balfour and Chaim Weizmann, and the Zeinatis had not hesitated to sell land to Zionist institutions. Still, the little boy's death did not alter the tribe's political stance. The Bedouin understood that the killing had been an error, and the incident did not prevent them from accepting a "voluntary transfer" proposal from Keren Kayemet LeYisrael. In exchange for land purchased for them in Transjordan and a grant of citizenship by Transjordan's ruler, Emir 'Abdallah, they agreed to sell the Zionists their land on the west side of the Jordan and move to the east side of the river. This is a rare example of an Arab population consenting to move out of Mandatory Palestine. The move took place in stages, ending in the mid-1940s.

Zeinati, who had promoted the plan, was shot dead in Haifa in December 1946 by emissaries of the National Fund, the Palestinian institution responsible for preserving Palestinian lands and preventing their sale to the Jews. It viewed Zeinati as a traitor (H. Cohen 2008). But that took place some seventeen years after 1929.

From Poland to Jaffa

Harusi did not lament the Ghazawiyya dead, nor the members of the 'Awn family murdered in Jaffa by the hero of his poem. Each nation mourns its own dead, not those of their enemies. The poet focused on the painful past that Hinkis had brought with him, "from the distant exile where he had known troubles and sorrow." This recalls Brenner, who, walking through Jaffa, felt as if he were rubbing shoulders with Ukrainian ruffians. Tzvi Nadav—who also arrived in Palestine during the Second Aliyah, helped found the self-defense force HaShomer, and served as a Haganah commander in Jerusalem during the 1920 disturbances—also made the connection between European pogroms and riots in Palestine. In 1920 he volunteered to make his way into the Old City of

Jerusalem along with Nehemia Rabin (Yitzhak Rabin's father) to help evacuate endangered Jewish families. Describing the scene on David Street, leading from the Jaffa Gate toward the Temple Mount, Nadav wrote: "We saw Jewish feathers [from mattresses and pillows] flying, the feathers that are such a clichéd symbol of Jewish existence, blown to and fro by every breeze. . . . We saw them [the Arabs] shattering burgled stores, an experience I know well from the Diaspora. . . . I thought to myself that the despicable British were acting on the model of Kishinev [where the Russian authorities stood by and allowed or even encouraged a pogrom]. Different insignia but the same method." In 1929 Nadav was a senior Haganah commander in Haifa. On guard duty, his thoughts wandered to his father's house in Russia and the pogrom that had ravaged their street, and to a desire for revenge:

I was close to sick for several days and dreamed of revenge in the form of remorse. Their conscience awakening. "They" sense what they have done. Remorse gnaws at them. "They" are imbued with a recognition that they did evil, insulted, humiliated a human soul. They come to me in alarm, plead for forgiveness for the awful crime of humiliating and hurting a human soul. My heart fills with compassion and love. I fill with compassion and love. I want to love everyone. I love them. I comfort them. . . .

Yes, revenge in the form of remorse. It seems to me that that would be the most soothing revenge I could ask for. Does a Bedouin woman not embrace her son's murderer [in a *sulha*, or reconciliation ceremony] as he kneels before her in submission, imploring and contrite, and accepts him as if he replaces her murdered son, forgives him? Does my heart really want blood? Images of spilt blood are before my eyes. People killed. The face of Yehezkel [Nisanov, a founder of HaShomer who was killed at Nadav's side at Merhavia in 1911] with a piece of brain spilling out over his forehead, and refusal wells up in my heart. No. I under no circumstances want blood. I recall a saying the Arabs use when they make peace: "*Wa-shu al-atgal min al-tagil*" — "What is heavier than heavy" [said in a Bedouin accent]. That's right, nothing weighs down a man's heart more than spilling blood. (Nadav's testimonies, HHA, testimony 58/48; testimony 35/13)

There it is. The experience of pogroms and acquaintance with the Arabs can also lead in a different direction. Nadav, a founder of a Hebrew fighting force, dreamed of forgiveness and absolution even when he longed for revenge. His model was the Bedouin *sulha* ceremony. In this sense Nadav was different than Brenner, who had no familiarity with Palestine's Arabs—for him, they were devoid of humanity. Nadav preferred a lesson his father had drilled into him over and over again: "Know this, my son. All human beings have a conscience. You just have to know how to awaken it. All people are born good." Nadav did not view the Arabs only as assailants, but the common wisdom in the Yishuv, certainly after 1929, was that violence and lawlessness were inborn Arab traits. An example follows.

Riot Culture

On the same day when Hinkis won his appeal, news came of the death of Arthur Balfour, who had drafted the famous declaration promising British assistance to the Jews in their establishment of a national home in Palestine, while disregarding the national (as opposed to the religious and individual) rights of the Arab inhabitants. The Jewish community recalled him with favor. The Arabs did not. "There are Arabs who have had no compunctions about publicly displaying their joy at this sorrowful event," *Davar* reported. "In the early evening two automobiles drove through Jerusalem bearing fifteen Arabs playing [the Zionist anthem] *Hatikva* and chortling wildly" ("Riot Culture," March 20, 1930).

Urfali, Same Cell, Same Fate

When his appeal was successful, Hinkis breathed a sigh of relief. He would not die. But he could not fully rejoice — he realized that he had many long years in prison ahead of him. Nonetheless, he was in a much better position than Yosef Urfali, another Jew who had been brought to trial for murdering Arabs on the Tel Aviv–Jaffa border in 1929.

The events in Urfali's neighborhood were recounted in detail by Riggs, the British police officer. Riggs related that when the riots started, on Sunday, August 25, at 10:30 a.m., the Muslim preacher Tubasi set out of the Hasan Beq Mosque for Manshiyya, a Jaffa neighborhood bordering on Tel Aviv, together with a large number of Arabs. Plainclothes detectives followed Tubasi. Riggs, as the officer in charge, proceeded to the border between Manshiyya and the Jewish city and set up a machine gun at the corner of HaCarmel Street, with the barrel pointing in the direction of Jaffa. Deputy Inspector Rashid 'Abd al-Hadi and six policemen were ordered by Riggs to patrol the area and report all suspicious movements to him. At 12:15, he testified, he heard shouts coming from the Cardboard neighborhood, where both Jews and Arabs lived. Riggs galloped there on horseback, calling to soldiers and policemen to follow him with the machine gun.

Urfali lived in the Cardboard neighborhood. When the riot ended, the bodies of two Arabs lay in the street — those of Mahmoud Tartir and 'Arafat Ramlawi. Witnesses fingered Urfali as their killer.

Urfali denied any connection to the deaths and maintained his denial under police interrogation and in his testimony in court. He suggested that Riggs and his men might have killed the two Arabs. But Urfali offered contradictory accounts of his involvement in the event. In his first account, he said that he had left his home on a quick errand to buy bread, then came back and hid there from the attackers. He heard of the deaths of Ramlawi and Tartir, he declared, only later from Arab friends who came to visit him. But then he changed his story and said that after running his errand he went not to his own home, but to that of his brother, along with another man, Ibrahim Ahmad. Urfali had not signed the first deposition he had given to the police; he signed the second with a fingerprint—*Davar* reported that he did not know how to read or write. In court Urfali was asked why his neighbors would have testified that they saw him shooting. He explained that they had conspired to implicate him in the crime (the file from the investigation can be found at czas25/4434 and isa p986/23).

The court did not accept his account and convicted Urfali of killing Tartir and Ramlawi. According to the court, Urfali shot Tartir without premeditation but during the heat of the confrontation, and he was thus liable for imprisonment rather than the death penalty. But, the court further ruled, Urfali had fired his gun twice more after the mob dispersed, aiming at Ramlawi, a man who had come to evacuate the wounded Tartir. That, the court found, had been murder with criminal intent—Urfali had had sufficient time to consider his actions, and yet he shot a man who presented no danger to his life.

Two witnesses tipped the scales against him. Tartir's mother testified that her wounded son ran toward her and collapsed, saying "Yusef Urfali. From the balcony." Hajj Hussein Hijazi testified he was in the street at the time and that after Tartir was wounded, he joined Ramlawi in trying to rescue him, at which time Urfali shot at them from his balcony. The witnesses contradicted one other in some minor details, but the court nevertheless sentenced Urfali to death. The sentence was handed down on November 20, 1929. Urfali immediately appealed. Eliash, who headed the defense team for Hinkis and the other Jews accused of crimes in the riots, represented Urfali as well.

Neighbors Telling Tales

The claim of neighbors trumping up charges came up in a similar context in the case of another Jew who lived on the Tel Aviv–Jaffa border, Yitzhak Auadis. He, too, was accused of shooting from his home, in his case in the Neveh Shalom neighborhood, at passing Arabs on the street. According to his indictment, however, he only wounded three of them, and hence he was not liable for the death penalty. Nelly Moshenson, coeditor (along with Moshe Shertok, later Sharett) of *Davar*'s English edition, wrote at length on this trial in 1929:

> It so happened that there was a man, Yitzhak Auadis was his name, a fishmonger by profession, who lived in Jaffa. . . . He is of typical Oriental appearance, tall, heavy, with impressive rolls of flesh, bald, with a nearly blond moustache. Auadis dressed in what is called a *kumbaz* [an ankle-length tunic] and tarboosh. A widower who

was not young, he lived with his grown children. One of his daughters kept house for him. One of his sons, who was named for his Arab godfather, had attended the French Catholic College des Frères school in Jaffa. Arabic was the language of the house, and it was Arabic Auadis used to fill in the gaps in his weak Hebrew.

There is thus reason to ask what about him bothered his Arab neighbors. They could in no shape or form, directly or not, hold him responsible for the Balfour Declaration. The man, like many of his kind, was an integral part of that block of humanity that constitutes the multifarious population of an Oriental city like Jaffa. Muslim Arabs, Christian Arabs, Jews, Greeks, Armenians, Italians, Egyptians, even Russians. . . . Yitzhak Auadis, fishmonger, was charged with incessantly firing a pistol from the window of his home in Jaffa's Neveh Shalom neighborhood on the day of the riots of August 25, and of wounding several people in the legs. When he was brought before Judge Plunkett he claimed that he was innocent. That that morning he had shut up his shop and taken his family to his sister's house in a distant neighborhood in Tel Aviv.

The trial lasted three days, because the prosecutor called many witnesses. They all had one thing in common. They could not adhere to their original stories under the judge's questioning. To their embarrassment, they deviated each time the defense attorney began to fire questions at them. They saw a hand holding a pistol in the window. They did not see it. They heard a shot. They heard three shots. There was a crowd. There were only a few loiterers. They were unanimous in declaring that none of them knew any of the others, that they did not even know there had been riots that morning, and that they had refrained from telling the doctor who treated their wounds and their families who had shot them, keeping this fact to tell the investigating magistrate. ("Auadis Trial," reprinted in *Davar*, July 3, 1936)

The investigating magistrate took note of the contradictions of the witnesses, both within the accounts given by each one, and between their several accounts, and he freed the suspect. Auadis was luckier than Urfali.

The Common Ground

Both men were what are today termed Mizrahim—Jews from the Islamic world. Both of them lived in mixed Jewish-Arab neighborhoods. Both spoke Arabic and had frequent conversations with their Arab neighbors. For Nelly Moshenson, Auadis's Mizrahi ethnicity was his salient trait. She could not understand why he had been attacked, she wrote, given that he had no connection to the Balfour Declaration—that is, to Zionism.

Are the Mizrahim Detached from Zionism?

That's what Moshenson thought. More than Auadis was a Zionist, she maintained, he was "an integral part of that block of humanity that constitutes the multifarious population of an Oriental city like Jaffa." Moshenson defined Zionism (not necessarily consciously) as a European movement with the goal of establishing in Palestine a Jewish national home of European character. From her point of view, a Zionist was a person who shared the Zionist and European conception of Jewish nationalism (in one of the many variants existing within Ashkenazi Zionism), identified with its goals, belonged to its institutions, and took part in the central Zionist activities of settling on the land and the "conquest of labor." The last point was one of the central doctrines of the socialist Second Aliyah—the demand that Jewish settlements and businesses in Palestine not employ Arabs if there were Jews seeking the same jobs. European Jewry was the Zionist movement's primary target audience. By the same token, some Jews from the Middle East and North Africa viewed Zionism as a foreign, European movement and for that reason did not join it.

This does not mean that these Jews felt no attachment to Zion—quite the opposite was true. Jews from the Islamic world settled throughout the Land of Israel, including Jaffa. Primarily, they were drawn to the Holy Land for a combination of religious, economic, and personal reasons prior to the emergence of political Zionism and wanted to live in it as Jews. The result was a major demographic shift in the port city. The Maghrebis constituted the great majority of the first Jewish community in Jaffa. They bought land from Arabs and built Jewish neighborhoods that constituted the first glimmerings of Tel Aviv. The first members and leaders of the Maghrebi community in Jaffa included Avraham Shlush, who came from Algeria in 1838 with his family and 150 followers; Rabbi Yitzhak Asouline and his family, who came in 1852; Hakham (Rabbi) Aharon Moyal, who led 180 followers to Palestine and settled in Jaffa in 1854; Rabbi Yitzhak Elbaz, who arrived in 1865; Rabbi Moshe Elkayam, who came with the students at his yeshiva in 1856; and Rabbi Ya'akov Shimol. All these men faithfully looked after the needs of Jaffa's Jews for years and arrived long before what is now called the First Aliyah. According to Mordechai Elkayam (1990), some of them were inspired by proto-Zionist figures such as Rabbi Yehuda Bibas, Rabbi Tzvi Kalisher, and Rabbi Yehuda Alkalai.

In his book, Elkayam seems eager to prove the Zionism of the Jews who came from the Maghreb—just as Yitzhak Betzalel was in his book on the Sephardim in Palestine at the end of the Ottoman period, *Noladtem Tzionim* (You were born Zionists; 2007)—and to serve as an antithesis to Moshenson and her ilk. (The terms "Mizrahi" and "Sephardi" are used frequently synonymously to refer to all Jews from the Muslim world, including those from the Maghreb. But originally "Sephardi" referred to the descendants of the Jews who were expelled from Spain in the fifteenth century and who settled in the Middle East. The term "Mizrahi" was not used during the Mandate period.) Elkayam points to the deep connection that the Jews of the Islamic world felt to the Land of Israel but does not disregard the tension these Arab Jews — that is, Arabic-speaking, culturally Arab Jews — felt in following the Zionist immigration from Eastern Europe, and he tells how they dealt with it.

Tension

Elkayam describes the three-way encounter in Jaffa between Arabs, local Jews, and Zionist pioneers. He does not say what year this description applies to, but apparently it was sometime during the Second Aliyah, at the end of the Ottoman period:

> The immigrants from the Orient dressed the same [as their Muslim neighbors]. They spoke the same language, the older people with a Moroccan accent and the young people with a Jaffa accent. The women went out on the street modestly dressed, just like the Arab women. They wore scarves over their faces and black dresses, so that you could not tell a Jewish woman from an Arab one. Like the Arab women, the Jewish women did not go out to shop in the markets and certainly did not walk the streets. The men did the shopping and provided all the home's needs. In this way the two communities kept the peace. Relations between neighbors were thus relations of mutual respect. An Arab who saw a lout hassling a Jewish woman would reprimand and sometimes even strike him.
>
> There were exceptions to this harmony, but it was violated by the immigrants from Russia. What stood out was the sight of their women and girls walking the streets with their faces bare, dressed immodestly in a way that everyone could see. Their appearance provoked, angered, and roused the passions of the Arabs. Jaffa's Jews were also shocked. Most of them were very pious and opposed women publicly exposing parts of their bodies. The flouting of moral customs that had been accepted for generations was jarring for both Arabs and Jews.
>
> Young Jews who saw the "enthusiasm" of Arab youths and their groping of Jewish women and girls took up their cause and admonished the Arabs. They asked their wives to advise the Russian women to behave more modestly so as not to anger the Arabs. But talk generally did not work. On more than one occasion fights broke out between Jewish and Arab youths over the honor of Jewish women. Sometimes the police even had to intervene.
>
> Relations between the Arabs and the "Moscobim" [the Zionist pioneers; literally, Muscovites] heated up. Every European Jew was immediately assumed to be a Moscobi. Incitement against Europeans as a whole began, on the grounds that they intended to take control of the country and dispossess the Arabs. This charge added fuel to the fire. The Jews of Jaffa, the Sephardim, would deny these accusations as baseless, explaining the settlement movement as seeking only to solve housing problems. (1990, 175–77)

Relations between Jaffa's long-standing Jewish population and its Arabs were not ideal, but they were smooth enough because of the groups' shared cultural background. The immigrants from Russia disturbed that harmony. They did not observe local mores. In addition, their arrival aroused fears that the Jews were trying to take over the country and push out the Arabs. The result was frequent fights between the *Moscobim* and the Arabs. The Jews of the established community had to try to mediate, explaining to their Arab neighbors that the immigrants from Russia had come to Palestine simply because they sought a solution to their "housing problem." It is an interesting claim. Did the Jews of Jaffa actually believe it? Not clear. Did the Arabs believe it? Certainly not. The 1929 riots are proof of that.

The stress the Arab Jews felt was multidimensional. There was tension between their familiarity with their Arab neighbors and their sense of Jewish solidarity; between their knowledge that European Zionism was detrimental to the trust between Jews and Arabs and their knowledge that that trust had its limits; between their sense of relative equality with the Arabs during the final years of Ottoman rule and the realization that the Jews of Europe did not see the Jews of the Islamic world as equal partners in their enterprise.

Partnership and Its Discontents

In fact, relations between Jaffa's Jews and the Eastern European Zionists were at first based on mutual understanding. When it first began operating in Palestine, Hovevei Zion (a movement that emerged among Jews in Russia and Romania in 1873 to further Jewish immigration to and agricultural settlement in Palestine, prior to Herzl's establishment of the Zionist movement) invited a member of Jaffa's Jewish Maghrebi community, Aharon Amoyal, to head its Palestinian office. During the second half of the 1880s, Amoyal labored, with the help of the European organization, to settle North African Jewish families in Nablus, Lydda (today's Lod), and Gaza. The community in Gaza, which became the largest of the three, remained there until 1929. But the honeymoon was a short one. With the emergence of the Zionist movement and its establishment of institutions, and the growing influence of Russian socialist Zionism, the Sephardim and Maghrebis were shunted aside. For their part, they distanced themselves more and more from organized Zionist activity, which they viewed as too militant toward the Arabs. Prior to World War I, prominent Sephardi activists rejected the conquest of labor. The goal was to provide livelihoods to Jews and to create a Jewish working class. The Sephardim argued that doing so would harm Jewish-Arab relations and demanded that the Yishuv open channels of communication with the Arabs. They were not taken seriously by the Zionist leadership (Jacobson 2003). Yosef Eliahu Shlush, a leader of the Jewish community in Jaffa, protested that the newcomers did not think that the Maghrebis were sufficiently Zionist. He was especially irritated because the Eastern European Zionists suspected him and his fellows of making common cause with the Arabs against Zionism. In articles and in his memoir, *Parshat Hayai* (My life story, 1931), Shlush lashed out at the way the pioneers were taking over the Yishuv; their failure to comprehend the fabric of life in Palestine; and their marginalization of the established Jewish population, whose standing and priority they dismissed.

Other members of the Sephardi elite, like Eliahu Elyashar, felt that the European Zionist leadership was largely responsible for undermining relations between Jews and Muslims. Elyashar voiced his frustrations in *Lihiyot 'im Falastinim* (Living with Palestinians; 1997). In an introduction to the work, Israel Bartal sums up Elyashar's views and feelings: "The leaders of the movement and of the Yishuv that ran matters from the beginning of the Mandate period were reluctant to include the Arab Jew and tended to deliberately avoid social and cultural contact between the Yishuv and the neighboring people. Not only did they disdain the customs of the Arab milieu, thus causing needless resentment and conflict, but they also displayed cultural arrogance and preferred a connection with distant Europe to connecting with their immediate surroundings" (1997, xv–xvi).

The writings of the Arab Jews of this period display a sense of inferiority vis-à-vis the recently arrived Zionists, who seemed so organized and dynamic —out to change the world, educated, and filled with a will to power. A unique encounter between the two groups took place at Havat Ruhama, a settlement in the northern Negev Desert, not far from Gaza. Nisim Elkayam, the father of Mordechai, was one of the founders of this settlement, and Maghrebi Jews who had settled in Gaza at Amoyal's initiative worked there alongside Second Aliyah pioneer laborers. Mordechai Elkayam's description helps explain the relations between the two groups:

> [The pioneers] were involved in constant political debate. This one represented one party and the other one represented another party. They all battled to get the votes of the workers. . . . Each party tried to instill in the [Jewish] Gazans its partisan idea and to get their votes.
>
> The Gazans profited from all the uproar. They were divided into small groups and each group received classes in Zionist history from a counselor from a different party. In this manner a school of small groups arose, in which classes were given and talks and lectures held in small classes as in the school in Gaza, and all this in the revolutionary atmosphere of the commune at Ruhama, in which the Gazans took part. It propelled the Gazans 200 years into the future. Their dormant intellects were awakened; they totally changed, to the point that they could no longer live with their

fellows, nor with their families in Gaza, who could not recognize them and who did not understand the change that had come over them. (1994, 208)

This passage gives us a sense of the fundamental assumptions of the integrationists: that adopting the European Zionist discourse constituted progress and that, as they saw it, this was not a blending of cultures but rather a matter of abandoning one culture and replacing it with another. The almost inevitable result was the alienation of the Gaza Jewish workers from their families and other members of the community from which they came. A book by another member of the established Jewish population of Jaffa, Aharon Shlush, has a title that sums up the process he describes — *MiGalabiya leKova' Tembel* (From *jellabiya* to pioneer cap; 1991) — as an abandonment of Eastern culture and adoption of Zionist culture. A corollary was choosing sides in the Zionist-Arab conflict, a conflict that up to that point had not been theirs, or at least not in the same way as the pioneers saw it.

Integrating and Mediating

The two writers, Elkayam and Shlush, had something in common: both were from leading families in Jaffa's Maghrebi Jewish community. But while Shlush's father moved to Tel Aviv and married a "Moscobi" woman, Elkayam's father moved to Gaza to lead the Maghrebi community there. Their lives, however, ran in parallel. Aharon Shlush, born in 1921, joined the Haganah as a teenager and continued to serve in the security forces after Israel's establishment, specifically in the new country's police force. His positions included head of the Minorities Division in the Gaza Strip when that territory was taken by Israel in the Sinai Campaign of 1956, head of the Special Missions Department in the National Police Headquarters, commander of the Jerusalem District, commander of the Southern District, and chief of the Investigations Division. Mordecai Elkayam served as a commander in the Haganah and Israeli Defense Forces (IDF); he was deputy military governor of the Gaza Strip in 1956 and governor of Jericho in 1976. Both were descendants of Arab Jewish families who chose to use their talents, connections, and knowledge to buttress the Zionist enterprise. In their later years, after integrating into that society, they wrote books recounting the history of their families and community.

And the Other Mizrahim?

Many other Mizrahi Jews did not integrate. They remained on the margins of Yishuv society. The poor neighborhoods of Tel Aviv, Jerusalem, Haifa, and other cities and towns were peopled by Mizrahi families that felt increasingly alienated from the Zionist establishment (but not necessarily from a sense of Jewish solidarity versus the Arabs). This alienation, which lasted through the Mandate period, derived both from the cultural disparity between them and the Ashkenazi mainstream and from the disdain with which they were treated. A year after Israel declared its independence, David Ben-Gurion summed up the social milieu in the IDF during the 1948 war:

> It was the first time that all the popular strata came together, and there was rabble among them. We are not aware of the extent to which the ruling echelon of the Yishuv lacks connection and knowledge of how the people live, and this applies to all levels. There is a "common people," people living in the [poor] neighborhoods, and we do not know them, we are ignorant of them and they are ignorant of us and we live in the upper atmosphere. Now, with the establishment of the army, we encountered each other. In these strata there are filth, illiteracy, and entirely different ways of thinking about everything (meeting of May 6, 1949, ISA, *Meetings of the First Government*, 5:2).

This was the state of affairs when the country was founded, even before the mass immigration that followed. Some four decades earlier, Yosef Brenner had had his protagonist Diasporin in *MiKan umiKan* (From here and there) argue against casting off Yiddish and making Hebrew the modern spoken and written Jewish language: "And beyond that . . . what good will one language do . . . one language for whom? Me and the Sephardim? What do I have to do with the Sephardim? Are we really the same nation as them? Say what you want — as far as I'm concerned, it's already a different nation" (1985, 2:1420).

A Different Nation?

There may have been a few Jews who felt that way, but on the political level the Zionist movement claimed to represent all the Jews in Palestine, and this is how the British viewed it (although the non-Zionist Haredi, or ultra-Orthodox, community was somewhat exceptional in this regard). Furthermore, Zionist emissaries were sent to all Jewish communities in the Middle East and slowly but meticulously worked to change the political identities and loyalties of the Jews of the Islamic lands (see, for example, Shenhav 2006). While the disaffection between the Yishuv's ethnic groups and classes did not vanish, the boundaries between the Jews and Arabs grew ever more salient as national identity grew stronger. The 1929 riots played a decisive role in this process of the Yishuv's consolidation around the Zionist movement.

1929 and Jewish Unity

No other factor was more influential in bringing the established Jewish communities in Palestine and the new Zionist community together under a single political roof than the riots of 1929. The Arab attacks forced the Middle Eastern and North African Jews living in Palestine, including those who had previously had reservations about the Jewish national movement, to cast their lot in with the Zionists, to ask for and accept their protection. To put it bluntly, in 1929 the Arabs created the Yishuv. This is true to a certain extent regarding the pre-Zionist Ashkenazi religious community in Palestine, often called the Old Yishuv, but much more so regarding the Jews of Middle Eastern origin who had lived within Arab society. Prior to 1929, not many Jews living in Arab countries were all that eager to cast off Arab culture and sever ties with their Arab neighbors. Instead, they looked for ways to integrate into the new environment that emerged in the Middle East following World War I. The same was true of some of the Mizrahi and Sephardi Jews in the Holy Land. In 1929 these Jews received a resounding message from their Arab neighbors: if you do not take sides against Zionism, you are its allies. If you identify on the national level with the European Jews, you have no place in Arab society. Even if Palestinian Arab spokesmen continued to stress that they distinguished between Jews and Zionists, and even if Arab society at some levels continued to differentiate between Mizrahim (and the Ashkenazim of the Old Yishuv) and the Zionist immigrants from Europe, for both Arabs and Jews the similarities among the Jews, of whatever community and origin, increasingly overshadowed their differences. This process had begun before 1929, but the riots were a turning point. During them the Zionist movement became the defender of all Jewish communities in Palestine and thus established its preeminence among these groups.

Acre as an Example

The Jewish community in Acre flourished during the 1920s, expanding from a few dozen to some 850 members. The veteran members of the community consisted of a small group of families that had come from the Islamic world, most of them from North Africa. They were joined in the early 1920s by two groups of Zionist pioneer immigrants from Eastern Europe. One group had organized as a commune to mine sand, while the other founded a fishing cooperative called HaKovesh (the conqueror). A group of Jewish fisherman from Salonika also settled in Acre (Sarugo 2010). And in 1923 Yehiel Weizmann founded the Nur match factory there, in which a small number of Jews worked alongside a large number of Arabs.

Relations between Acre's Jews and Arabs were fairly good, partly because the Islamic religious leadership was headed by Sheikh As'ad al-Shuqayri, one of the most vociferous opponents of the virulently anti-Zionist mufti of Jerusalem, Hajj Amin al-Hussayni. Al-Shuqayri maintained good ties with Zionist institutions and opposed violence. He rejected the mufti's request that he organize demonstrations in Acre to oppose the Jewish takeover of the Western Wall. On September 8, 1929, *Ha'aretz* reported that despite the good relations, tension had been evident in Acre following the demonstrations in Jerusalem. The Arab workers at the Nur factory told their Jewish colleagues ("who had in the past given them strike funds") that they would slaughter them. One of the leading firebrands, according to *Ha'aretz*'s report, was Habib Hawa, a colorful and somewhat dubious character. His daughter, Raymonda Tawil, would gain prominence in the 1970s as an Arab journalist and feminist poet (1979). Her daughter, Suha Tawil, married Yasir Arafat, chief of the Palestine Liberation Organization (PLO).

Another Palestinian nationalist activist in Acre was Sheikh Ahmad al-Shuqayri, a son of Sheikh As'ad al-Shuqayri and an opponent of his father's conciliatory stance. "Every day during that time I gathered people at a café or in the city's central square or on the street and I explained to them how serious the situation was, and I called on them to fight both imperialism and Zionism," he wrote in his memoirs (1969, 116). The riots were one of the first events that shaped the consciousness of the young al-Shuqayri, who thirty-five years later founded the PLO, which he headed for four years.

What Does That Have to Do with the Mizrahim in Acre?

Throughout his book, al-Shuqayri stresses the difference between Zionists and Arab Jews and takes pride in his good relations with the latter. But this was largely a theoretical distinction. In practice, in 1929 the attackers treated all Jews the same. When tensions increased in the city, a reporter for *Ha'aretz* wrote, Zionist Jews began to be especially careful while walking in the street. The established Jews, for their part, continued to feel at home. It quickly became clear, however, that this sense of security had no basis in reality. The venerable mukhtar of the city's Jewish community, Avraham Haim Tzuri, left home on the day of the riots just as he did every day, confident that no one would harm him, as a longtime inhabitant of the city. When he returned and entered his home he found his family under assault: "The rioters attacked his house, breaking all the items in two of its rooms. They were unable to break into the third room, where 23 people were sheltering, because Mr. Tzuri jumped from the window on the second floor into the street and shouted for help, and the police soon dispersed the rioters." *Ha'aretz* stressed what seemed to it an important point:

> It should be noted that they attacked the house of Tzuri, the mukhtar of the Jewish community, who has always had peaceful and friendly relations with the Arabs. His family speaks Arabic at home, some of his children attend Arab schools, and when the Arabs collect donations for a cultural or philanthropic project they do not forget

to solicit him—yet they displayed no gratitude and his family was but a step away from death.

Also Mr. Farji, whose children attend only Arab schools and who keeps his distance from all other Jews and, being wealthy, is a respected man and member of the Acre city council, was not spared and was forced to take cover along with all the other Jews.

Tzuri and Farji represented different Mizrahi attitudes toward Zionism. Tzuri was in close contact with the pioneers and aided their absorption into the city, while Farji had nothing to do with the Zionist community. Yet the Arabs presumed that Jewish identity trumped Arab identity even for a man like Farji. They assumed that Mizrahi Jews supported the idea of a Jewish return to Zion even if these Jews did not belong to, or take part in, Zionist institutions and did not support the manner in which the Zionist movement operated. Even when they were aware of the opposition of some Mizrahi Jews, both in Palestine and elsewhere in the Islamic world, to the Zionist project of establishing Jewish sovereignty in Palestine, the Arabs nevertheless felt that, when it came time to choose between Arab and Jewish nationalism, the Mizrahi Jews in Palestine would choose the latter. That was the principal reason why these Jews, who lived for all intents and purposes as Arabs in their daily lives, were also attacked. To a certain extent, these Jews were considered even more dangerous than the European Zionists—they were a fifth column within the Arab community. Below we will see that the rioters in Safed and Hebron also made no distinction among Jews according to their ethnicity or time spent living in Palestine. The reasons for this will be examined in depth.

And the Result?

A number of things resulted from the attacks on Mizrahi Jews. They enhanced Jewish cohesion and made religious and national identity more important than cultural identity. On the institutional level, the riots prompted growing numbers of Mizrahi Jews to join Jewish militias—both the Haganah and the breakaway Haganah Bet that eventually became Etzel. Shevah Yekutieli immigrated to Palestine in 1923. In 1929 he was responsible for the Haganah's armory in Haifa and commander of a contingent of fighters. In September 1970 he provided testimony in which he related that up until 1929 the Mizrahi Jews did not participate in Haganah activities and were closer in their lifestyle to the Arabs than to Ashkenazi Zionists:

There were no members of the Sephardi community in the Haganah. The Sephardim did not mix with the Ashkenazim. The European boys with their shorts were alien to them. They lived in *hamulot* [extended families or clans], with Arab culture, with

Arab clothes, and with the Arabic language. They did not contribute to our funds. They always charged that we brought them trouble. Because they lived well with the Arabs. They ate the same things as the Arabs. After six in the evening you didn't see any of them. Until six in the evening their cafés were full. We—after work, we dressed in their clothes, went to visit them, and saw how they lived.

Beginning in 1929 the Sephardim began joining the Haganah. The Arabs began to do with the Sephardim what they did with us. They [the Sephardim] had to leave Ard al-Yahud [Haifa's old Jewish neighborhood; literally, the Jewish land] and they were provided with shelter on HaPo'el Street. We bought mats for them. They were the ones who suffered most from the Arabs. The Arabs burned down their wooden storage sheds. The young people began to connect with us. They didn't go back to Ard al-Yahud. They lived on HaShomer Street. (HHA, testimony 103/23)

It was clear to the members of Haifa's old Mizrahi community that the Zionists had "brought them trouble." But, like most of the Jews in Palestine and the Arab countries, they underwent a process of Zionization. Prior to World War I and immediately after the war, they still tried to straddle the gap between their Jewish and Arab identities, and to a certain extent to fashion a bridge between the Zionists and the Palestinian Arabs. But heightening tensions between the Jewish national movement and the Arab national movement following the Balfour Declaration forced them to choose sides. Even though many of them felt alienated from the Zionist movement and its institutions, the gap between them and the Palestinian national movement, which opposed Jewish immigration, was even greater. As a result, some members of the younger Mizrahi generation were drawn into Zionist activity and adopted the pioneer ethos. But even to those who stayed on the sidelines, it was clear that their lot had been cast with the Zionists. And in 1929 Palestine's Arabs were well aware of this. The Arab attacks on the Mizrahi communities and the Ashkenazi Old Yishuv in 1929 firmly ensconced the Arab Jews in the Zionist camp. In this regard, the attacks led to an irrevocable change in the identity of the pre-Zionist Jewish community. In other Middle Eastern countries the point of no return came later, at the time of the 1948 war, as described in the work of Moshe Behar (2007).

Each Other's Creations

It is a common view in Zionist discourse that Zionism created Palestinian nationalism. Gilad Sharon, son of former Israeli Prime Minister Ariel Sharon, put it this way: "They are a byproduct of our Zionism" (*Yediot Aharonot*, March 13, 2011). But it is important to be precise here: the Zionist movement did not *create* Arab nationalism in Palestine but rather shaped it, since the Arab national movement in Palestine had to wrestle from the start with Zionism. Similiarly, Zionism was shaped by the Palestinian national movement. That is, through its violent opposition to Zionism, the Palestinian Arab national movement strengthened Jewish solidarity and made the value of solidarity in the face of an enemy the cornerstone of the Zionist ethos. In other words, Israeli Zionism and the Jewish community in Israel as we know them today are a product of Palestinian nationalism, and vice versa.

Urfali: An Appeal, and Another, and Another

Urfali could know none of this in 1929. His priority was appealing the death sentence imposed on him. For a moment he seemed to have succeeded—on January 25, 1930, the appeals court accepted his attorneys' request to procure the testimony of more witnesses and to remand the case to the trial court for an additional hearing. But the new hearing was painfully disappointing for Urfali. The Jaffa court scheduled a date for the new witnesses to testify, but most of them did not appear. The court then reaffirmed the death sentence. Urfali thus became the only Jew sentenced to death on charges stemming from the 1929 riots whose death sentence was confirmed after an appeal.

A Jew Was Sentenced to Death in 1929?

It's a fact, if one that Israeli collective memory largely ignores. Nevertheless, we should not deduce from this that Urfali was indeed guilty, just as we should not presume that Hinkis's acquittal, like that of many Arab murderers, meant that he and they were innocent. In any case, it is essential to bear in mind that the events in Jaffa and Abu Kabir were not representative of the 1929 riots as a whole, but exceptions: most of the Arab dead (unlike the 'Awn family and a few others) were involved in attacks on Jews, whereas most of the Jewish dead were unarmed. There is nevertheless an advantage in presenting these events side by side—it helps us see both similarities and differences in the ways in which the Jews and Arabs experienced the events of 1929, and the diverse ways in which those events have been told of and written about up to the present day. Everyone knows that, as far as the Jews were concerned, the disturbances of 1929 were a nationwide Palestinian pogrom aimed at Jews qua Jews—and they had good reason for believing this. If that is the case, the killings committed by Jews during the disturbances, even the most morally offensive of them, clearly fall under the general rubric of self-defense. But how do the same events look to the Arabs?

Like Self-Defense, of Course

The Palestinians too viewed the 1929 riots as part of a movement of self-defense. The first paragraph of al-Dabbagh's account, quoted at the beginning of this chapter, points to the common wisdom among Palestinians about what happened. The bloody events of 1929 erupted because of Jewish attempts to take control of the Western Wall (al-Buraq), in contravention of the binding status quo and despite the fact that the spot belonged to the *waqf*, the Muslim religious trust. The riots were set off, the Muslims maintain, by Jewish provocations in Jerusalem that reached their climax with a massive procession to the Wall. This claim of self-defense is consistent with Islamic logic and the Qur'an's command:

190. وَقَاتِلُواْ فِي سَبِيلِ اللّهِ الَّذِينَ يُقَاتِلُونَكُمْ وَلاَ تَعْتَدُواْ إِنَّ اللّهَ لاَ يُحِبُّ الْمُعْتَدِينَ

191. وَاقْتُلُوهُمْ حَيْثُ ثَقِفْتُمُوهُمْ وَأَخْرِجُوهُم مِّنْ حَيْثُ أَخْرَجُوكُمْ وَالْفِتْنَةُ أَشَدُّ مِنَ الْقَتْلِ وَلاَ تُقَاتِلُوهُمْ عِندَ الْمَسْجِدِ الْحَرَامِ حَتَّى يُقَاتِلُوكُمْ فِيهِ فَإِن قَاتَلُوكُمْ فَاقْتُلُوهُمْ كَذَلِكَ جَزَاء الْكَافِرِينَ

Fight in God's cause against those who fight you, but do not transgress: Indeed, God does not love transgressors. Kill them wherever you encounter them, and drive them out from where they drove you out, for persecution is more serious than killing. Do not fight them at the Sacred Mosque unless they fight you there. If they do fight you, kill them — this is what such disbelievers deserve. (al-Baqara 2:190–91)

These verses underline the distinction between a defensive and offensive war in Muslim law. This is not the place to discuss how Islamic thought on this issue has developed over the ages. What is important for the matter at hand is to understand that one of the principal motives for the attack on the Jews in 1929 was — in the Arabs' perception — the desire and duty to defend Muslim holy places, given that the Jews had risen up to fight them first. The murder of an Arab family in Jaffa by a Jewish policeman and the lynchings of Arabs by Jews in Jerusalem are frequently cited in this context so as to depict the riots as Jewish aggression to which the Arabs responded in self-defense.

Whatever the case, there is no disputing that the aggression began in Jerusalem, and we will go there next in an effort to understand why the Arabs viewed the Jews as aggressors, whereas the Jews believed that they were under attack.

JERUSALEM

Friday, August 23, 1929

In which we will follow rising tensions in the Holy City to its violent eruption, consider the involvement of Rabbi Avraham Yitzhak HaCohen Kook and Mufti Hajj Amin al-Hussayni, follow the tracks of the mysterious man who saved the neighborhood of Meah She'arim from a mob of hostile Arabs, and meet many other inhabitants of Jerusalem—Jews, Muslims, and Christians.

First Things

The Wailing Wall, which is one part of the whole western wall of al-Haram al-Sharif [the Temple Mount], has been an Islamic holy site since the Prophet, may prayers and peace be upon him, descended there on his steed al-Buraq on his night journey. The tranquility and mutual understanding between Jews and Arabs regarding this site have been maintained over the years since the Arab conquests led by 'Omar ibn al-Khattab, and in the time of Salah a-Din and in the Mamluk period. (Samrin 2003, 164)

So Ghaleb Samrin opens chapter 7 of *Qaryati Qalunya* (My village Qalunya). The title of the chapter is "The People of Our Village Qalunya and Their Jihad against the English and the Jews before 1948." Qalunya was located just west of Jerusalem, on the north side of the main road to Jaffa. The Jewish settlement of Motza was founded next to it. During the 1929 disturbances, Arabs from Qalunya murdered seven of their Jewish neighbors.

Samrin's opening sentences present the traditional (though not the only) Palestinian view of Jerusalem's sacredness to Islam and of Muslim tolerance of the city's Jews. As is the case with Ahmad al-Shuqayri in his memoir about Acre (1969), Samrin prides himself on the good relations that prevailed between Jews and Arabs under Islamic rule. But this familiar litany stops abruptly when the author offers an unusual account of the involvement of the inhabitants of his village in the 1929 disturbances. It is an account written from the point of view of the assailants, and its tone is manifestly unapologetic. But before proceeding to Motza, let's take a look at Jerusalem. On the way, I'll offer a short account of

Muslim-Jewish relations in the city and say something about each group's relation to its holy sites.

The Western Wall has two names in Arabic. One is Ha'it al-Mabka (the wall they weep at), which resonates with the common English term, the Wailing Wall, referring to the custom of Jews who visited there to clutch at the wall and cry. The sight was described by an American writer, William Curtis, who visited the wall at the beginning of the twentieth century and wrote of it in *Today in Syria and Palestine*:

> The saddest sight in Jerusalem is the wailing of the Jews over the ruins of the temple [sic]. It has become a good deal of a formality, however, and attracts a large number of spectators, who sit around upon benches prepared for them, laughing, smoking and taking snap shots [sic] with their kodaks [sic] in an irreverent way, while a touching custom, which has prevailed for centuries, is observed. The wailing place is at an ancient gate called the Gate of the Prophets, and under a retaining wall erected by the Romans, probably on foundations laid by Solomon to sustain the terrace upon which the great temple stood. It is partly hidden by excavations, and reached by a narrow winding road through the Jewish quarter. The ceremony takes place every Friday afternoon between 4 o'clock and sundown, and also upon certain festivals, when 200 or 300 Jews assemble, many of them barefooted and in sackcloth and ashes, and weep and wail, kiss the stones of the wall and bemoan the downfall of Jerusalem. (1903, 392–93)

The wall's other Arabic name, its Islamic one, is al-Buraq, after the wondrous winged steed on which, according to Muslim tradition, Mohammad rode on his night journey from Mecca to Jerusalem. When he reached the Holy City, Mohammad hitched his horse to the wall, to the same ring to which the biblical prophets tied their mounts. Detailed descriptions of the events of that night are quoted in the important collections of traditions such as *Sahih Muslim* and Ahmad Ibn Hanbal's *Musnad* (1978). Thus the western supporting wall of the Temple Mount, or al-Haram al-Sharif, compound gained its Arabic name. The night journey is called al-Israa. Later that night Mohammad ascended from Jerusalem to heaven. Along his way he met the prophets who had preceded him — among them Moses, Abraham, and Jesus — who told him of their experiences and offered him advice. This journey upward is called al-Mi'raj. The Muslims commemorate the night of al-Israa wal-Mi'raj each year on the twenty-seventh day of the month of Rajab.

Everything I have written up to this point is the subject of endless dispute.

One Argument

Did Mohammad ever visit Jerusalem? The relevant verse in the Qur'an does not state explicitly that he did. Here it is: "Glory to Him, who made His servant

The Temple Mount (al-Haram al-Sharif)
(Matson Photograph Collection, Library of Congress).

travel by night from the sacred place of worship to the furthest place of worship [or "the uttermost mosque"; al-Aqsa in Arabic], whose surroundings we have blessed." This is the first verse in chapter 17, Surat al-Israa (The night journey, known also as The children of Israel). Some commentators on the Qur'an understand the expression "the uttermost mosque" to refer to the celestial mosque, which has nothing to do with Jerusalem. But most commentators construe it to mean Jerusalem, both because that is the tradition handed down to them by their teachers and because the rest of the chapter addresses the fate of the Children of Israel. They entered the Holy Land at God's command, but their Temple was destroyed and they were exiled from it because of their sins. The verse's reference to the "surroundings we have blessed," or the "blessed land," offers another reason for exegetes to claim that the place of worship visited by Mohammad was in Jerusalem.

Holy or Not?

Some claim that Jerusalem has no special sanctity in Islam. They base this in part on the fact that the city is not mentioned by name even once in the Qur'an.

But Muslim tradition makes it clear that the community of believers that took form around Mohammad sanctified Jerusalem. In fact, the prophet's followers faced Jerusalem while praying during the first sixteen months after his proclamation of the new faith. That being the case, the absence of the name "Jerusalem" in the Muslims' most holy book does not necessarily denote its status in Islam. But if Jerusalem is so important to Islam, wouldn't the Qur'an mention it by name, as the Torah does?

In fact, the Torah does not mention Jerusalem by name, either. Yet all Jewish religious scholars are certain that the Five Books of Moses refer to it and have no doubt at all regarding the city's sanctity. How could that be? They accept traditions that identify Shalem, mentioned in Genesis as the realm of Malchitzedek, with Jerusalem. They also accept the traditional exegesis that the phrase "the place that He will choose," which appears frequently in Deuteronomy, refers to Jerusalem. In the same way, Muslims as a general rule accept the traditions that claim that the uttermost mosque, al-Aqsa, refers to Jerusalem.

According to the Islamic interpretation that is most widespread today, the name of the holy precinct in Jerusalem had been al-Aqsa even prior to the Muslim conquest in 640. That is what the verse refers to. According to some scholars, the mosque and the compound in which it sits was named al-Aqsa after the conquest, so as to forge a link between the site and the verse in the Qur'an.

Another Dispute

Where was the wondrous steed tethered? Today it is common wisdom among Muslims that al-Buraq, the winged horse, was tied to the Western Wall, right in the area where the Jews make a custom of praying. It is not clear that this was the prevailing version of the story in earlier times. David Yellin, a Jewish educator and scholar in Jerusalem and an expert on Arab literature and history, testified as an expert witness before the Western Wall Commission, which the British appointed to study the history and the status of the holy place. Yellin claimed that, according to Muslim tradition, the site where Mohammad hitched al-Buraq was on the east side of the Temple Mount, close to the Golden Gate. The implication was that the Muslim leadership had sought to enhance the sacredness of the Western Wall for no reason other than to impinge on Jewish rights there. Yellin's analysis was published in several languages, and a prominent Egyptian scholar, Ahmad Zaki Pasha, who had served as secretary to the Egyptian cabinet in the first decade of the twentieth century, promptly published a pamphlet rebutting each of Yellin's claims (Zaki 1930). Yellin won high praise for his scholarship from Zaki, who apparently knew him personally. But the Egyptian refutes the Jewish scholar's claims one by one.

The reverberations of this debate are still felt today. The Palestinian-American historian Rashid Khalidi notes ironically that the debate over where an imaginary winged horse was tied up proves the extent to which serious scholars can get carried away when they debate religious claims to Jerusalem (1997, 216, note 25). In any case, even if the Muslim inhabitants of Jerusalem believed at various times that Mohammad had tied his steed inside the sacred compound or at its eastern wall, it is clear that in the 1920s they believed that the hitching post was at the same place where the Jews prayed.

A More Comprehensive Dispute

Samrin stresses the understanding and amity that prevailed in Jerusalem under Islamic rule, in the spirit of many of the best Muslim writers who trumpet the integrity and munificence of Muslim rulers, and in particular the protection they provided to their Jewish and Christian subjects, who fell under the rubric of "religions of the book." An entirely different view is that the members of these communities suffered persecutions and humiliations, due to the xenophobia that is built into Islam. Bat Yeòr's *The Dhimmi* (1985) offers the latter perspective.

The contest between these two positions is fundamentally a dispute about history, but often the positions of the antagonists are shaped by their own life experiences or religious and political views rather than research. A more inclusive view of the premodern age (not just of the period in question) shows that no religious group was ever granted equality when it was a minority living under a ruler of a different faith. Jews and Christians did not enjoy equality in the Islamic lands, just as non-Christians did not in Christian realms. Jews, Christians, and Muslims all believed that their religion was the one true faith and that their own community thus had the right to rule over, kill, or expel nonbelievers.

As a rule, Sunni Muslim sovereigns were generally tolerant, partly because Muslim religious law, *sharia*, requires rulers to defend those who practice the religions of the book, mainly Jews and Christians. But the sovereign's protection is conditioned on the acknowledgment by these non-Muslims of the supremacy of the Islamic faith and their acceptance of a lower status. Until the advent of the modern age this arrangement was accepted by all parties, if for no other reason than the lack of an alternative. The practical effects of this may be summed up as follows: Jews and Christians did not enjoy equality under Islam, but by and large they were able to survive. Another way of putting it is that, if the standard for comparison is the ideal of freedom, brotherhood, and equality, the Jewish position under Islamic rule was a difficult one. But their position under Sunni rule was on the whole better than under Christian rule (for a more comprehensive account, see M. Cohen 1994; Lewis 1984).

Jerusalem as a Case in Point

The restrictions imposed on Jews by the Ottoman authorities included a prohibition against their entering the Temple Mount, on the ground that it was a holy place, al-Haram al-Sharif, reserved for Muslims only. It is difficult to date the inception of this proscription. During the early period of Islamic rule Jews were permitted to pray on the Temple Mount. There is even evidence that they were invited to light the lamps on the Dome of the Rock after its construction in the seventh century. But at some point, apparently beginning with the Mamluk conquest of Jerusalem in 1266, Jews were banned from entering the site. In addition, in some eras, Jews were required to dye yellow their 'amamas, the common headdress in Muslim countries, to distinguish them from Muslims (Christians were required to dye theirs blue). Jews who did not observe this stricture were prosecuted. In *Jewish Life under Islam*, Amnon Cohen writes that the purpose of such distinguishing garb was not to humiliate the Jews but rather to keep each religious community distinct, as well as to make it more difficult for Jews to enter the Temple Mount (1984, 72–73).

Cohen may be a bit too forgiving on the issue of this marking of Jews by a dress code, but whatever the case, the fact that a Jewish community could reside in Jerusalem was a Muslim innovation. Both the Byzantines, who ruled the city prior to the Muslim conquest, and the crusaders, who took it from the Muslims and ruled it for a time, forbade Jews to live in the city. A lesser-known fact is that under the British Mandate, Christians still forbade Jews from entering the Church of the Holy Sepulcher and the street leading to it. Nor were Jews allowed into the Christian compound on Mount Zion.

Christians Constrained Jews under Islamic Rule?

Yes. Here are two interesting accounts. One is that of Laurence Oliphant, a British journalist, scholar, and diplomat of Zionist sympathies who settled in Palestine, in the Druze village of Daliat al-Karmil just east of Haifa, during the last quarter of the nineteenth century. In *Haifa*, he wrote that the Jewish boy who served as his guide on a visit to Jerusalem accompanied him when he ascended to the Temple Mount but was forbidden to join him when he entered the plaza before the Church of the Holy Sepulcher. Oliphant concluded from this that the city's Muslims were more tolerant than its Christians (1887, 196).

Another account is that of Agustin Arce, who studied the restrictions of movement that were imposed on Jews in Ottoman Jerusalem, and mentioned that some of these strictures remained in force during the Mandate period. Arce recalled that he witnessed Greek and Armenian monks attacking a Jew who entered the Holy Sepulcher compound in 1927 (1979, 220). Clearly, opposing Christian approaches coexisted—the anti-Jewish attitude displayed by these monks and the pro-Zionism advocated by Oliphant and others, which in various guises had champions in British ruling circles. But the differences between these different takes on Christianity were shunted into the background by the dispute between Jews and Muslims, which touch on the existential roots of each faith.

The Roots

The core religious dispute between Jews and Muslims, then and now, is very simple to state: which religion is the true religion. The fundamental assumption subscribed to by both Jews and Muslims is that God granted them the Land of Israel or Palestine because they have the true faith. Many Jews believe that God's promise to Abraham, "Unto thy seed I will give this land" (Genesis 12:7), and the injunction to the Children of Israel as they were about to enter the Holy Land, "Behold, the Lord thy God hath set the land before thee; go up, take possession" (Deuteronomy 1:21), remain in force. According to Muslims, however, God granted the land to the Children of Israel, but they lost their right to it because they disobeyed God's commandment by turning their backs on his prophets —from Isaiah, Jeremiah, and Zechariah to Jesus and Mohammad. What, then, is the disposition of the Holy Land? According to the Qur'an, in the Sura of the Prophets (al-Anbiyaa, 21:105), "the righteous will inherit the land"—that is, those who accept the revelation of Mohammad.

In the age of nationalism these claims took on a new guise, but their religious dimension did not disappear. Both the Jewish and Palestinian national movements were based in large part on religious sentiments and did not always separate religion and nationhood. Nationalism thus did not replace religion as a focal point of identity, but rather merged with it. The events of 1929 offered a good demonstration of this.

August 1929: The Jewish Demonstrations

In his book, Samrin is clearly not troubled by the debates between historians about the precise place where Mohammad tied his horse or the status of Jews in Muslim society. He is among those fortunate writers — Jews, Arabs, and others —for whom the facts are neither obscure nor open to doubt. Samrin believes that there is a single truth, the one that he learned from his father. One claimant, the group to which he belongs, is right. So whoever tells the story just as he does is honest. Whoever tells it otherwise is a liar or inventor of narratives. His duty, as he sees it, is to preserve and foster his community's heritage. His certainty that he possesses the absolute truth is evident both in his account of interfaith relations in Jerusalem under Islamic rule and in his telling of the events of 1929. Like Mustafa al-Dabbagh and all other Arab writers on 1929, Samrin ascribes great importance to what the Jews did in mid-August:

[The Jews] staged demonstrations in Jerusalem and Tel Aviv and shouted provocative slogans at the Arabs and Muslims, such as "The Wall is our Wall." Prior to this the [Jewish] Committee for the Wall called on the entire Jewish people everywhere in the world: "O Jews scattered throughout the entire world. Awake. Do not rest and do not remain quiet until the entire Western Wall is returned to us." . . . From then on the Jews focused on turning the Arab Palestinian–Zionist conflict into a religious conflict, in order to enlist the interest and mobilization of world Jewry, and especially of the Jews of the United States, so that they contribute generously to the construction of the Jewish national home in our land of Palestine and to our expulsion from it. (2003, 165)

The claim that the Jews had an interest in turning the conflict into a religious one is not unique to Samrin. 'Abd al-Wahhab Kayyali says the same.

Kayyali's Analysis

Kayyali is the author of *Ta'rikh Filastin al-Hadith* (A history of modern Palestine), a comprehensive work published in 1970, which has gone through many editions since. His fundamental perspective is that of an Arab nationalist, and his methodology that of a professional historian. In the chapter he devotes to the 1929 disturbances, he endeavors to present the events from both the Zionist and Arab points of view. He believes that the Zionists sought to challenge the status quo on the Wall as a way of buttressing Diaspora Jewish support for Zionist institutions in Palestine. As evidence, he quotes from a letter Chaim Weizmann wrote while on a fundraising trip to the United States in 1928, in which the Zionist leader related, prior to the riots, that the dispute over the Western Wall roused strong feelings among Jews in every location he visited (Kayyali 1970, 198). This claim is interesting in and of itself, but it is also interesting to note the similarity between it and the Zionist claim that the Arab national leadership deliberately ignited the dispute over the Wall, invoking Islamic rhetoric as a way of consolidating its public support.

Kayyali was a prolific and important Palestinian historian. Born in Jaffa in 1939, a decade after the riots, by the time he was ten years old he was a refugee in Jordan. He moved from there to London, where he received his master's degree and then pursued a PhD at the University of London. While his ideology was pan-Arabist, he joined the Palestine Liberation Organization (PLO) soon after it was founded, becoming one of its central figures and serving on its Executive Committee and on the Palestinian National Council. He edited a number of periodicals, some published by the PLO; founded an institute for Arab studies; and authored many works of scholarship, including a book on the kibbutz movement. Kayyali was murdered in Beirut in 1981 by unknown assailants, apparently Palestinians.

An Alternative Analysis

Yehoshua Porath, one of the first Israelis to study the Palestinian national movement in depth, maintains that it was the Arab leadership that wanted to fire up its public over the wall. He accepts the position of *Sefer Toldot HaHaganah* that the mufti incited the Arab mob (Dinur 1973). And he argues that the Shaw Commission, which cleared the mufti of responsibility for the riots, was biased against the Jews. However, Porath maintains, the Jewish interest in keeping the peace at the Wall was tactical: calm would enable them to continue their strategy of "peaceful penetration" of the Western Wall compound, with the goal of changing the status quo in their favor. The interests of the Supreme Muslim Council and its leader, Grand Mufti Hajj Amin al-Hussayni, were precisely the opposite, in Porath's account. By inciting the Muslim public, they sought to force the British to halt the Jewish effort to take control of the Wall. "Peaceful penetration" was, by the way, the term used by Leonard Stein, secretary of the World Zionist Organization, with regard to the Jewish strategy regarding the Wall (quoted in Porath 1974, 262).

So What Actually Happened?

In chapter 13 of *One Palestine, Complete* (2000), Tom Segev does an excellent job of reconstructing the events at the Wall during the year preceding the riots. He relates that, at the end of the summer of 1928, during the Jewish High Holidays, it came to the attention of the British district commissioner for Jerusalem, Edward Keith-Roach, that Jewish worshipers at the Wall had erected a divider to separate men and women. Keith-Roach notified the Muslim religious authorities. He also instructed Police Constable Douglas Duff to remove the partition. "From his memoirs, Duff emerges as a violent man, a racist, a misogynist, and a fool," Segev writes (2000, 295–96). Duff carried out his orders with brute determination. The Jews felt humiliated, and the Muslims believed they had won this small battle in an ongoing campaign.

Both sides set out to defend their shrines. Both established committees to defend their holy sites. The Muslims ratcheted up their presence in the area. The Jews did the same. One side staged public prayers, and the other followed suit. One organized rallies and demonstrations, and so did the other. Both sent telegrams to King George V and his prime minister.

The Importance of the Divider

Orthodox Jews separate men and women during prayers. Christians do not. The Muslim custom is similar to that of the Jews, which apparently is rooted in the practice at the Second Temple. In most Orthodox synagogues, the sexes are divided by a curtain or a solid divider. No such divider stood at the Western

Wall, where men and women prayed side by side. Rabbi Avraham Yitzhak Ha-Cohen Kook, the Ashkenazi chief rabbi of Palestine, told the Shaw Commission that the situation disturbed an important visitor—Rabbi Menachem Mendel Gutterman, the *admor* (Hasidic spiritual leader) of Radzymin in Poland. Rabbi Kook reported that Rabbi Gutterman "came to the Wailing Wall to pray; he noticed there was no partition between the men and women worshippers, and in his innocence he told the beadle [*shamash*, the functionary responsible for the physical arrangements at the site] to erect that screen. In all Orthodox Synagogues it is an old custom to make a partition between men and women" (quoted in Commission 1930, 2:740).

The Wall in the 1920s

In contemplating the site of the conflict it is important to keep in mind that today's immense plaza that spreads out before the Western Wall did not exist then. To get to the site one had to walk through a crowded Muslim neighborhood, the Maghrebi quarter, which had houses that nearly abutted the Wall. The space in front of the wall was only about four meters wide, the width of an average room. The length of the section of the wall available to Jewish worshipers was about thirty meters. This space was surrounded on all sides by the homes of the Muslim Maghrebi community.

Jerusalemite Maghrebis

In Jerusalem there was a large community of Maghrebi Muslims, who came to the city from all over North Africa. It was centuries older than Jaffa's Maghrebi Jewish and Muslim communities. Pilgrims, religious scholars, mystics, and simple folk had journeyed from the Maghreb to Jerusalem ever since North Africa accepted Islam. And since Islam is a religion of redemption and because, according to Muslim tradition, the events of the end of days are to take place in Jerusalem, many thought it the right place to await the arrival of the Mahdi (the Messiah). Some of them were familiar with the tradition from the sayings of the Prophet Mohammad cited in the previous chapter: "There will be a *hijra* after *hijra*, to the place that your father Ibrahim moved to" (Ibn Hanbal 1978, 2:84).

How Did the Area Become "Maghrebi"?

This question of ownership, possession, or sovereignty has several aspects. The first is: how is it that a person, community, or nation gains ownership of any territory or site? Is it by dwelling there for many years? By force of arms? By holding a deed from a land registry? By government fiat? By divine promise (If so, how does one know whether God gave the land to a specific nation? What happens when there are conflicting claims or understandings about God's will?)

Can ownership expire, and if so, how? What is the connection between national sovereignty and private ownership of land? All these questions are valid and important. I will address only the legal aspect of the issue. From a legal point of view, the area to the west of al-Haram al-Sharif, or Temple Mount—including the parcels adjacent to the Western Wall—was allocated to the Maghrebi community by the Ayyubid sovereign al-Malik al-Afdal Nur a-Din in the thirteenth century. To the best of our knowledge, permanent Maghrebi settlement in Jerusalem commenced after the city was retaken from the crusaders by Salah a-Din in 1187. North African Muslims knew very well of the conquest of Jerusalem by the crusaders in 1099. They took part in the Muslim religious awakening that followed that event. Like other Muslims, they felt the pain of the slaughter of Jerusalem's Muslim defenders, the city's fall to foreigners, the transformation of the al-Aqsa Mosque into a church, and the use of al-Haram al-Sharif's underground tunnels as stables for the horses of the Knights Templar. It would not be surprising, then, if some Maghrebis answered Salah a-Din's call to arms and took part in the conquest of the city in 1187, placing their expert seamanship at the disposal of the Muslim fleet.

Salah a-Din encouraged the Maghrebis, as he did Muslims in general, to settle in Jerusalem and elsewhere in the region, to strengthen the Muslim community in the Holy Land. Nur a-Din, his son, followed in his footsteps. He granted the Maghrebis a plot of land to the west of al-Haram al-Sharif, where they made their homes. This was the original Maghrebi waqf. Over the years other prominent Maghrebis who owned land in the city and its environs bequeathed their property to the Maghrebi community through the waqf system. Some lots were designated for the construction of housing for the members of the community; others were cultivated, and in those cases the income from the land was used for the upkeep of homes and other buildings in the Maghrebi quarter and the financial support of its inhabitants. One person who bequeathed property was Shu'aib Abu Midyin, one of the great North African Sufi mystics, who owned land in Jerusalem. His grandson did the same. This was the conventional way for Muslim sovereigns and property owners to make donations for the general welfare. These and other sorts of donations provided the Maghrebi quarter, next to the Western Wall, with a firm foundation. Over the years some 130 residences were built that were densely populated by numerous families, many of them poor. The neighborhood also had a ten-room *zawiya*, a Sufi meeting house, which was used both to shelter the homeless and for the performance of Sufi religious rituals (Tazi 1984).

For many years the Maghrebis, like the rest of Jerusalem's Muslim inhabitants, viewed themselves as duty bound to defend the city from foreign invaders. That was a central component of Muslim identity in the city, and in fact in the crystallization of Palestinian identity as a whole. Recalling that this was the reason why many Muslims settled in the Holy Cities of Jerusalem and Hebron during the years of conflict with the crusaders makes one more sharply aware of the depth of this aspect of Palestinian identity. Yet, of course, the same area had been sacred to Jews from ancient times.

The Jews and the Western Wall

Earlier, apparently up until the Mamluk period, the custom of Jewish pilgrims was to direct their prayers at the Temple Mount from the Mount of Olives to its east, or from the Temple Mount enclosure's southern retaining wall, next to Hulda's Gate. During the Ottoman period Jews began praying in the area of the Western Wall. The first tensions between the Maghrebis and Jewish worshipers were documented at the beginning of the eighteenth century. In 1727 the leaders of the Maghrebi community filed suit against the city's Jewish leaders, complaining that Jews who habitually prayed at the Western Wall littered the neighborhood and worshiped at a volume that disturbed Muslims who were studying the Qur'an. During the trial it emerged that the Jews had never received a permit to pray there. The *qadi* (the Muslim judge who heard the case) ordered the Jews to desist from entering the Maghrebi neighborhood and from praying at the Wall (A. Cohen 1996, 116–18). In the years that followed, an accepted practice developed at the site. Jews were allowed to pray there on the condition that they not disturb the residents of the neighborhood, and on the understanding that they not claim title to the site. But in the nineteenth century the Jews were no longer satisfied with this arrangement: they wanted to make the Western Wall their own.

Buyers Only: Jewish Attempts to Purchase the Wall

Jerusalem's Jews grew more self-confident in the mid-nineteenth century as their numbers grew and under the custodianship that the British assumed over them. Sir Moses Montefiore, a figure who more than any other symbolizes the British-Jewish connection, was the first to attempt to buy the Wall, in 1875. A decade later another European Jewish philanthropist, Baron Edmond de Rothschild, tried to do the same. On the eve of World War I the Zionist movement carried on the effort (Kramer 1998). The attempts continued after the British conquest. On September 10, 1918, the Zionist functionary Mordechai Ben-Hillel HaKohen reported to the Zionist Organization that more and more of the city's Muslims were coming to realize that the Western Wall would pass into Jewish hands. He also said that he had made contact with a man who was prepared to serve as an intermediary in the transaction (HaKohen's letters are preserved in NLI, HaKohen papers, 4-1068/305). But his elation was without foundation

—the attempts led nowhere. The Maghrebis must have had in mind the charter Shu'aib Abu Midyin wrote for his trust: "It is forbidden for every man who believes in God and the Day of Judgment, and knows that he will be taken by his Lord, [whether] ruler or subject or community leader, to abrogate this trust. And God will help whoever preserves this trust and will give him a perfect reward. And whoever acts against it has defied the word of God, and will be considered a rebel, and the curse of Allah will justly pursue him" (Tazi 1984, 225).

In the months that preceded the 1929 riots, the Zionist Executive in Palestine was negotiating the purchase of a property to the north of the Wall, to improve access to the site. According to memoirs published in Hebrew (Broide 1997; Frumkin 1954), a member of the al-Khalidi family had agreed to sell a house in a complex transaction that was approved by the head of the Zionist Executive, Colonel Frederick Kisch, as well as Chaim Weizmann. But by the time that the agitation surrounding the Wall went into high gear, the deal had not yet been concluded and negotiations ceased.

Jews Also Opposed the Deal

Not only Arabs opposed the purchase. So did members of the Yishuv's radical right wing. One such person was Abba Ahimeir, who after the 1929 riots would—along with Uri Zvi Greenberg and Yehoshua Heschel Yevin—found Brit HaBiryonim, a small group of radical Jewish nationalists. On October 8, 1928, following the incident of the divider at the Wall and prior to the outbreak of violence, Ahimeir, who wrote a column in the daily newspaper *Do'ar Hayom* titled "On Questions of the Moment (From the Journal of a Fascist)," devoted a long installment to the question of the Western Wall:

Again a proposal has been made to redeem the Western Wall by paying a full price for it, again this Diaspora method has been placed on the agenda: "I will buy everything with gold," the Diaspora Jew always says. . . . But what is perhaps permissible with regard to the [Jezreel] Valley and the Sharon [plain] is forbidden with regard to the Wall. There are things, my friends, that it is forbidden to buy even though there are 4 million Jews in America. We need to obtain the Wall through our political power, if we still cannot get it by those same classic means by which little Serbia became great Yugoslavia. And if our political pressure is not sufficient, and if the millions of our compatriots in New York, Chicago, Warsaw, Paris, and London find that it is more urgent for them to devote themselves to business and jazz and this national insult is not their insult, then it would be best for the Wall to remain in the meantime in its current situation.

Ahimeir believed that the Wall had to be liberated with military force. Barring that, one could make do with having official title to the Wall transferred to the Jewish people via an international diplomatic decision. But purchasing it was inconceivable, as it already belonged to the Jewish people. Similarly, as we have seen, the sale of the Wall was inconceivable to most Arabs—they could not even accept placing benches and a divider in the area designated for prayer. They understood that the Jewish agenda was much broader. They did not entirely understand what the Jews were after, but they sensed that it was not good for them.

Developments at the Flash Point

For Jerusalem's Muslims, then, the Wall symbolized the danger of a Jewish takeover of their city. The Maghrebis increased their hounding and provocation of Jews passing through their neighborhood to pray at the Wall, and the Haganah, protecting the Jews, responded with gunfire. One night in 1927 two Haganah commanders stole into the Maghrebi quarter and planted a primitive bomb—a tin bucket full of explosives and pieces of metal—in the doorway of one of the neighborhood sheikhs. The house was largely destroyed in the explosion, but no one was hurt (Dinur 1973, 2:253). In 1929, when tensions at the Wall escalated, the Muslims responded to the placement of benches and a divider at the Wall by mounting a building project. After receiving a permit from the British authorities, they renovated a mosque and zawiya close to the Wall, with doors opening toward the Jewish prayer area. Muslims increasingly crossed the site and made their presence felt.

At the edge of the Temple Mount compound, close to the gate that led from the Maghrebi quarter to the sacred precinct, the Abu Sa'ud family, which managed a number of waqfs in the area of al-Haram al-Sharif, held a double, nonpolitical celebration in mid-August 1929—two women in the family, the cousins Hiba and Zahwa, had given birth to sons in the same week. The women agreed that they would both call their babies Yasir. One of them would later be known as Yasir Abu Sa'ud, while the other would make a career for himself as Yasir Arafat. Still another cousin gave birth to a girl, whom she named Fatima. Fatima's brother, 'Azem Abu Sa'ud, spoke about these three babies in a eulogy he delivered at Yasir Arafat's funeral in 2005. He noted the symbolism of Arafat's birth in Jerusalem at the height of the disturbances (and in doing so tried, without success, to end the debate over where Arafat was born).

In tandem with the family celebration, Sheikh Hasan Abu Sa'ud, an associate of Mufti Hajj Amin al-Hussayni and one of the city's most prominent preachers, carried on with his religious and political work. In his sermons he called on believers to visit al-Buraq. And, in fact, the paved area next to the Wall, which had previously been used only by a handful of Maghrebis whose homes lay at the edge of the compound, soon became a busy byway. The Mandate government's chief secretary, Harry Luke — filling in for the British high commissioner, John Chancellor, who was away on vacation when the riots broke out — described the atmosphere for the benefit of the Shaw Commission:

> Things began to get a little difficult at the Wall, as far back as May, when the projected buildings, the new buildings, down there were causing a certain amount of disquiet. . . . Here is a report . . . "Inspector Langer, the Jewish [police] officer down there, report[ed] . . . that on the day in question (27th July, 1929), while he was on duty at the Wailing Wall with a British constable, a Jew, Ephraim Jacob Mizrachy, arrived and opened the door of left [sic] Moghrabi [sic] Quarter and looked inside and he was slapped on the face. Both persons, accused and complainant, were sent to Inspector Misbah el Daoudi, and they were reconciled. . . ."
>
> Then here is a report dated 5th August: "At about 1200 hours on 27th July, 1929, some Jewish visitors visited the Wailing Wall. Five of these visitors attempted to enter the Moghrabi zawiyah [sic] for sight-seeing. The Moghrabis refused to allow them to enter, and both nearly began fighting, had not the British police on duty intervened. . . ."
>
> "The following occurrences took place at the Wailing Wall on 3rd August, 1929: A certain Moghrabi attempted to pass through the worshippers of the Wailing Wall while prayers were in progress and was smoking a cigarette. One of the worshippers approached and requested him to wait for a while until the prayer is over. The Moghrabi, in disobeying the request, got hold of a stone and attempted to throw it at the Jew. He was arrested, prosecuted and sentenced to seven days' imprisonment." (quoted in Commission 1930, 1:305)

Incidents of this sort became routine at the Wall. The Betar movement's procession on the fast of the Ninth of Av (August 15), 1929, was a protest against such indignities. Its slogan was, according to al-Dabbagh, "The Wall is ours. Woe to anyone who defiles our holy site" (2002, 4:265).

The Prophet Mohammad's birthday that year fell on the day after the Jewish fast of the Ninth of Av — that is, on Friday, August 16. The Muslims celebrated the occasion on al-Haram al-Sharif, in front of al-Aqsa. They staged a demonstration in response to the Jewish procession, and some of them, led by Sheikh Hasan Abu Sa'ud, descended to the Wall and burned Jewish holy books and the notes and supplications that Jews traditionally placed between the Wall's stones. The Muslim demonstrators had a clear message: al-Aqsa and al-Buraq are ours — woe to anyone who defiles our holy sites.

On Similarities and Differences

Can one compare the conduct of Jews and of Muslims on the eve of the massacres of 1929? Yes, one should compare them, if one wants to understand what happened in 1929 and since then. A comparison of the demonstrations and the arguments shows that the emotions of the Jews and those of the Muslims were of the same sort, involving national pride, love of homeland, and devotion to holy places. These feelings also came from another common source: fear, hostility toward strangers, a sense of superiority, and a desire for control. Their methods were also similar, at least at this point.

Rabbi Kook and the Maghrebis

The feelings of the Jewish protestors, and the far-reaching nature of their demands, were expressed by Rabbi Kook in an interview he gave to *Do'ar Hayom* just after the fast. Here is the item from the newspaper:

> Even though the rabbi had not yet eaten, he devoted an hour and a half to a conversation with Meiri [the newspaper's correspondent], heard details about the demonstration, and expressed his profound gratitude for this youth and for all the measures he had taken, because these measures demonstrated "national pride and Maccabean zealousness," which is "the eruption of the holiness of Israel's sublime soul, which has entered into the ranks of our youth in most of its types and classes," and the desire "to actually sacrifice his life for the redemption of our Holy Place." Tears were in his eyes at the moment that he was told that the national anthem had been sung for the first time before the Western Wall, that the national flag had been flown in honor, while standing in silence for a few moments before a huge crowd of thousands of people, and that the youth swore to defend the Western Wall. . . .
>
> "It is unacceptable that the status of this holy site," the rabbi continued, "which is venerated by the entire Jewish people much more than the opulent synagogues and 'temples' of the Jews all over the world, remain endlessly in this insulting way. It is unacceptable that this holy site be permanently surrounded with such grimy and ugly courtyards and alleys, which serve as breeding grounds for every pollution and disease. We must," the rabbi declared, "explain to the government that it is obligated by our general situation in the Land of Israel and the entire world to expand the boundary on this side of the Wall, where our position before the remnant of our Temple is so miserable and deficient. There is nothing to prevent such expansion other than the secular 'waqf' of the Maghrebi beggars. Is it really conceivable that legal logic cannot find some means of compromise that will lead to the expropriation of the location of our Temple in a fair and conciliatory manner by the government? That is, really, the elementary duty of the Mandate government." ("A Conversation with Chief Rabbi Kook," *Do'ar Hayom*, August 18, 1929)

The article appeared the following Sunday. Rabbi Kook stressed in this interview, and at other opportunities, that the Jewish demand was to enlarge the space for prayer at the Wall, and that he was leaving the question of the Temple Mount to heaven. He maintained that the government should carry out the expansion, compensating the Maghrebis for evacuating the site. But these fine distinctions between the present and the indefinite messianic future did not impress the Muslims in and around the city.

Find the Differences

The neighborhood that for the Muslims was the environs of al-Buraq, where they huddled to be close to the city's holiest site, was dismissed by Rabbi Kook as a slum maintained by a nonreligious trust, full of filthy alleys breeding contagion and disease. The Jewish rally that the Muslims experienced as unadulterated hooliganism was, for the rabbi, the "eruption of the holiness of Israel's sublime soul." What the rabbi termed, elsewhere in the article, as "the fine moral state" of Hebrew youth was, as far as the Arabs were concerned, nothing more than belligerence and arrogance.

Time Warp: The End of History?

Less than forty years after this interview, Rabbi Kook's dream came true. In 1967, at the end of the Six-Day War, the centuries-old Maghrebi quarter was bulldozed by the Israeli army, and its hundreds of inhabitants ejected. Cabinet ministers who came to visit the Western Wall on June 11 were astonished to see that the neighborhood had been razed even before they had made a decision on the matter, but they were pleased (Raz 2012, 113). The wreckage was quickly trucked away and the area paved with stone, producing the Western Wall plaza that exists today.

The demolition of the Maghrebi quarter can be seen as an act of revenge for the community's involvement in the progress of events that led to the riots of 1929, the implementation of a fifty-year-old plan, or the conceit of victory. Some will argue that there was a real need to demolish the quarter. But they will be those who leveled the neighborhood, not those whose homes were destroyed.

Nonetheless, history does not stand still, nor can we predict its progress or know whether it has a preplanned end. In any case, it has not reached its endpoint. Nevertheless, there are a number of proposals regarding what the Temple Mount and its environs will look like when that happens. A documentary broadcast on the Palestinian Authority's television station on August 10, 2011, displayed a photograph of the Western Wall plaza with a voice-over telling of its future: "They [Israelis] know for certain that our [Palestinian] roots are deeper than their false history. We, from the balcony of our home, look out over [Islamic] holiness and on sin and filth (Jews praying at the Western Wall) in an area that used to have [Arab] people and homes. We are drawing our new maps. When they [Israelis] disapper from the picture, like a forgotten chapter in the pages of our city's history, we will build it anew (residential area). The Mughrabi [*sic*] Quarter will be built here (on the Western Wall Plaza)" (quoted in Marcus and Zilberdik 2011).

There you have it. In the view of many Jews, Muslim history in the Land of Israel is shallow and much of it fabricated, while the Palestinians see it as having deep roots. Jewish prayer and dancing at the Western Wall seem to many Jews, including the disciples of Rabbi Kook's disciples, an expression and fulfillment of the site's sanctity and of the Jewish people's profound attachment to the remnants of its Temple. To Palestinian planners, however, they are a source of pollution and sin — almost the same words that Rabbi Kook used regarding the Maghrebi quarter.

Continuing the Account of Samrin of Qalunya

Samrin wrote:

> [In their deeds and declarations in 1929] the Jews showed that their ambition was to seize control of the Islamic sites sacred to us, and especially the noble al-Buraq, and to rebuild Solomon's Temple on its site, on part of the precinct of the blessed al-Aqsa. The inhabitants of Palestinian cities began to stage demonstrations, while fellahin from our villages commenced offensives and clashes, battles and the destruction of settlements, and attacks on the Mandate police and the British army. (2003, 165)

Solomon's Temple

In writing about the ancient Jewish Temple, Samrin does not use the common current Arabic term for it, al-Haikal al-Maz'um (the imaginary temple), which incorporates the claim that the Jews in fact never had a Temple on al-Haram al-Sharif. His choice of words is worth noting, given the current Palestinian and Islamic discourse on the issue, in which ordinary people, religious scholars, and political leaders all assert repeatedly that the claim that a Jewish Temple ever stood on al-Haram al-Sharif is a lie promulgated with the intention of reinforcing Zionist propaganda and taking control of Islam's shrines. Most of the Palestinians who say this are not aware that their denial is a new phenomenon, and that even the Supreme Muslim Council, under the leadership of Hajj Amin al-Hussayni, never voiced any such doubts. For example, *A Brief Guide to al-Haram al-Sharif*, published by the Supreme Muslim Council in 1925 for the benefit of tourists, states that "its identity with the site of Solomon's Temple is beyond dispute" (Supreme Muslim Council 1925, 4). Guidebooks put out by the Supreme Muslim Council up until 1990 agree.

The Temple as a Trigger

Samrin's basic claim is worthy of examination. He argues that what set off the events in Jaffa and Jerusalem and the strife in Hulda, Qalunya, Gaza, He-

bron, and Safed, and what fired up hundreds of Arabs to descend on their Jewish neighbors and kill them, was the belief that the Jews wanted to destroy the
al-Aqsa Mosque and build a new Temple in its place. The time has come to see
whether this claim is true.

True or False?

Many Arabs "know" that it is absolutely true, just as many Jews "know" that
it is false. Here is a quote from a speech delivered by Haim Arlosoroff, head of
the Jewish Agency's Political Department, in November 1931:

> A few months later [after the end of World War I], Dr. Chaim Weizmann arrived in
> Jerusalem, as the head of the Zionist Executive, and in a speech he made at an official
> event hosted by the governor of the Jerusalem District on April 27 he said: "Jerusa-
> lem is a holy sanctuary for the Jews, and as such—and for other reasons—the Jews
> respect the religious sentiments of all other communities that also see this land as a
> holy one. It would behoove all of them to know that the Jews do not even conceive
> in any way of harming the holy places to which the Muslim and Christian worlds
> direct their gazes." . . . The Jewish National Council [the Jewish communal govern-
> ment under the British Mandate] made a similar declaration following the incident
> in question [the placement of the divider by the Western Wall in 1928:] "We state it
> with a pure heart and full confidence that no Jew has ever thought and is not think-
> ing now in any way whatsoever of impinging on Muslim rights and their holy places."
> (quoted in Al-Wikalah al-Yahudiyyah 1931, 4–5)

Arlosoroff made this speech when the Arab press again claimed that the Jews
were seeking to seize Muslim holy sites. Later in his speech, he said that he did
not know whether Muslim leaders who spread such false rumors were aware
of truth and were deliberately spreading falsehoods, or whether they truly believed that Jews intended to seize the mosques—which would call their powers
of judgment into question. Either way, he said, they were not worthy leaders. A
pamphlet containing an Arabic translation of Arlosoroff's speech was issued in
a large printing (ibid., 7). Zionist emissaries and agents distributed it to Arabs in
Palestine and adjoining countries.

What Do Leaders Know?

We could pose Arlosoroff's question regarding the Arab leadership to him.
Did he in fact believe what he was saying, or did he say it for political purposes?
Could he correctly claim that "no Jew has ever thought and is not thinking now
in any way whatsoever of impinging on Muslim rights and their holy places?"
Did he know, for example, about an underground group in Jerusalem that was,
about the same time, plotting to plant a bomb on the Temple Mount? And about

the Haganah's role in getting rid of the group's ringleader? It's an event I find no mention of in history books. His account may not be entirely accurate as it does not completely accord with another surviving report. Nevertheless, it indicates something of the mood of the time.

Aryeh Botrimovitch was a member of the Ein Harod Company of the Labor Battalion, a communal labor organization established by socialist Zionist pioneers in Palestine in 1920. His nickname was Butra. In 1925 his company went to work in Jerusalem, where he enlisted in a Haganah liquidation team. I will have more to say about his deeds during the riots below. But here is his account of how he took part in the kidnapping of one of the plotters, at around the time that Arlosoroff made his speech:

> I recall that they came and told me that there was a group of people in Jerusalem planning to blow up the Mosque of Omar [the Dome of the Rock, the shrine adjacent to al-Aqsa]. A friend of mine named Lyova (Aryeh) Abramson (a driver in the South [Transportation Cooperative]) referred me to Sa'adiah Kirshenbaum. When I met him he told me that there was a guy, the leader of that group, who needed to be liquidated (I was an expert at liquidation), but "not in a brutal way. . . ." I took my car, drove over to that person, and Sa'adiah sat next to me. It was at night. When I called him to come outside and told him that my friend and I wanted to join his group, after we told him that we wanted to join his group, he told us details about his plans to blow up the Mosque of Omar. We put him in the car and we told him we'd teach him how to drive (he was an Ashkenazi guy, I don't know his name). We went to him in Romema. Abramson with Avraham Zilberg [Tehomi, a leader of the Haganah in Jerusalem, a member of the Odessa group that advocated military activism, and a founder of Etzel in 1931] went in a different car and waited for us behind Beit HaKerem. Sa'adiah and I and that guy drove to a certain place, where Avram and Abramson were waiting. They got out of their car, covered the boy with a blanket, put him in the car, and drove off.
>
> I was left alone in the field in the middle of the night. The guy's walking stick and a shoe that slipped off his foot remained in my car. I saw two figures in the distance, and when they got closer it turned out that they were two British policemen. I managed to toss the stick and the shoe into the field and I began to pretend I was working on the car. They came up to me and asked what I was doing. I told him that the car wasn't working. When they left me I drove to [Haganah leader Yitzhak] Ben-Zvi's house in Rechavia. When I got there I saw bloodstains in the car (from them dragging him out by force) and Rachel [Yana'it, a senior Haganah figure and Ben-Zvi's wife] gave me cotton wool and alcohol and helped me clean up the blood. (HHA Botrimovitch testimony 27/8)

This is another of those surprising documents, like the passage from al-Dabbagh on the 'Awn family. Here is evidence of a Jewish underground that was plotting to blow up a mosque on the Temple Mount during the British Mandate, and of a Haganah assassination squad that made the key conspirator disappear. What can we learn from this story (even if we cannot be sure about the details)? First, we learn that there were Jews in the Yishuv who wanted to jump-start the messianic redemption of the Jewish people and who set out to turn their mystical longing into action—all this in contradiction of the official statements quoted above and the official line of the political leadership. In fact, the existence of such sentiments should be no surprise, given Judaism's long history of longing for the return to Zion and rebuilding of the Temple. We also learn that the Yishuv's mainstream, or at least the Haganah command in Jerusalem, was very concerned about people acting on such messianic longings—so concerned that such Jews were prepared to kill a fellow Jew to keep a plan to blow up a Temple Mount mosque from being discovered, much less carried out.

And Apropos of Liquidations

This was not the first time that a Jew had been liquidated by the Haganah in Jerusalem. In fact, the socialist component of the Haganah used such deeds to position itself as the principal power in the Yishuv. A previous instance was that of Rabbi Ya'akov Yisrael de Haan, a Haredi poet, homosexual, and fierce anti-Zionist opponent of Jewish rule in Palestine. Just before a scheduled trip to London to lobby against Zionism, he was murdered in 1924 after meeting in Transjordan with that country's ruler, Emir 'Abdallah. With profound conviction in the justice of their cause, members of the Haganah killed Jewish activists who tried to undermine the model it had fashioned: in one case, the head of a messianic conspiracy, and in the other, a Haredi opponent of Jewish sovereignty. Both these assassinations took place against the background of the relations between the Yishuv and Palestine's Arabs, as they were then taking form. But the Haganah's repression of messianic tendencies among Palestine's Jews did not prevent the country's Muslims from sensing that such a messianic awakening was in progress, sweeping up some members of the Yishuv.

Messianic Awakenings

Jewish history is replete with waves of messianic fervor, especially during devastating wars, conquests, and clashes between nations. It blossomed during the Islamic conquests of the seventh century, under the false messiah Shabbetai Zvi in the seventeenth century, and during the Napoleonic wars. The British victory in World War I, together with the appointment of the Jewish Zionist Herbert Samuel as the first British high commissioner in Palestine, intensified expectations that the end of days was imminent. The story of Samuel's first sabbath in Jerusalem, in 1920, was told and retold by those who experienced it. As it happened, it was the Sabbath of Comfort (Nahamu), as the sabbath following the Fast of the Ninth of Av is called. On this day a passage from Isaiah promising the return to Zion is read in synagogues. Samuel walked from his lodgings at the Jaffa Gate to the Hurva Synagogue in the Jewish quarter. Max Nurock, Samuel's Jewish secretary, who accompanied him (after helping Samuel practice the blessings recited before and after the reading of the Torah and of the haftarah, the selection from the prophets), offered this account in an interview in the third installment of the television documentary *Pillar of Fire*:

> My breath even today stops when I think of how this scene looked. All windows in these narrow streets . . . windows from both sides of the street, were full of Jews looking and crying and shouting and weeping with joy. Carpets on the roadway, flowers everywhere, flags at every point. This was their *nasi* [prince, who] had come to them. And we walked along into the Hurva synagogue, which was crowded *ad efes makom* [with no room left]. Not a seat could be obtained. So when the call came forth "*y'amod HaNatziv HaElion*" [may the high commissioner come forward], Herbert Samuel rose and the whole congregation rose with him and he went upon the bimah and he started reciting the *brakhot lifnei kri'at haMaftir* [the blessings before reading the last of the sections of the Torah reading]. And he certainly recited them very well, I take some credit for that, and he came to the famous words: "*nahamu nahamu ami yomar Elohikhem*" [Be comforted, be comforted my people, says the Lord (Isaiah 40:1)], at that point the congregation as it were shuddered, vibrated, quivered, and from the whole congregation there rose — I could feel it — rose a great sigh, a *bat-kol*, to the high heavens, to the dome of the Hurva, and in that moment, in that golden moment, the Jews inside that synagogue and all who knew of it outside felt that the hour of redemption had come. (Lussin 2005)

The elation continued, and the sense of impending salvation intensified, when Rabbi Kook read the blessing after the haftarah, an ancient Jewish prayer asking for the privilege of experiencing the sublime joy of the redemption. It reads in part: "May you, the Lord our God, exult us with the prophet Elijah your servant, and the kingship of the House of David your anointed one [messiah], may he quickly come and redeem us. On his throne no foreigner will sit and others will not inherit his honor." Surrounding the new Jewish ruler of the Holy Land, Jerusalem's Jews felt that the end of their enslavement to gentile nations was approaching, that foreigners soon would not rule above, on the Temple Mount, and over the Jews huddled in prayer at its foot, by the Western Wall.

And at the Same Time

Palestine's hundreds of thousands of Arabs were not at the Hurva Synagogue that day, but they were everywhere around it, on Jerusalem's streets and in its

High Commissioner Herbert Samuel in Jerusalem
(Matson Photograph Collection, Library of Congress).

neighborhoods, in the villages ringing the city, in the Hebron hill country and in Nablus, on the coastal plane, on Mount Carmel, and in the Galilee. They did not hear the blessings over the haftarah nor the reading from Isaiah, but the sense of those words reverberated in the streets and in Arab hearts. They were keenly aware of the connection between the Zionist awakening that had shaken their lives and the ancient Jewish messianic belief in the renewal of the Israelite monarchy. They also understood the connection between these beliefs and British policy. They understood quite well that they would pay a price for the modern return to Zion. They did not know the poem written in 1924 by Uri Zvi Greenberg, "Jerusalem under the Scalpel," which compares the Dome of the Rock on the Temple Mount to an artificial head on Jerusalem's neck instead of its real head—the Temple: "Your head is gone / your head has been splattered / A mosque has been attached to your neck / a house of splendor for Muslims / like a gravestone on a costly torso soaking up the blood underneath" (1990–2013,1:63). No one had translated it into Arabic. But the Arabs of Palestine could feel that some Jews were losing patience with the presence of the mosques on their sacred mountain. The Arabs could not disregard this messianic passion, which was not restricted to abstract thought. It was translated into action in the form of repeated attempts to purchase parcels in the area surrounding the Western

Wall, to reinforce the Jewish presence close to the site of the former Temple, and to bring about Jewish independence on the soil of Palestine.

Jewish Independence in Palestine

It is hardly difficult to understand why the Jews wanted independence. It was a reasonable alternative to the experience of many Jews of the time—a life of subordination to others, generally one of inferior legal status, and often one of constantly confronting physical threats. It is hardly difficult to understand why the Arabs of Palestine opposed it—they understood that large-scale Jewish immigration would turn them into a minority in their own country, into subjects still ruled by foreigners.

Arab Independence in Palestine

Were the Palestinian Arabs free before the advent of Zionism? After all, prior to the British conquest in 1917, Palestine was ruled by the Ottomans, before that by the Mamluks, before that by the Ayyubids, before that by the crusaders, before that by the Seljuks, and before that—in other words, the Arabs of Palestine had never been independent.

That's one way of looking at it. But could they in fact have been independent? That is, how may a regime be properly described as foreign? In our day a foreign regime is considered to be the rule of one nation over another. But that understanding of the term comes from the age of nationalism. In a more fundamental way, the term "foreign rule" refers not only to an objective situation—rule by a regime from somewhere else—but also to a subjective one—a regime whose subjects do not accept its legitimacy. What determines whether people feel that their ruler is legitimate? On the ideological level, it has to do with whether their worldview is like that of the ruler—that is, the extent to which the population and the people governing it have the same perceptions of good and evil and the same ideas about how the world should be ordered and for what purpose. On the practical level, it depends on the extent to which the population is integrated into and involved in the regime and its institutions.

In these ways, Muslim rulers, even if they came from far off, were not necessarily seen as foreign in Palestine. Muslim empires that aspired to fortify the Islamic world, including Jerusalem, and that fostered belief in Allah and his prophet Mohammad, saw eye to eye with Palestine's Muslims about the future of the city and shared their vision of justice, God, social order, and the end of days. Muslim inhabitants of Palestine could thus identify with and accept the authority of their Muslim rulers, as long as they did not feel that they were being exploited. Under most of the Islamic dynasties that ruled Palestine, and certainly under the Ottoman Empire during most of its four centuries of rule, the

Muslims of Palestine were subjects of the sultan who enjoyed equal status with all his other Muslim subjects. They were not denied rights because of their collective identity. Rather, they were part of the governing society. The local elite held positions in the imperial administration and climbed to its highest levels. So even if the Palestinian Arabs under the Ottomans were not independent in the national sense, the concept was not particularly relevant to them prior to the nineteenth century. It is therefore not precise to say that Palestine's Arabs lived for centuries under foreign rule.

This changed as the Ottoman Empire declined during the nineteenth century and the concept of nationalism made its way into the Middle East. People's definitions of themselves changed, and as a consequence their concept of who was foreign also changed. Arab nationalists began to cast a more critical eye on the Ottoman Empire (on differing Palestinian perceptions during the waning of the Ottoman state, see Doumani 1992). What is more important for our topic here is that the idea that started spreading through both Jewish circles and on the international stage — the idea of the establishment of a Jewish state in the Holy Land that would rule over the Muslims and Christians who lived there — heralded a real revolution. This was seen as a program to impose on the country's inhabitants a foreign regime in the full sense of the term. It was taken as an attempt to subordinate the Arabs of Palestine to a political culture with values opposed to Muslim values. It was an obvious attempt to establish a political structure in which non-Jews would, by definition under Zionist rule, be relegated to being a minority living in the shadow of foreigners.

So What's the Connection with the Temple?

For the Arabs of Palestine, the danger of being subjugated to foreign rule was serious enough in and of itself, even without any connection to harm that might be done to the al-Aqsa Mosque. But the idea that the Jews would build their Temple on al-Haram al-Sharif seemed the severest possible harm the Arabs could imagine: it would be for them a shameful religious defeat following on the heels of political weakness. It meant bringing havoc to every convention and assumption by which they had lived their lives, and it could be regarded as proof that Islam was not the true religion. The Islamic obsession with the Jewish desire to rebuild the Temple — which was sometimes more intense than the internal Jewish debate on the subject — seems to have been an apprehensive reaction to the expectation that this worst of all possible scenarios might actually take place.

And the Jews?

When it came to holy places, different Jews had different hopes. The messianic religious discourse was entirely foreign to some of them. They had come to

Palestine only because they had nowhere better to live. Others sought to create a productive and healthy Jewish society, one in which the Jews would not be a minority; these, too, did not put the Temple on their list of priorities. Alongside both these groups were Jews who envisaged a messianic redemption. It is hard to read the Jewish public and determine how many Jews felt, and at what intensity, that they wished to be involved in a messianic religious movement focused on the Temple Mount. Whatever the case, there was certainly a spectrum with, at one end, those who aspired to the rebuilding of the Temple and who believed that action should be taken to bring that about and, at the other end, people who felt no connection at all to the Temple. Most of the Jews seem to have been somewhere in the middle, subscribing to the two different propositions. For example, there were those who expected that the Temple would be built but opposed taking action to do so. Others saw the Western Wall and Temple Mount together as a central Jewish national symbol but accepted the mosques on the Mount as an irrevocable fact; thus they focused their efforts on restoring the Wall alone to Jewish ownership.

The dividing line in opinion on the holy places did not coincide with the line dividing secular and religious Jews, if only because secular Zionism itself stood on a religious foundation. The opposing sides were divided more on priorities than on doctrine. Amnon Raz-Krakotzkin, an Israeli historian, offers an incisive characterization of secular Zionism in his article "Ein Elohim aval Hu Natan Lanu et haAretz" (There is no God, but he promised us the land):

> The national-historical mind-set identified as secular . . . is based on viewing Zionist settlement and sovereignty in the Land as a Jewish return to their land, and the completion of Jewish history and the realization of Jewish prayers for redemption. . . . Secular Zionism indeed cast off Jewish tradition and defined itself on the basis of an utter negation of everything considered "religion," but it did this while viewing nationalism itself as the ultimate interpretation of religious myth, based on a return to Judaism's biblical sources. (2005, 71–72)

Inside Evidence

In May 1932 the House of Lords, sitting as a court of appeals, heard the arguments of the Zionist land purchase and settlement organization, Keren Kayemet LeYisraʾel, against a court ruling that required it to pay taxes on its income. Keren Kayemet was represented by Norman Bentwich, a British Zionist Jew who in the 1920s (including 1929) served as the Mandate government's attorney general. He told the House of Lords that his client should be exempted from tax payments on the ground that it was a religious organization. Judaism, he argued, was a composite of religion and nationalism. God's promise to Abraham was the fundamental tenet of Judaism, and religion was the background to Jewish settlement in Palestine. The goal of Keren Kayemet, to settle Jews on the soil of the Holy Land, was thus a fundamental part of Judaism, and assistance in achieving this goal was therefore a religious activity, not merely a political one (*Do'ar Hayom*, May 17, 1932; hearing preparation file, CZA KKL5/5475). In other words, Zionism was an arm of Judaism, and Zionist activity was the actualization of a religious precept. So the Zionists maintained, although not all Jews agreed with them. Neither did the House of Lords, by the way, which rejected the appeal without delving into the theological claims.

What about the Place of the Temple?

The attitude toward the Temple Mount was more complex. On the official level, Article 6 of the agreement that Chaim Weizmann reached with the leader of the Arab national movement, Faisal ibn Hussayn, in January 1919 stated that "the Mohammedan Holy Places shall be under Mohammedan control" (CZA z4/2989). That meant, ostensibly, that the Zionist movement was renouncing its claim to the Temple Mount. Furthermore, many Jews simply repressed thoughts of the Temple Mount. But not all of them, of course. Yitzhak Shalev, a poet, was one Jew who directed his gaze to the Mount. In his poem "Jerusalem Symphony," published in 1951, he described what he felt, as a boy, when — sometime around 1929 — he visited the wall encompassing Jerusalem's Old City:

> The Messiah's gate — closed . . . ("And tell me, my teacher, who closed it?")
> And the boy's heart is heavy, blurry with sorrow and pain
> And like an echo from afar the teacher's voice came to him, saying
> "Here is the site of the Temple" . . . He shook himself and saw: Omar's mosque
> And gritted his little teeth and wept inside, in silence. (1951, 56–57)

Anger and pain, pain and sorrow. Are these religious emotions? Are they national ones? Can the two be distinguished in a religion and nationality like Judaism?

Here is another small example of the difficulty of parsing religious and national sentiment in Jerusalem under the Mandate. Fifteen months after Samuel was appointed — on November 2, 1921, the fourth anniversary of the Balfour Declaration — Arabs in Jerusalem staged violent demonstrations and attacked Jews. Yana'it supplied her comrades with weapons and set out herself for the Old City:

> I am hiding a small pistol under my clothes and rush back to the Old City. At the entrance to the Street of the Jews Yehuda Zariz runs up to me, agitated and breathing heavily. He tells me about the action just carried out on Maidan Street [called Batei

Mufti of Jerusalem, Hajj
Amin al-Hussayn (Matson
Photograph Collection,
Library of Congress).

Mahaseh Square today]. "We sat there," Yehuda said, "on the ready at the Hurva, and suddenly we heard a cry: 'The Arabs are breaking through to Maidan Street.' We set out at a run. We ran and shouted 'In the name of the God of Israel.'" Yehuda took a deep breath and repeated: "We're running with our weapons in our hands, rallying ourselves 'in the name of the God of Israel.'" I looked into his eyes. Yehuda, a member of Po'alei Tzion Smol [a Marxist-Zionist faction] was spurring on [his friends] in the name of the God of Israel. (Yana'it Ben-Zvi, Avrahami, and Etzion 1973, 29–30)

This is the "Jewish spark" that some people believe in, the dual consciousness of many Zionists — and this is the same Rachel Yana'it who was involved in the liquidation of the founder of the Jewish underground who wanted to plant a bomb in a Muslim shrine on the Temple Mount.

The Mufti

The mufti, Hajj Amin al-Hussayni, shared the view that Zionism was a melding of religion and nationality. Like Uri Zvi Greenberg, he maintained that control of the Temple Mount was fundamental to Zionism. The mufti thus concluded that Zionism had to be fought by all possible means. Following the 1929 riots, he explained why he had appealed to religious feelings and justifications in his war against Zionism. Religion, he maintained, was the Jews' principal motivating force, and the Bible was the basis for their national claim to Palestine. Their primary aspiration was to build a new Temple where the mosques of al-Haram al-Sharif stood. Under the circumstances, he said, he had to counter the Jews with religious claims of his own (Porath 1977, 194).

The Truth of Rumors

To sum up, the rumors that the Jews wanted to demolish the mosques were not very well founded. Some Jews wanted to do that, but the Zionist movement, as a movement, did not aspire to reestablish the Davidic dynasty and build a new Temple in place of the mosques. Furthermore, mainstream Zionism then took severe measures to suppress the idea of building a new Temple, including the kidnaping of the head of the radical underground who plotted to bomb the shrines. But Muslims took note of deeper currents in the Jewish psyche and saw that the centuries-old Jewish dream of redemption had not evaporated when the British Mandate began and perhaps had grown even more potent. The Muslims knew that building a Temple was a conscious or unconscious wish for many Jews. That was an important motivation for the Palestinian Arab offensive (a counteroffensive, in their view) in 1929.

We Are the Victims

That's what the Jews felt regarding both British policy as a whole and the 1929 riots. That's what the Arabs felt, too. I've already said that the Jews viewed the Arabs as the aggressors and themselves as people who had no choice but to fight for their lives. The Arabs felt that the Jews were aggressors who had come to rob them of their country and push them out of it. Each side also claimed that the British favored the other. When, on September 1, High Commissioner John Chancellor issued his first statement on the riots, terming the acts of the Arabs "savage murders," the Association of Arab Lawyers responded with sarcastic questions: Is there any difference between the barbarism of each side? Had the Jews murdered their victims in accordance with the finest traditions of Western culture? (Kayyali 1988, 144). At the same time, the Arab Executive Committee, the representative body of the Palestinian Arabs, claimed that it was the Jews who had been the first to kill women and children — the first fatality in the riots, it claimed, had been an Arab woman, 'Aisha, wife of 'Ali al-'Atari, whose body was found near the Jewish neighborhood of Meah She'arim (CZA S25/4184). But both sides claimed that the first fatality had been in their camp.

The First Fatalities

For the Arabs to claim priority, 'Aisha al-'Atari would have to have been killed on Friday. But her body was found on Saturday, two large stones lying on her crushed skull (see the list of dead in Jerusalem, in TNA CO 733/180/471). There was also a dispute over whether the first adult male killed had been an Arab or a Jew. The Jews had a certain advantage in the argument. They could claim that the first fatality had not been on the day the riots broke out, but a few days earlier, when seventeen-year-old Avraham Mizrahi was murdered in a street fight with Arabs not far from Jerusalem's Bukharan quarter. *Do'ar Hayom* reported this death:

> Yesterday afternoon the fields next to the Bukharan Quarter witnessed a ferocious and brutal Arab attack on Jews. A group of young people were playing soccer in one of the fields near the neighborhood. There were also onlookers who stopped by to watch the game. Suddenly a group of Arabs appeared, some of whom live near the neighborhood and others from the village of Lifta. They suddenly attacked the players and the audience with clubs, rocks, and daggers without any cause and as a result many of the Jews were injured.
>
> One Jewish boy, seventeen-year-old Avraham Mizrahi, employed in the Kadima Garage, was stabbed in the back by Arabs and brought, mortally wounded, to the government hospital. (*Do'ar Hayom*, August 18, 1929)

Davar Reports from the Field

Do'ar Hayom's editor at that time was Ze'ev Jabotinsky, the founder of the Betar movement that took part in the procession to the Western Wall on the Ninth of Av. The newspaper played a central role in promoting national pride during the months of conflict over the Wall. Some accused it of provocation. The labor movement daily, *Davar*, offered quite a different account of the incident:

> Comrade V from Tel Aviv, who was present at the site of the altercation, near the Maccabi athletic field, also spoke with the injured Kurd [Mizrahi] and gave us the following details: Three Kurdish [Jewish] boys who live in the area were walking through the vegetable gardens belonging to their Arab neighbors, between the Bukharan Quarter and the Sanhedria neighborhood. One of the boys picked a squash from one of the gardens. Two young Arabs, owners of the garden, began shouting and cursing him. The pickers cursed back. The exchange turned into a fistfight. The two Arabs fled to the side of the field and the Kurds chased them. Six older Arabs immediately set out after them and a knife and rock fight began, in which one young Kurd suffered a fatal knife wound. The others were injured by rocks. (*Davar*, August 18, 1929)

The area to the east of the Bukharan quarter, the area of today's Shmuel Ha-Navi Street, then belonged largely to Arabs from the village of Lifta, in the valley to the west, and parts of it were cultivated. Presumably this was not the first time that a passerby had taken something to eat from a neighbor's garden. When neighborly relations are the norm, a person caught picking a squash from someone else's field without permission apologizes and even offers politely to pay.

When relations are especially good, the owner of the field refuses payment and even offers a few more vegetables and a glass of water. Neither was the state of Jewish-Arab relations in August 1929. From the Arab point of view, the taking of the squash was one small detail in the Zionist story—Jews were coming and arrogantly trampling Arab land, stealing the fruits of their labors, and when Arabs stood up to them, the Jews attacked, confident of their morality and the justice of their cause, or simply out of thuggery.

Comparing Accounts

Two Hebrew newspapers offered two different versions of the incident, different down to even the most basic details. Did the Jews bear some responsibility for the outbreak of violence? Did it take place on Jewish or Arab land? Who were the casualties? Presumably the two newspapers were basing their reports on similar information. If so, their differences serve as an illustration of two different views of the role of the press—critical reportage or self-congratulation and victimization. There is another difference as well, at least in this particular case: *Davar* cited the ethnic affiliation of the Jews in the fight (they were Kurdish Jews—that is, Mizrahim). *Do'ar Hayom* did not.

A Word about Mizrahim

The Mizrahi ethnicity of the Jews who got into the fight is notable. As we saw in the first chapter, some Mizrahi Jews maintained that they had good relations with their Arab neighbors and claimed that the European Zionists were those who provoked the conflict. However, according to the account of Mordechai Elkayam from Jaffa in the first chapter, and in the case of the Bukharan quarter, it was Mizrahi Jews who were involved in the quarrels. At first glance, this contradicts the idea that the Mizrahim were well integrated into the Arab environment—but only at first glance. Actually their involvement in clashes to defend national honor, the honor of their women, and their territories is part and parcel of neighborly relations in the Middle East as elsewhere. In addition, their intimate relations with Arabs led some Mizrahi or Sephardi activists to suggest a complex approach to the "Arab question." Eliahu Elyashar, mentioned above, is a good example—a community leader who supported negotiations and compromise with the Palestinians but heatedly opposed restraint during the Arab Revolt of 1936–39, arguing that holding back would be seen as a concession that could lead to an escalation of Arab aggression (1997, 66–73).

What Did Both Newspapers Keep under Wraps?

Each newspaper described the events differently, but neither reported the raid that followed Mizrahi's injury, when dozens of Jews attacked and burned shacks and tents that Lifta's Arabs had erected on their land near the Bukharan neighborhood, and assaulted the family of one of the Arabs there, 'Ali 'Abdallah Hasan. Hasan had shut himself up in his house, but a band of Jews managed to break in and stabbed him repeatedly. A Jewish neighbor, Shimon, who owned a nearby grocery store, tried to hold the attackers back and was beaten. But he managed to rescue Hasan's wife and children and hide them in his house (Commission 1930, 1:40).

Mizrahi's Death and Funeral

Two seriously wounded victims, one Jew and one Arab, were rushed to the hospital. Both fought for their lives. Segev quotes a diary entry written by the high commissioner's aide-de-camp: "It was most desirable for the maintenance of the status quo that they should both die" (2000, 310). That was not to be. Hasan lived, while Mizrahi died of his wounds the following Tuesday, close to midnight. The police wanted to bury him immediately, before dawn. So did the Zionist Executive. Mizrahi's family refused. They wanted a national funeral, befitting a Jew who died a martyr. The wishes of the family and their supporters prevailed. The funeral took place the next day, in the late morning. Thousands of people attended, and it turned into a nationalist demonstration.

At right about that time the Sixteenth Zionist Congress convened in Zurich, and as a result the Zionist leaders were not in Palestine. The Zionist Executive's accountant, Yeshayahu Broide, was filling in for the chairman. He had never viewed himself as a leader, certainly not as a person to stand at the head of the Yishuv during such an emergency. He was the brother of Yosef Haim Brenner's widow, Haya. His grandson Gideon Broide (1997) wrote that Yeshayahu had not come to Palestine inspired by Zionism, and that in 1909 he had even left Palestine to seek his fortune in South Africa, where he studied accounting. But during a visit to Palestine he was asked to join a team conducting a review of the Bezalel Academy of Art, which had run into financial difficulties. After that he was appointed the financial officer and vice-chairman of the Zionist Executive. That was how he found himself in such a senior post when the riots broke out. His position made it incumbent on him to take part in Mizrahi's funeral. He testified before the Shaw Commission that he and his associates tried to calm tempers but found it difficult to do because the crowd was so angry:

> I was with the procession at the beginning. . . . I tried to lead them on and then I noticed 20 or 30 steps away from me one man got on the shoulders of the people and tried to make a speech.
> [Questioner:] What sort of man was he?
> [Broide:] He was a very ignorant man. I thought he was a porter. He did not know

what to say; first he started to attack the Executive saying nothing is being done, which was the very general cry at that time, and for the moment all I had in my mind was to get him down by force or otherwise. It struck me at the moment that I should tell him what to say. I told him to say "Trust the Executive; they will do everything that is necessary." The man had no words, he did not really know what to say and was happy to have something to say. He was terribly excited and he said every word I told him. First of all it calmed him down because it was not the stuff he wanted to say in his excitement. Then I told him another sentence that he believed everything would be done. And then he calmed down. (quoted in Commission 1930, 2:595)

But the crowd did not calm down. They tried to diverge from the route the British police had prescribed for the procession. Policemen beat Jews, injuring more than twenty. The next day, Thursday, tempers rose even higher: "The government [handed down] an order to Arab leaders to calm the storm that had arisen among the Arabs, and apparently Arab leaders promised that Arab preachers in Jerusalem and its environs would that day call for quiet and order. Recall that the government also made a request to Rabbi Kook that he calm the Jews, and he responded that he saw no need to do so, because the Jews had no intention of attacking anyone" (*Ha'aretz*, August 23, 1929). This article appeared on Friday, when the violence that earlier had barely been held back erupted in Jerusalem and spread through the entire country.

Rabbi Kook, One Moment Previously

Rabbi Kook, who said that "the Jews have no intention of attacking anyone," seems to have believed that sincerely but naïvely. He lived in the higher spheres and might have lacked a good understanding of what was happening on Jerusalem's streets, where young Jews had set fire to Arab homes and attacked Arabs on the boundary between Lifta's fields and the Bukharan quarter. It is hard to fathom what he thought about these events. Did he see such violence as a proper way of defending Jewish honor? That seems doubtful. Did he try to avert it? There is no evidence to that effect. Had he used his prestige, could he have prevented it? Hard to know. He chose the easiest solution: disregard and denial. The religious Zionist daily *Hatzofeh* followed this tradition of disregard when, in an article published on the forty-seventh anniversary of the riots, it proudly quoted the rabbi's response to a British proposal that he issue a public statement against violence: "Rabbi Kook was the only one to grasp the disgrace inherent in such a declaration, and defended Jewish honor in his pointed response: 'The Hebrew Yishuv does not need such statements. Acts of violence are not its custom'" (*Hatzofeh*, August 13, 1976).

The Start of the Riots: Diverging Truths

The question of how the riots began on Friday has no single answer. The Jewish version is that the Arabs started it. The Arab version is that the Jews started it. I have already noted the human tendency to accept the story that is the common wisdom in one's own society. I have also noted the corollary to this way of thinking, the belief that the other side is lying. Here is a more well-grounded possibility: Jews waylaid Arabs in Meah She'arim and Rechavia, and Arabs simultaneously—but in larger numbers and in more localities—attacked Jews at the Jaffa and Damascus Gates and other parts of the city.

Mufti Hajj Amin al-Hussayni's Version

On Friday, villagers from the Jerusalem area streamed into the city to attend prayers at the al-Aqsa Mosque. Mufti al-Hussayni testified before the Shaw Commission that, on their way to the prayer service, fellahin passed through Jewish neighborhoods, as they had always done. But,

> on [that] Friday as a special case many of them who passed through the Jewish quarters, which was their only route, were assaulted. . . . [A]nd some of them were threatened and were only saved by the Police. . . . Such was the situation when I arrived at the Haram at 11 o'clock. Some of them came and surrounded me and complained against the assaults or insults that they had been subjected to. I pacified them and asked them to keep quiet. I undertook to them that the Government would safeguard their rights. . . . And then I entered Al-Aqsa with the worshippers, and in order to ensure that they would all be within the Mosque and keep quiet, I asked one of the leaders who has a good voice to read the Koran, because it is the habit, when the Koran is read, that the whole of the worshippers, or audience will listen and keep silence. . . . I also asked Sheikh Said Shawa Effendi, who was the preacher of the Mosque of Al-Aqsa and gives his sermon on Friday, I asked him to include in his address, or to make the greatest part of his address an appeal to the worshipers and those persons present to keep the peace and be quiet. He did that and his address was most effective. (quoted in Commission 1930, 1:506–7)

Peace and Quiet? The Mufti?

The mufti told the Shaw Commission that he tried to keep things calm. Note how he constantly repeats the word "quiet" in his testimony. Historians, like the mufti's contemporaries, have differed on the role he played in the events of August 1929. *Sefer Toldot HaHaganah* depicts him as the brains behind the riots (Dinur 1973), and the same claim was made by one of the mufti's closest assistants, 'Izzat Darwaza. In this view, the mufti was only paying lip service to keeping the peace when he urged Arabs to stay calm. (Darwaza, of course, made this claim to promote the mufti as a hero, while *Sefer Toldot HaHaganah* did so to pillory him.) The commission, like critical Palestinians, maintained that the mufti (like his contemporary, Sheikh 'Abd al-Qader al-Muzaffar) did not plan attacks on or massacres of Jews, among other reasons because he needed the support of the British, who had appointed him to his post and who paid his salary.

Looking back on the riots from today's perspective, given the assistance the mufti gave the Nazis during World War II, it is difficult for many people to accept that the mufti might have exerted a calming influence. But there is a reasonable case to be made that the mufti's venomous antisemitism (as opposed to his inalterable anti-Zionism) developed only in the mid-1930s.

In a PhD dissertation on the 1929 disturbances written in 2007, Rana Barakat persuasively argues that the mufti sought to position himself as protector of Islam's holy places. He fanned the flames in the conflict over al-Buraq, she argues, but from the start of the crisis he operated within the bounds of the status quo. In other words, he did all he could to pressure the British to resolve the dispute in the Muslims' favor, but he had no interest in mass Arab violence. But the Palestinian Arab public, especially the rural population, refused to put their trust in the British. The mufti lost control of events. Popular resistance to the mufti's conciliatory policy was evidenced in a number of accounts given to the Shaw Commission. For example, when Sheikh Abu Sa'ud sought, at the mufti's request, to sooth the tempers of the worshipers in al-Aqsa, some fellahin and Maghrebis shouted at him: "We absolutely do not accept these words. Except that we should go for the Holy War." Then Sheikh Ya'qub al-Jilani ascended to the platform and screamed: "Do not listen to these words. This speaker is telling lies. . . . Do not take note of what our leaders say, because they are unfaithful or traitors" (quoted in Commission 1930, 1:90, 104). A week earlier Abu Sa'ud had led a demonstration at the Wall, but now, when he tried to prevent an explosion, he was shunted aside.

George Antonius, a Christian Arab of Lebanese extraction, served as one of the four assistants to the Mandate government's chief secretary. (Almost a decade later he published *The Arab Awakening*, which remains a classic text about Arab nationalism.) As part of his assignment, he accompanied the mufti in the early afternoon hours that Friday as he went from the Nablus Gate to Herod's Gate and to al-Aqsa. Antonius told the commission that the mufti had done everything in his power to calm the crowds, but that they did not always listen to him. Stones were even thrown at his car as it made its way between the two gates (Commission 1930, 1:399).

The Haganah and the Mufti
But the Haganah's official history pictures the mufti as the mastermind behind the riots. The Zionist Executive's internal correspondence shows that or-

ders were given to collect information on incitement in the mufti's speeches (ISA/P 694/3) and present them to the Shaw Commission. In the field, the attitude toward him was more complex.

When the violence broke out, Efrayim Tzur was sent at the head of an armed squad to defend the Shimon HaTzadik neighborhood, located next to the Arab neighborhood of Sheikh Jarrah on the east side of Jerusalem. He related the following incident:

> I saw the mufti returning to his home with his entourage. I suddenly wanted to kill him. I sent one of the neighborhood kids, Shvili, a budding thief, to the Haganah command [at the offices of] the Jerusalem Jewish Committee with a note for Rachel Yana'it. I wrote that I could and wanted to get rid of the mufti. The boy equipped himself with a knife, stuck it in his mouth like a wild man, and set off. The response he brought back was in the negative: "For heaven's sake don't do it." (HHA testimony 117/12)

Tzur's intense desire to kill the mufti grew out of the common wisdom — common mostly among the Jews — that the mufti was the man who had fanned the flames and set the attacks in motion. There were later opportunities to assassinate him. Ya'akov Pat, a senior Haganah operative, told of a chance encounter with the mufti at the Haifa train station. Pat was on his way to Egypt to serve as a security guard for Chaim Weizmann and his entourage, who were on their way to visit Palestine:

> The train was a bit late and I wandered back and forth on the platform, and then my gaze landed on three honorable Arabs standing on the platform, also waiting for the train. I took a good look at them and my heart started pounding—here stood the mufti and beside him Sheikh al-Muzaffar, a well-known propagandist from Jaffa, and another man. I tensed up. My hand felt for my pistol. I said to myself: "Has the hand of fate arranged it that at precisely this moment, when I have a weapon on me, I have encountered the enemy? If so, I am duty-bound to kill him." . . . Everything was foggy and blurred. It was as if I had been overcome by a fever. I didn't know what to do. Then, suddenly, my thoughts cleared. I realized that I had no sanction to do this while I was on duty and pursuing a mission. The opposite. It was clear to me that it would be an act of perfidy. And, as if I had been touched with a magic wand, peace came over me. (HHA testimony 75/14)

Back to Friday: The Mufti's Version

Following the prayer service, the mufti continued with his meetings. He told the Shaw Commission how he did all he could to clear the atmosphere during the rest of the day as well:

Subsequently I came to the [Supreme Muslim] Council meeting. In this room I had a number of visitors, about 10. I was glad and I was congratulating them that everything had passed by peacefully and nicely. At that moment, Mr. Moody [deputy secretary of the Mandate government], Subhi Bey al-Khadra [an attorney and a member of the Arab Executive Committee, from Safed], and Mr. Aabani came to see me. Mr. Moody told me that there was a crowd at the Damascus Gate and he asked me to go and assist him to pacify the crowd and disperse them. I at once went with him to Damascus Gate. We found many people assembled there. I saw there Major [Alan] Saunders [acting commandant of the Jerusalem police force] moving round in that place. I went to a step and made an effort to address the crowd. I asked them to keep quiet and to disperse to their homes. My words were effective on them, but at that moment a wounded man was brought in and a further wounded man also whom the people saw.

[Questioner:] How were they wounded, were they Arabs or Jews or what?

[Mufti:] Wounded Arabs.

[Questioner:] How were they wounded?

[Mufti:] They were shot, the result of fire shots. I saw that they were covered
with blood. The crowd were more excited on seeing the blood on these two
persons and the people shouted: "The Jews are killing our brethren!" At that
moment I could not do anything more, and with Mr. Moody I took the car and
accompanied by Subhi Bey al-Khadra came to this building [of the Muslim
Council]. (quoted in Commission 1930, 1:506)

Were These the Riot's First Casualties?

It's hard to say. Neither is it clear whether they were innocent passersby or Arabs who took part in an attack on a Jewish neighborhood. Perhaps these were the men hit by the shots fired by Moshe Alperstein, about whose courage we will hear shortly.

The question of whether the first fatality was a Jew or an Arab, a question that preoccupied the commission—is really more of a propaganda issue than a critical fact. The riots were not, after all, a series of killings, each one caused by a previous one. In their early hours, the disturbances involved a few Jewish attacks on Arabs and many more Arab attacks on Jews throughout the city—in the Bukharan quarter and Meah She'arim, on Jaffa Road, in Yemin Moshe, and in the Nisan Bek compound next to the Old City; in the Old City and on the outskirts of Lifta along the road leading west out of the city; at Kibbutz Ramat Rachel in the southeast and Bayit VeGan in the southwest; in Mekor Hayyim; and many other places. We do not know everything, and not all of what we do know can be recorded here. It's important to keep in mind the limitations and inadequacy of our knowledge. And it's important to keep in mind that, in real time, neither Jews nor Arabs involved in one clash knew what was happening at the same time in other parts of the city.

In any case, when the prayer service at al-Aqsa ended, masses of Arabs, armed with clubs and sticks, surged out of the Old City. They claimed that they had armed themselves in self-defense. One source says that Fakhri Nashashibi, one of the mufti's leading opponents, stood at the Jaffa Gate with other people and tried to prevent the crowds from attacking Jews (*Palestine Bulletin*, September 2, 1929, in CZA L59/85). He did not succeed.

Jaffa Gate

Exhibit number 130 presented to the Shaw Commission was the "Deposition of Constable White regarding Incidents in Jerusalem on the 23rd of August, 1929." It appears as an appendix to the commission's report:

> I was called down there [to Jaffa Gate] at about 13:30 hours. The crowd was there then, and I tried to force the crowd on to the main road. Two Jews dashed across the road through the crowd; they were attacked with sticks. I ran into the crowd and pushed them back beyond these two men. Corporal Shalom of the Palestine Police came then to my assistance. The two Jews were then stunned by the blows of the sticks. We carried them to a shed. We closed the doors. In the meanwhile, we were blowing our whistles for assistance. . . . The crowd then numbered about 200. Some had knives, some stones, and some swords. Most of them carried heavy sticks. This crowd gathered right around us. Corporal Shalom was then injured by a stone. We remained there as long as we possibly could and were forced about two meters beyond the doors. They got into the shed and then stopped throwing stones. When they rushed into the shed, they killed the two Jews. . . . I was called to identify several Arabs at the Prison, but I could not recognize any of them as being in the crowd. (quoted in Commission 1930, 2:1,100)

The two men killed were brothers, Yosef and Yehuda Rotenberg, aged thirty-three and thirty-one. Master plasterers and whitewashers, the two men had come to Palestine from Lithuania. They were buried in a mass grave that was dug to contain several of the Jewish dead from the 1929 riots in Jerusalem.

Jaffa Gate—Yemin Moshe

Not all the Muslim worshipers who emerged from the Jaffa Gate took part in the attack on the Rotenberg brothers. Some tried to return to their homes. Residents of the villages to the south of the city made their way, as usual, onto Hebron Road, the first section of which runs through the valley between the Old City walls and the Jewish neighborhood of Yemin Moshe. They testified before the commission that the inhabitants of the Jewish neighborhood attacked them and prevented them from proceeding along the road. Shmuel Tavori of the Haganah said that Yemin Moshe was attacked from several directions at once and that he ordered the use of grenades and pistol fire to protect it (Yana'it Ben-Zvi, Avrahami, and Etzion 1973, 70–72). This is another example of two versions of events that may well be consistent, even if they seem at first to contradict each other. Arabs indeed attacked the neighborhood. Jews indeed prevented passersby—including innocent ones, and sometimes by force—from crossing the neighborhood. At the end of the day there had been one Jew killed there, and at least one Arab—apparently one of the attackers—killed close by.

Jaffa Gate—Jaffa Road

The villagers who lived west of Jerusalem, principally those from Lifta, also exited the Old City at the Jaffa Gate. They set off to the west, toward Jaffa Road. Sergeant Alan Sigrist reported what happened:

13:00.—Outside the Jaffa Gate the mob approximately 400 strong; Moslem fellaheen were shouting and waving swords and knives and trying to break through the Police cordon and make their way up Jaffa Road. They were prevented from doing this, but eventually Major Munro allowed 60 or 70 fellaheen to proceed up the Jaffa Road in order that they might return to their village of Lifta. He instructed me to take a tender and three British Police and follow them up the Jaffa road in case of trouble.

13:30.—The Arabs passed up the road and I followed them very slowly and they kept order and remained quiet. Opposite the Municipal Gardens, however, near the door of the Carmel Oriental Wineshop, were standing 3 or 4 Jews and after the Arabs had passed about 20 yards they yelled out "Boos," "Boos," etc. Instantly the Arabs turned back, and led by an Arab about 6 feet 6 inches in height, very well built and dressed in a blue serge jacket with native trousers, they fell on the Jews, and at the same time with my Police I attacked the Arabs and after liberal use of our batons we drove them off. One of the Jews was knocked down; afterwards I heard he was dead, and I sent a stretcher for him from the Government Hospital. (quoted in Commission 1930, 2:972)

The dead man was Eliahu Raitan. Born in Jerusalem in 1902 to parents who had come to Palestine from Bulgaria, he attended elementary school in Jerusalem and high school in Alexandria, Egypt. He then studied bridge and road engineering in Paris. Raitan was considered one of the most talented engineers in Jerusalem. Itamar Ben-Avi, founder of *Do'ar Hayom*, had been standing beside him and was also beaten, as was another journalist, Wolfgang von Weisel. At about the same time another Jew was critically wounded not far from Jaffa Gate; he later died from his wounds (the commission had a hard time ascertaining his name). He had had difficulty exiting Jaffa Gate in the direction of the western (Jewish) side of the city, was beaten by Arab demonstrators armed with sticks, got up, was beaten again, and collapsed. This was repeated two more times before British policemen stationed nearby arrived and evacuated him to the hospital. Two Arab passersby, Hanna Karkar and Khalil Dahudi, were also killed in the early afternoon near Meah She'arim. We will return to them below.

Sergeant Sigrist continued to serve in the Jerusalem police. He had a reputation for extreme brutality. In 1936, leaders of the Arab Revolt that broke out that year decided to get rid of him. That June two young Palestinians, Bahjat Abu Gharbiyya and Sami al-Ansari, ambushed him near the Rockefeller Museum, just outside the Old City on its northeast side, shooting at his car. Sigrist was wounded; his bodyguard returned fire and killed al-Ansari. Abu Gharbiyya remained active in the Palestinian cause, both the armed struggle and the political campaign, for many years more. He offers an account of the attack on Sigrist in his memoirs (Abu Gharbiyya 1993).

Lifta and Jerusalem, Land and Faith

The area where Raitan was beaten to death, on the edge of the Nahalat Shiva neighborhood, had once belonged to the villagers of Lifta, just as the area of the Bukharan quarter and Meah She'arim had. Few now remember that Lifta's lands once extended from what is now the western entrance to Jerusalem east along both sides of Jaffa Road, almost up to the Old City walls and, to the northeast, up to the bottom of Mount Scopus. In 1866 fourteen inhabitants of Lifta sold the plots that became Nahalat Shiva to Esther, daughter of Eliahu Yosef Rivlin, and the wife of Aryeh Leib Hurwitz. A few years later other Lifta villagers sold tracts of their land to the entrepreneurs who built Meah She'arim (A. Cohen 2003, 288–307).

The attack by the Lifta villagers near Nahalat Shiva was not the only case of descendants of Arabs who sold land attacking the descendants of Jewish land purchasers. The same thing occurred in Meah She'arim; in Motza; in Jerusalem's Gurji courtyard, inhabited by Caucasian Georgian ("Gurji," as they were called at the time) Jews; and to a certain extent in Hebron. Perhaps the violence resulted from the fact that the selling and purchasing families remained neighbors, or perhaps because of something deeper, once the Arab sellers understood that they had been involved in no innocent real estate deal but rather a larger Jewish project of returning to their ancestral land. It took them a couple of years to realize that this project would lead, at best, to their subordination to foreign rule or, at worst, to their dispossession of all their land.

Boos

Sergeant Sigrist testified that the Jews called "Boos" at the Lifta Arabs passing by and then were attacked. Another British official, Leslie Charles, recounted that Jews armed with sticks stood along Jaffa Road, waiting to beat Arabs. In his report, the jeers came from a small group of Jews standing on the sidewalk. Such accounts smack of blaming the victim. Von Weisel, who stood beside Raitan when he was stabbed to death, told the commission that the catcalls came from inside the building in which the wine store was located and were part of an argument between Jews — some of them wanted to close the entranceway to keep other Jews from entering, while still others booed them and demanded that the door be kept open for any Jews outside who might need refuge. Von Weisel had a difficult time answering some of the questions put to him by the commission's interrogators. "My eyeglasses fell off and I am very shortsighted," he admitted (quoted in Commission 1930, 1:241).

Wolfgang von Weisel

Von Weisel was a Vienna-born physician, journalist, and Zionist. He was a close associate of Jabotinsky, and the two were cofounders of the Revisionist Party, which advocated the establishment of a Jewish state on both sides of the Jordan River. Von Weisel had served as an artillery officer in the Austro-Hungarian army, and prior to his immigration to Palestine he had been secretary of Keren Kayemet's Austrian branch. His Hebrew name was Binyamin Ze'ev, identical to the Hebrew name of the founder of the Zionist movement, Theodor Herzl, who had been a frequent visitor to the von Weisel home during Wolfgang's childhood. At the time the prayer service in al-Aqsa came to an end, von Weisel happened to be in Steimatzky's bookstore, near Zion Square at the entrance to Nahalat Shiva, along with Greenberg. The sound of the crowd stirred his journalistic instincts and sent him to Jaffa Gate, where he saw a Jew being beaten to death. Von Weisel then turned west, along Jaffa Road to the Municipal Garden, where he was attacked by the Lifta villagers.

There is no denying von Weisel's nose for news. A week earlier he was the only newspaper reporter to witness the burning of Jewish holy books by Muslims at the Western Wall. He had had years of experience, having written his first article — on Yemenite Jewish immigration to Palestine — when he was eleven years old. On Jaffa Road he saw the Liftans heading west toward their village, accompanied by policemen. He saw a small group of them suddenly turn back, among them an especially tall and muscular man, to beat and stab a Jew standing at the entranceway to the building. The man was Raitan:

Practically at the same moment, when I was aware of this attack, I was attacked myself by two Arabs hitting with stick[s] at my head.
[Questioner:] What happened then?
[Weisel:] I fortunately had a very good topee hat and the topee hat took the force of it. I knocked down one of them and arrested the second one.

[Questioner:] You warded that attack off?

[Weisel:] Yes. . . . Then I shouted to a policeman a few yards in front of me to seize the Arab I had taken, but he was too busy pushing the people forward to listen to me. The Arab tried to free himself from my hands but did not succeed, then I continued to shout: "Policeman, arrest this man! Arrest him! Come and take the man." But instead of the policeman, a young Arab came up, he stepped round me, and stabbed me in the back. . . . After that, one or two minutes later, an English policeman took the Arab from me; he did not arrest him but pushed him forward in the procession and the Arabs left in the direction of the Russian Compound. (quoted in Commission 1930, 1:226)

The dagger penetrated von Weisel's left lung and he required a lengthy hospitalization. At a later session of the Shaw Commission he was asked about his political views and about Arab attitudes toward Zionism. He spoke of the need to boost Jewish immigration and claimed that his ideas were acceptable to the Arabs. He noted, however, that in the last year or two the Arabs had begun voicing their opposition to the Jewish influx. Yet von Weisel attributed this phenomenon precisely to the fact that the flow of immigrants had waned. When large-scale immigration resumed, the Arabs would once again become cognizant of the benefits of Zionism. On this matter he differed from Jabotinsky, who in his essay "The Iron Wall" (1923) had evinced full comprehension of Arab opposition to Zionism.

Von Weisel spoke as an expert. He termed himself a man who understood the Arabs. He had visited Jabal al-Druze, Hejaz, Amman, Egypt, and the Persian Gulf. He had been the guest of Emir 'Abdallah and of Palestinian Arabs. According to his granddaughter Niva von Weisel, he tried to persuade the Zionist leadership to purchase military gear to equip two divisions, to organize 30,000 pioneers, and to conquer Palestine:

In 1922 von Weisel immigrated to Palestine, where he served as an instructor in the first course for commanders in the Labor Battalion, in accordance with a training program he had become acquainted with during his time in the Austrian imperial army. Many years later the Austrian ambassador asked him why he had not returned to Vienna after the war. Von Weisel replied: "When I was a student in Vienna, there were graffiti on the walls and doors of the toilets: 'Jews, get out!' And I take toilet literature very seriously."

From 1924 onward, as correspondent of the respected Vienna newspaper *Neue Freie Presse* and the Ullstein publishing house's representative in the Near East and Islamic world, von Weisel set off on a brilliant journalistic career, with his articles appearing throughout the world and translated even into Chinese. He was received by the "caliph of all believers," the king of the Hejaz, Hussein, while he [held the title] king, and was the only European to dine with the caliph at his final royal dinner before going into exile. He was also the guest of King Ibn-Sa'ud, stayed at the home of Sultan al-Atrash, the leader of the Druze rebellion, and was a regular visitor at the palace of the emir of Transjordan, 'Abdallah, and served as his personal physician. . . . At all times and everywhere von Weisel thought as a Zionist and took advantage of his position and his status as a person who was at home in the courts of the Arab kings for the good of the Zionist movement. He believed that he would be able to bring the Arabs around to recognizing the Zionist enterprise. He proposed to King Faysal of Iraq the transfer of the Arabs of Palestine to cultivate the land of Iraq, received his blessing, and was even permitted to publish a news item promoting the matter, but encountered the opposition of the British and the pro-British Zionist leadership led by Weizmann. (von Weisel, n.d.)

The idea of transferring Palestine's Arabs to Iraq was in the air at the time. Not only Von Weisel proposed it; a number of Zionist officials toyed with the idea. The claim that official Zionist institutions opposed it is surprising, given that the Zionist Office for Arab Affairs, headed by Yitzhak Ben-Zvi, drafted a similar proposal on November 22, 1931 (CZA J1/2216). The British Palestine Royal Commission of 1937 (known as the Peel Commission) also recommended a transfer of Palestine's Arabs from areas designated for the Jewish state.

Was Von Weisel Really an Expert on Oriental Affairs?
There is reason to doubt von Weisel's fluency in Arabic. He told the Shaw Commission about a meeting he had with Ruh Imshi, a Jerusalem sheikh, saying that the man had not wanted to converse with him for long (Commission 1930, 1:233). We can be fairly certain that there was never an Arab by that name in Jerusalem. Von Weisel's account makes it clear that he had indeed sought to interview a sheikh. The journalist apparently began by asking for his interviewee's name. The impatient personage told him "*Ruh, imshi*" (Arabic for "Scram, go away"). Von Weisel thought it was the sheikh's name.

The Divider at the Wall: Von Weisel's Version
Von Weisel offered the Shaw Commission an interesting take on the divider incident. He related that there had long been only a Sephardi shamash at the Wailing Wall. Rabbi Kook had appointed an Ashkenazi shamash as well. The Sephardi official was angered by this, as his income came from donations he gathered from worshipers and now he would have to split them with the newcomer. But in the end the two men reached an accord—the Ashkenazi shamash would pocket donations received from Ashkenazi worshipers and the Sephardi shamash those from his own people. But, as Rabbi Kook told the commission

(and as discussed above), soon before Yom Kippur of September 1928 the admor of Radzymin arrived to pray at the Wall along with many of his followers—who had brought a large number of donations. The Sephardi shamash wanted a cut of the income, but his colleague refused—an agreement was an agreement, he said. With the holiest day of the Jewish year approaching, the admor asked that a divider be erected at the site to separate men and women worshipers. The Ashkenazi shamash knew that doing so would violate the status quo but did so anyway. Von Weisel believed that the shamash was given a generous gift to encourage him to respond to the admor's request. The Sephardi shamash asked for a share of that income as well but was refused. On the eve of Yom Kippur the Sephardi shamash told some Arab acquaintances that his Ashkenazi colleague was building "a new wall" next to al-Buraq. Apparently his intention was to indicate that if he were still the only official responsible for the site, things like this would not happen. But the report reached the mufti, who had no interest in the issue of who should be shamash or whether it was a Jewish custom to separate men and women during prayers. His agenda was to protect the Islamic holy sites and to enhance his image as the protector of Islam in Palestine. The mufti immediately told the British, who used unnecessary force to remove the divider. Von Weisel published this account in *New Palestine*, a periodical put out by the American Zionist Organization. The journalist sent the article to the magazine on August 21, two days before the outbreak of the violent riots, but it was published a few weeks later. Rabbi Kook, for his part, told the commission that the Ashkenazi shamash had appointed himself to the post years before the riots and was not in any way subordinate to the chief rabbinate (Commission 1930, 2:740).

Petty Stuff

This may seem petty, but it's part of the larger picture. Life consists of great events and the little things that happen around them—and vice-versa. The Sephardi shamash, by the way, was attacked and beaten by the Arab demonstrators who descended from al-Haram al-Sharif to the Wall on the Friday prior to the riots, on the Prophet Mohammad's birthday. The small amount of money he had in his pockets was stolen. He was rescued by an Arab who took him into his house (*Ha'aretz*, August 18, 1929).

In any case, let's get back to the important things.

The Beginning of the Riots, Outside Nablus Gate

While the Liftans were heading down Jaffa Road, hundreds of other worshipers left the Old City through Nablus Gate. They found themselves facing the Gurji courtyard, just outside the Nablus Gate, within the Nisan Bek compound.

Was this before the mufti arrived at the plaza in front of the gate and tried, according to several accounts, to mollify the crowd? Or did it happen afterward? Did the mufti really try to calm them? We have no authoritative answer, but we do have an account of what happened in the Gurji courtyard. It is not detailed, but it makes it clear that the crowd was not calm:

> At 12:30 an Arab mob of huge proportions stormed the neighborhood. They broke into houses and began to kill, rob, and burn. Meshulam Shvili and Hannah Salanshvili [Tzvina-Shvili] and her young son in her arms were killed by gunshots. They killed the boy after gouging out his eyes. After looting all the houses they went into the synagogue, ripped up the Torah scrolls, the ark and the ark curtain, and destroyed the rest. Eliahu Sasson, who lived close to the synagogue, went in to save the Torah scrolls and was killed immediately by the rioters.
>
> Also killed, in addition to Meshulam Shvili, Hannah Salanshvili, and Eliahu Sasson, already mentioned, were Ya'akov Ben-Shim'on, Reuven Wolfe (died of his injuries), H. Weiner (a Jew from England), Menahem Savlani, and Shmuel Ganani (died of his injuries). (Amikam 1929, 21)

The attack actually seems to have begun considerably after 12:30 p.m. The prosecution witnesses at the trial of the murderer of Hannah Tzvina-Shvili testified that the attack began at 2:00 (*Davar*, April 9, 1930). Any number of hypotheses can be proposed to explain the disparity. Perhaps the mob started to gather at 12:30 but the attack on the neighborhood began an hour and a half later. Perhaps, in the framework of the dispute over who started it, Yisra'el Amikam moved up the time so as to place this Arab attack on Jews prior to the lynchings that Jews committed against Arabs. But the description of the murder of the mother and her baby son also requires a closer look.

Hannah and Her Baby Son

On September 4, a few days after the British permitted newspapers to resume publication, *Ha'aretz* printed the story of the Shvili family. The father was a driver, and on the Friday of the riots he had set out from Nablus to Jerusalem. His car was attacked near Ramallah, and he was slightly injured and evacuated to the Jewish settlement of Neveh Ya'akov, where his wounds were bandaged. "Immediately on arriving in [Jerusalem]," the newspaper reported, "he rushed to his house to tell his family that he had gotten through safely. And he found his entire family (who lived in the Gurji courtyard next to Nablus Gate) slaughtered: the driver's wife, his small sons, his brothers and uncle had all been killed by the Arabs in their first attack on this Jewish quarter."

According to this account, not just one son was killed but all of them. Which version is more likely to be true? What really happened there?

Critique of the Press

Tense situations spawn rumors. In the initial hours following a violent event there is often a great deal of haziness about what actually happened. *Ha'aretz*'s account was published a good ten days after the incident, but the pressure of events nevertheless made it difficult to investigate and find the facts. As a matter of fact, in the same issue *Ha'aretz* published a list of the Jews killed in Jerusalem, but the names of the Shvili children do not appear there. Apparently the editor did not notice the discrepancy. Perhaps he was under pressure or simply inattentive, or perhaps the story was too dramatic for him to cut. Readers who were alert — as readers ought to be — might have noticed and realized that they should not believe everything a newspaper publishes. But perhaps there was something to the lurid story? Perhaps it was more accurate than the list of names?

What Really Happened?

The mother was murdered. All her children survived, including the one she held in her arms. The attackers stabbed him in the face and he was blinded in one eye, but not killed. In the summer of 2011, at the age of eighty-three, his testimony was recorded and posted on YouTube. His name is Shmuel Tzfania (Tzvina-Shvili) and his excruciating story explains the version in which he was killed. Here is a transcript:

> We lived here by Nablus Gate and there was this thing they called the mufti, Hajj Amin al-Hussayni, and he was in the Mosque of Omar and incited the Arabs, it was on Friday the seventeenth of Av 1929. He incited them and told them "*idbahu al-yahud*," slaughter the Jews, and they went out of the Mosque of Omar shouting all the way "*idbah al-yahud*," "*idbah al-yahud*," until they reached Nablus Gate and the first neighborhood they reached was the Gurji courtyard. And they began the massacre from our neighborhood. I had a mother, may peace be on her, she held me in her arms, I was then about one year old and I was in her arms, but before that she concealed, hid my brother and sister under the bed. My sister now tells me that even when they began murdering Mother, stabbing her, she wanted to cry, but my brother shut her mouth and that was how they were both saved. They did not discover them. They murdered my mother with many knives, and I was in her arms the whole time. At the same time that they murdered her they also gouged my eye out. That was on Friday, and it was already late. They took them, my father was a cab driver and he drove a cab back from Nablus. On the way they injured him as well. Injured him in the neck. When he came home he saw that all that was left to him were his two children, my sister and my brother. They took them [the neighborhood's dead] afterward to the morgue and I was there, and on Saturday night they were about to bury them

and they opened up the morgue and heard the voice of a baby crying and that was me. They immediately, it was right next to a hospital, called in a nurse and she took me and they took care of me and here I am before you today.

What I want to say is that you should know that then we didn't have, we weren't occupiers, we didn't have arms, we didn't have anything. But there are murderers who are called Arabs and they don't like Jews and will never like Jews and there will never ever be peace with them. That's the way it is. That's what I want to tell. That's the whole story. (Tzfania 2011)

You can't get more primary than this primary source. The testimony of an adult describing how his mother was murdered when he was one year old, as she was holding him, who as a baby spent a night in a morgue among the bodies of his family and neighbors. But even evidence like this needs to be analyzed and put into context. The speaker's personal experiences are not a testimony in the strict sense of the word, but rather a memory that was reconstructed with the aid of others. And the personal account must be separated from the political commentary he heard at second remove. For example, his testimony on the mufti's actions is not actually a testimony, nor is it his unique account. It is a story composed of accounts he heard years later, just as other Jewish children of that time did. Whatever the case, he offers a personal account of facts and feelings that is vital to understanding the time and the riots and their consequences.

"They . . . Will Never Like Jews"

At the end of the Mandate period, Tzfania joined the Haganah but then decided to leave it and join the radical Lehi underground. "During the War of Independence I was a machine gunner in the Church of Notre Dame," he told the magazine *Besheva'*. "I sniped at Legionnaires [Transjordanian soldiers] who were at Nablus Gate, by our houses, the Nisan Bek homes. Thank God, I did my part" (quoted in Lax 2009, 24). Following the Six-Day War he signed an open letter published by wounded and handicapped veterans of Israel's wars, declaring that "we will not consent [to] and will not tolerate the concession of any part of our liberated homeland" (*Ma'ariv*, September 3, 1967). Soon after the war he took part in an initiative to settle Jews in houses in Ramallah and its suburbs that had been abandoned by Palestinians. He and his partners corresponded with cabinet ministers, among them Menachem Begin, who was enthusiastic about their plan. Minister of Religions Zerach Warhaftig supported them, and Prime Ministers Levi Eshkol and Golda Meir promised to discuss the initiative (*Ma'ariv*, May 27, 1969). The project did not proceed as Tzfania and his colleagues had hoped, but this is not the place to tell that story. Our subject is not post-1967

Jewish settlement to the north of Jerusalem, but rather how a survivor of the 1929 riots reacted to his trauma.

Back to 1929 and the Gurji Courtyard

About a third of Jerusalem's Jewish dead in the 1929 riots were killed in the Gurji courtyard. British police officers (according to an unnamed Jewish policeman quoted in *Do'ar Hayom*, September 9, 1929) arrived while cries of the assailants and the wailing of the victims still rang in the air — but the law enforcers did nothing to halt the killing. Acting Police Commandant Saunders confirmed before the Shaw Commission that though the Muslim attackers were visible from his headquarters, no order was given for live fire to stop them (Commission 1930, 1:16, 33–34). Haganah personnel who responded to an alarm about the slaughter arrived tragically late. "When we got to the neighborhood, there were already dead and wounded and desecrated Torah scrolls," testified Ya'akov Waxman-Sagi (HHA testimony 37/1). "We advanced into the neighborhood. On the way we encountered an Arab with an ax. We thought he was one of the rioters, but he called us over to help Jews who had hidden in his house."

The Gurji dead were killed on the first day of the riots, and the Arab with the ax was one of the first Arabs to rescue Jews. A week earlier, as we have seen, it was a Jewish grocer in the Bukharan quarter who rescued his Arab neighbor from a Jewish mob. The truth is that almost everywhere that killers raged there were also rescuers from the same nation the killers came from. This is a very important fact about 1929, not one to be taken as a given. I will seek to explain below what motivated these people.

Even in the Maghrebi Quarter

Clashes between Arabs and Jews occurred that Friday, following the prayer service at al-Aqsa, within the Old City as well. There, however, the Haganah was sufficiently organized and the onslaughts were repelled. The only Jew killed that weekend in the Old City, testified a Haganah deputy commander, Meir Sharvit (HHA, testimony 59/75), was an elderly man who, unawares, was making his way to synagogue on Saturday morning. At the roots of the dispute that led to the riots were the rival claims of the Maghrebis and the Jews in the area of the Western Wall; yet, signally, these did not prevent acts of cross-national friendship there. "Several Jews aged 100 to 105 congregated in the Maghrebi courtyard," Rabbi Mordechai Weingarten related (HHA testimony 115/34). "They remained there with very little food, and Arab neighbors provided them sustenance via the roofs, alerting them to the fact that they were in danger of being killed. For that reason the Arab neighbors had to get them out of there. But the old men would not agree to leave, and the rescuers arranged them a protective wall next to the gate to the courtyard." Here was another instance of Maghrebi brotherhood in the midst of the massacre.

The Early Hours in the Bukharan Quarter

Khamis Salem al-Sayyed, a porter from the Old City, offered the following testimony in court:

> I know Khalil Burhan [Dahudi al-Dajjani]. He worked with us carting produce to the Jews in Meah She'arim, the Bukharan neighborhood, Beit Yisrael, and Zikhron Moshe. I remember the first day of the riots in Jerusalem. It was Friday and on that day I was with Khalil. At about ten in the morning we left Jaffa Gate and walked toward the Bukharan neighborhood to collect money and [empty] boxes. . . . We began to walk along the lower road, by the flour mill. Before we reached the mill a number of Jews saw us and began to walk after us. We walked on the descent and they ran after us. We heard them calling out: "Gul, beat them." They had boards and iron rods. We went into Meah She'arim. I ran in front and the late man [Burhan] ran after me. The Jews threw stones and "pots" at us from balconies and windows. I heard a shot. The late man let out an "aaah" and fell. I heard only one shot. I continued to run without noticing who was running after me. I knew that the four defendants were among the pursuers. . . . I continued to run and went into the house of a Jew and waited there until the late afternoon. Then the people of the house told me that I'd better go. When I went out, there was a Zionist Jew who wanted to beat me. The people in the house shouted at him and prevented him from doing it. I ran toward the Ethiopian church. (Zionist) Jews ran after me. When I reached the door of the church I pushed it and went in. (ISA/P 3050/20)

"(Zionist) Jews"

The parentheses are in the original Hebrew document. The witness was trying to characterize the people who chased him and killed his companion, but when it happened the delineations between different kinds of Jews were no longer clear to him. It's not easy to tell them apart. There are the old kind, who were divided into different ethnic communities, and there are the new Jews, the Zionists. Either al-Sayyed was confused or the person who translated his testimony in court, or who recorded the proceedings, was confused. These were not the Jews who knew their place very well, the ones al-Sayyed and his forefathers had known. There was now a new breed of Jew in the land, Jews who chased down innocent Muslims and killed them. In other words, they were not really Jews, they were Zionists. Or maybe they were Jews who had been incited by the Zionists? In any case, fundamentally, they seem to have been Jews. Or maybe actually Zionists?

Al-Sayyed gave his testimony before H. Kemp, an investigating magistrate before whom four Jews were indicted for the murder of the produce merchant al-Dajjani.

The Survivor and His Rescuer

Al-Dajjani was killed. Al-Sayyed survived. He related that Jews hid him in their home. The police located the family that saved him and summoned the woman who gave him refuge to testify. The court record names her as Mina, wife of Shlomo Albert and daughter of Rabbi Leibele. She testified:

> I remember the first day of the riots. It was Friday. I was at home all day. A man came that day to hide in my home. He was an Arab. I will recognize him if I see him. Now I see him in the courtroom (she points at Khamis). He appeared between 1 and 2 and stayed until 4 or 4:30. A man arrived and wanted to beat him. I shouted at him and he went away. I offered the Arab tea. He refused. I offered him clothes belonging to my husband to disguise himself. I showed him the way to Ethiopia Street and he went. He did not tell me what he was scared of and I did not ask him. He was frightened. He did not drink tea but he asked for water and I gave him some. (ISA/P 3050/20)

So, just as Arabs saved Jews in 1929 — in Mekor Hayyim, in Motza, in Hebron, and elsewhere — there were also Jews who saved Arabs. We already mentioned Shimon, the grocer in the Bukharan quarter, and now we have Mina Albert.

I have not been successful in turning up any more information about Mina Albert or Shimon the grocer. No one extolled their deeds. *Davar* devoted a special column titled *Orot MeOfel* (Light from the darkness) to Arabs who saved terrified Jews from danger. No Jewish source said anything about Jews who saved Arabs. Perhaps the Jewish writers did not want to admit, even implicitly, that Jews had lynched innocent Arabs.

The Time of the Event

On October 30, 1929, the investigating magistrate handed down his judgment:

> The proofs in this case indicate that a man named Khalil Burhan al-Dahudi (a.k.a. al-Dajjani) and another named Khamis al-Sayyed were attacked by a Jewish mob in Meah She'arim in Jerusalem and the first was murdered. It is important to note that the pursuit and murder took place between 12:30 and 1:30 on Friday August 23, and that the two Arabs were conducting themselves as usual and peacefully before the chase after them began, while they were occupied with their normal tasks. They were not aggressive and did not create any sort of provocation. Everyone knows that between 1:15 and 2 that day there were clashes between Arabs and Jews close to the entrance to Meah She'arim, not far from the scene of the crime. But at the time of the

pursuit of Khamis and Khalil, and at the time the latter was murdered, there were still no confrontations between Jews and Arabs. (ISA/P 3050/20)

The accused men, four Jews from the Bukharan quarter, were brought before the special court established for crimes committed during the riots. The prosecutor in their case was a police officer, Bechor Shalom Sheetrit, a Jew born in Tiberias whose family had come there from Morocco. Sheetrit spoke Arabic and was given a special appointment as prosecutor after the riots; he would later serve as a judge in the Mandate judicial system. He was also elected to the first Knesset on the Sephardi and Mizrahi slate and was appointed police and minorities minister in Israel's first government. Eight years prior to the 1929 riots he served as an interrogations officer. In that capacity he disguised himself as an Arab livestock merchant in order to investigate the murder of Yosef Haim Brenner (HHA, Sheetrit testimony 134/5).

Sheetrit also served as prosecutor in the trial of a group of Arabs from Qalunya charged with murdering members of the Maklef family of Motza, which will be described in detail below.

Gershom Scholem and the Al-Dajjani Murder

Gershom Scholem, the great scholar of Jewish mysticism and Hasidism, lived in 1929 where Ethiopia Street intersected with Meah She'arim. Not far, that is, from the site of al-Dajjani's murder. Scholem belonged to Brit Shalom, a small group of Jewish intellectuals who advocated equality between Jews and Arabs under the Mandate administration and later, when the time was right, in a unitary binational state. In April 1926, in what he termed his first political statement since arriving in Palestine, Scholem signed a petition calling for a reduction of British military forces in the country, which should be replaced, he said, with a civilian police force (Scholem 1989, 61). On the Friday when the riots began he may have regretted that there was no British force large and strong enough to prevent the killings. Whatever the case, despite having heard of the Arab assault on Meah She'arim, Scholem set out for that neighborhood to fetch the meal that his longtime cook had prepared for him. He testified immediately after the riots what happened on his way back:

As I continued down Ethiopia Street I noted, about fifteen meters from the corner of the new street that leads to Nevi'im [Prophets] Street, the body of a wounded Arab. I reached home at between 1:35 and 1:45. I had left home at 1:25 and it takes me about twenty minutes to walk in both directions. . . . Our maid was all worked up and related that she had seen them killing the Arab not far from our home. We talked about the attack on Meah She'arim and the riots of that day. I went over to the home of Dr. Trio to ask him to examine the wounded Arab, but he had already set out for

Hadassah Hospital. I went to the home of Dr. Rosenthal who lived across the street so as to call the police. I called the British police and asked them to come and take the Arab's body. They told me that it was not their business and that I should seek elsewhere (I believe they mentioned the government hospital). We sat down to eat lunch.

Later, when I saw that the wounded man was still on the street, I decided to go inform the Meah She'arim police station. That was much later than 2 p.m. When I reached the corner where the Arab lay, I saw a truck driven by a Jew. Dr. [Mikhail] Shammas [a Christian Arab physician], along with several Jews, stood by the Arab's body. I and a couple of other Jews helped Dr. Shammas lift the body of the Arab to the truck. I did not continue on to the police station. At least an hour had gone by between my first noticing the Arab and the time he was evacuated to the hospital. (CZA L59/115)

Al-Dajjani lay wounded for a long time; perhaps quick action would have saved his life. But the people hearing the testimony had a more important question to answer — was the first person killed a Jew or an Arab? They asked for Scholem's testimony in an effort to establish the time of al-Dajjani's death.

Mikhail Shammas

Shammas, a graduate of the American University in Cairo, lived not far from Scholem. He and Scholem hoisted the body on the truck, Shammas testified before the Shaw Commission on November 23. He was asked about the precise time he had eaten and how many times he had looked at the clock that day. But the rest of what he said in his testimony was no less important. While he was dining, he heard noises outside. When he finished his meal, he went out on his balcony and saw two men pulling something along the street. At first he thought it was a sack. When they got closer, he saw that they were dragging a person. Behind them were six or seven men wielding sticks and beating the wounded man:

[Questioner:] Hitting him where?
[Shammas:] On the back and on the head with sticks. When I saw that I shouted at them with excitement.
[Questioner:] What did they do?
[Shammas:] At that they let go the man on the ground and left him.
[Questioner:] Now can you say what sort of people they were who were dragging this man and those who were beating him?
[Shammas:] The men who were dragging the body were all Jews, they belonged to a group of Jews known as the Halutzim [Zionist pioneers].
[Questioner:] Are you quite familiar with the various types of the inhabitants and of Jews?
[Shammas:] Yes. . . .
[Questioner:] Was there any other type [of Jew]?

[Shammas:] The others were a mixture of Ashkenazim and Yemenites.

[Questioner:] You say that they dropped the man?

[Shammas:] They dropped the man and went down the road again, but they did not leave him alone. They kept coming back and hitting him on the head with the sticks. (Commission 1930, 1:386–87)

Scholem and Shammas saw al-Dajjani's body after the attack on Meah She'arim had begun, not before. But it seems that inhabitants of the neighborhood had already injured him. Al-Dajjani may have hidden while wounded until being discovered by the Halutzim, who dragged him up the street and continued to beat him.

Meah She'arim: The Onslaught and the Rescue

A short time after al-Dajjani and his companion were attacked in Meah She'arim, the Friday prayer service at al-Aqsa came to an end and hundreds of Arabs streamed out toward Nablus and Herod's Gates and from there in the direction of Meah She'arim, shouting and waving knives and clubs. We do not know whether they had already heard of the lynching. They tried to enter the neighborhood's main road to attack the inhabitants. A Haganah detachment rushed to the scene to prevent the mob from breaking into Jewish homes. One member of this force was Aryeh Botrimovitch, mentioned above as the man who abducted the instigator of the Jewish underground plot to blow up the mosques on the Temple Mount. He contributed a firsthand account of the events:

We received an order to get off next to the Italian hospital and to stop the Arab attack on Meah She'arim. We got off: [Moshe] Alperstein, [Levi] Spiegelman, and myself. I had a Par [Parabellum pistol, also called a Luger] and Alperstein had a Par and two grenades. We stood not far from the Landau School (at the corner, where Mandelbaum Gate now is) and advanced toward Meah She'arim. When the Arabs began to stream from the direction of Nablus Gate we let them approach, and when we received an order from Levi, Alperstein threw a grenade and I began to fire with the Par. The number of dead was two or three, and there were injuries as well. The Arabs retreated. We returned to base. There was a nurse with us, Ahuva Wittenberg (now in Tiberias). She brought us into a room and calmed us down. . . . On Saturday morning I was sent with Alperstein to patrol in the city. I took my Par, we got off at the Russian Compound to patrol, we saw Arabs, and without receiving an order from anyone we "finished" them and ran off. (HHA, Botrimovitch testimony, 7/9)

Alperstein, the Man and the Legend

Moshe Alperstein was, according to this account and others, the man who saved Meah She'arim, but he was recognized as such only by his close friends.

He is an anonymous hero whose name does not appear in history books. He never got promoted and did not receive a senior position in the army or government after the founding of the state of Israel. Where did he vanish to? Did he simply descend into oblivion like most fighters in most battles? Haim Be'er proposes a solution to the mystery in a digression in his essay "Ir Lo Museget" (The unachieved (or inconceivable) city). Alperstein, Be'er reports, was a Haredi Jew who had secretly enlisted in the Haganah:

> The tortuous life of this man of twists and turns, Comrade Alperstein and the saint R. Aharon. He later came to be known in Meah She'arim as Rabbi Aharon Fisher, a God-fearing teacher of young boys and one of the Haredi champions who fought ferociously against the libertines at the National Council polling place, but his name was whispered at night like a legend, the legend of Moshe Alperstein, a bold fighter in the service of the Haganah, who excelled at dangerous combat operations against the Arab rioters in Hebron, Jerusalem, and Motza. In 1925 [!] he took part, so the story goes, in the execution of de Haan and a few months later named his son Ya'akov Yisrael after that saint, may God avenge his blood, a son who would later be appointed one of the esteemed members of the Edah Haredit Religious Court in Jerusalem. (Be'er 1993, 202–3)

Father of the Head of the Edah Haredit Religious Court?

Be'er identifies Alperstein as Rabbi Aharon Fisher, whose son was later appointed to the Edah Haredit Religious Court, and relates that the father joined an underground Jewish militia, but without adopting secular Zionist doctrines. According to this version, he openly battled against Zionism and secretly served as a legendary soldier alongside the Zionists in their struggle with the Arabs. Here is more information about him from a book by two Haredi authors, Yocheved Salmon and Yehudit Golan, *Elef 'Olamot* (A thousand worlds):

> The Arabs continued to advance down Shivtei Yisrael Street, led by an Arab sheikh hoisted on the shoulders of one of the Arabs, waving a huge sword and whipping up the mob to embark on a jihad against the Jews. The English, for their part, offered no response to the bloodbath that was about to break out, and just vanished from the scene.
>
> Suddenly, at Reb Shabtai Bachrach's flour mill, located on the south side of Meah She'arim (today's Breslov yeshiva), a youth named Alperstein appeared. The youth, who put his life on the line for his brethren, drew a pistol and fired at the leader of the mob. The Arab fell to the ground, dead.
>
> At that instant the Arabs panicked, turned on their tracks, and fled, abandoning for the moment their murderous plans, each man for himself escaping the death-shooting pistol. A grenade thrown at them — by Jewish Haganah men — killed

three more rioters and the flight turned into a terrified rout, with the Arabs trampling one another to death.

It later turned out that this "Alperstein" was no other than Rabbi Aharon Fisher, father of the eminent Rabbi Meir Tzvi Fisher, today the rabbi of [the Jerusalem neighborhood] Har Nof; Rabbi Yisrael Ya'akov Fisher, may the memory of the righteous be a blessing, who was the head of the rabbinic court of the Edah Haredit; Rabbi Moshe Fisher, rabbi of [the neighborhood of] Batei Broide and its surroundings; and Rabbi Shlomo Fisher, head of the Itri Yeshiva. Rabbi Aharon had been an expert sharpshooter in his childhood in Romania. He named his son Rabbi Ya'akov Yisrael after the saintly Rabbi Ya'akov Yisrael de Haan, who was murdered by thugs. (2003, 236)

An Astounding Revelation

In fact, in certain circles this story is well known. It has also appeared in a memorial book published in Rabbi Aharon Fisher's memory as well as on a number of websites; in resource material published by the Kfar Etzion Field School; and in a scholarly religious journal (Sternberg 2003, 368), where there is also material regarding, among other things, the rabbi's service in the Romanian army and his refusal to violate the Sabbath even while in mortal danger. But these sources contain some inconsistencies. For example, was de Haan murdered by Zionist thugs, as Salmon and Golan have it, or by Fisher himself, as Be'er maintains? Was he an unknown schoolteacher, as Be'er suggests, or one of the great men of his generation; a friend of de Haan and a close associate of Rabbi Yosef Chaim Sonnenfeld, founder of the Edah Haredit, the communal organization of anti-Zionist Haredim in Jerusalem, as Rabbi Yehiel Sternberg wrote?

More Haganah Stories about Alperstein

Nor is there any shortage of stories about Alperstein on the non-Haredi side. Gedalia Armoni met him in Jerusalem's Bayit VeGan neighborhood a few days after he repelled the invasion of Meah She'arim, as Armoni relates in recorded testimony:

In 1929 there was in Jerusalem a rapid mobile response force. One day the Arabs set fire to a grain silo at Tel Yosef [a communal farm in the north]. Somewhere in Bayit VeGan, Rachel [Yana'it] gets up before the guys and tells them about the silo, tells them and cautions, weeps and laments, "our silos are burning." One of the guys was a kid named Alperstein. A strong guy, tall and with broad shoulders. He stands there listening to Rachel shouting amid her tears "our silos are burning" and he, this hero, sobs, begins to run, grabs a can of kerosene. There was an Arab house in Bayit VeGan at the time. He ran off shouting that he would burn that house down with everyone inside. He was dangerous. . . . He's running off to burn down the house, and the guys saw that it was a bad situation and begin to block him. He's got two pistols, a big one under his clothes and a little one in his pocket, he grabs both pistols in front of the guys and shouts, leave me alone. . . . They see it's not good and tell him, we need to ask headquarters. We need permission from Haganah headquarters. Of course, the answer [from headquarters] was, no way. And then he declares: an order is an order — and he calmed down. (HHA, testimony 36/16)

Bayit VeGan in 1929

Bayit VeGan was an isolated Jewish neighborhood in southwest Jerusalem. The closest Jewish neighborhood was Beit HaKerem. Three Jews were killed in Bayit VeGan in 1929: Mordechai Ben-Menasheh (Dagestani), who served as the Bayit VeGan guard; David Vilnai, a student at the David Yellin Teachers College, who went to Bayit VeGan to participate in its defense during an Arab attack; and Police Sergeant Yudelevitz, after whom the poet Emmanuel Harusi named his infant son after learning of both the death and the birth while he was on guard against the Jaffa mob that sought to ravage Tel Aviv.

The members of a mobile rapid response force led by Sa'adiah Kirshenbaum arrived in Bayit VeGan at about this time. Kirshenbaum later related: "We found a group of our guys there acting against Arab positions in the area, and had not only inactivated them but also caused them many losses. Women and children were also killed" (HHA testimony 120/30). During the weeks following the riots, Jews from Bayit VeGan were charged with the murder of Arabs, and Arabs were tried for murdering Jews. The accused on both sides were released, either for lack of sufficient evidence or because they were found innocent. In at least one case Jews testified in court that a specific set of Arabs had shot at them, but other Jews testified in the same trial that the Arabs in question had helped them and were not involved in the attack in any way (*Davar*, February 20, 1930). In any case, the killers of the Jews and of the Arabs who died in the Bayit VeGan area were not found, or else they managed to fool the court and escape conviction. The British police also searched for Alperstein, whom they wanted to arrest for carrying weapons illegally and for killing Arabs near Meah She'arim, but they were unable to find him.

The Real Comrade Alperstein?

Some Haganah veterans in Kiryat Haim, a town on the Gulf of Haifa, are bemused by Alperstein's adoption by the Edah Haredit and the claim that his name was an alias used by the senior Rabbi Fisher. The main reason they raise their eyebrows is that Alperstein lived in their town from the 1930s onward and many people there still remember him, even though he died young in 1953. Meir Mizritzki served with Alperstein in Meah She'arim in 1929, and his son Yair was a classmate of Alperstein's son Uri. Yair Mizritzki-Meiraz wrote me a letter saying that "Moshe (Misha) Alperstein was a real person whom I knew personally." He sent me the following account:

[My father] did not tell me the following story, either, of his own volition — until Misha Alperstein died. All the leaders of the Haganah from Jerusalem at that time attended his funeral. We were astounded. . . . After the funeral I asked my father: Why did all of them come? This is his story:

The 1929 riots. As a member of the Haganah, he [my father] was sent with fifteen of his buddies to defend one of the Haredi neighborhoods adjacent to the Old City. Their combat gear was sticks and a single underground pistol. The pistol was given to my father, who was considered a responsible, serious, and disciplined person. This small contingent of defenders found itself facing, in a narrow alley, an inflamed mob of hundreds of Arabs, waving cutlasses and clubs and shouting "*Itbah al-Yahud.*" . . . My father knew that if the mob got out of the alley and spread among the neighborhood's houses the Haganah men would be like a drop in the ocean. At the very least dozens [of Jews] would be injured and killed. And there was a large chance that the Haganah men would be among the first. He understood with simple logic that the only way to stop the mob was to shoot at it while it was still in the alley, to at least wound the leaders and inciters at the head of the crowd. A moral problem: my father was unable to persuade himself to kill people who, at this moment, had not yet hurt anyone. . . .

My father hesitated and agonized. The mob was already 20–30 meters from the entrance to the Jewish neighborhood. Suddenly Alperstein went up to my father, grabbed the pistol, advanced with an erect back toward the first of the rioters, and from a range of about five meters emptied the entire magazine at them. I don't know how many were hit by the bullets, obviously many were trampled in the flight to the rear. The neighborhood was saved. . . . My father remained divided his entire life — he had acted precisely in accordance with the norms, with the training he had been given, the orders he had received . . . but it wasn't he and his comrades who had saved Jerusalem, it was Misha Alperstein! (Meiraz 2007)

Is this narrative more reliable than the Haredi version? There are some similarities — the hesitation of the man holding the gun at the fateful moment, and the initiative of one of the other men standing nearby. Can one or the other version be validated? In this case, not in every detail. On the one hand, it is clear that Alperstein and Rabbi Aharon Fisher were two different people, as the latter died in 1942 while the former remained active in the Haganah in 1948 and was buried in 1953. But that doesn't mean that Rabbi Fisher didn't come to the rescue of Meah She'arim. It may well be that he fought bravely against the Arabs, just as he did to prevent Haredim from taking part in the elections to the Jewish

National Council. Maybe that is the source of the confusion. Or maybe his story of military valor is just a myth.

What's the Lesson?

Legends and rumors are easily crafted, and events and people are easily omitted from history. The story of Alperstein is also a reminder of the different ways that different communities tell the same story—in this case, Haganah veterans on the one hand and the Edah Haredit on the other. And, of course, it also tells us how much people, whether religious or not and of all communities, need heroes.

It looks as if we know who Alperstein was and what he did in Meah She'arim in 1929. But several other incidents took place nearby that now require our attention.

The Desecration of the Nabi 'Ukkasha Mosque

Nabi 'Ukkasha is the name of a Muslim tomb and mosque located in the neighborhood of Zikhron Moshe in central Jerusalem, between Strauss and Yeshayahu Streets. 'Ukkasha bin Muhsin was one of the companions (*sahaba*) who gathered around the Prophet Mohammad. 'Ukkasha arrived in Jerusalem with the Islamic army of conquest, then died and was buried in the city. The same compound includes the tomb of Husam al-Din al-Qimari, who arrived in Jerusalem some 500 years later as an officer in Salah a-Din's army. In the 1920s both Jews and Arabs lived in the area, but gradually most of the Arabs moved away. Some of them rented or sold their properties to Jews. The only Muslim family that remained in the immediate area was the family of the imam who preached at the mosque. His relations with his Jewish neighbor, Moshe Mizrahi, were tense—Mizrahi wanted to open a pub in his building. The imam objected, citing a law forbidding the opening of leisure establishments within fifty meters of a house of prayer. The dispute was brought to court in the summer of 1929. In the meantime the disturbances began, and the isolated Muslim site became a target of the hostility of Jews in the surrounding neighborhoods. One group planned to blow it up, but the Haganah commander Yosef Hecht headed them off. Nevertheless, there were further attempts to destroy the mosque. Shlomo Ze'evi—father of Rehavam Ze'evi, later a general in the Israeli Defense Forces and a politician—who was a member of the Jerusalem Jewish Committee, sent two men to guard the compound. The two were David Yellin's son, Avinoam Yellin (who was murdered by an Arab assailant in 1937 while serving as the head of Hebrew education in the British Mandate department of education), and Reuven Ben-Zvi. They seem to have arrived too late. Vandals managed to get into the compound and destroyed part of the mosque, desecrating

Nabi ʿUkkasha Mosque, Jerusalem, August 1929
(Matson Photograph Collection, Library of Congress).

sacred books and curtains (HHA, Yosef Hecht testimony, 98/11; Shlomo Zeʾevi testimony, 21/3).

In a letter to al-Hussayni that can be found in the archives of the Supreme Muslim Council and that was published in the journal *Hawliyat al-Quds* (Hammuda 2011), the imam of the mosque offered a detailed account of the destruction. He added that a large sum of money had been stolen from his home, as well as his store of cheese. Yosef Hecht's testimony corroborates that last allegation: "We found a pantry in the sheikh's house, mostly olives and cheese, and we confiscated it for the benefit of the [Jewish] refugees [from Jerusalem's Old City and Hebron]."

In 1948 the mosque was abandoned, and the Israeli city council of Jerusalem used it for storage. In 1993 the president of the sharia religious court in Jerusalem, Qadi Ahmad Natour, sent a letter to Prime Minister Yitzhak Rabin protesting the neglect that mosques on the west side of the city were suffering. One of them was Nabi ʿUkkasha, which, he said, had become a den of drug addicts and sexual perverts. Ten years later, when the deterioration of the site continued, the Islamic Movement in Israel, led by Sheikh Abdalla Nimer Darwish, petitioned the Israeli Supreme Court — via Adalah, the Legal Center for Arab Minority Rights in Israel (Adalah 2007, 23) — demanding that all abandoned mosques in the country be recognized as holy sites and receive appropriate public funding.

The suit was rejected, but the government promised to allocate funds for preserving and buttressing the mosques and abandoned Muslim cemeteries. In the winter of 2011, Nabi 'Ukkasha was desecrated once again. A Star of David was painted on one of its walls, along with the slogan "A good Arab is a dead Arab." Which takes us back to 1929.

The Death of Hanna Karkar

The story of the discovery of Hanna Karkar's body was recounted to the Shaw Commission by the British policeman William Dove. He related that on the Friday afternoon of the riots he was called on, along with other lawmen present at police headquarters in the Russian compound, to leave their offices and arm themselves. They were driven to the residence of the British high commissioner, which was then located at Mahanayim, a house at the corner of Prophets and St. Paul Streets (St. Paul is today's Shivtei Yisrael Street, and the home that was used then as the high commissioner's temporary residence now houses offices of the Israeli Ministry of Education). They immediately dispersed several dozen Arabs who had gathered there. They were sent northward, where they joined 200 or so Arabs who had gathered in an empty lot across from the entrance to Meah She'arim. Jews stood on the roofs of their homes in the neighborhood and pelted Arabs who approached with stones. Eight British policemen separated the Jews and the Arabs:

> [Dove:] We stood along the Mea Shearim Road facing the Arabs and I heard a shot from behind me. I turned around and saw a Palestinian policeman bending over an Arab who lay against the wall of the shops of the Mea Shearim Quarter.
> [Mr. Silley:] What was the state of this Arab?
> [Dove:] He was in a very bad state. It was obvious he was dying.
> [Mr. Silley:] Was he wounded?
> [Dove:] He was covered with blood but I could not see where he was wounded.
> [Mr. Silley:] What did you do?
> [Dove:] I called the tender, put him in, and took him to Government Hospital. I handed him over to Dr. Sternberg, who examined him as he lay in the tender and said he was dead.
> Chairman: Was he dead?
> [Dove:] The doctor said he was dead; he must have died on the way.
> Mr. Silley: What time was this, do you know?
> [Dove:] I should say about a quarter to one.
> Chairman: How was he injured? You suddenly looked round and saw him on the ground.
> [Dove:] He may have been there before we arrived. The Arabs went away to the

The Shaw Commission, Jerusalem, 1929
(Matson Photograph Collection, Library of Congress).

waste land on our right and we turned our backs to Mea Shearim. He may
have been there and we had not noticed him because we were followed by the
Arabs.

Sir Henry Betterton: Is it not the same case we heard of from Dr. Shammas?

[Dove:] No.

Chairman: How was he injured?

[Dove:] He was covered with blood and dust, I could not say.

[Chairman:] I am trying to identify this incident. Had he been shot?

[Dove:] No, he had not been shot. He was either killed by sticks or stones.

Chairman: This is some incident we have not had.

Mr. Silley: It is. What did you do then?

[Dove:] After I carried the dead body to the doctor he was placed in the mortuary
and we returned to Mea Shearim, the tender driver and myself.

[Mr. Silley:] Now, so far as you know, had there before that been any attack by
Arabs on this quarter?

[Dove:] There were no signs that I could see.

[Mr. Silley:] There were no signs of any attack having been delivered before this?

[Dove:] There may have been an attack but there were no signs of it. (Commission
1930, 1:416)

Hanna Karkar (Courtesy of
the Karkar family, Jerusalem).

Dove's cautious language, here and in the rest of his testimony, was com-
mendable. He explained that he arrived on the scene to block an Arab assault,
but he said that the Arabs were armed only with sticks. He did not see any signs
of a previous Arab attack, but he did not rule out the possibility that there had
been one. He told about shots that were fired at the beginning of the incident by
Jews, about large stones being thrown by Jews from their roofs, and about additional shots fired at the Arabs (we may presume that these were Alperstein's). He
also mentioned improvised bombs that repelled the mob. But he observed that
the man who died might well have been struck down prior to the attack.

The commission's discussions focused on when the Arab was killed. The Jewish member of the panel tried to prove that it had occurred after Jews had already been killed near Jaffa Gate. Dove's testimony indicates an earlier hour. In
other words, the dead Arab mentioned by the British policeman seems to have
been killed before the Arab violence began. We cannot prove this categorically,
and the commission also found itself unable to decide which account was correct (see also a later session, Commission 1930, 2:845–46). In any case, later that
day the dead man's wife identified him, after she arrived at the hospital looking
for him. His name was Hanna Karkar.

Karkar came from Lydda's Arab Orthodox community. A short time before
the riots he had moved to Jerusalem, taking up residence in a compound that
his sect's patriarchate had established in the Old City. He, too, has become a legend. Mustafa al-Far, in *Madinat al-Lidd* (The city of Lydda), numbers Karkar
among the fallen heroes of the "al-Buraq Rebellion" (2009, 369–70). Karkar, al-

Far relates, served as a driver for the British army. When he heard that Jews and Arabs were battling each other and that the British were assisting the Jews, he decided to take matters into his own hands. His British commanders ordered him to drive his truck to Jerusalem, loaded with forty British soldiers designated as reinforcements for the Jewish forces. Karkar drove at high speed and at one of the bends in the road he deliberately flipped his truck over, killing himself and a good portion of the soldiers. He became a symbol of Muslim-Christian solidarity, and al-Far quotes a song that was sung about his act of heroism: "Christians and Muslims are united and ready. The Jews are at the gates — down with the Balfour Declaration."

But this legend has nothing to stand on. Karkar did not work for the British army and didn't drive a truck. He had commercial relations with Jews and had gone to Meah She'arim on business. He largely dismissed the tension then prevailing in the city. Perhaps because he was intent on supporting his family, which had recently grown larger — his third son had been born earlier that year (so his grandson, who bears his name and lives in Jerusalem, told me). Karkar was dressed that day in traditional Arab garb and was thus easily identifiable, so he was beaten to death.

The attorneys for the Arab Executive Committee tried to argue that the murders of Karkar and al-Dajjani, along with other attacks on innocent Arabs, were what set off the riots. The Zionists countered with the claim that the mufti had incited the violence. Placing these two claims side by side serves as a reminder of an important principle that political debates often disregard: explanations of events are generally complementary rather than mutually exclusive. In 1929, the atmosphere was charged as a result of the agitation and provocations surrounding the conflicting Jewish and Arab claims about the Wall. The mufti was not the only figure to engage in provocation — other Muslims advocated violence, as did some groups of Jews. When blood was spilled, passions were stirred up even more. And inflated rumors that the Jews had murdered dozens of Arabs in Jerusalem spread throughout the country, reaching Hebron as well.

3 HEBRON

In which we meet the varied Jews of Hebron and examine their connection to the Zionist movement and their relations with the city's Arabs. We walk through the courtyards in which Arabs slaughtered Jews and stand face to face with the brutality of the murderers and the selflessness of the rescuers. We will read what Hebron Arabs wrote about the slaughter and try to understand what a massacre is. Only the biggest question will remain: Why?

Reports that Arabs had been murdered in Jerusalem reached Hebron on Friday afternoon. Highly exaggerated, the rumors claimed that Jews had killed huge numbers of Muslims. Dozens of Arabs congregated at the Hebron bus station, seeking to ride to Jerusalem to defend their brethren or join the offensive against the city's Jews. The police kept them from setting out. In the meantime, gangs of rioters began roaming through the city, throwing stones at Jewish houses. One of the groups made its way to the Slabodka-Hebron Yeshiva. Yeshivas, seminaries where Jewish men study religious texts and the Talmud in particular, traditionally observe a summer recess in the month of Av, so many of the students had left the city. Others were in their homes, preparing for the Sabbath. Only two diligent prodigies were studying in the yeshiva itself. The attackers entered the seminary's main hall, threw stones, and stabbed to death the younger of the two students, Shmuel Halevy Rosenholtz.

That was the prelude to an anxious night. Then, on Saturday morning, many hundred Arabs from Hebron—known as the City of the Patriarchs—and the surrounding area stormed Jewish homes, breaking into them and killing sixty-six men, women, and children. The massacre lasted for less than two hours. Some of the victims died on the spot. A small number survived a short while before dying of their injuries. Some died instantly, others only after enduring horrible agonies. Some were longtime inhabitants of the city, others newcomers. Some were Ashkenazim, others Sephardim. Sixty-six members of the small

Jewish community in Hebron were murdered, and the survivors were evacuated from the town. It was the beginning of the end of Hebron's ancient community.

The question is, why?

Why?

Why did the Arabs of Hebron kill scores of Jews? How could they slaughter their neighbors and acquaintances in cold blood? Did the stories about what had happened in Jerusalem infuriate them so much that they lost their senses? Was it long-standing hatred of the Jews on the part of Muslims that motivated the carnage? Or were the motives economic? Was it a spontaneous uprising, or had the Arabs of Hebron long been planning this bloody campaign, which claimed as victims both visitors who did not live in the city and long-established residents, among them people who had faithfully tended to the city's Arabs? One example was the pharmacist Ben-Zion Gershon. Here is an account of his murder, from Pinhas Grayevski's *Halaley Bat 'Ami* (The slain of the daughter of my people). It is not easy to read:

> For forty years, this Jew dressed the wounds and treated the illnesses of the most wretched Arabs, generally without asking for any compensation, as he received a salary from the community or from Hadassah. Over his lifetime, this man saved hundreds and thousands of Arabs from dying of diseases of all kinds, from going blind or becoming handicapped. . . . On the day of the riots Arabs broke into the home of this poor Jew, and instead of having mercy on him for being one-legged, they cut off both of his hands. The very same Arabs whose eyes had been cured by him of trachoma and blindness stood over him and gouged out his eyes. The same Arabs whose wives and daughters he had saved from miscarrying and from gynecological illnesses now seized his eldest daughter, raped her, and killed her. They also stabbed his wife four times with a knife and brought a nail-studded club down on her head. (1929, 18)

Why would they have killed Gershon? Why did they kill his friends and neighbors? Why did they rape his daughter? Did they really do these things?

Rapes and Doubts

Any charge of rape should be examined carefully. A. Barzin in *Yizkor 'Am Yisra'el et Kedoshei Av TaRPa"T* (The Jewish people remember the martyrs of 1929) relates that Esther Gershon, Ben-Zion's daughter, had been betrothed some three months before the riots "and began preparing her clothes and belongings for her marriage, which was set for the Sukkot holiday" (1930, 190). But the riots broke out two months before the wedding, and her home was attacked: "Esther struggled valiantly with the murderers, who sought to abuse her. When they were unable to overcome her, they drove knives into her ribs and belly. She died after convulsing for five minutes" (ibid., 191).

According to this account, the bride-to-be grappled with her assailants and managed to prevent herself from being violated. Are there any criteria for preferring one account to the other? Here's yet another description of a rape in Hebron: "And in the Old City, in the 'Jews' Court,' which is the Jewish ghetto, all the homes were looted. . . . One young woman was attacked by Arabs. She fainted. A medical examination proved that thirteen men abused her." The source for this account is *Megilat HaDamim* (The scroll of blood), which memorialized the students of the Hebron Yeshiva (Schwartz 1994, 78). The story is appalling, but it raises questions. Did the author indeed have medical reports available to him? Can doctors determine how many people took part in a gang rape? How likely is it that these details are precise? Or is the writer deliberately exaggerating to make the story even more shocking and terrifying? Should historians endeavor to discern the truth?

We may presume in the case of a massacre in particular, some people will naturally suppress instances of rape even if they in fact occurred, while others will claim that rapes were committed even in the absence of solid facts. Readers of these accounts can ponder what their sources might be and choose which to trust. Arab sources categorically deny the charges that Arab rebels raped Jewish women in 1929 (*Filastin*, September 8, 1929). Ostensibly supporting their claim is the fact that in the series of trials conducted by the government after the riots there was not a single charge of rape, while hundreds of people were accused of murder, assault, and looting. However, these Arab declarations are not based on any thorough investigation of the facts. Rather, the writers seek to present the Arab community as an enlightened one. The British judicial system, for its part, did not show itself to be very effective at investigating the crimes committed during the riots and bringing the perpetrators to justice. The only testimony to be found in an official document that hints at an attempted rape is found in a report that the chief of the Hebron police force, Raymond Cafferata, submitted to the Shaw Commission (Commission 1930, 2:985). Cafferata related that, on entering the Jewish quarter to halt the murders, he found in one house a Jaffan Arab policeman in civilian clothes, 'Issa Sharif, standing with a dagger over a bloody woman. Sharif fled into another room, but Cafferata shot him dead. Was this an exceptional case or evidence of a more widespread phenomenon? We don't know. We have to accept the fact that we have no way of determining all the details about the Hebron massacre, and thus we have no way of determining which accounts are more truthful and which are less. My best guess is that there were instances of rape, but that it was not as widespread as reported in Hebrew-language sources.

Jewish Versions, Arab Versions, and British Versions

Cafferata's testimony casts his own action in heroic terms. He stood against the mob nearly alone, moved with agility from position to position, and repelled the attackers. In appreciation of his work he was awarded a medal. But the Jews of Hebron would have none of this. They reviled the police chief. At the start of the riots he had treated the leaders of the community rudely and derisively. They held him responsible because the riots had broken out on his watch. Furthermore, he had failed to prevent killings that took place before his eyes. One of the most tragic of these was the murder of the Heichal brothers, Eliahu-Dov and Yisrael-Aryeh, who, fleeing the mob, ran up to Cafferata and grabbed his horse—yet were torn away and stabbed to death (Commission 1930, 2:985; Ben-Zion 1970, 416). It may have been such incidents that lay behind the rumors, still accepted as true today by some elderly Hebron Muslims, that Cafferata had both egged on the murderers and killed them as well.

But even disregarding Cafferata's performance, the Hebron riots serve as an illustration of a key point in the reading of history that must be comprehended if Jewish-Arab relations are to be understood. True, in Hebron, as opposed to in Jerusalem, there is no ambiguity whatsoever regarding who the assailants and victims were. Yet Jews and Arabs view the disturbances in entirely different light and write about them in completely different ways. Jewish writing on the riots offers exhaustive, if not always precise, blow-by-blow accounts of the massacre of Hebron's Jews. Palestinian writers show no interest in such details. They do not ask who killed whom and in what way. For the Jews, what happened in Hebron that day was a monstrous slaughter of innocents and a seminal event in the country's history. For the Palestinians, the day's occurrences were just one event in a series of Arab uprisings against the European-Zionist attempt to dispossess them and just some in a series of murders on both sides. Each side remembers primarily its own dead; the killings its own members committed, and under what circumstances they did so, are repressed. That might be quite natural, but it is important to stop for a moment to consider it. Other than in exceptional cases, nations do not perpetuate the memory of massacres they committed, only those committed against them.

The Exceptional Cases

No need to go far to find exceptional cases—we can stay in Palestine. Most of the killings and massacres that Jewish fighters committed against Arabs have been repressed in Israeli society. Yet two specific events have won a place in Israeli—not just Palestinian—collective memory, to the point that they get mentioned in Israeli school books. They are the killing of inhabitants of the village of Deir Yasin in April 1948 by Jewish fighters and the slaughter of dozens of the inhabitants of Kafer Qasim, all of them Israeli citizens, by Israeli Border Guard troops in October 1956.

Such incidents do not get imprinted on the national memory automatically. The war crimes committed by Jewish militias in Deir Yasin became common knowledge in Israel mostly because of internal rivalries in the Jewish community. The Haganah and Jewish Agency wanted to discredit Etzel and Lehi and thus accused them of carrying out the massacre. In the process, the number of victims was inflated to about 250 — by all sides. Etzel and Lehi wanted to terrify the Arabs; the Jewish Agency sought to vilify the breakaway militias; and the Palestinian Arab leadership wanted military aid from the Arab states and international protection against the brutality of the Jews. Decades passed before the Palestinian historian Sharif Kana'na examined the records and put the number of dead at about 100 (Kana'na and Zaitawi 1987). Some of these were killed during the battle between Jewish and Arab forces that took place in the village, others during the mop-up operation when the village was taken by Jewish forces, and still others were killed in cold blood after the fighting was already over.

The Kafer Qasim massacre entered Israeli discourse through the front door. It is studied by Israeli high-school students and by cadets in the Israeli Defense Forces (IDF) officers' course. The purposes of such instruction is to set moral standards for future Israeli soldiers and commanders and to convey to soldiers that decisions about who to kill and when are to be made by the country's leadership and not by each army unit on its own. But these are the exceptions that prove the rule: for the most part, in all wars, including the Israel-Palestinian conflict, massacres are forgotten by the side that committed them and memorialized by their victims. That is the case, for example, with the massacres that Arab forces committed against a convoy of medical personnel on its way to Hadassah Hospital in Jerusalem and at Kibbutz Kfar Etzion in the spring of 1948, and the massacres the IDF committed in Arab villages in the Galilee when that area was taken in the autumn of that same year. Such incidents are remembered by and large only by the victims. Why? It's not only a matter of deliberate, official efforts to commemorate a nation's own victims and relegate those of the other side to oblivion, as many people mistakenly think. There's a much simpler reason: people feel intense pain when someone close to them dies, and much less pain, if any, when a person distant in time, space, and ethnicity is killed (especially if that person belongs to an enemy nation). Thus in cases of massacres against one's own people, or one's own friends and relatives, the great pain becomes part of the group's collective memory.

Deir Yasin: 1929 and 1948

A few days following the riots, *Haʾaretz* (September 11, 1929) called on the British to impose collective punishment on Deir Yasin, just as they had done with other villages. According to contemporary Jewish reports, several dozen inhabitants of Deir Yasin took part in 1929 in attacks on the nearby Jewish neighborhoods of Givʿat Shaʾul and Beit HaKerem:

> At 2:30 [on Friday, August 23], some 30–40 Arabs were seen on the descent from Deir Yasin opposite us. They went down into the valley and prepared for an assault. A group of Jewish defenders hid at a corner on the slope down from Beit HaKerem and began to shoot at them, without hitting any. . . . The exchange of gunfire continued until 8:30. In the meantime, several machine guns arrived with the English army. A machine gun was set up and opened fire in the direction of Deir Yasin. The soldiers took a local car, drove to the village, and opened fire on Arabs and then came back . . . on the Jewish side several were wounded over Friday and Saturday in Givʿat Shaʾul. One (Yaʾakov Leib Dimentstein) was badly wounded and died. (Amikam 1929, 28–29)

What happened in the village after Jewish forces took it in April 1948 can be seen as a response to what happened in 1929. Etzel's deputy commander of the operation in Deir Yasin, Yehuda Lapidot, wrote the entry on the 1929 riots for the online Hebrew encyclopedia *Daʿat*. (Lapidot n.d.). In his account, Deir Yasin played a central role in the 1929 riots. The founder of the Kach movement, Meir Kahane, defended the massacre committed in the village, claiming that "Arabs from Deir Yasin led and organized the attack [on Jewish neighborhoods in western Jerusalem in 1929], but the village became world famous only twenty years later, in 1948, when it received its payback for the many Jews its inhabitants killed" (Kahane 1980).

Kahane exaggerated. The people of Deir Yasin did not kill "many Jews," as Kahane claimed—only Dimentstein. In any case, here again is another example of inaccuracy, as well as evidence of the effect that the Arab attacks of 1929 had on Jewish fighters in 1948. We will see further examples of this below.

Comparing Massacres

Comparisons can offer a view of the common parameters of different events. While massacres committed by Arabs, Jews, Latin American dictators, American forces in Vietnam, or the Stalinist regime might all be different, they all have one thing in common: the slaughter of defenseless people. And in general, the slaughterers present their actions as necessary for their self-defense. For the most part, they seem to really believe this. And that is connected to the reason why the massacre in Hebron is not and cannot be a seminal event in Palestinian consciousness.

Why Not?

Because, as we saw in chapter 1, people's fundamental, overarching view of the world determines how they perceive historical details. And in the Palestinian conception of history, the massacre in Hebron is a small part of a larger campaign of self-defense. This is not to say that all Palestinians see it the same way. Some completely ignore the massacre, others see it as an act of heroism, and still others are pained by the human suffering it caused. And, of course, some of Hebron's Arabs rescued Jews during the riots, an act much more important than any condemnation of or statement about the massacre. The different attitudes derive from the opposing ways in which Jews and Arabs perceive the larger arc of events in Palestine or Israel. A typical example of this can be seen in the following two passages on the riots. The first comes from *Ha'aretz* and the second from *Filastin*. Here is *Ha'aretz*:

> It was not we who set the fire
> It was not we who sought blood and loot
> It was not we who set man against man, community against community.
> We were attacked everywhere, city and country. (September 2, 1929)

This was a response to a week of bloodshed. It is of interest because just a week before the riots, *Ha'aretz* had harshly condemned "the fanners of flames in both camps" (August 18, 1929), and because the editors knew of the lynchings that Jews had committed against Arabs in Jerusalem and of the murder of the 'Awn family by Hinkis. In other words, the editors knew that it wasn't true that "we" had been attacked in all cases. But they preferred to publish a declaration that accorded with the image of the Yishuv that they sought to paint. They did so by offering their readers a picture in black and white.

Ten days later an editorial in *Filastin* responded to Chaim Weizmann's declaration that, after reparations were paid, it might be possible to reach an understanding with the Arabs:

> What kind of reparations do you expect after treacherously murdering Arab women and children and stirring up these disturbances, in which you used rifles and pistols and bombs against people bearing only sticks and stones?
>
> What sort of understanding do you expect with the nation you are trying to eject from its country, on the grounds that it is the Land of Israel? Can there be understanding between an assailant and his victim? Between a homeowner and a burglar who has broken into his home? Between the murdered and the murderer with blood dripping from his fingers? . . .
>
> O naïve Jews, hear the last word of the Arabs. No understanding between you and us is possible without the revocation of the Balfour Declaration. There will be no

understanding until you understand that Palestine is not part of wild Africa, and that murdering people [here] is not easy like in Rhodesia and the other countries inhabited by Negroes, who evince no resistance. (September 12, 1929)

This passage presents the common Arab view of the riots quite clearly. It states who the aggressor is (the Zionists), who the victim is (the Arabs), and who created the animosity between them (the British), putting everything in the context of colonialism. That is the general framework; within it the Jews are charged with inciting the riots by killing women and children. Is that accurate? Not really. But, as with *Haʾaretz*, it is a general value system and worldview that informs *Filastin*'s articles and editorials, not historical details.

Within this general perceptual and emotional context, there is no real discussion of the killing of defenseless people. Questions about the murder of Gershon, the pharmacist; the brutality of his killers; and the murders of dozens of other Jews in Hebron seem trivial. Such details become dim within the larger picture, in which ideology outshines massacres. But such a way of thinking is not unique to the Palestinian Arabs. It is the way in which massacres are almost always viewed by their perpetrators.

Massacre: A Definition

The study of massacres presents many serious difficulties, according to Jacques Semelin (2007). One is emotional. Most scholars cannot but be shocked by the deeds they are researching, which makes it difficult for them to analyze events dispassionately. Another obstacle is presented by the nature of massacres: they seem to be devoid of logic and impervious to justification. How, then, can they be fit into a causal framework? Nevertheless, Semelin writes, it is important to understand the political, economic, and cultural conditions that give rise to such events.

First of all, however, the term "massacre" has to be defined. Semelin's analysis leads to the following definition: A massacre is the murder of defenseless people in a distinct time and place, when the killers are not in danger. Everyone can agree on this, but it leaves some questions unanswered. How many victims does it take for a killing to become a massacre? Semelin quotes other scholars to the effect that, under certain circumstances, the murder of a single person can be considered a massacre. He notes that human rights organizations in Guatemala have decided that the murder of as few as three people, in accordance with the above definition, constitutes a massacre. A seminal event in American history, the Boston Massacre, had only five victims. Others place the minimum at ten.

Another question: How proximate does the danger to the attackers have to be for killings not to be considered a massacre? This comes with a subsidiary question, because in many cases massacres include acts like cutting off limbs, rape, and other abuses. Are such acts a necessary component of a massacre — that is, if they do not occur, does that mean the act is not a massacre? Another element is the physical proximity of the murderers and their victims. Some definitions of "massacre" restrict the word's application to cases in which the murderers are located in the same place as their victims and do not use firearms but rather knives, clubs, and axes. Others maintain that all killing of defenseless people should be classified as a massacre, including, for example, the bombing of civilian populations from the air.

And for Our Purposes?

The events in Hebron in 1929 fit even the most restrictive definition of the term "massacre." Unlike the lynchings in Jerusalem and the attacks in the Tel Aviv–Jaffa area, where there were roughly equal numbers of Jews and Arabs and both sides were armed to one extent or another, in Hebron the Jews numbered just a few hundred and lived among the tens of thousands of Muslims who populated the city and its hinterland. And except for a single pistol in the possession of Eliezer Dan Slonim, held for self-defense, the Jews were not armed.

Here is another detailed account of a kind that cannot be found in the Palestinian literature. It tells what happened to the Slonim family of Hebron on that horrible Sabbath in August 1929:

> And here — hundreds of murderers also surround the home of E. D. [Eliezer Dan] Slonim, charging at it furiously. The air reverberates with a horrifying and ghastly scream, a long, fearsome wail drenched in despair. Here, in this house, some seventy people have found refuge, students at the yeshiva and heads of families, who thought this to be the safest place, because E. D. Slonim, may his memory be a blessing, was very much respected by the Arabs, as manager of the Anglo-Palestine Bank, whose principal customers were Arabs. . . .
>
> They [the Arabs] pelted the house with stones for about fifteen minutes. A terrible, horrifying, heartbreaking scream was interwoven with the voices of the murderers and deafened the ear. But suddenly a hole appeared in the door and shots thundered. A bullet hit the hand of Mr. Y. Yaini. A second bullet struck the face of Mr. H. Volansky and injured him severely. He fell in a pool of his own blood. A bullet sliced through the belly of the yeshiva student Yisrael-Mordechai Kaplan and inflicted a deadly wound . . . horrific calls of "*Shema Yisrael*" accompanied by despairing cries and howls shook the house . . . but now the murderers broke into the house through the roof. The yeshiva students Dov Lipin and Alter Sher, who held the door [to the roof] shut until the last minute and faced the murderers as they broke into the house[,] fell dead on the stairs. At the same moment the main door was also

broken down. Mr. E. D. Slonim fired his pistol. An iron rod landed powerfully on his head, the pistol dropped from his hand, and he fell in a pool of his own blood. The silence of death filled the house. . . .

In this house, the Slonim house, twenty-four people were killed and thirteen injured, many of them severely. Many inhabitants of Hebron, storekeepers and heads of families, friends and acquaintances of E. D. Slonim, took part in this brutal slaughter. (Ben-Zion 1970, 413–14)

The Slonim home was the principal site of the slaughter: more than a third of the victims killed in Hebron died there. Thought to be a refuge, it became a death trap. The man who was perceived as "very much respected by the Arabs" was killed on the spot. *Sefer Hevron* (The Hebron book), from which this passage is taken, relates that leading Arabs offered him protection if he would turn over the yeshiva students, the foreigners, who were in his house, but he chose to die with his fellow Jews rather than to hand them over. "We Jews," he told the Arabs, "are not like the Muslims. We are a single nation. There are no foreigners among us" (Ben-Zion 1970, 412).

Sefer Hevron

Sefer Hevron was edited by Oded Avisar, scion of an old Hebron family. The members of the Jewish community that had fled Hebron decided to write the book at a meeting they held in Jerusalem in 1958, when Hebron was under Jordanian rule. The volume would serve as a memorial book, similar to those produced by survivors from Jewish communities that had been destroyed in the Holocaust, Avisar said at this gathering. Testimonies and documents were slowly gathered, and money to produce the book was collected. Twelve years later, when the project was completed and the book published, Hebron was under Israeli rule, and it was one of the first sites of Israeli settlement in the territories occupied in 1967.

David Ben-Gurion was asked to write the introduction to the book. Under the title "Jerusalem's Sister," Ben-Gurion quoted and explicated biblical verses relating to Hebron. He concluded with the statement: "We would be making a horrible and terrible mistake if we did not settle Hebron, Jerusalem's neighbor and predecessor, with a large and growing Jewish community within the shortest period of time." And in the spirit of traditional Zionism he added: "It will also benefit the Arab neighbors (Ben-Gurion 1970, 15).

1929 and the Reestablishment of Hebron's Jewish Community

It would be hard to say that the reestablishment of a Jewish community in Hebron in 1968, and its subsequent expansion, has been a blessing for the city's

Arabs. It's doubtful whether it has been a blessing for the Jews. Whatever the case, the founders of the new community directly linked their initiative to the events of 1929. On the fortieth anniversary of the massacre, the following advertisement appeared in the Hebrew press: "On the Sabbath, 18 Av, forty years ago, the Hebron martyrs were slaughtered. Today, too, the city produces many terrorists. Only a large-scale Jewish settlement has a chance of changing the face of the city. The heritage of our nation's forefathers and the cries of the martyrs obligate the builder-sons of the state of Israel" (quoted in Avisar 1970a, 495). Let's set aside the use of the massacre as a justification for Jewish settlement in the city after 1967 and return to the event itself, that Saturday in 1929, and the fundamental, primal question: Why?

The Palestinian Version of the Question

In the words of Tareq al-Ja'bari, a student at Hebron University who wrote a master's thesis titled "Thawrat 'Am 1929 wa-Majriyyat Ahdathiha fi al-Khalil" (The 1929 uprising and the progress of events in Hebron): "And here we face a great question: The Jews of Hebron, on the eve of the events of 1929, were manifestly religious Jews who did not share the Zionist appetite for expansion, and whose relations with the inhabitants of Hebron were characterized by cooperation and acceptance. What, then, caused the inhabitants of Hebron to disregard the good neighborly relations that they had granted the Jews, to rise up against them 'in savage acts of murder, and to carry out a great slaughter against the city's Jews,' as the high commissioner put it?" (1999, 10).

Ja'bari paraphrases the words of High Commissioner John Chancellor in the first proclamation he issued after the massacre (JTA, September 3) and offers his readers a British perspective on the events. In the introduction to his thesis he stresses that he writes out of a sense of national duty and hostility to Zionism, but he is also committed to the truth. His study, he says, is not meant to be an apology to the Jews, but neither is his purpose to justify the acts of his forebears. This is a fairly common genre of historical writing (*Sefer Toldot HaHaganah* is another example): an attempt at factual precision without undermining the fundamental truths of the writer's national discourse. Ja'bari also asks: Why?

Why It's So Hard to Explain: A Proposal

Ja'bari asks the question, but his study does not include the graphic depictions of atrocities that appear in the Hebrew accounts, nor does he try to explain them. Why? Because they can't be explained. How can one explain why a human being would castrate an elderly rabbi? How can you explain why a group of men rapes a girl? Maybe no explanation should be attempted. Or maybe it is beyond the competence of the historian to do so. I suggest the following way of looking at the Hebron massacre and massacres in general: they have two levels, or two kinds of acts. One kind is "normal" acts of killing that grow out of the collective desire of a specific group to strike out at its enemies. The second is acts of perverted brutality carried out by individuals who take the opportunity presented by the conflict to act out their twisted desires. Members of the aggressor group will not necessarily, even at the remove of a generation or more, criticize the killing itself, which they see as motivated by their collective's interests. At the same time, they will choose to disregard atrocities because these, in their view, are not true expressions of the will of their collective but rather aberrations used by the enemy to vilify their legitimate struggle. Ja'bari, like other Palestinian scholars, takes a general view of the event, seeing both the killing and the acts of rescue while disregarding the difficult details.

Before delving into his explanations, let me present the explanation offered by another resident of Hebron. Actually, he lives in Kiryat Arba, the Jewish settlement established adjacent to Hebron shortly after the West Bank was occupied by Israel in the 1967 war. Elyakim Haetzni was born in Germany in 1926; served as a member of the Knesset for a short time in the early 1990s; was a leading member of the Yesha Council, the coordinating body of Israeli settlements in the West Bank and Gaza Strip; and was an activist in the reestablishment of the Jewish community in Hebron.

Haetzni's Explanation

In 1999, Haetzni published an article in which he termed the willingness to make concessions to the Arabs in peace negotiations as the "1929 syndrome." He offered this historical explanation for the Hebron massacre:

> Somewhere there is a list of all human material and spiritual pleasures: love and hatred, eating and sex, gratitude and revenge, construction and destruction and, very high on the list, the spilling of Jewish blood. A day-old Jewish baby has something that many in the alien world around him lust for: Jewish blood. In many cases it is an uncontrollable urge. Consequently, a person who holds within him this most desirable fluid and who wishes to live must be suspicious, cautious, and always alert to keep his blood, that is, his life, in a vault where there are no illusions and great clarity of vision, and his country needs to be armed to the teeth and not to make any allowances for anyone, especially in the matter of territory, for any payment, including that of "peace": "and guard your lives very well" [Deut. 4:15]. (Haetzni 1999, 35)

The passage expresses Haetzni's view that anti-Jewish sentiments and the thirst for Jewish blood are existential characteristics of non-Jews. They are primal urges that motivate gentiles no matter what the Jews do. The 1929 riots served as proof of his claim. He had, he related, often spoken with his Arab neighbors in Hebron about the riots. He offered an account of one such conversation, with a man "who spoke honestly":

> In a quiet and straightforward way the man told me that, in fact, the Arab majority had indeed lived for many years in peace and quiet with the small Jewish community, although [the Arabs] kept [the Jews] on a short leash and saw to it that "they [did] not get uppity." He did not say why it had to be that way, and I didn't ask. But, he added, when a yeshiva established itself in the city (the Slabodka-Hebron Yeshiva) a few years before 1929, and brought in students even from the United States, the Arabs felt that the Zionist menace had reached Hebron and decided to put an end to it. . . . I did not bother to ask why, if that were the case, they slaughtered and destroyed and expelled a non-Zionist Jewish community, because it was clear from what the man said that in his view the difference between one Jew and another was meaningless. Had I asked, he would not have understood my question. (ibid, 32–33)

Comprehending Questions, Comprehending Answers

The reply made by this Arab, who is not given a name or an identity, in fact contradicts in every detail the assumptions made by Haetzni. The Arab makes clear distinctions between Jews — specifically, between the established Jewish community and the new immigrants who had arrived in the city. He displays no thirst for Jewish blood and relates that the Muslims of Hebron had no problem coexisting with the small Jewish community of the town. Furthermore, the Arab speaker offered a rational (if certainly disputable) reason for the attack on Hebron's Jews — the decision by the Slabodka Yeshiva to relocate from Lithuania to Hebron, along with its students and their families. He understood the move as part and parcel of the Zionist project of seizing control of Palestine, and he was very much aware that the move was supported by the old Jewish community. This is a preliminary, partial, and possibly insufficient answer to our difficult fundamental question. Note that Haetzni simply ignores it. He senses the sincerity of his interlocutor, but he does not pause to comprehend the answer he has been offered. And he does not continue the conversation.

Why does Haetzni stick to the position he held before the conversation rather than attend to the answer he was given? What causes him to conclude that the Arab was incapable of understanding his questions? We can suggest three reasons. The first is his position that the gentiles thirst for Jewish blood without any connection to historical circumstances. If that is the case, then explanations grounded in historical context are invalid a priori. The second reason has to do with the natural human revulsion that Semelin points to — the difficulty of accepting rational explanations for massacres (especially for people who are not on the killing side). The third reason is the inability to listen to an Arab explanation that is detached from the Jewish point of view. In this case, Haetzni cannot accept the Arab identification of the yeshiva with the Zionist enterprise, because according to standard Zionist criteria it is crystal clear that the yeshiva was not Zionist.

Slabodka, the Mussar Movement, and the Land of Israel

The Knesses Yisrael Yeshiva, better known as the Slabodka Yeshiva, after the town near Kovno where it was located, was founded in about 1880. Its founders and teachers developed a unique ethical philosophy they called Gadlut HaAdam (greatness of person), the central principle of which was a focus on a person's good traits rather than his or her bad ones. According to this outlook, a human being had the right and even an obligation to enjoy life in this world, within the framework of Jewish law.

The unstable political situation in Lithuania following World War I prompted the seminary's leaders to move it to the Holy Land. An exceptional decision for the time, it was motivated in part by fundraising considerations — the assumption was that it would be easier to solicit donations for a yeshiva in the Land of Israel than in the United States. But there was also a spiritual and national motive: one of the institution's leading rabbis, Moshe Mordechai Epstein, was a member of the proto-Zionist organization Hibbat Tzion and believed that Jews were enjoined by their faith to settle in the land of their fathers.

The news of the yeshiva's planned move quickly spread throughout the Jewish world. Hundreds of former students and students at other yeshivas asked to join in the move but were turned down, mainly for financial reasons. Teachers and students mulled over whether the yeshiva's new home should be Jerusalem, Tel Aviv, Petah Tikva, or Hebron. Tel Aviv was too secular, they felt, and Jerusalem's Haredim did not want them, believing the yeshiva to be dangerously influenced by modern ideas and practices — such as shaving. In the meantime, Slonim lobbied hard for Hebron and persuaded the Knesses Yisrael administration to relocate the yeshiva to the City of the Patriarchs, along with 130 students. The yeshiva opened its doors in Hebron in 1925, and by 1929 it had 194 single and married students. Most of these intended to devote their lives to Torah study. A small number were the sons of Lithuanian Jewish families living in the United States who wanted their young men to receive a yeshiva education before embarking on careers (Tikochinsky 2009). The newcomers injected new life into the shrinking Jewish community of Hebron.

Shrinking Hebron

As the Jewish community throughout Palestine grew in the early twentieth century, the Hebron community disintegrated. Consider the numbers: In 1890,

The Sephardi Synagogue,
Hebron, August 1929
(Matson Photograph
Collection, Library
of Congress).

1,429 Jews lived in Hebron—810 Sephardim and 619 Ashkenazim. By 1923, just
before the yeshiva's relocation, there were only 413 Jews, 306 Sephardim and
107 Ashkenazim (Avisar 1970c, 71–72). Some of them had moved to the big city,
Jerusalem, or elsewhere in Palestine. Others had been compelled to leave the
country during World War I because they were citizens of countries that were at
war with the Ottoman Empire. Still others went overseas, mostly to the United
States and Australia, in search of a better life for themselves and their children.
This was the situation that prompted Slonim to write: "Hebron Must Be Saved"
(*Ha'aretz*, July 10, 1924).

Slonim was twenty-five years old when he published his call to action. Like
his father Ya'akov Yosef before him, he launched a career as a public figure and
writer at a young age. His campaign to bring the yeshiva to the city was not what
might have been expected of him, as his family belonged to the Chabad sect of
Hasidim. The Lithuanian yeshivas were the intellectual centers of opposition
to the Hasidic movement, and the rivalry was fierce, involving at times excom-
munications and even violence. Hebron's Jewish community, divided between
Sephardim and Chabad Ashkenazim, now added a third element, a Lithuanian
yeshiva.

Chabad and Hebron

In the nineteenth century, Hebron was the center of Chabad Hasidism in the Holy Land. Most of the members of the sect who lived in Palestine were in Hebron, and they constituted a majority of the city's Ashkenazi Jewish population. That had not always been the case.

As the Hasidic movement became consolidated in Eastern Europe in the second half of the eighteenth century, small numbers of its devotees began arriving in the Holy Land. In 1777 several of the movement's leaders arrived there, with a number of followers and hangers-on. Numbering about 200 in all, they settled in the Galilee and established the Hasidic community in the Land of Israel. At the beginning of the nineteenth century, Chabad found itself in conflict with the rest of the Hasidic community for both religious and financial reasons. As a result, some fifteen Chabad families left Safed in the Galilee and settled in Hebron alongside the Sephardi community, which had arrived and integrated itself into the city following the Spanish expulsion in 1492 (Yaari 1960). This took place while the founder and leader of the Chabad movement, Rabbi Schneur Zalman of Liadi, author of the philosophical and mystical work *Tanya*, was still alive. In the generation that followed, his son and successor, Dov-Ber, known as the Mittler (middle) Rebbe, sent more of his followers to Hebron, and in 1845 his daughter, Menuha Rachel Slonim, arrived and came to be known as the "mother of the Ashkenazi Yishuv in Hebron." Chabad had become the largest Ashkenazi community in the city. And, as in Europe, it stood at the forefront of the fight against Zionism.

Chabad and Zionism

At the time the Zionist idea began spreading through the Jewish communities of Eastern Europe, the admor of Chabad was Shalom Ber Schneurson (1860–1920), the fifth in the movement's line of leaders. A fierce opponent of the new political movement, he viewed Zionism as a great menace, a movement that had as its goal severing the connection between the Jewish people and God. He considered Zionism opposed to Jewish religious law, halakha. His source text for this position was a passage in the Babylonian Talmud in which the sage Rabbi Yosi bar Hanina relates that, when the Jewish people went into exile, God imposed two oaths on the Jews and one on the gentile nations to which the Jews were sent into exile: "One, that Israel shall not go up [all together as if surrounded] by a wall; the second, that whereby the Holy One, blessed be He, adjured Israel that they shall not rebel against the nations of the world; and the third is that whereby the Holy One, blessed be He, adjured the idolaters that they shall not oppress Israel too much." The simple understanding of the passage is that the Jews must not seek to hasten the messianic redemption — that is, must not return collectively to the Land of Israel—by force, and that it must accept the yoke of foreign rule by not rebelling against the gentile nations. On the face of it, Zionism, the central doctrine of which was collective action to settle Jews in the Land of Israel, seemed to violate these two oaths and was thus opposed to the divine will. The Chabad admor was not the only important rabbi to take this position—so did Rabbi Yoel Moshe Teitelbaum, the admor of Satmar, and many others. Religious Zionists offered a variety of explanations for why their movement did not violate these oaths. One of them, for example, was the argument that the endorsement by the League of Nations of the establishment of a Jewish national home in Palestine meant that the Zionists were not rebelling against the gentile nations. The anti-Zionists had responses to these justifications, one of which was that what was important was the opinion of the gentiles living in and around the Holy Land, not that of the League of Nations. This is not the place to delve deeper into this dispute. What is important for us is that the Chabad community in Hebron was firmly opposed to both Zionism and the Western enlightenment.

Examples of this abounded in the city's daily life. The Zionist group Tze'irei Hevron (Young Hebron, composed mostly, but not solely, of young Sephardim) tried to establish a modern Jewish school in the city under the aegis of the French-Jewish Alliance Française, which ran such schools in other cities in Palestine and the Middle East. Chabad stymied the plans. Following the death of the founder of the Zionist movement, Theodor Herzl, in the summer of 1904, the members of Tze'irei Hevron wanted to hold a memorial service for him; the city's rabbis refused to allow it. Tze'irei Hevron sponsored free evening classes for the Jewish community's young people and opened a lending library. A Sephardi rabbi, Haim Hizkiya Medini, came out against both the classes and the library, as did the city's Chabad rabbis, led by Rabbi Shlomo Leib Eliezerov.

Rabbi Eliezerov

Eliezerov was born in Latvia to the Kazarnovsky family and came to Hebron in 1873, when he was ten years old. He was a member of a prominent Chabad family, closely connected to the Slonim. He changed his family name to Eliezerov, in honor of his father Eliezer, during a period he spent in Bukhara as an emissary of the admor. He served as Hebron's Ashkenazi rabbi in the decade before World War I. During the war he went back to Bukhara, and he returned to Palestine after the British occupation. But not to Hebron—the Chabad community there had collapsed during the war. Instead, he settled in Jerusalem. Settling in the Bukharan quarter, he generally attended prayer services at that neighborhood's Musayoff Synagogue. He was famous for the enthusiasm with which he recited the standard morning blessing in which observant Jews thank God for not making them gentiles (Halperin 1980, 225). Singling out this blessing for particular devotion reflected Chabad's emphasis on the ties that connect all Jews and Jewish superiority to non-Jews.

Back to the Question of Zionism

To advance the fight against Zionism and *maskilim*—the advocates of Jewish enlightenment inspired by the secularizing and rational trends in Western European culture—the admor of Chabad ordered, on the eve of World War I, the establishment of a Chabad yeshiva in Hebron—in Hebron and not in Jerusalem (Ratzabi 1996, 84; Landau 1985). The yeshiva opened its doors in 1912 in a building known as the Romano House, after the wealthy Turkish-Jewish family that had built it forty years previously. The family had come on hard times and put the property up for sale. Competition for the house was intense—interested buyers included the house's Arab neighbors, Christian missionaries, and the Alliance Française, which wanted to open a modern school there. But the Chabad community beat the others and celebrated its victory over the gentiles and, in particular, over Zionist and secular Jewish influence. This brings us back to our core question: if the Jewish community in Hebron opposed Zionism, why were the Arabs so upset?

What Did the Arabs Want?

To sum up: the Chabad community in Hebron stood in the vanguard of the battle against Zionism, and the Slabodka Yeshiva stood aloof from it. Why, then, were their members attacked by the Arabs? Why did Muslims cease to view these anti-Zionist Jews as protected minorities (*ahl al-dhimma*), as they had in the past? It's the question that both Ja'bari and Haetzni ask. The question is a vitally important one, and, taking a long view, here is a possible answer: True, the "Torah world" in Eastern Europe and in Palestine's Jewish community stood opposed to Zionism. While the Zionist movement advocated what its members called the "productivization" of the Yishuv—that is, the idea that the Yishuv should, through its own labors, support itself—the Old Yishuv, as the religious community was called, continued to live off donations from Jewish communities abroad. While the Zionist movement aspired to establish a national home, Chabad and other religious groups rejected the modern national idea. While the Zionist movement was strongly influenced by socialism, liberalism, and other European schools of thought, the Old Yishuv—both Hasidim and Lithuanians—rejected all Western ideologies. The secular Zionist deprecation of religious observance was a horrible sacrilege for the Haredim. For the Zionists, religious Jews were stuck in the past, but many rabbis perceived adherence to tradition as the ideal way to live until the coming of the Messiah.

That gap sounds unbridgeable. But it only sounds that way. The lines between the Zionist movement and its Jewish opponents were not in fact that sharply drawn. Just as the tension between the established Sephardi population and the socialist pioneers did not outweigh their common Jewish identity, either to themselves or to the Arabs, so the differences between the "secular" Jews of the Zionist movement and the movement's Orthodox opponents did not override what they had in common. Jews differed about religious observance, the need for political activism, and the place of religion in public life. But as fundamental as these divisions were in intra-Jewish discourse, they were dwarfed by the consensus regarding their people's position in relation to the non-Jewish world and to the Land of Israel. There were some things that all kinds of Jews shared, that shaped the attitude of Palestinian Arabs to the country's Jews, that blurred the distinction between Zionists and non-Zionists and led the Arabs to view all Jews as a single public. Zionists and Haredim all agreed that: (1) the Jewish people are a nation, not just a religion; (2) Jewish history is continuous — that the Jews of today are the heirs of the nation founded by the patriarch Abraham and by Moses; (3) the Jewish people have a profound connection with the Land of Israel, anchored in the Bible, whether that is seen as a historical or a sacred work; (4) no matter what their differences, Jews are responsible for one another, in particular during troubled times; (5) the purchase of land and the construction of homes, institutions, and new communities in the Land of Israel is legitimate, necessary, and praiseworthy; (6) Jewish learning, whether traditional or cultural, and however balanced with labor, is essential to Jewish life; and (7) in the end, whether in the messianic age or sooner, the Jews will be sovereign in their land, and it is the responsibility of Jews to further this end, whether by spiritual or practical means.

It should be no surprise, then, that for the Arabs of Palestine — who rejected the right, whether secular or religious, of the Jews to sovereignty in Palestine in the present or in the future — the distinction between Zionists and non-Zionists looked ephemeral. While to the Jews themselves this split seemed earthshaking, even unbridgeable, from the outside, to the Arabs, the two groups looked at best like barely distinguishable shades within one large Jewish public. The battle within the Yishuv over women's suffrage, the debate over holding a memorial service for Herzl, and the "language wars" over the use of the Hebrew language in everyday discourse (just to offer a few examples) meant nothing to the Arabs of Hebron and to the Arabs of Palestine as a whole. There was one big fact that united all the Jews, whether Iraqi rabbis, North African immigrants, socialist pioneers, Hasidim, Central European intellectuals, national extremists, Maghrebi fishermen, or Zionist functionaries — they all wanted to expand the Jewish population and to turn Palestine into a Jewish homeland. Even if not all of them saw the goal as the establishment of a Jewish state, and if not all of them viewed the

Arabs as enemies, their activities, taken together, looked to the Arabs of Palestine as a menace to them, a menace that seemed all the more dire following the Balfour Declaration and the British conquest.

Haredi Immigration as Alternative to Zionism

The view that the Slabodka-Hebron Yeshiva was a Zionist institution, even though it did not see itself as such, is a cornerstone of a study by Shehada al-Rajabi at al-Najah University in 2000, titled *Al-Jaliya al-Yahudiyya fi al-Khalil 1917–1936* (The Jewish community in Hebron, 1917–1936). Al-Rajabi, a native of Hebron, discussed the massacre committed against Hebron's Jews using a wide variety of both Jewish and Arab sources, including interviews with elderly people in Hebron and documents from the Central Zionist Archives. He concludes that the Slabodka Yeshiva's move to Hebron was manifestly Zionist in nature and was initiated by Zionist figures in Hebron, chief among them Eliezer Dan Slonim and his father Ya'akov Yosef Slonim. Al-Rajabi's conclusion is diametrically opposed to Haetzni's view and seems to be more solidly grounded. In his study of the yeshiva, Shlomo Tikochinsky, an Israeli scholar, relates that on arriving in Hebron, the seminary's students began studying the laws of the Temple and its sacrifices. Yitzhak Sapir, grandson of Rabbi Slonim, also writes that in the 1920s the Hebron community integrated Zionism with a Haredi lifestyle (Tikochinsky 2009, 198–99; Sapir 2006).

For Example, Rabbi Eliahu Mani

The fuzzy lines between Haredi and Zionist were exemplified by many members of the Old Yishuv in Palestine as a whole and in Hebron in particular. Take Rabbi Eliahu Mani, who arrived from Baghdad in 1848. After moving to the Holy Land, he purchased land in Hebron and its environs with the purpose of strengthening the city's Jewish community. In this activity he received support from Rabbi Yehuda Alkalai, a proto-Zionist thinker. Mani also disregarded the Ashkenazi-Mizrahi divide and worked hand in hand with Rabbi Akiva Schlesinger, a Haredi rabbi who had moved to Jerusalem from Hungary (Mani 1970, 103).

And Rabbi Ya'akov Yosef Slonim

Rabbi Slonim was born in 1880, during the golden age of Hebron's Jewish community that dawned as a result of the work of leaders like Mani. But by the time he was a teenager the community was fading, both materially and spiritually. He worked hard to shore it up. In his early days as a public figure, at the end of the nineteenth century, he tried to persuade Zionist institutions to help Hebron's Jews make their livelihood as farmers.

When the Chabad yeshiva in Hebron opened in 1912, Slonim, a descendant of Rabbi Schneur Zalman of Liadi, was appointed its secretary. Despite Chabad's anti-Zionism, Slonim maintained connections with Zionist institutions and gave his son Eliezer Dan a general as well as a Jewish education. In the years around World War I, he searched for land that could be purchased and settled, working in coordination with Zionist land-purchasing organizations. Following the British conquest, he helped gather intelligence on Hebron's Arabs and engaged in covert political activity. Among his projects was the founding of National Muslim Associations, Palestinian Arab groups that were founded with covert Zionist backing in order to undermine the Palestinian national movement (H. Cohen 2008).

Slonim was not alone in this activity. The committee that Hebron's Jews founded to operate among the Arabs included among its members Rabbi Meir Kastel; Rabbi Meir Franco; and the author Yitzhak Shami (ISA P3139/20), whom the Palestinian sociologist Salim Tamari (2008) has cited as an archetypical Arab Jew who integrated both cultures into his life. Hebron's Jews contributed financially to Zionist efforts as well. Dozens of Hebron's Jews, both Sephardim and Ashkenazim, made donations to Keren Kayemet during its campaign of February 1923. One of the largest donors was Eliezer Dan Slonim (*Do'ar Hayom*, February 25, 1923).

Donations and Mutual Responsibility

Hebron's Jews did not give only to Keren Kayemet. Two decades previously they had raised money—even though most of themselves lived off charity—for the Jews who were injured and orphaned in the Kishinev pogrom of 1903. The collection was organized by Rabbi Eliezerov and the city's Sephardi chief rabbi, Haim Hizkiya Medini. They told the Hebrew newspaper *Hahavatzelet* (August 14, 1903) that they were aware that the sum they had collected was very small, but they wished to give the injured a sense of brotherhood and the feeling that they shared their pain, and that the entire Jewish people mourned for the dead. In 1929, following the Hebron massacre, the German Jewish community declared a public day of fasting, Warsaw's Jews staged a demonstration in front of the British embassy until they were dispersed by armed cavalry, and a protest rally was staged in New York City (*Ha'aretz*, September 1, 1929). A little more than a decade later, when the dimensions of the Holocaust became clear, the Jews of Palestine and the entire world observed a public day of fasting. So the pendulum swings.

Hebron's Jews and Zionism, Continued

The British commission of inquiry into the disturbances of 1929 also took an interest in the extent to which the Jews of Hebron were Zionists. Franco, who testified before the commission, was asked by Reginald Silley, an attorney for the Arab Executive Committee, whether he thought of himself as a Zionist. Franco said: "We are all Zionists. In our services, in our prayers, three times a day we mention the name of Zion and we hope for the rebuilding of Zion" (quoted in Commission 1930, 2:853). When asked what the words "the building of Zion" meant, he said that they expressed faith in the coming of the Messiah. He thus made a clear distinction between the general ancient aspiration for a return to Zion and the institutionalized Zionist movement, which was one possible manifestation of this aspiration but not necessarily the only important one. However, it is important to keep in mind that the word "Zion," in its religious context, does not refer just to the Holy Land as a whole, but specifically to the Temple Mount as well, and "the building of Zion" means, in part, the rebuilding of the Temple.

As long as the idea of building Zion was a vision of future days that Jews did not work practically to achieve, it constituted no threat to the Arabs of Palestine. In the 1920s, both the Arabs and the Jews in Palestine began to sense that a sea change was taking place before their eyes. The Jews' hopes of redemption and a return to Zion had won the support of Great Britain, a world power. Jews of all kinds — Zionists, Lithuanians, Chabad Hasidim, socialists, Revisionists, and those from the Islamic world — sensed that a transformation was in the making. And the Arabs felt that the land was being pulled out from under them.

Did That Justify the Massacre?

Absolutely not. It only explains why the riots in Hebron should not be seen as an assault by irrational savages on a peaceful community that was no threat to anyone. For the Arabs, the combination of the expansion of the Jewish community, the Balfour Declaration, and political changes in the Middle East constituted a very real threat.

And Why Specifically in Hebron?

There were attacks in other places as well. In Hebron the Jews were a smaller minority with no capacity for self-defense. Beyond that, according to al-Rajabi (2000), Hebron's atmosphere was more highly charged than elsewhere in the country for a number of reasons:

> - Provocations by yeshiva students, and the arrogance displayed by the American students. This was why the violence was directed primarily at them.
> - The arrival of armed Haganah personnel in the city, and the concealment of arms in the vaults of the Anglo-Palestine Bank.
> - Family ties between Muslim families in Hebron and Jerusalem, which prompted an immediate response in the former city when rumors or reports reached people there about the murder of Muslims in Jerusalem.

> Jewish control of Hebron's economy via the Anglo-Palestine Bank, and interest-bearing loans provided to Arabs by members of the Jewish community.

Let's look at some of these claims.

Loans

Money lending was an important business for Hebron's Jews, as both Jewish and Arab sources testify. The Anglo-Palestine Bank provided loans just as all banks do. But both before and after its establishment, individual Jews also loaned money at interest to Arabs. So did Hakham Reuven, the remarkable protagonist of Menasheh Mani's heartwarming 1963 novella *Hevron veGiboreha* (Hebron and its heroes). Menasheh was the grandson of Rabbi Eliahu Mani and one of the founders of the Zionist-*maskil* Young Hebron Association. Menasheh Mani began his career working at the Anglo-Palestine Bank, eventually being promoted to a senior position at the renamed Bank Leumi. He was well acquainted with both the Jewish and Arab communities in Hebron and had a profound understanding of monetary matters. Here is his description of his book's central character—a man respected by all, a community functionary, and a benevolent and charitable man:

> The deeds and business transactions of Hakham Reuven were of many shades, if not of many kinds. To put it succinctly: Hakham Reuven was a banker, peddler, and a community functionary. How? On weekdays he went around to the many Arab villages in the Hebron area: Zif, Yatta, Halhul, and others, selling his wares to the fellahin, lending them money, and instead of interest receiving from them chickens and the products of their coops and fields. . . . He was very influential among the Arabs, because of his countenance, his character, the wisdom they found in his speech, and his manly bearing. (1963, 104–5)

This is how Hakham Reuven and daily life in Hebron are described at the beginning of his story. However, as national tensions grew, Hakham Reuven's Arab friends began to grow distant from him. Following World War I, they came to his house along with an educated urban Arab to say that they suspected him of cheating them in his accounts, demanding that he forgive all the loans he had made. "Even if you are a Jew, justice is stronger than you," they told him, "and even if our country is sold to all of you, the force of justice is still stronger than the force of a Jew" (ibid, 131–32). The author identifies, of course, with his protagonist, but that does not prevent him from letting his Arab characters voice the feelings he had heard expressed by the Arabs he knew. They were apprehensive of the power of wealthy Jews, anxious at the prospect that they could lose their country, momentarily certain of their own strength due to the backing of the urban effendis, and aggressive in the way that people are when they become aware simultaneously of their strength and their inferior position. But Mani was not the only Hebron writer to chronicle lending money at interest. So did Yehuda Leib Schneurson in his memoir.

Yehuda Leib Schneurson

Schneurson was the scion of the Chabad admors, just like the Slonim and Eliezerov families were. His father was the proprietor of the Eshel Avraham Hotel, which boasted the most famous accommodations in Jewish Hebron and was a popular summer vacation site for Jerusalem's Jews. During the massacre the Muslim Kurdiyya family saved Schneurson's life. He testified in court about what he saw from the window of their house (appeal file 12/30, TNA CO 733/181/4). He later left the country for a time, and when he returned he joined the Revisionist movement. When Avraham Stern founded Lehi, Schneurson joined the organization, and during the British manhunt for Stern, Schneurson was one of the few who knew where he was hiding. Schneurson's age and background led his fellow Lehi operatives to call him *saba* (grandfather). In 1980 the Lehi veterans association published his memoir, *Hoy Hevron, Hevron* (O Hebron, Hebron). The introduction was written by Israel Eldad, the organization's ideologue. Eldad noted that Schneurson bridged the Old and New Yishuv, between Haredi Judaism and maximalist Zionism, between yeshiva study and fighting spirit.

Schneurson was a man of firm opinions. At the end of the Ottoman period he met an important Arab thinker in Damascus, Mohammad Kurd Ali (who would later become Syria's first education minister). Schneurson wrote: "I presented myself to him as a Zionist and told him that the Land of Israel had no significance for his people, nor did they have any need for it. They had never built things there and never would" (1980, 53). Such declarations manifested Jewish pride but were devoid of any real understanding or knowledge of history. Their primary effect was to make it clear to the Arabs that they were fighting a war to the death with the Jews.

But even if his account of the Arabs' connection to Palestine is deficient, his firsthand testimony about the livelihoods of Hebron's Jews is very interesting. The Jews lent money to Muslims and charged interest, he reports. But he adds that the Muslims liked to take loans from Jews because the Jews were willing to receive interest payments in kind (for example, in wheat, barley, and wool) and because they charged less interest than Arabs.

Money and Blood

Making loans at reasonable interest rates enables people to engage in long-term economic activity. That is why both Muslim and Jewish religious scholars found ways to permit lending at interest despite injunctions against it in the Torah and Qur'an. In Ottoman Palestine quite a few prestigious Arab families used their ability to give loans to impoverish the less well-off, at times confiscating the lands of those who could not make their payments. The British tried to regulate interest, and al-Rajabi found documents in the Central Zionist Archives demonstrating that the Jews of Hebron felt that they had been hurt by the legislation that set a ceiling on interest rates (2000, 46–47). However, these restrictions seem to have enabled the Anglo-Palestine Bank, owned by the Zionist Organization, to expand its activity. The manager of the Hebron branch, Eliezer Slonim, granted Arab effendis loans on easy terms. Schneurson relates that, in mid-August 1929, when tensions in the city heightened, he wanted to request help from the Zionist security institutions, but Slonim prevented him from doing so. Slonim said that the Arabs would not harm him because they profited from their relations with him. "I spoke with him about this and tried to disabuse him of this belief," Schneurson wrote. "I tried to make it clear to him that when an Arab is seized by the urge to murder he does not think of financial gain. But he stood his ground and opposed asking for help by telephone from Tel Aviv, arguing that the Arabs would learn of this immediately and there was no point getting into a conflict with them. Eliezer Dan also prevented me from going to Jerusalem and asking for help in person" (1980, 53).

This is one of the painful intra-Jewish points of controversy among the survivors of the massacre. Could the massacre have been averted? Were the community's leaders too complacent? No one doubts Slonim's efforts to expand the Jewish presence in Hebron or his success of bringing the Slabodka Yeshiva to the city. Everyone acknowledges that he put his life on the line when the riots began on Friday. He may well have chosen to die with the people who hid in his house even when the Arabs offered him an opportunity to save himself. But did he assume too much personal responsibility? Did he put too much trust in his economic relations with the Arabs, believing that they would save the city's Jews? Did he really prevent Schneurson from calling for help? Or, as other sources claim, did Haganah defenders indeed arrive in Hebron, only to be turned away by Slonim?

Here is the account of Baruch Katinka, an engineer and a Haganah operative, one of the proprietors of the construction company that built Mufti al-Hussayni's mansion and the Palace Hotel that he owned. In *Me'az ve-'ad Henah* (From then to now; 1961), Katinka related that he had been dispatched to Hebron two days before the massacre to reinforce the defense of the Jewish community. He said the same in testimony he provided to the Haganah History Archives:

> About two days before the slaughter in Hebron we were told that we had to go to Hebron and transfer ten to twelve fellows with weapons so as to organize a defense

of the place. . . . We arrived in Hebron after midnight. We woke up Slonim and told him that we had brought arms, bombs and a *musolinka*—a kind of tommy gun with two barrels—and men. He began to shout and swear at us, that if there was a need for men and arms he would ask for them, but he didn't need them because the Arabs were in his hands and needed credit and would not raise their hand against him. On the contrary, new faces in Hebron would only be likely to provoke people.

While we were arguing there was a knock on the door and two Arab policemen entered and told us that the people who had arrived in the automobiles were to report to the police station. . . . The two guys with the small suitcases containing the bombs remained in Slonim's house. We told them good-bye and drove off. The next day they also returned to Jerusalem because Slonim forced them to go back. The next day at six in the morning the slaughter took place. (HHA testimony 120/27)

According to this version of events, Slonim gave too much weight to the Arabs' economic dependency and refused to accept Haganah personnel and their weapons. Sapir (2006) wrote in an article in the magazine *Eretz Aheret* that Rabbi Ya'akov Yosef Slonim, Eliezer Slonim's father, claimed to his dying day that this story was false. But Avraham Ikar, a Haganah commander in Jerusalem, also said that a Haganah detachment had been dispatched to Hebron. He testified that during the riots he had been arrested in Jerusalem with a gun and bombs as he moved between the forces that he had sent to outlying neighborhoods. In court he confirmed what the policeman who had arrested him claimed—that he had been armed:

I told [the policeman] that after Hebron every Jew needed to have a weapon and that I would repeat that here [in court]. . . . When I said that a murmur ran through the crowd. The judge also turned his glance to the crowd and then for a short moment there was silence. There was another reason to say this. About a week before the outbreak of the riots we send a contingent of comrades to Hebron, and the Jews of Hebron not only did not receive them nicely, but pleaded with them to return to Jerusalem, because their presence was likely to provoke the Arabs. The fellows were not given a place [to stay] and they had no choice but to leave. . . . I wanted to make people realize that there was a need for arms and in doing so to clear us of the charge that we had abandoned Hebron. (HHA testimony 71/44)

The last sentence came in response to a right-wing propaganda offensive that followed the massacre. It may also testify to the Haganah's feelings of guilt about not having saved the Jews of Hebron. "Grandfather" Schneurson wrote that the story of the Haganah detachment that came to Hebron with arms was an utter falsehood. According to his account, he called the offices of the Jerusalem Jewish Committee, where the Haganah central command was located, and asked them to send help to prevent the destruction of the Hebron Jewish community. According to Schneurson, the response was that the Arabs of Hebron were opponents of the mufti and that they thus presented no danger to the Jews of Hebron (1980, 66). *Sefer Toldot HaHaganah* offers its own take on the story. It says that two members of the defense force arrived in Hebron and proposed to Slonim that armed reinforcements be sent, but that Slonim rejected the offer after consulting with Jewish and Arab notables (Dinur 1973, 2:320). Malka Slonim-Sapir, the mother of Yitzhak Sapir and daughter of Ya'akov Yosef Slonim, recalled Haganah personnel arriving in Hebron on the eve of the riots. But, she said, her father the rabbi and her brother Eliezer Dan were not in the city. She maintained that when the Haganah men left to walk around the city they left their weapons in the bank with her sister, fearing that if the local police found the guns on them they would be confiscated. These memories came back to her when she visited Hebron immediately after the Six-Day War (*Ma'ariv*, June 16, 1967).

We have no way of determining who is right or what actually happened. We saw that al-Rajabi maintains that one of the reasons that Hebron's Arabs were angry at the Jews was the arrival of armed Jews bearing crates of arms and ammunition that were hidden in the vaults of the bank. He also writes that a group of defenders remained in the Slonim house, implying that the arms were actually used by Hebron's Jews. But al-Rajabi does not base his claim on Arab sources, but rather on *Sefer Toldot HaHaganah* (Dinur 1973) and *Sefer Hevron* (Avisar 1970b), which he does not read carefully enough. In any case, even if the Haganah men brought arms to Hebron, it seems very likely that they took them back when they left the city, and certainly no use was made of them during the riots.

And the Provocations of the Yeshiva Boys?

Al-Rajabi interviewed a number of Hebron elders who lived through the massacre. One of them told him that students at the yeshiva had stirred things up and often caused fights by peering into the homes of their Arab neighbors, in violation of the accepted mores in all places and certainly in conservative Hebron. Does that sound totally unfounded? To a large extent, yes. Why should yeshiva boys peer into the homes of the city's Arabs or ogle their daughters? But, like many claims that seem fabricated, a thorough examination reveals that there is some truth to the charge, if you take into account the different social standards of the two populations. An intimation can be found in a book on the Jews killed in the massacre, *The Martyrs of Hebron* (1930), by Leo (Leib) Gottesman, an official at the yeshiva who lived in Eliezer Slonim's home. In a chapter devoted to his host, Gottesman related that on more than one occasion Slonim was called on to obtain the release of a yeshiva student from jail after he had mistakenly entered the home of a Hebron Arab. The students seem to have gotten lost while walking through the unfamiliar city. They walked into the yards of houses where women were present. From the point of view of the yeshiva boys, they had made an innocent mistake with no malicious intent. For the Hebron Muslims this was a grave act of trespass and a violation of *hurmat al-bayt*, the sanctity of the home and its women—that is, a serious provocation. So there you have it: on the simple level of everyday life, the same actions are perceived in entirely different ways.

Another man interviewed by al-Rajabi claimed that everyone in the city hated the yeshiva students, "to the point that no one had anything to do with them" (Rajabi 2000, 93). That does not accord with the memory of Dov Cohen, a student at the Slabodka-Hebron Yeshiva who came there from the United States. He authored a memoir rich in documentation and detail about his period of study in the city. In his account, the Hebron Arabs did indeed boycott the man who had rented his building to the yeshiva, but not the students themselves. On the contrary, he wrote, the students' relations with the Arabs were "quite excellent": "It once happened that after we finished our shopping in the village of Tarqumia, a group of residents of the village came out to greet us with dancing and drums! When we investigated the reasons for this celebration, they told us that they were doing it in our honor, in order to express the esteem in which the people of the village held the yeshiva students" (D. Cohen 2009, 205–6). The story sounds pretty strange, but Cohen's book gives the impression of being very reliable, so there seems to be no reason to take the story as the imaginings of a young American Jew. It seems reasonable to assume that he indeed saw the villagers dancing and that the students asked what they were celebrating. And someone seems to have told them that it was for them—whether seriously, as a joke, or simply to be polite. By the way, one of the aspects of Cohen's book that lends it credence is the careful distinction he makes between eyewitness testimony and hearsay, between facts and rumors. For example, in his account of how Meah She'arim was saved on the day the riots began, he relates the story that Rabbi Aharon Fisher, the father of the president of the Edah Haredit Religious Court, "fired a pistol directly into the mouth of the sheikh, the leader of the procession, who walked at the head," but Cohen precedes this by saying that "so it was told" (D. Cohen 2009, 212). In other words, he does not claim it is a proven fact.

What is no less important is that when Cohen describes good relations with the Arabs of Hebron, he also tells the other side of the story.

Rabbis and Arab Boys

On the eve of each new month the yeshiva, including Rabbi Moshe Mordecai and Rabbi Leibzik, would go to pray at the Machpelah Cave. We were welcomed there. I recall that the Arab beadle of the cave would guard the gold cane of the head of the yeshiva, and would even allow us to go farther up than the famous limit of the seven steps, sometimes one step higher and sometimes more, I think up to the eleventh. Every possibility of moving up one more step was considered a great achievement. It was an exceptional thing, but he received the sanction of the appropriate authorities. He would also keep watch on the Arab boys, who sometimes threw rocks at the heads of the worshippers, so that they not interfere with our prayers. I think he was compensated by the yeshiva. (2009, 207)

This was the nature of the good relations that prevailed between the Arabs and Jews in Hebron. There was a certain amount of commercial cooperation, positive social interactions and good neighborly relations, and a prohibition against Jews entering the city's central holy site, sacred to both Muslims and Jews. That site was the Tomb of the Patriarchs, known to the Jews as the Machpelah Cave and to Muslims as the Ibrahimi Mosque (Ibrahim being the Muslim version of the name of the Patriarch Abraham). Beyond the humiliation that this proscription involved, the inferiority of the Jews was perpetuated also by the pastime Muslim boys had of throwing stones at Jewish worshipers. In the City of the Patriarchs the prohibition against Jewish prayer inside the shrine was meant as a physical expression of the Muslim claim to be the real heirs of Abraham's faith, as the Qur'an states:

> People of the Book, why do you argue about Abraham [being Jewish] when the Torah and the Gospels were not revealed until after his time? Do you not understand? You argue about some things of which you have some knowledge, but why do you argue about things of which you know nothing? God knows and you do not. Abraham was neither a Jew nor a Christian. He was upright and devoted to God, never an idolater, and the people who are closest to him are those who truly follow his ways, this Prophet [Mohammad], and [true] believers — God is close to [true] believers. (The Family of 'Imran, 3: 65–68)

According to this passage, the claim that Abraham was a Jew is false, because he lived before the revelation of the Torah. In other words, he did not belong to any of the ancient religions but was father to them all. The only ones who follow in his path, according to the Qur'an, are the Muslims, because they are the only ones who accept the prophecy of Abraham and the prophets who followed in his path — including the last one, Mohammad. The Jews, who rejected Mohammad's call, are not true believers. For this reason they are forbidden to enter mosques. In the early centuries of Muslim rule Jews were in fact permitted to enter their ancient sacred sites, such as the Temple Mount and the Tomb of the Patriarchs, even though they had been converted into mosques, but the Mamluk sovereign Baybars, who fought the crusaders and significantly reduced their in-

Abraham Entertaining the Three Angels by Rembrandt (Gardiner Greene Hubbard Collection, Library of Congress).

fluence in the country, decided in 1267 to bar the Jews from both of them. More than six centuries of this ban and thirteen centuries of Muslim rule had perpetuated the perception that the Jews were religiously and socially inferior. Muslim boys thus viewed it within their rights to molest Jewish worshipers, throw stones at them, pull at their beards and sidelocks, and engage in other similar degrading actions. The Muslims thus demonstrated their sense of superiority and their closer relationship to Abraham, the forefather claimed by both Jews and Muslims.

But

The Tomb of the Patriarchs was not just the site of a conflict over a forefather's love. It was also a place of partnership. Here is an example: In July 1914, a short time before the outbreak of World War I, the Ottoman Sultan Mehmed V had new coverings made for the tombstones marking the burial places of the Patriarchs and Matriarchs. All Hebron prepared for the important ceremony, in which both Jews and Muslims participated. When the procession bearing the coverings passed through Hebron's streets on its way to the Machpelah Cave, Jewish schoolchildren stood on one side of the street waving Ottoman and Zionist flags and their Muslim counterparts stood on the other side. According to one report, "Avraham Franco, a teacher in the gentile school, made a speech in fine Arabic, in which he welcomed the arrivals in the name of the Jews and the schools, and also blessed His Royal Highness, who had generously sent as a remembrance these coverings for this holy site, to which the eyes of the entire world looked. 'And even though we, the Jews, do not enter it,' he continued, 'our souls are nevertheless tied to it from both far and near'" (*Hatzefira*, August 16, 1914, quoting an article in *Herut*).

The Seventh Step, the Admor, and Moses Montefiore

The closest the Jews were allowed to get to the tombs of the Patriarchs was the seventh step of the stairway that led up to the shrine. For the Jews, this was a symbol of their humiliation, but al-Rajabi and al-Ja'bari present this as a Muslim gesture toward the Jews—even though Muslim law forbid them to enter mosques, they were allowed to ascend to the seventh step. The rabbis and teachers of the Slabodka Yeshiva were able, with the help of some greasing of palms, to go up as far as the eleventh step. Over the years only a handful of Jews managed, with or without permission, to enter the inner compound. Ten days before the riots broke out the Chabad admor, Rabbi Yosef Yitzhak Schneurson, did so on his only trip to the Holy Land. Eliezer Dan Slonim obtained a special exception for him and a few of members of his entourage (D. Cohen 2009, 198–99).

Rabbi Schneurson thus succeeded where the British Jewish financier and philanthropist Sir Moses Montefiore and his wife Judith failed. As British nobility, the couple were permitted to ascend to the Temple Mount. But their visit to Hebron ended differently, as their journal shows. They arrived in the city in June 1839 with an impressive company of Ottoman officials. During the huge celebrations that the city's Jews staged, as the couple climbed the steps toward the shrine:

> On reaching the steps of the Mosque, even before we had dismounted, there was a great cry against us entering. We nevertheless ascended the steps, and entered the passage leading to the interior of the Mosque. It was filled with people, all screaming and threatening us with sticks. But the situation soon became much more serious. The Mussulmans began to beat back those of the Jews who had followed us, and the screams were truly frightful. The soldiers of the Governor of Beyrout and the janissary from Mr Moore, the English Consul, behaved admirably; they struck right and left with all their might, and the entrance gate was soon closed. We remained inside, and following the Governor, attempted to enter the Mosque, but we were for some time prevented by the cries of the people, which were greatly increased by a dervish, who threw himself before the door, shrieking in a most frightful manner, and calling on the people not to allow us to enter. (Montefiore and Montefiore 1983, 1:184)

Montefiore, his wife, and their secretary understood at this point that it would be best for them to leave. They turned to leave from a different entrance than the one they had come from. The governor followed them, apologizing again and again, "but Sir Moses would not speak to him, as he (the Governor) was bound in honor and duty not to have subjected us to such an insult" (ibid.). The Jewish philanthropist's visit to the holy site led to an attack on the city's Jews. Several were injured, but no one was killed.

Another Hasidic leader, the admor of the Gerer sect, had an experience more like that of the Montefiores and not like that of the Chabad leader. In 1935 Admor Avraham Mordechai Alter visited the Holy Land for the fifth time and went to pray at the Machpelah Cave. He was shoved by a local policeman when he ascended to the eighth step. His disciples, who tried to defend him against the policeman, were arrested and brought to trial (*Do'ar Hayom*, October 3, 1935).

And since we are talking about the Tomb of the Patriarchs, let us note that the first non-Muslim to enter the shrine (with permission) in the modern age was the prince of Wales during his visit to Palestine in 1862. The head of the shrine's guard greeted the prince with a declaration that it was his responsibility to prevent unbelievers from entering the mosque, but then he said that he could not turn away the eldest son of Britain's queen. This was more than a piece of flattery —it expressed his unease at Britain's increasing influence in the Holy Land. The Muslims who accompanied the prince sighed painfully when they heard this. The sheikh of the tomb appealed to Abraham to forgive the intrusion (Stanley 1863, 155).

Abraham's Grave? The Tombs of the Patriarchs?

We have no way of knowing whether Abraham forgave the shrine's keepers for letting the prince of Wales enter his tomb. Another question that is hard to answer is whether Abraham is, in fact, buried in the Machpelah Cave. In other words, is there complete consensus about the identification of the Machpelah Cave as we know it today with the tomb of the patriarchs and matriarchs mentioned in Genesis? At first glance, the answer would seem to be yes. More precisely, setting aside the academic debates about whether Abraham and Sarah, Isaac and Rebecca, and Jacob and Leah were historical figures, there is reliable evidence that this site has been identified as their tomb since ancient times. It certainly precedes the Roman period, when King Herod built the monumental structure that still stands above the cave. In the case of the tomb of the fourth matriarch, Rachel, which stands on the outskirts of Bethlehem, there are other traditions and scholarly proposals regarding her place of burial. There are no such alternative traditions and proposals regarding the Patriarchs' tomb.

Only once has doubt been publicly expressed about the site. An Israeli archaeologist and the son of an archaeologist, Yigal Yadin, a former chief of staff of the IDF, was quoted as declaring at a press conference in New York that the

identification of the site as the Tomb of the Patriarchs was no more than a tradition, and that he did not believe it to be true. He said this in October 1967, about
a hundred days after the IDF had conquered Hebron. When the story hit the
newspapers, Minister of Religions Zerach Warhaftig and his ministry's director
general, Shmuel Zwehil Kahane, swiftly condemned Yadin: "Professor Yadin,
what do you have to do with the holy sites of the Machpelah Cave and Rachel's
Tomb? Go talk about Masada and archaeological sites and leave holy sites to the
care of the Ministry of Religions" (quoted in *Ma'ariv*, October 17, 1967). Yadin
later issued a clarification — he did not, he said, make light of tradition, but since
there was no scientific proof that the patriarchs had been buried in the cave, he
could not declare that to be a scientific truth (*Ma'ariv*, November 10, 1967).

The Seventh Step: The End

The months that followed the Six-Day War were the final days of the existence of the seventh step. When the war ended, masses of Jews traveled to Hebron. They ascended to the seventh step and then delighted in being able to
climb even higher. Malka Slonim-Sapir, the daughter of Rabbi Slonim and a survivor of the massacre, was one of the first to go there: "I went to Hebron. They
let me go only to the Machpelah Cave. At the seventh step I halted. I could not
make my feet move. I was used to [stopping there after doing so] hundreds of
times in my childhood. They shouted at me, 'Get moving, woman, why are you
standing there?' My feet refused to move. Afterward I went further, for the first
time in my life, and I didn't know what I was doing. I was as if in shock" (quoted
in *Ma'ariv*, June 16, 1967).

Some sixteen months later, during the week of the Sukkot holiday in October
1968, a hand grenade was thrown into a crowd of Jewish visitors at the Machpelah Cave. Forty-seven people were injured. IDF bulldozers arrived at the site
and began to demolish the adjacent houses. They also destroyed the stairway
on the shrine's eastern side, including the emblematic seventh step. The order
seems to have been given by the general in charge of the IDF's Central Region
Command, Rehavam Ze'evi, an officer for whom the 1929 riots had been a seminal experience.

Ze'evi, 1929, and Montefiore

Ze'evi belonged to a group of high-ranking IDF officers that can be called the
1929 generation, a group for whom the riots were a childhood memory, part
of the terrain into which they were born. As we have seen, on Friday, August
23, 1929, Yemin Moshe, where Ze'evi lived, was attacked by Muslims who had
emerged from the Old City on their way to Hebron. Ze'evi was then three years
old. His father a Zionist activist who, later in August 1929, was sent by the Haga-

nah to Safed to assist the Jewish community there. The defense of Yemin Moshe
— built with the support of Montefiore and located on a hill facing the Old City's
Zion Gate — was placed in the hands of a Haganah operative nicknamed 'Aziz
Effendi, who liked to dress in an *'abayah*, a traditional Arab robe. Later, under
his real name, Pesach Bar-Adon, he would pursue a career in archaeology. But
as a young man, he spent many months living among the Bedouin of the Jordan
Valley. Ze'evi's mother later related that at the time of the attack on the neighborhood, Bar-Adon drew a pistol out of his *'abayah* and fired into the air. When
British soldiers in the area heard the pistol shot and came to look for the illegal
weapon, Bar-Adon hid it under Ze'evi's pillow. When a British policeman entered
his room, the boy's mother pinched his cheek to make him cry. The policeman
was deterred from searching the room and the pistol was saved (Shashar 1992,
16). This story does not, however, accord with the fact that Bar-Adon, by his
own testimony to the Shaw Commission (Commission 1930, 2: 844–45), was in
the Beit She'an Valley at the time of the attack and reached Jerusalem only a few
days later. Still, it's a good story, which Ze'evi himself recalled in 1948 when he led
a raid on the village of Zir'in in the Jezreel Valley and Bar-Adon accompanied
him as a military correspondent. Twenty years after the war of 1948, thirty-nine
years after 1929, Ze'evi headed the Central Region Command and ordered the
demolition of the seventh step, to mark the end of the age of Jewish inferiority.

Religious Superiority and Inferiority

Proscriptions on nonbelievers that forbid them entrance to religious sites are
not unique to Muslims. Jewish religious law, for example, forbade gentiles from
entering the Temple Mount. Neither was the idea of religious superiority born
with Islam; it was a feature of the monotheistic faiths that preceded it as well.
Since we are dealing with Hebron, it would be instructive to consider the view
of relations among religions and peace advocated by Rabbi Shlomo Ben-Hamo,
which he presented as *the* Jewish position in an anthology that was published
in commemoration of the fiftieth anniversary of the massacre in Hebron. In his
contribution, Ben-Hamo declared that "the vision of peace is the dearest wish of
the Jewish people," adding that "unlike the gentiles, Jewish aspiration for peace
does not derive from weakness and fear, but out of love, compassion, and a desire to improve the world." He went on to present the implications of this view
for Jewish-Arab relations in our time: "So long as they [the Arabs] do not recognize our authority, our national reestablishment, and our national existence,
as well as our moral superiority, attempts at peace are useless talk, because the
Supreme will desires *the submission of Ishmael to his master Isaac* [emphasis in
the original], and so long as there is no such submission, enmity and hatred continue toward us and toward our state" (Ben-Hamo 1979, 25).

Ben-Hamo's Judaism partly derives from that of his teacher, Rabbi Tzvi Yehuda HaCohen Kook, son of Rabbi Avraham Yitzhak HaCohen Kook, the chief Ashkenazi rabbi of Palestine at the time of the riots. It demands that non-Jews recognize Jewish superiority and declares that peace will be possible only when the gentiles accept this hierarchy. The same hierarchical view can be found in important streams of Islam, and it is natural for adherents of monotheistic religions to believe that their religion is the only true faith.

Let's return to Hebron in 1929, a time when Muslims feared that the Jews were refusing to accept the divine injunction regarding their inferiority to Islam. We will look at who was murdered by the Arabs of Hebron to discern whether the Muslims distinguished between different kinds of Jews.

Motives and Distinctions

The Slabodka Yeshiva, as we have seen, was viewed by the Arabs as a beachhead for Zionist settlement in Hebron. It was thus considered a legitimate target. But the attack was not guided by a single analysis of the facts or by a single motive. Here is what Yehuda Schneurson was quoted as saying in the first issue of *Do'ar Hayom* to appear after the British lifted its ban on the publication of local newspapers:

> While we were in one of the rooms we saw that a large mob of rioters were following Sheikh Taleb. At their head was Sheikh Taleb Maraqa and he was shouting: "You Muslims, here you have before you ten Americans who have millionaire parents in America, here is Eliezer Dan Slonim who blinded the Arabs with his credit at the Anglo-Palestine Bank. Slaughter the Jews! Drink their blood! Today is the day of Islam! It is the day that the Prophet commanded. Allah and the Prophet call on you to avenge the blood of your Muslim brothers killed in Jerusalem! *Allah akbar!* Kill Jews! Come up with me. Here before you are beautiful Jewish girls!" (quoted in *Do'ar Hayom*, September 2, 1929)

According to this account, Sheikh Taleb Maraqa used every possible justification for attacking Jews. There was the cultural one, attacking the American millionaires who had come to settle in the city; the economic one, exploitation by the bank; the religious one, the Islamic precept of slaughtering Jews (a possible, but not necessary, interpretation of Islam); the sexual one, the opportunity to rape beautiful women; and blood, revenge for the killing of Muslims in Jerusalem. The crowds who streamed toward the homes of the Jews were moved by all these motives, above all of which floated the thing that had set attackers on their way throughout the country — great apprehension that the Zionists' intention was to turning the land into a Jewish one.

Maraqa headed the Hebron branch of the Muslim-Christian Association (the organization that Rabbi Ya'akov Yosef Slonim had sought to vilify with the help of his Muslim friends) and represented his city in Palestinian national institutions. He was brought to trial for incitement to violence, and many of his admirers attended his trial to support him. During the trial, Maraqa denied all the charges against him. In his testimony he related that on that Saturday morning he had drunk tea with Eliezer Dan Slonim and the Schneurson family at the Eshel Avraham Hotel. He had emerged from the hotel arm in arm with Slonim, who headed for his house next door. Later in the day, Maraqa claimed, he had not even been in the area where the killing took place. His defense attorney, George Salah, interrogated him regarding the charges against him:

> Salah: The accusation is that on Saturday you provoked the killing of Eliezer Slonim and his family. Is that true?
> Maraqa: No.
> Salah: There is another accusation, by Sultana [Gozlan]. [That] you told people to kill her. Is that true?
> Maraqa: No.
> Salah: Were you among the people who attacked the Slonim home?
> Maraqa: No.
> Salah: Were you among the people who attacked the Abushedid house?
> Maraqa: No.
> Salah: Did you incite anyone to attack these houses?
> Maraqa: No. (*Sefer haMishpatim* 1930, 65)

The defense included Maraqa's claim that the city's elders had opposed the killing of the Jews. The sheikh spoke at length about the long friendship between the city's Jews and Muslims and claimed that Zionist elements in Jerusalem who wanted to incriminate him had persuaded Hebron's Jews to testify against him.

The court convicted Maraqa of some of the charges against him, but not of the main ones. It ruled that the prosecution had proved that he had spoken to the crowd, but not what the contents of the speech had been. He was sentenced to two years in prison. So we return to the question of the assailants' motives and goals and how they were manifested during the hours of horror.

Rajabi: The Target—Zionist Men

The number of Zionist Jews killed in the Hebron Intifada was 57, all of whom were buried in Hebron. Some 70 people were injured and sent to hospitals in Jerusalem. There 7 additional people died of their wounds, and were buried in Jerusalem. . . . When one examines the names of the dead, it shows that most of them were not inhabitants of Hebron, and that most of the wounded were not members of the old Jewish community in the city but rather Zionist immigrants who had arrived a short time previously in the city, from Europe and America. The number of dead among the Ashkenazi community was 57 out of a total of 64 Jews killed. The conclusion is that the Hebron Intifada was not directed against the Jews in general, but rather against the adherents of the Zionist movement, most of whom were Ashkenazim. (Rajabi 2000, 130)

This is an attempt to offer a reason for the massacre. Al-Rajabi, like Ja'bari, Haetzni, and me — indeed, like anyone who investigates or takes an interest in the riots — seeks to understand what caused the Arabs of Hebron to murder their Jewish neighbors. Al-Rajabi's explanation is a simple one: the Arabs did not murder their Jewish neighbors but rather their Zionist enemies. That seems to be how some of the attackers that Saturday saw it. Since, according to al-Rajabi, the attack in Hebron followed the Jewish attack on Hebron Arabs in Jerusalem the previous day, the Arabs viewed their actions as reasonable. Al-Rajabi also tries to minimize the horrific nature of the killing: "This intifada was accompanied by theft from both Jewish and Arab stores, and women and children were certainly not deliberately killed, as can be seen by the small number of women and children among the dead and wounded. Nor did anyone mutilate the bodies of the dead, and no one dishonored Jewish women. Furthermore, the homes of Jews were not destroyed, and as a general rule their homes were not looted, and in the cases in which this happened, they were individual initiatives" (2000, 123). It is worth examining all of al-Rajabi's claims. Let's begin with the question of whether Hebron's Arabs refrained from attacking the members of the established Jewish community.

No. "Arab Jews" Were Also Attacked

Al-Rajabi's claim that the number of non-Ashkenazi members of the old Jewish community who were killed was only seven is not precise. Thirteen members of the Sephardi community, some of them born in Hebron and some of them immigrants from the Islamic world, were murdered by Arabs. If Chabad's adherents (like Rabbi Slonim and his family) are included as part of the established community (as they should be), the number of victims who were not recent arrivals is even higher.

It is true that in Hebron and throughout Palestine there were local Jews who had no connection with the Zionists, for whom life with the Arabs seemed more comfortable and proper than Zionist political activism, and for whom Zionism upended their cultural world and damaged their social and human ties to the Arabs. It is also true that in Palestine and the surrounding countries the Arabs did not immediately identify the Jewish neighbors they knew, and with whom they were sometimes friendly, with the Zionist pioneers arriving from Eastern

Europe who were trying to change the nature of the Holy Land. Furthermore, Arab political and cultural discourse in fact distinguished between the pioneers and local Jews ("local" sometimes including all the Islamic lands and the Ashkenazi Jews who had lived there for generations), as did Zionist discourse. But all of this was true in quiet times, not tense ones. As political competition between the peoples increased, and along with it the tension between them, Jews and Arabs grew distant, and each side gathered around the national movement that offered to represent its members. This was the general case, and it was all the more so during bloody clashes. Then distinctions such as the ones above lost all validity.

The year 1929 was a cusp. It was the year in which the bloodshed made it clear to both Jews and Arabs that Jews were closer to other Jews, no matter of what community and belief, than to anyone else. For example, Dov Cohen related that when he first saw Eliahu Abushedid, the Jewish owner of a small grocery store in Hebron, he did not know if he was Jewish or Arab (2009, 186). But when the Arab mob attacked Abushedid, his Arab visage, garb, and culture did not save him, nor did his acquaintance with many of the city's Arabs:

> They [the Abushedids] called out to the policemen and the people on the street by their private names and cried for help. No one came to their aid. They strangled the head of the family. He defended himself with all his strength and cut off the fingers of one of the rioters. His two sons did the same. He called out to them that if any of them were to remain alive they would know against whom to avenge his blood. One woman of the family was stabbed and the murderers smashed her with their shoes and trampled her body. The rioters held one baby by his legs and slammed him against the wall until he died. . . . Of this entire family remained one fifteen-year-old boy, who recognized 24 of the rioters as inhabitants of the city. (Amikam 1929, 53)

The Killing of Children

The account of what took place in the Abushedid and Gozlan homes makes it clear that the fate of Jews who were culturally Arab was no better than that of the students at the Slabodka Yeshiva. It also supports the claim that children were deliberately murdered, contradicting al-Rajabi's claim. But Amikam's account is flawed by a certain amount of exaggeration, as were testimonies from other places where massacres took place in 1929; indeed, the phenomenon is common to all massacres. In testimony that was filmed when he was more than eighty years old, Yehuda Abushedid, Eliahu's son, who was ten years old in 1929, offers this account of what happened:

> They broke into the house and I see them, it's as if I see them now. Masses of people with swords in their hands. Real swords and knives. They entered. My father and

mother were there, my little brother, seven years old, who was always attached to his mother, and another brother. That brother managed to evade them and ran away to the other side of the street. Across the street lived my older married brother. There the Arabs guarded them. They didn't guard us. And they came in. They broke in. I was badly wounded. . . . The result was that that, like, [after the assailants] left, I went out with my mother and my little brother, and I see my father sprawled [he chokes back a sob], sprawled on the ground, badly wounded in his head. I look for my other brother. He is in a room with his hand cut off and his wife badly wounded. He had a girl, seven months old, who they left in the carriage. They didn't touch her. And that's it. We went out. We left everything behind. (Abushedid 2012)

The first notable difference between this testimony and that published by Amikam is that more than one of the family's children survived. Second, this account also supports the claim that the attackers did not distinguish between Jews of different communities. The third point that stands out is that, according to Yehuda Abushedid, the rioters refrained from killing babies. Furthermore, this is not the only account we have of a baby being spared. Not only was Abushedid's baby nephew spared, but so was three-year-old Shlomo Gozlan. In her chilling testimony at the trial of the Hebron murderers, Sultana Gozlan related how the assailants passed over Shlomo. The killers gored and beat her Hebron-born husband, Ya'akov, to death, as well as killing her eldest son Moshe, while her baby son, she recalled, wandered from room to room, among the murderers and victims, wailing and screaming. Sultana did her best in her testimony to ensure that her family's murderers would be convicted. The fact that she had no interest in depicting the Arab attackers as merciful lends credence to her statement that they spared the life of her younger child (court file 47/29, TNA 733/181/4: 34).

The List of the Dead: A Cautious Reading

The list of sixty-six fatalities that appears in *Sefer Hevron* includes fifty-four men and twelve women (Avisar 1970b). In other words, the number of women killed is much lower than the number of men. The list includes three children: Devora Lazarovsky (five years old, killed with her father Betzalel and her uncle Yisrael), Menahem Segal (two years old, killed with his father Nahman), and Aharon Slonim (five years old, killed with his father, Eliezer Dan, and his mother, Hannah).

Do these numbers indicate that the killers aimed principally at men, and only here and there murdered small children and women, as al-Rajabi proposes? Can we conclude that some of the murderers hesitated when they brandished their knives and axes and found themselves facing children, while others did not?

There are other possible explanations for the low proportions of women and children among the victims. One is the fact that the balance of men to women in the community was not equal because of the existence of the Slabodka Yeshiva, whose students were primarily unmarried young men. This would in and of itself skew the number of victims to the adult male side. But the evidence presented here indicates that there were nevertheless murderers who chose, at the height of the massacre, not to kill small children.

One More Thing about the Mizrahi Question

In contradiction of the version of events accepted by Hebron's Arabs, one source charges that Hebron's established Arabic-speaking Jewish population was in fact the principal target of the attackers. The testimony is hearsay and is difficult to verify, but it should be weighed. It comes from Gershon Nedivi, who claims that he heard it from Baruch Katinka of the Haganah. Katinka told Nedivi that a Jewish Agency intelligence operative, Aharon Haim Cohen, who visited Hebron disguised as an Arab, heard that Sheikh Maraqa had told his flock a few days before the riots that the Jews were planning to seize the Machpelah Cave. Cohen quoted Maraqa as saying: "It is precisely the Jews who live among us and who have nursed the milk of our mothers—it is they who are liable to take revenge on us more than the Moskobim, and it is thus an imperative to slaughter them first" (Nedivi 1983, 41).

Who Were the Attackers?

The testimonies refer to hundreds—some say thousands—of Arabs who roamed the streets of Hebron, going from one Jewish house to another, armed with clubs, knives, and axes. It seems almost certain that hundreds participated in breaking into the houses. A few dozen committed the actual murders. In my conversations with Palestinian Arabs in Hebron in recent years, they have stressed that the killers came from the surrounding villages, while the Arabs of Hebron itself protected their neighbors. That is not true. Many of Hebron's notables stood by the homes of the Jews, heard the screams, and did nothing to save them, with just a few exceptions (Sultana Gozlan spoke at length about this in her testimony in court). Eleven of those sentenced to death for their involvement in the massacre were members of Hebron families, most of them long-standing ones: Halwani-Tamimi, Nasser a-Din, Sharabati, Ajuri, al-ʻArafe, al-Khatib, Farrah, ʻAweida, Jamjum, al-Zir. Some of the defendants who were acquitted by reason of doubt also came from Hebron families.

Some of the murderers were never arrested. Many of those brought to trial were acquitted. Ibrahim Abu Gharbiyya was one of them. Along with another eleven men, he was accused of taking part in the murder of four people: Eliahu

Abushedid and his son Yitzhak, and Ya'akov Gozlan and his son Moshe. Victoria Gozlan, Ya'akov's daughter, testified that she had seen Abu Gharbiyya among the murderers. She told the court that a large group of Arabs broke into their home through three of its doors. She ran to hide in the bedroom. As she ran, she saw Ibrahim Abu Gharbiyya and 'Id Abu Shawarib stabbing her father. Four other men assaulted her brother and stabbed him to death.

Ibrahim Abu Gharbiyya was arrested. One of his nephews was Bahjat Abu Gharbiyya, mentioned in chapter 2 in connection with his role in the Arab Revolt of 1936–39 and his service in 1948 as one of the commanders of the Palestinian forces in the Jerusalem region. Bahjat, thirteen years old at the time of the massacre, went to visit his uncle in jail from time to time, to bring him provisions. He attended the trial as well, and the proceeding made a huge impression on him. In his memoirs (1993, 18), he writes that it was an important stage in shaping his militant nationalist consciousness. Like other Hebron Arabs, he claims that the victims were Zionist Jews who had recently arrived in the city. As we have seen, this is not true. All four of the people that his uncle was accused of murdering were Arab Jews who had been well integrated into Hebron's Arab community. During the attack, when they pleaded for their lives, they addressed their attackers by name.

The Arabs who saved Jews also came from Hebron's old established families, such as the Kurdiyya family that saved the Schneursons. The reports sent by Hebron's Jews to the Zionist institutions include the names of such saviors, some of whom acted as individuals and others as representatives of their families. Among these were members of the following clans: Abu Haikal, Abu Zina, Hirabawi, Shahin, Tahbub, Bader, al-Khatib, a-Zaru, Zeitun, Hammuri, Kawasmi, Zghayyir, Abu Munshar, and Abu Shkhidam. One member of the Maraqa family, the head of which was accused of being the principal provocateur, defended his Jewish neighbors (for the lists of Arabs who saved Jews, see Ben-Zion 1970, 424–26). Some of these people were injured while protecting their Jewish acquaintances. One of these was Abu Shaker 'Amru, who defended Rabbi Ya'akov Yosef Slonim. 'Amru was not originally from Hebron but from the town of Dura to the south, but his family had a long-standing connection with the city and its Jews.

Abu Shaker 'Amru and the Rescue of Rabbi Slonim

The 'Amru family of Dura had, in the nineteenth century, dominated the rural area of the Hebron highlands. Sheikh 'Abd al-Rahman 'Issa 'Amru was acknowledged as the sheikh of sheikhs in the area; the Jews of Hebron called him *der Shvartzer Rebbe* (the black rabbi), and this is how he appeared on the payroll of the Chabad community. He also periodically asked for—and received—expensive gifts from Hebron's Jews. He lived up to his self-appointed status as their defender on at least one occasion—during the battles between Ibrahim Pasha and the fellahin rebels, he helped the Jews repossess property that had been stolen from them (Slonim 1970, 309). In later years, other members of the 'Amru family also held leadership positions, among them Subhi 'Amru, who served for many years as a government minister in Jordan; and Nabil 'Amru, who served as a member of the Palestinian Authority's cabinet. Members of the family have also worked at the grass-roots level, including 'Issa 'Amru, who is now the coordinator of nonviolent resistance activities to the Jewish settlement in Hebron and who is frequently arrested by the IDF.

In 1929 some members of the 'Amru family lived near the Jewish neighborhood in Hebron, not far from Romano House. Malka Slonim remembered:

A short time after my injured father and I returned home and shut ourselves up inside, our neighbor Abu Shaker suddenly appeared, mounted on his white horse. He hitched the horse up and sat on the steps to our house, looking and examining the surroundings. Afterward he knocked on the door and said: "Don't open, I just want you to know that I'm here! I won't let anyone touch you! Don't open the door! Close all your windows and shutters! May God be with you!" We sat silently, shut up in the house, and he, Abu Shaker, reported to us what was happening: "The scoundrels are killing the Jews," he said in a choked voice, "and no one will help. The police are on their side. The British police are escorting the killers to the homes of the Jews. . . ."

The mob reached us, we heard them howling murder. We heard them blazing with hatred and blood lust. We also heard Abu Shaker's voice: "Get out of here! Here you will not enter! Here you will not kill!" They shoved him. He was old, maybe 75, but he had a strong body. He struggled with them, lay down at the entrance to the house, by the door, he shouted at them, "Only over my dead body will you pass here! Only over my body!" One of the rioters waved his knife over Abu Shaker's leg and shouted, "I'll kill you, traitor!" Abu Shaker was not frightened: "Kill me! Kill me! Here is the family of the rabbi, which is my family. Kill me! I won't move!" The knife came down. Abu Shaker's leg was torn. His blood flowed out. He did not moan in pain. He did not cry out, only said: "Cut me! I won't move!" The rioters consulted among themselves, there was a second of silence, and afterward we heard them leaving. We knew that we'd been saved. We wanted to bring our savior into the house, to bandage him, to thank him. He refused. He said, maybe others will come. My mission has not yet been completed. (quoted in Ben-Zion 1970, 417)

Hebron: The End, for the Time Being

Afterward, quite a long time afterward, the Hebron police, led by Police Chief Cafferata, came to their senses and began to hold back the attackers with live fire. Both looters and killers were deterred. They left the homes of the Jews, leav-

Jewish Old Cemetery, Hebron (Matson Photograph Collection, Library of Congress).

ing behind dozens of bleeding bodies. The streets emptied. The survivors slowly emerged from their hiding places. Some rushed to search for their loved ones. Others treated the wounded and wept over their dead.

The police brought all the Jews to Romano House. The dead were buried in the local cemetery. The wounded were evacuated to Jerusalem for treatment, and the rest of the community was taken to Jerusalem as well. Hebron was emptied of its Jews.

A Temporary Return

The refugees from Hebron lived in Jerusalem for months, supported by public funds and bearing in their hearts the memory of their city and the pain of the murder of their loved ones. About a year after the massacre they slowly began to return to Hebron. It would be difficult to say whether they were moved by a sense of religious or national calling, or whether it was the difficulty of living as refugees in Jerusalem that prompted them. Perhaps it was just the natural urge of people to return to the city of their ancestors, their hometown. The Jewish national institutions did not organize the return. In fact, they doubted whether it was a good idea. Shmuel Charles Pasman, who was the head of a special fund set up to aid the riots' victims, opposed the move because the renewed community would lack an economic basis for their survivors. The Slabodka Yeshiva, which had employed members of the community in service roles for its students, had decided to relocate permanently to Jerusalem. Nor did Pasman see money lending as a viable business for the community. "It would not be proper," he said, "to continue to engage in this 'profitable sector'" (letter dated November 18, 1930, CZA S25/4472).

Aharon Haim Cohen, an intelligence operative for the Zionist Executive in Palestine, spoke to Jews about the return and traveled to Hebron to talk to the Arabs as well. He reported that some of the Arabs expected that the Jews would return, assuming that this would restart commercial activity in the city, which had ground almost entirely to a halt. But Cohen's Arab interlocutors expressed frustration at the fact that most of the returnees were poor, old, and unemployed. By June 1931 there were ninety-six Jews in the city, including fifty-four children. Most of them lived off charity from Jewish communities overseas, distributed by Hakham Haim Bajayo, the head of Hebron's Sephardi community (CZA S25/4472). In the years that followed the community grew a bit. But the big plan supported by the Zionist leaders Menachem Ussishkin and Yitzhak Ben-Zvi, as well as Chief Rabbis Ya'akov Meir and Kook, to expand the urban community and establish a Jewish farming community nearby did not come to pass. The hoped-for funds did not arrive, and the majority of the Zionist leaders opposed the community's return (Arnon 2005). The Jews who returned to Hebron did not serve as a Zionist vanguard—instead they resumed life as a minority under Arab and British protection.

In 1933, when the Arab leadership called for demonstrations against the British and Zionists, Haganah personnel arrived to protect the Jewish community in Hebron. This time they were welcomed by the Jews. One of the men was Moshe Alperstein, the man who saved Meah She'arim in 1929 (HHA testimony 5/9). Jewish homes were not attacked in 1933, and he did not have to use his gun again. But the Jews slowly drifted out of the city. When the Arab Revolt broke out in April 1936, all the Jews were evacuated from Hebron except for the Ezra family, who remained there until the UN partition resolution of November 1947.

In 1950 a local Hebron magazine, *Sawt al-Khalil*, commenced publication with Mayor Mohammad 'Ali al-Ja'bari as its chief editor. An article in the first issue, by the governor of the city, Mohammad al-Ma'ayta, proudly proclaimed that Hebron had successfully rid itself of its Jews (Ma'ayta 1950, 11). His joy was, as we have seen, premature. But that is a jump forward in time. Let's return to 1929, to what happened that morning in the Jewish farming village of Motza.

4 MOTZA

> In which we will visit Motza, a peaceful hamlet to the west of Jerusalem. We will hear how inhabitants of the adjacent Arab village, Qalunya, massacred the Maklef family and their guests. We will try to understand what the Qalunyans had against the Motzans and see the murderers acquitted. And we will hear much false testimony.

At the Very Same Time

The Arabs of Qalunya beset Motza at the very same time that Hebron's Arabs attacked that city's Jews. Ghaleb Samrin, a native of Qalunya who was mentioned in chapter 2, offers a lengthy account of the events of those days in *Qaryati Qalunya*:

> The news of the demonstrations in Jerusalem and the clashes between Jews and the inhabitants of Lifta reached all Palestine's cities and villages [on Friday] in an exaggerated and inflated form. The rumors spread by British soldiers were that Jews had attacked Muslims when they emerged from prayers at al-Aqsa Mosque and had killed hundreds of them, both there and in the village of Lifta, next to us, and that induced the inhabitants of our village to cut the phone lines along the Jerusalem-Jaffa road and to throw stones at government vehicles, which led to an additional rise in tensions. On Friday night a decision was made to attack the settlement of Motza, at the south end of our village, on the morning of Saturday August 24, 1929. (2003, 166)

The hyperbolic rumors (for which Samrin and many other Arabs, including some from Hebron and Safed, blame the British, but for which the Jews blame the mufti and his agents) incensed the village. The inhabitants began to plot an attack on their Jewish neighbors. The zero hour was set for the next morning, giving some of the villagers an opportunity to warn friends in Motza.

The Pride of the Qalunyans

Samrin continues: "Our fathers in Qalunya were the first to attack a Jewish settlement. . . . [They were the first to comprehend] that armed action was the only way to restore our rights. I would not be exaggerating if I said that the inhabitants of our village, Qalunya, were the first Arabs to engage in a military initiative. Their partners, but not their predecessors, were the inhabitants of Hebron who attacked the Jewish quarter there and who killed more than fifty Jews at the very same time" (2003, 166–67). That is not accurate. Samrin ignores the riots of 1920 and 1921, as well as the previous day's attack on the Gurji courtyard in Jerusalem. Even in the environs of Qalunya it was not the first attack. Emek Ha'Arazim, a small Jewish farm east of Motza, had also been attacked on Friday. One of its residents, Yitzhak Landberg, was wounded when he tried to repel Arab shepherds who had deliberately trespassed on the farm's cultivated fields. Taking Landberg with them, the rest of the farm's inhabitants fortified themselves in the home of the Yedidya family. A large band of Arab villagers from the surrounding area besieged the house:

> Then Isma'il appeared. Isma'il was a close neighbor and a constant friend. He lived in adjacent Bayt Tolma and did not consent to the slaughter. Isma'il placed himself between the victims and the attackers and after parleying with them, and at the price of four hunting rifles that were inside the house, the villagers left. In the meantime night fell and Isma'il transferred all the besieged [Jews] to his home. From this moment they came under his protection, eighteen Jews, eighteen men, women, and small children. They [Isma'il and his people] dressed [the Jews] in Arab garments and they slept in Isma'il's house on Friday night, 18 Av. On Saturday morning the villagers again raided Emek Ha'Arazim's six houses, looted them and then burned down what was left. But the inhabitants of Emek Ha'Arazim themselves were still hiding as guests in Isma'il's home. (Broza and Broza 1994, 143)

It's another dumbfounding rescue story: another courageous man saves his neighbors. Samrin ignores the attack on Emek Ha'Arazim, perhaps because its inhabitants were saved.

Yitzhak Landberg

Yitzhak Landberg's name is familiar to many Israelis. It is the original name of Yitzhak Sadeh, who served as a senior Haganah commander and was one of the authors of its offensive strategy during the Arab Revolt of 1936–39. In 1941 Sadeh founded the Palmach, the Yishuv's elite strike force. But, in fact, the Yitzhak Landberg who lived in Emek Ha'Arazim was not the future general but rather his cousin.

When the riots broke out in 1929, Sadeh was working at the salt factory at Atlit, just south of Haifa, one of a small number of Jewish workers in the midst of a largely Arab workforce. That Sunday morning he had not yet heard that his cousin had been injured. He got up and, as was his daily habit, went for a swim in the sea. When he returned to the beach he saw dozens of his fellow Arab laborers gathered around the spot where he had left his clothes, bearing their work tools in their hands. He feared that they intended to attack him but, pretending that all was normal, he emerged from the water, dried himself off, and got dressed. Sensing tension in the air, he thought it best to leave right away, so he walked quickly to the nearby station and took the train to Haifa. There he was assigned to replace a junior commander who had hesitated to respond when, a few hours before, an Arab mob had beaten to death a Jewish worker, Yisrael Groyer. Sadeh took a different approach. He sent his men out into the field to change the balance of terror and to put fear in the hearts of the Arabs rather than allowing the Jews to be the frightened ones (HHA testimony 74/66). They carried out motorized incursions into Arab neighborhoods, shooting at the gathering crowds. Levi Avrahami, the senior Haganah commander in Haifa and later chief of police in the Israeli Jerusalem District, took part in these actions and his testimony (HHA 2/7) indicates that he and his fellows made no distinction between assailants and innocent passersby. Haifa's Arab community included both belligerent and moderate elements, the latter growing in part out of many years of Jewish-Arab cooperation on building and maintaining the train system (Lockman 1996, 159). Sadeh's force seems not to have taken this into account.

But all this took place afterward, on Sunday, and far to the north, in Haifa. Let's get back to Motza on Saturday morning, when the Arabs went on the offensive.

The Attack on Motza: The Belligerents' Version
Samrin relates:

The inhabitants of the village [Qalunya] launched their attack in the early hours of Saturday, August 24, 1929. . . . The attack first concentrated on the home of the Broza family and on the home of Michael Steinberg, the mukhtar of the Jewish settlement, as well as on the shingle factory that he owned. News of the attack reached the Jews on Friday night, and two of them, Matityahu Broza and Moshe Maklef, took the warnings seriously and immediately set out for Jerusalem to ask for aid from the Zionist Executive. They returned with ten armed and well-trained members of the Haganah, commanded by Eliezer [Broza and Broza (1994) give the name as Yehoshua] Lerman. This aid force managed to defend the inhabitants of the settlement who acted in accordance with its instructions and gathered in a single house. They were saved from the death that would have awaited them had they remained in their homes, isolated and scattered over a space of more than thirty dunams [three hectares].

The assailants from Qalunya did not have arms appropriate for such an attack; all the weapons they had were a sword held by Ahmad 'Awidat, a dagger in the hands of Nu'iman 'Abdallah Dirbas, a club in the hands of Mahmud Hamdan, a knife with Ahmad Hamad, and a rifle brought by Ahmad Mahmud Hamdan from his uncles' village, toward the end of the attack—but most of the people had only sticks and stones. May Allah have mercy on the souls of all of them.

The first of the attackers was Nu'iman Dirbas. He was well acquainted with the ins and outs of the Jews' houses because he had worked for them for a long time. He was the first of the villagers to be killed in the attack, killed when Bentzion Broza shot him dead with his pistol. Sa'id Khader Dirbas, who was next to him, bore him to the wide space in the valley. Nu'iman was buried in the village's old cemetery. (2003, 167–68)

The Brozas' Version

Motza: Sipur Eretz-Yisra'eli (Motza: A story of the Land of Israel; 1994) was written by Meir and Tsori Broza, two members of one of the oldest of the farming village's families. The book relates the story of Motza from the start. The first plots of land were purchased in 1860 by David Yellin (the grandfather of the David Yellin we met in chapter 2) and Shlomo-Yehezkel Yehuda; the former was born in Poland, the second was a scion of a prominent Baghdad family. They bought the land for their children, Yehoshua and Serah, who had married (a demonstration that whatever divisions there were between Jews from the Islamic world and those from Europe, there was also economic cooperation and, if rarely, also marriage). The Brozas tell of the purchase of additional land and the expansion of the village; of the visit made by Theodor Herzl in 1898 and the tree he planted there; and of relations between Jews and Arabs, in times of peace and of trouble, in 1929 and the Arab Revolt of 1936–39. Their account of the land purchase is of special interest.

From Whom Was the Land Purchased?

The people of Qalunya and Muslim notables in Jerusalem sold the land to the Jewish settlers. Remember, the Islamic legal ban on selling land to Jews is a modern ruling. True, in early periods there were legal authorities who forbade selling land to Jews and Christians, but that was a minority opinion. During the second half of the nineteenth century, a number of changes occurred simultaneously. Palestine's population mushroomed and with it the demand for land; Western powers reinforced their presence in the country; and the Zionists began planning a large-scale Jewish settlement in it. The country's Arabs slowly came to the realization that the sale of land to Jews was not merely an individual transaction in which an asset was transferred from one person to another, but rather something that had much wider implications. It could help the Jews establish a foothold in the country and take control of it and its inhabitants. If this was the case, then the sale of land to Jews was certainly forbidden under the standards of religious law, and unacceptable from a moral and national point of view.

In the 1860s, awareness of this situation was still in its infancy, and the inhabitants of Qalunya could not know the future. As a result, a number of them sold land to Serah Yellin who, as an Ottoman subject, was legally permitted to purchase land without restriction. The transaction was registered in the Islamic court of Jerusalem (the texts of the documents can be found in A. Cohen 2003, 270–77). The method was much like that used by the Jews who bought the land on which Jerusalem's Nahalat Shiva neighborhood was built from the inhabitants of Lifta. In 1890, so Motza's old-timers tell, the Jewish settlers played a little trick on the fellahin of Qalunya to enlarge the settlement's territory.

A Real Estate Sting

The trick that Yehoshua Yellin and his associates played on the people of Qalunya in 1890 is related in the Brozas' book. Yellin became friendly with a leading Arab from Jerusalem who built himself a summer house next to the Qalunya springs. The man was *naqib al-ashraf*, the leader of the descendants of the Prophet Mohammad who lived in the city. ("Naqib al-ashraf" is a traditional Islamic title; during the Ottoman period the person who bore it was also invested with political, economic, and sometimes military power.) The naqib, like Yellin, was aware that, according to the Ottoman land law promulgated a few years previously, the ownership of untilled land was forfeited to the state. The two of them decided to dupe the Qalunya villagers.

The Brozas do not name the naqib al-ashraf, but at that time the post was held by Ahmad Rasem al-Hussayni. Adel Manna, a Palestinian Israeli historian, mentions him in his important lexicon, *A'lam Filastin fi Awakhir al-'Ahd al-Uthmani* (Palestine's scholars at the end of the Ottoman period; 1995), noting that by this time the position's importance had waned. Nevertheless, the naqib was still able to maneuver between Jews and Arabs and still wanted to accumulate capital. He thus agreed to assist the Jews in the land transaction. The Brozas relate that the naqib sent a Turkish soldier to the village who demanded, in the name of the government, that the mukhtar prepare a list of fallow land and the names of the owners of these plots—including plots that the owners had not wanted to sell: "The fellahin, utterly fearful over losing their lands, approached —who else—the naqib al-ashraf. They now preferred to get paid, even if a pittance, for their land rather than to have it confiscated. They thus offered their plots at a low price, assuming that he would know how to deal with the authorities. . . . The effendi registered 184 dunams [18.4 hectares] in the name of the planned Jewish village" (Broza and Broza 1994, 25). The incident illustrates, in this early case, two of the characteristic features of Jewish land purchase, ones that remain salient today. The first is exploitation of provisions of land laws in ways that are opposed to the spirit of the law and detrimental to the owners of the land. The second is the use as intermediaries of Arabs who are prepared to collaborate with Jewish settlers. The Brozas write of this matter-of-factly as a family tradition demonstrating cleverness and resourcefulness. From Qalunyans' point of view, it was a cynical and cruel exploitation of their plight for the purpose of dispossessing them of their land.

Is There an Alternative?

Did the Jews have any other choice, in Qalunya and elsewhere? That is, could they have bought up land more fairly? If their aim had been simply to settle on the land in accordance with local custom and live side by side with their neighbors, it seems likely that they could have done so in modern times just as they had done in the past. But because their goal was either to establish a Jewish state or to create a Jewish majority, two goals the Arabs opposed, they could proceed only through a subterfuge. Did they have a right to do so? That is a difficult question to answer without putting it in a larger context. Let's put it this way: on the fundamental level, it is unacceptable for the wealthy and powerful to use their advantages to take possession of land from the weaker people who actually till it. But what makes the issue more complex, and perhaps less unambiguous, is the question of whether there are conditions under which such an injustice can be justified. In this particular case, the question becomes whether the persecution of the Jews in Europe and their inferior status in the Islamic world could authorize deceptions aimed, if only in Jewish eyes, to save the lives of their fellow Jews and the Jewish nation. This specific question in the case of Yehoshua Yellin and the fellahin of Qalunya is an early example of the elemental moral questions that Zionist activity would pose to both its supporters and opponents.

What Does Morality Have to Do with International Relations?

Writers about international relations are divided on the question of what place moral considerations have in the interactions between countries. But when the subject of discussion is the Zionist movement, it is almost impossible to avoid moral questions. There are three reasons. The first is that the Zionist claim that the Jews have a right to sovereignty in the Land of Israel was based, in part, on moral arguments. The second is that the Zionists fostered a conception of themselves as, unlike the Arabs, occupying the moral high ground.

The third relates directly to the 1929 disturbances, which led Zionists to claim that Palestine's Arabs were fundamentally immoral actors who attacked helpless Jews. Thus it is impossible to address the events of 1929 without addressing moral issues. Since the debate over the morality of Zionist practices cannot reasonably begin from the moment that the first Jew was killed, the events that preceded 1929 have to be reexamined. That produces a primary question, one that the story of Motza and Qalunya exemplifies: did the Zionist aspiration of founding a Jewish state that could cure the Jews of the malady of living as a humbled minority justify injury to the Arab inhabitants of Palestine? This question leads to another one: did the Arabs have a right to oppose Zionist settlement? And that in turn leads to a third question: if nonviolent resistance does not or cannot succeed — due to, in this case, the support the Zionists enjoyed from the European powers — to what extent were the Arabs justified in opposing Zionism by force? And if they were justified, what targets were legitimate? Only armed Zionists? All Jewish males? Every Jew in Palestine? (These questions themselves, it is important to keep in mind, are based on universal conceptions of morality, as opposed to religious discourse on the right to the Holy Land. The latter, as we saw above, does not take equality between Arabs and Jews as a given and does not accept moral standards that come from outside the tradition of each faith.)

The Answers

The Jewish Zionist and Arab answers to these questions have been and remain opposed. The Zionists think that their right to the land is unarguable, and that the Jews' plight elsewhere is so difficult that injury to the Arabs could be justified. Early Zionists also stressed that, whatever injuries the Arabs might suffer, they would also benefit, and some Zionists called on restricting the injury to every extent possible. The Arabs as a rule did not accept the premise that they should give up their homeland because of the suffering of Europe's Jews. Most of them did not receive the impression that the Jews were seeking to minimize the damage caused to the Arabs. On the national level, the Arabs justified their opposition by arguing that they were the majority community in the country and thus had the right to determine its fate, according to the international norm of national self-determination. On the religious level, the Muslims maintained that the Jews' historical and religious right to the land had expired when that stiff-necked people rejected Mohammad's call to Islam. On the moral level, they argued that if the Jews suffered in Europe, it was an issue Jews needed to take up with the European nations. Under no circumstances could it justify an infringement of the individual and national rights of the Arabs of Palestine.

At the same time that they opposed mass Jewish immigration to Palestine, the Arabs declared that they were prepared, in principle, to grant full equality to the country's long-established Jewish population, along with the rest of the country's inhabitants. But that was not what Zionists sought. They wanted Palestine to become a refuge for the Jews of Eastern Europe and a national home for Jews everywhere in the world. It is that intention that made the Arabs feel that their fight against Zionism was self-defense, and that they had every right to use violent means to achieve their ends.

Full Consensus?

Not all the Arabs rejected completely Zionist immigration to Palestine. Nor did all the Jews want to rule over the Arabs. There were Jews of the Old Yishuv from both Ashkenazi and Sephardi communities, as well as immigrants from Europe who hoped to live in equality with the country's other inhabitants. Some Jewish groups worked to achieve a compromise (unsuccessfully, because even these conciliators were not prepared to forgo the fundamental Zionist tenet that Jews be allowed to immigrate to Palestine in large numbers). Nor did all Arabs maintain that violence should be used against the Jews. In every society different views exist in parallel, and individuals revise their positions over time or waver between positions, among emotions, and between logic and emotion. Alongside Arabs who were fully and deeply persuaded of the Arabs' exclusive claim to Palestine and who believed that they were justified in using violence to defend their country from foreigners, there were Arabs who aided Jews in land purchases even after the Arab national movement declared this to be the highest treason. Some of them thought that Jewish immigration would indeed benefit the Arabs, as the Zionists claimed. Others put personal gain before the good of their nation. Still others developed personal connections with and loyalties to Jews and acted in concert with them in various ways. There were also Arabs who believed in the possibility of coexistence between the two nations. Whatever the case, the plots on which Nahalat Shiva, the Bukharan quarter, and the Gorji courtyard were built, like the land of Motza and parcels in Hebron, were sold to the Jews during the twilight period when the national idea had not yet become fully ensconced in the hearts of the country's Jews and Arabs.

Motza, Herzl, and Hajj Amin al-Hussayni

Samrin addresses the dawn of Zionist settlement in his book. He notes the role played by members of the Muslim urban elite in transferring Arab lands to the Jews, but he does not provide full details. In this he carries on a Palestinian tradition of treating sensitive subjects obliquely. Nevertheless, throughout his book he stresses the selfishness of the urban landowners, contrasting their behavior with the readiness of the fellahin to make sacrifices. Although Samrin could not have been ignorant of the fact, he does not mention the al-Hussayni family's involvement in land sales. Some of the al-Hussaynis seem to have felt guilty about their actions and found a way to cope with their feelings.

For example, Su'ad al-Hussayni, the daughter of Grand Mufti Hajj Amin al-Hussayni, claims that her father, in his youth, was the man who uprooted Motza's most famous tree, called Herzl's cedar. In his youth, she relates, the future mufti learned horseback riding at his family's fields in Qalunya. He and his friends resolved to express their hostility to Zionism by chopping down the tree.

In fact, the tree wasn't a cedar but a cypress, which gained its name after being planted by the Zionist visionary Theodor Herzl on November 2, 1898. "A few Arabs helped us, together with the [Jewish] farmers Broza and Katz," Herzl recorded in his diary. The Brozas write: "Herzl was extremely moved. He embraced the sapling he was handed, his hands trembled with emotion and tears flowed from his eyes" (Broza and Broza 1994, 48–49). But the tree survived for only seventeen years. In August 1915, during World War I, it was cut down. Some Jews charged that Qalunya Arabs felled it, others accused the Turks, while others maintain that Jewish anti-Zionists had a role in the deed.

In claiming the deed for her family, Su'ad al-Hussayni even names the two friends of her father's who helped cut down the tree—the brothers Ragheb and Rushdi al-Imam. These details lend credence to the story, which appears in a biography of Hajj Amin written by Taysir Jabrah of An-Najjah University (1995).

This account can be accepted or rejected. We will set aside the mufti's youth and return to the heat of that afternoon in August 1929, on the terraces of Motza, where shots rip through gunpowder-scented air.

The Massacre in the Maklef House
Samrin's account continues:

When the attackers perceived the defense force of ten soldiers and its firepower, they understood that the defenders could kill them all, so they turned to the southern part of the settlement and attacked the Maklef house. . . . The assault on the house was led by Ramadan 'Allan and Mahmud Taleb.

Seven Jews were killed in this house: five members of the Maklef family itself —the father, Aryeh Maklef, known as Nimr; and his wife, the mother of the family, Haya; their son Moshe Maklef; and his two sisters, Mina and Rivka. Killed along with them were two rabbis who happened to be in the house at the time. The attackers surrounded the house. Haim Maklef shot at them with his gun until a bullet lodged in the chamber, and then he began to use the rifle as a club. That is how he killed the martyr 'Ali Mahmud Hamdan Lakah, who was the first who reached the door of the home, advancing from among his fellow assailants while shouting "*Allah akbar*" (2003, 168).

Pay close attention to the wording. Seven Jews were killed. It doesn't say by whom, or how. The account, detailed up to this point, suddenly turns frugal. The passive voice replaces the active, and the richness of the narrative disappears. But when Samrin describes the Arab dead, he uses the active voice, naming the perpetrator: Haim Maklef killed 'Ali Lakah, leader of the assault, just as above Bentzion Broza killed Nu'iman Dirbas. Who killed the Jews? And how?

That's What Haim Maklef Tells Us

On Saturday morning, prior to the attack, Haim Maklef took the milk produced by the family's cows to Jerusalem. He was the milk supplier for Jerusalem's Hadassah Hospital. After returning to Motza he went to the home of Steinberg, the Jewish mukhtar, to see if the requested reinforcements had arrived. Danger was in the air. He heard screams from his house and warily made his way there. *Davar* quoted his court testimony. It's not easy reading:

Mohammad Matar (al-Khatib) tried to shoot me, he held out his pistol at me, I hid in the house. While I was on the porch they did not shoot at me. They ran up to the house and I hid.

Among the first who entered the porch was Mohammad Samrin, holding a sword. He approached Mother and stabbed her with the sword and I heard her sigh. Before wielding the sword he cried out "Tidhbahu li-klab [slaughter the dogs]."

I ran into my room (on the house plan he points to his room) where my sister Mina was. While I was in the room three Arabs came up to the window, one of them ripped open the *muskitar* [a cloth mosquito screen], they inserted two pistols and shot my sister, who fell on her face, dead.

Next to the wall outside there was a bench and the murderers stood on it. Their names: 'Ali Salih and Mohammad Matar. The third was Husni Barakat who ripped the *muskitar* with a dagger.

I turned to the door of my room and saw Mohammad Samrin and Jamil Jum'a, who cut through the metal-wire screen of the door with forty-centimeter swords that they held. There were other Arabs with swords but I could not see them or recognize them.

When I saw that there was no hope I entered the living room so as to run away through the porch . . . in the living room the residents of the house stood by the partition [between the living room and the porch]. I demanded that they move and opened the door to the porch. In the living room were Rabbi Zalman Shach, Miriam Sirkis, Tzipora Yafeh, my sister Hannah, my brother Mordechai, and Rabbi Glazer, who was hiding under the bed. . . .

When I returned to the house I didn't find any Arabs and here's what I saw: by the fence across from the stairs were Father and Mother bent over and my brother Moshe supine. I raised Father's head, which fell again, because he was dead. Mother called to me: Haim, Haim! Save Moshe and save me. Father had a round hole on the top of his head close to his forehead, and a piece of brain was visible outside, and over his left eye there was also a cut. There was no blood on his head, but a little blood above his eye. There was no sign of blood on Moshe. Mother's left breast was cut from the top to the bottom, apparently with a knife. Over her left eye was a cut and another cut on her mouth on the right side, four centimeters in length, made by a knife or sword. Then I went up to the house. I saw my sister Rivka in the kitchen lying dead, her tongue hanging out. I saw a gunshot on her face, I don't remember if on the right or left side. From there I went into my room and saw my sister Mina lying on her face. I tried to lift her up but she was no longer alive. (quoted in *Davar*, September 22, 1929)

Haim Maklef offers us the details of the killing that Samrin kept from us. Samrin did not write who raised a sword against whom, who stabbed what girl, and who killed the mother who tended to the Arab village's sick. The available evidence indicates that Ghaleb Samrin's father, Mohammad, called al-Badawi or Abu 'Abdallah, was one of the murderers.

Mohammad Samrin, Al-Badawi

According to stories collected by Ghaleb Samrin, his father had loved guns from the time of his youth, specialized in sniping, and believed with all his heart that an armed struggle was the only way to save Palestine. Mohammad Samrin continued to engage in belligerent activity in the years that followed 1929. His good friend, Abu Ibrahim, told Ghaleb about the time when Mohammad, acting on his own, killed four Jewish workers who were driving past Motza at the beginning of the Arab Revolt, in 1936. The impulse to murder the Jews had come to him when, during the funeral of a Qalunya woman, Hasna Hamad, just outside the village, a truck waving a Zionist flag passed by. The young Jewish men sitting on the truck were chanting something rhythmically, which the villagers understood to be "Palestine is our land and the Arabs are our dogs" (2003, 178). Mohammad Samrin decided to take revenge against those Jewish laborers:

> On the day set for the operation, he set out with his rifle hidden under his black 'abayah and headed for the spot he had chosen, over one of the well-known sharp turns near al-Qastel. . . . He waited for the truck. Not long thereafter the vehicle appeared, driving quickly down the descent, passengers riding on it. Swiftly, without hesitation, he fired a single shot and hit the driver. The truck wove from side to side as the workers on it and inside shouted, and at this time, and quickly, he emptied his magazine at the workers — and the truck soon turned over on the side of the road, by the upper spring. . . . Abu 'Abdallah testified that from that time on he never heard any Jews taunting Arabs on that road. (ibid., 178–79)

Mordechai Maklef in
the British army, 1944
(Central Zionist Archives).

Jeering "Palestine is our land and the Arabs are our dogs" was not a common practice in Zionist circles; perhaps there was a misunderstanding in this case. There seems, however, to be no reason to doubt Samrin's skill as a sharpshooter. Haganah sources tell of a similar incident, although there are significant differences in the details. Apparently the shooting Samrin tells of was the same one in which Dudu Nishri, a student, was killed and two of his friends wounded in an ambush near Qalunya. Nishri served as a Haganah security guard in Motza Ilit; Ya'akov Pat, the Haganah commander in Jerusalem, mentions the shooting in testimony he provided to the Haganah History Archives (HHA testimony 84/65). If this is indeed the incident Samrin reports, then only one Jew rather than four was killed, and the other victims were wounded.

Samrin's talent as a sniper was on display on other occasions as well. His talents won him the position of bodyguard to the mufti in 1948. But he was not just a gunman—he was also a pious Muslim. It was his piety, his son relates, that would not allow him to kill small children. He thus saved the young son and daughter of the Maklef family. That young boy, Mordechai, later rose in the ranks of the Haganah, the Jewish Brigade (a unit of the British army composed of Jews from the Yishuv), and the Israeli army. He served as a commander in the battles of Haifa and the Galilee in 1948 and was appointed chief of staff of the Israel Defense Forces (IDF) in 1952.

They Saved the Children?

Here is Ghaleb Samrin's account of how the children were rescued:

> Mohammad Matar al-Khatib joined the attackers in the early afternoon, after return-
> ing to his village, Qalunya, from the village of Ayn Karem. He took part in the attack
> on the Maklef house without having planned or expected to do so. He also took part,
> along with Mohammad Samrin, in saving the lives of the two children, four-year-old
> Hannah and five-year-old Mordechai. My father [Mohammad Samrin], may he rest
> in peace, and his friend and cousin Mohammad Matar, were of high Muslim morals,
> so that they did not hesitate to rescue these two children from one of the attackers
> who for a moment thought to kill them. In 1952, Mordechai Maklef was appointed
> chief of staff of the Israeli army and took part in the killing of Arabs [and in the 1948
> war] had taken part in the conquest of Haifa and the eastern Galilee. (2003, 168–69)

In Maklef's own memoirs, and in the testimony provided by members of his
family and other survivors, there is no mention that Arabs from Qalunya rescued them. According to the family's version of events, the elderly Rabbi Shach,
who was the family's guest for the Sabbath, was the man who saved the two children—he told them to jump from the balcony and flee. The rabbi himself was
murdered in the house.

We thus have two different accounts of who saved the children, with the historian unable to decide between them. But once again these are two versions of
events that are not mutually exclusive. It could well be that the children jumped,
as Rabbi Shach told them to do, but that one of the villagers saw them and
wanted to kill them. Mohammad Samrin and his companion may have stayed
that villager's hand, just as some of the murderers in Hebron refrained from killing children. But it is also possible that Ghaleb Samrin's account is a fabrication
meant to demonstrate the morality of his father and other Arabs. After all, both
the Jews and the Arabs in the Holy Land constantly proclaim that they hold the
moral high ground.

The Motza Survivors, 1929–48

Mordechai Maklef fought in World War II in the ranks of the Jewish Brigade. The formative incident of his life was the murder of his defenseless family.
He gained military experience fighting German forces that were slaughtering
his helpless fellow Jews. After returning to Palestine after the war, he was appointed to the staff of the Carmeli Brigade and served as an officer in the conquest of Haifa in April 1948. There are contradictory versions of the conduct of
the Jewish forces during the battle for the city. Some stress the attempts by the
city's Jewish leaders to prevent Haifa's Arabs from leaving the city and minimize
Haganah attacks on Arab civilians (Karsh 2001). Others stress the shelling of

the city's Arab inhabitants by Haganah forces as one of the principal causes of Arab flight from the city (Fogelman 2011; W. Khalidi 2008). Some cite the order given to the Carmeli Brigade's 22nd Battalion to kill any Arab they saw and put to the torch everything in Arab neighborhoods that would burn (Eshel 1973, 138; Pappé 2006, 95). This unprecedented order was not carried out, and in any case Maklef was not the man who drafted it. Members of his family relate that he did everything in his power not to let his experience in 1929 affect his military actions or his views about the Israel-Arab conflict (Ron Maklef, personal correspondence with the author, 2014).

Members of the Broza family also fought in 1948. Ghaleb Samrin relates that Bentzion Broza, who faced off the attackers in 1929, left Motza forever after the massacre. He adds that Broza was killed in 1948 in a battle not far from Motza along with nineteen of his comrades. Samrin's account is based on the facts, but it is not precisely correct. The Broza killed near Motza was the Palmach soldier Yonatan Broza, Bentzion's son. He was killed along with nine of his comrades when they attempted to extricate a squad of soldiers who battled the forces of 'Abd al-Qader al-Hussayni. From the point of view of family history, it can be seen this way: a scion of the al-Hussayni family, which had been involved in selling the land on which Motza was built to the Jews, in 1948 commanded the Palestinian Arab forces (the Holy Jihad militia) that sought to raze the Jewish settlements in the Jerusalem mountains that stood on that very land. Members of the Jewish families attacked in 1929 were among the Jewish soldiers who defended those settlements.

In 1929, the war of 1948 was still hidden in the clouds of the future. For the Jews who found themselves under attack in Motza and elsewhere, the establishment of a Jewish state was a vague hope. For the attackers, it was a nightmare that spurred them to action.

Let's return to Motza in 1929.

The Motza Massacre: The End

On that Saturday afternoon in August 1929, the men of Qalunya completed their massacre in the Maklef house. They set it on fire, and torched other houses also, the owners of which had hidden at the Broza home. Then the Qalunyans left the settlement. The cowering Jews saw the attackers bearing furniture and goods off to their village, where their women welcomed them. The Jews regrouped and took refuge in the Steinberg shingle factory. A small Haganah force, led by Yohanan Ratner, arrived to help them. Ratner, born in Russia in 1891, had lived through pogroms during his childhood in Odessa. He had studied architecture in Germany and served in the Russian army during World War I, reaching the position of staff officer in a combat division. In 1923 he set off for Palestine and joined the Haganah. In 1948 he attained the rank of general in the IDF, serving as head of the General Staff's Planning Branch. The start of the 1929 riots found him in Jerusalem, from where he was sent to Motza when word arrived of the attack on the Maklef home. When he arrived, he found the mother wheezing and unconscious. The rest of the survivors were huddled in the local factory, as Ratner recalled:

> Our situation was very bad. The factory was not at all appropriate for our purposes —thin brick walls that any bullet could penetrate—while the rest of the homes were built of thick stone. . . . I wanted to tell people to get out of there before it was too late, but it was impossible to move them. The large fortress-like building enticed them, and they had a logical reason—that the Arabs of the village would not attack the factory that was the source of their livelihood. The owner of the factory even went so far as to appeal to us not to shoot. He still hoped to reach an agreement with "his" Arabs from the village. Otherwise he'd face an economic catastrophe, as he did not believe that he could manage with Jewish laborers. He was an experienced man, not without wisdom. But he had not grasped the changes—patriarchal relationships had vanished, and he was no longer dealing with Ahmed or Mahmud from Qalunya (they themselves had changed) but with emissaries of the mufti, people from outside, motivated by sincere national feeling. (1983, 238)

Over the course of the afternoon shots could be heard from time to time, coming from the direction of the village. Ratner called in evacuation vehicles and reinforcements. Toward evening the people of Motza sent their wounded to the hospital and prepared their dead for burial.

"Sincere National Feeling"

Ratner comprehended something that many others had not at that time. That is why his analysis differs from what was then the prevailing Zionist view of what motivated the Arabs in Jaffa and elsewhere. He understood that the assailants were not killing for a pack of cigarettes or an opportunity to loot. They were on a national mission, spurred by authentic national feeling, as primal as it might have been.

The Trial

The British rounded up suspects in Qalunya a few days after the attack. During their sweep they killed and injured several villagers—ironically, ones who had not participated in the killing. Sixteen men were brought before an investigating magistrate and charged with murder. The director of the investigation, who prosecuted the case before the magistrate, was Bechor Shalom Sheetrit, the police officer from Tiberias discussed in chapter 2. You may remember that he served as prosecutor in the trial of the Jews accused of murdering Khalil Burhan al-Dajjani.

Tiberias

This offers an opportunity to digress briefly to Tiberias. Of the four Jewish Holy Cities (Jerusalem, Hebron, and Safed are the others), all of which had ancient Jewish and Muslim communities, Tiberias was the only one in which no blood was shed during the 1929 disturbances. The city's Jewish and Arab leaders issued a public appeal to the members of their communities to keep the peace, and they did (almost—one yeshiva was torched by Arab demonstrators, according to the *Sefer Teveriah* [The book of Tiberias; Avisar 1973]). The Jewish signatories to the letter were the rabbis of the Maghrebi community, Ya'akov Hai Zrihan and Meir Vaknin; Tiberias's Jewish mayor, Zaki Alhadif; and a representative of the Ashkenazi community, Ya'akov Veinberg. The Muslim signatories included the local mufti, Sheikh Taher Tabari; Yusuf al-'Akil; Qasem Shahin; and Khalil al-Khartabil.

The inhabitants of the city's rural hinterland were not parties to the agreement. Arabs of the Lower Galilee attacked the Jewish farming village of Hittin. The commander of the Tiberias police at that time was Tzvi Shapira, who would later become a prominent attorney in Haifa. He related in testimony he gave to the Haganah History Archives that fellahin and Bedouin tried to make their way into Tiberias itself to attack the Jewish community: "I drove around the roads and came to the aid of Jewish settlements desperate for help and protection. Each day I went from Tzemach to Tiberias and arrested all the Arabs I found carrying weapons. Others I drove away and I beat suspicious ones and warned them not to return to Tiberias. . . . I did my work only with the help of Jewish and Christian policemen, with the exception of one sergeant, Salah Zu'bi (a Muslim Arab), who was brave and very dedicated, and thanks to his devotion to me I was saved several times from death" (HHA 180/11). Zu'bi was murdered by Arab rebels in 1937, just like Halim Basta—who in 1929 defended the Jewish settlements in the area of Ben Shemen.

The Motza Trials: The First Decision

The investigating magistrate in the pretrial proceeding against the Motza assailants decided to charge twelve of the detained men with first-degree murder (*Do'ar Hayom*, September 26, 1929). They were tried before the special court created to hear the cases resulting from the 1929 violence. The defendants included Mohammad Matar and Ghaleb Samrin's father, Mohammad (called al-Badawi), who, according to Samrin's book, took part in the attack on the Maklef home. Dozens of witnesses were called by the prosecution and defense. The record of the trial covers 470 pages. The prosecution sought to prove that the accused men were the murderers. Its witnesses, the survivors from Motza, told about their friends from Qalunya who had warned them in advance—thus seeking to prove that the murders had been premeditated. They also described the attackers and named names. The accused men were their neighbors, and they knew them well. According to the defense, however, four of the defendants had not even been in the village that day, but rather had been in other villages nearby. Those who had been in Qalunya never went to Motza, the defense attorneys claimed, and thus did not participate in the murder. The defense claimed that the attackers had been Bedouin without any connection to Qalunya.

Mohammad Samrin (Al-Badawi) Testifies

In his book, based on oral testimonies about his village, Ghaleb Samrin proudly noted the involvement of Qalunya's men in the 1929 riots. That contrasts starkly with what the Qalunya defendants and witnesses told the court. Here is how Mohammad Samrin, Ghaleb's father, responded to the prosecution's interrogation in court:

> I remember the Saturday when the riots occurred. I was at home in Qalunya. With me at home were my wife Fatma and my young daughters. I am a laborer and take any work that comes. On that Saturday none of the village men were working because the tax collector was in the village and everyone was busy getting money.
>
> —You stand accused of the murder of the Maklev [sic] family.
> —Mr. Maklev and his family are my friends.
> —Did you bear a sword that day?
> —No.
> —Haim Maklev says that you stabbed his mother.
> —That's not true. I know the whole family. They are my friends. On Friday night I had a very sharp toothache and I did not sleep all night, so I slept on Saturday morning from about ten to two in the afternoon.
> —Did you have any dreams while you slept?
> —No.
> —Did you hear gunshots on Saturday?
> —I heard a few shots at about ten and then I went to sleep.
> —Did you see anything unusual when you woke up?
> —I heard women screaming in the home of Nu'iman Dirbas's family. My daughters told me that Nu'iman was killed by Mr. Broza.
> —Haim Maklev says that at the time that you say you were sleeping, you were in the Maklev home with a dagger in your hand together with Mohammad Matar [al-Khatib] and others.

—It's all a lie. Mr. Broza arranged all those testimonies.

—Didn't you say that you are a friend of the Jews?

—Mr. Broza killed Nu'iman and arranged the whole thing in order to save himself and so that his crime would be considered self-defense.

—Did Mr. Broza also arrange the burning of the Jewish homes and the murder of the Maklev family?

—I don't know. (*Davar*, January 22, 1930)

Qalunya: The Judicial System I

Haim Maklef was one of the witnesses who clearly recognized Mohammad Samrin in his family's home. Maklef heard him shout "Slaughter the dogs!" as he stabled Maklef's mother, Rivka. Passages from his testimony were quoted above. In court, Maklef said that he had beaten 'Ali Lakah, one of the assailants, with a stick. Recall that, in his book, Ghaleb Samrin maintains that Maklef beat Lakah on the head with the butt of a rifle, after his weapon jammed. Maklef denied having a rifle in his possession but acknowledged using a stick as a weapon. Immediately following his testimony, the Arab lawyers demanded Maklef's arrest on suspicion of murdering Lakah, and the police complied. The reporter for *Davar* added: "By the logic of the Jerusalem police, a man should watch his family being murdered, including women and an old man of eighty, and not raise his hand until they come and murder him as well" (December 1, 1929). The prosecution team also realized the absurdity of the arrest and consented to release Maklef on bail. Similarly, Bentzion Broza, accused of murdering one of the attackers in his house, Dirbas, was arrested and then released on bail.

A Nine-Year-Old Boy Testifies

Mordechai Maklef was later called as a witness:

Mordechai Maklev [*sic*], the surviving Maklev. The guard at the door announces that the boy is crying and is afraid to enter. He is brought into the courtroom and his eyes are full of tears. The judges gaze affectionately at the small witness. Presiding Judge McDonnell tells him that he needs to tell the truth, that he must not tell a lie, especially in court. The boy giggles and says: I know.

In accordance with the prosecutor's questions, the witness relates: I remember the Saturday on which the Arabs attacked our house. At the time I was on the small balcony with my sister Hannah. I hadn't yet eaten lunch. We wanted to set the table. I saw the Arabs running on the side of the village and on the side of the road straight at our house, and when they were close to the house I went into the living room because I was scared of them. . . . I heard Mother and Rivka shouting to Salih [al-Zir] What do you want of us. . . . In response to the prosecutor's question the witness replies that he is sure that he saw Salih Zir by the gate to the garden.

—Why did you look specifically at the door of Haim's room?

—I looked there because Mina fell there.

—When you went into the living room, what was Mina doing?

—She wasn't doing anything because they shot her right away.

Would the Court Believe Him?

The prosecution summed up at the end of January 1930. Then the defense offered its summation. The basic defense argument was that all the Jewish witnesses were lying. Fa'iz Haddad, the defense attorney, highlighted the contradictions among the testimonies heard in the trial and claimed that the Jews had named specific people from Qalunya simply because they knew them, or because Jewish policemen had coached them to do so (*Do'ar Hayom*, January 24, 1930). The Arab murderers in Safed made the same claim, as did the Jewish defendant Yitzhak Auadis from Jaffa.

Haddad did not tell the truth. It was not his job to do so. We know that the facts were not as he presented them because we have the testimonies that Ghaleb Samrin collected. Inhabitants of Qalunya told him about a premeditated attack on the Jews of Motza, in which Ghaleb's father and Mohammad Matar al-Khatib took part. They also told him that the two villagers who died, 'Ali Lakah and Nu'iman Dirbas, were killed leading the assaults on the Maklef home (in Lakah's case) and the Broza home (in Dirbas's case). In other words, the defense witnesses and the defendants lied in court—which is hardly unheard of. The question is whether the court was able to tell truth from falsehood. The inhabitants of Palestine, both Jews and Arabs, awaited the court's decision. Would it convict the accused men or believe their version of the events? The court did not have the benefit of Samrin's book, which was not published until 1993. It had to decide between the two opposing versions of events presented to it.

Liar!

The court was aware that witnesses do not always tell the truth. Qalunya's mukhtar tried to provide alibis for a number of the defendants and also claimed that he had not heard of the murder of the Maklef family until Sunday. Judge de Freitas retorted: "Let me offer you my compliments. You are the biggest liar I have ever heard in my life. I have already heard plenty of liars in Palestine, but you are the biggest one. Go back to your village and everyone will know that you are a liar. You are a disgrace to your gray hair. Leave" (quoted in *Davar*, January 10, 1930).

Lies: The Haifa Version

As we saw with the Hinkis trial in Jaffa, neither side in the conflict felt duty bound to tell the truth at all times. Here is an interesting testimony from Haifa, offered by Yosef Arman, a Haganah commander in that city who was involved in weapons procurement and intelligence collection. He tells of an incident that does not appear in other sources, in part because it never reached the courts. It involved an Arab sheikh by the name of Mahmasani, who was killed by a Jewish police sergeant. The only witness to the event was an Arab named Rashid Yasin. Arman recalled:

> I was assigned to go to the hospital to sway him to change his testimony in return for a sum of money. I was told that if I promised him compensation, he would almost certainly listen to me. I went to him and told him that no matter what happened he would remain handicapped and unable to work, and if he would consent to change his testimony, he would receive a good pension from the Palestine Jewish Coloniza- tion Association for the rest of his life. And after much talk and many promises he was persuaded and, in accordance with my instructions, summoned the prosecu- tor-general and staged the writing of a will, since he was about to die and wanted to confess before his death that the things he had said before were entirely false and that nothing of the sort had happened, and that he had not seen the sergeant and so on and so forth, and so it was. (HHA testimony 6/20)

That's how it worked.

And the Testimony of the Supreme Court Justice

Safed-born Zvi Berenzon, who later served on Israel's Supreme Court, was twenty-two years old in 1929. He taught Hebrew and mathematics at the Scottish College in his home town. During the riots his family home was attacked and burned to the ground. The next chapter will focus on what happened in Safed, but here the testimony Berenzon offered at the trial of a Safed Arab can serve as another example of how witnesses conducted themselves in the trials that re- sulted from the 1929 riots:

> I was a prosecution witness at one of the trials. On the second floor of our house there was a balcony from which I could see what was happening on the street and I indeed saw one of the Arabs below, walking around and calling out various cries and waving a sword. The truth is that I saw him from a distance of about 200 meters and I did not see who it was, but all the other Jews identified him and testified against him at the trial. He was a respectable Arab, owner of a store in Safed. Shamefully, I also testified against him. But there were enough testimonies of others who identi- fied him with certainty to convict him in court. I did not hesitate to testify against

him because I did indeed see and hear the sight [*sic*] of a man going around with a drawn sword in hand calling out "*itbah al-yahud* [kill the Jews]." From this instance I learned that in such cases, when everything is done in anger, one has to take care not to believe every incriminating testimony. (Berenzon 2000, 66)

This was the system of testimony coordination that the British Mandatory courts had to cope with.

Qalunya: The Judicial System II

On January 23, 1930, precisely five months after the riots broke out, the court handed down its verdict on the Motza massacre. Presiding Judge Michael Mc-Donnell began to read out the judgment: "Before announcing the verdict, I wish to say a few preliminary words. This trial has lasted some two months, over forty to fifty sessions. All the participants have worked hard and we thank both the prosecutor-general and the defense attorneys for assisting us. The duty of the court is to enforce justice, and if the people of the various communities in Palestine wish for the enforcement of justice, they must know that when they come to testify in court they must come with clean hands" (quoted in *Davar*, January 24, 1930).

An Interim Comment to the Judge

Why should the inhabitants of Palestine believe in foreign justice and submit themselves to it? The Arabs, after all, believed that the British had come to give the Jews power over them, and the Jews felt that the British were abandoning them to the mercies of the Arab majority. Both sides sensed that the British interest was not in justice but in ruling the Holy Land. At the same time, both the Jews and the Arabs felt profoundly that justice was on their side with regard to the great question of who had the right to Palestine. They felt the same about the specific questions discussed in court, such as their right to bear arms and to use it to defend themselves and their country.

The Judge Continues

The twelve prisoners indicted under Section 170 of the Ottoman Criminal Code Ordinance and Sections 3–4 of the Amended Criminal Code Ordinance of 1927 stand accused of participation in the murders of members of the Maklev [*sic*] family and other individuals who were in the Maklev house in Motza, and in abetting this murder [*sic*]. The task of the prosecuting attorney is to bring the court proofs without a shadow of a doubt according to which people can be convicted of murder. . . .

We do not maintain that Matityahu Broza's testimony was false, but it was not solid and we cannot rely on it. Shmuel Horowitz's testimony cannot help us much, since he has lived in Motza for only seven years and does not know the local inhabitants well, and was acquainted only with Salih [al-]Zir. Haim Maklev's testimony contains much that makes no sense. Accordingly, we have determined that the prosecutor-general has not proved guilt to us via these witnesses.

The defendants are acquitted. (quoted in *Davar*, January 24, 1930)

Then came the cheers and the embraces and the congratulations, and the families of the defendants cried out "the state is with us" and "Allah is with us." The families of the dead felt humiliated and angry. They were not the only ones to feel that way. "Who spilled the blood of the Maklef family?" *Davar* protested (January 24, 1930). Rabbi Avraham Yitzhak HaCohen Kook and Joseph Klausner of the Hebrew University and the Committee for the Defense of the Western Wall vented their rage in *Do'ar Hayom*. They had a strong argument: if the defendants from Qalunya were not the murderers, then the police should be out searching for the real culprits ("Public Opinion on Maklef Trial," January 26, 1930).

Two months later, a court acquitted the Jewish defendants accused of lynching al-Dajjani in Meah She'arim. Reporting on the ruling, *Do'ar Hayom* raged at the fact that the suspects had been kept in detention for half a year (March 26, 1930). As one might expect, the newspaper did not demand that the police find the true murderers.

5 SAFED

In which we will head northward to this Galilean town and see how Jews and Arabs lived there side by side for many years, and what the Arabs and the Jews say about those days. We will, once again, try to understand how friends turned into enemies, what got etched onto the hearts of the children of 1929, and how memory of that year influenced the fighters of 1948.

In Safed, like Hebron and like Motza, Arabs attacked their Jewish neighbors, Jews whom they had often welcomed into their own homes. It happened five days after the massacre in Hebron, when the country had calmed almost completely. On Thursday afternoon, in full view of several Arab policemen and sparse British security forces, Arab bands stormed into Safed's Jewish quarter, descending from neighborhoods higher up on the slope on which the city stood and ascending from the Amud River channel below. For nearly an hour they went from house to house with knives and axes, killing and maiming, dousing the houses with combustibles and setting them afire. Thirteen Jews were killed in Safed during the 1929 disturbances, most of them in this brief violent episode. Another three Jews were burned to death in nearby Ein Zeitim, and two others were shot dead on the roads into the town. The flames from the homes of the Jews were spread by the wind toward the Arab neighborhoods, one of the reasons the attack stopped so soon.

Mazal Cohen was one of the dead. A eulogy for her by her brother (Menachem Raphael) appeared in *Davar*. More than a painful tribute to a sister brutally murdered, it is a valedictory for Jewish-Arab coexistence in the Galilean mountains, in the city of the Jewish mystics and pious Muslims, merchants and peddlers, and idlers and laborers of both faiths:

> For a quarter of a century I have spoken their language, perused their books, learned their way of life, observed their ways and manners, yet I did not know them. . . . Who injected into your inner beings this twisted spirit, to stride with drawn swords at the

head of a bloodthirsty throng and to lend a hand to murdering innocent people who lived with you securely for generations, who just yesterday were your companions and friends. . . .

You always said that you considered native-born Jews to be your brothers, that you would love them, that you would respect them, because you share a single language and way of talking with them, and that you bore a grudge only against those who came anew to grasp the shovel and plow, who with the sweat of their brows turned the wastelands into blooming gardens, against those who lit up the darkness and who did not discriminate between their brothers and yours, giving succor and healing your maladies as well in their medical institutions, against those who brought to this country the culturally and humanly good and beautiful, the light and magnificence to which your eyes too opened, wakening you from your long slumber. . . .

And how is it that you, the murderers of Safed, beset like beasts of prey solely those inhabitants of the city who have been integrated there for generations, turning their homes to heaps of ruins, mercilessly killing women and the old and the weak, who never did you any harm, taking the lives of people whose mother tongue is your language, and whose way of life is yours, different from you only in religion. . . .

I have lived among you for a quarter of a century, I have been your guest, I have attended to your confidences and thoughts, and I did not know you. (M. R. Cohen, "I Didn't Know Them," *Davar*, October 13, 1929)

The Motif Returns

The speaker's hurt over losing his sister was enormous, and to it was added his pain at how his neighbors and friends had turned on him. How could they have abetted such vicious murders? M. R. Cohen reaches a precise and understandable conclusion: he had not truly known his neighbors, nor had he understood that the gap between them was so great. But what gap did he mean? In his view, it was a moral disparity. The Arabs had revealed their true faces—they were despicable and treacherous murderers. But the eulogy suggests another source of the difference between Jews and Arabs, a political one. Each side experienced differently the change that Palestine underwent during the first decade of British rule. According to Cohen, Zionism brought culture and progress to the inhabitants of the land. The Arabs saw this same process as one of conquest and exploitation. For them, the transformation of the wastelands into blooming gardens meant Jewish confiscation of their land. The idea of equality that the Jewish pioneers brought with them was a bad joke for the Arabs—did not the Jews plan to establish a Jewish state and deny the Arabs their national rights?

Without intending it, Cohen highlighted the core of the separation of the Arab Jews from the other Arabs, the beginning of which we considered in chapter 1 from the point of view of Mordechai Elkayam of Jaffa. At that time, during the Second Aliyah, members of the established Jewish population found themselves divided between loyalty to their fellow Jews and to their own tradition and culture, which had much in common with the local Muslims and Christians. But thanks to the influx of pioneering Zionists during the early years of the British Mandate, the Yishuv grew in number and strength. The old-timers were proud of this. More accurately, they felt uncomfortable with the alien values that the pioneers brought with them and disliked the condescension and alienation with which the European immigrants treated the native Jews. They were frustrated by the fact that the foreigners were appropriating the resources of the country's Jewish community. Yet, despite all this, they saw much that was positive in the newcomers. They were brethren who had come to redeem the soil of the homeland, striving toward the promised redemption, coreligionists bearing the banners of progress and modernity. Most importantly, they were fellow Jews whose arrival would help turn the Jews into a majority in their ancestral land. The feelings of the established Jews about the pioneers were thus completely different from the feelings of Muslim and Christian Arabs, who viewed the pioneers as arrogant foreign invaders whose goal was to eject Palestinian Arabs from their own country. In the context of the times, at the climax of the consolidation of national identities, any indication of identification with Zionism by the longtime Jewish inhabitants of Palestine was understood by their Muslim and Christian neighbors as a declaration of war against Arab nationalism, as well as against the rights of the Palestinian Arabs to their land. Hence it made no difference that these Jews had long been part of the Arab cultural sphere. For the Palestinian Arabs, then, the Jews of North Africa and the East became one and the same as the Jews from Eastern Europe, for better and for worse. That was the situation throughout the country, Safed included.

1921: The Jews of Safed Sign Off on Zionism

The Jews of Safed, or at least the community's leaders, had made their political choice in the summer of 1921. The leaders of the Palestinian national movement had traveled to London for a series of meetings with the British regime, their goal being to bring about the revocation of the Balfour Declaration. While the Arab delegation was in London, it declared that it represented all the longtime inhabitants of Palestine: Muslims, Christians, and Jews. The Zionist leadership was alarmed and sent emissaries to collect pledges of support from the leaders of the old Sephardi communities in Hebron, Jerusalem, Safed, Tiberias, Jaffa, and Haifa. The petitions stated that these Jews viewed the Balfour Declaration as "the beginning of the fulfillment of a generations-old prophecy," in the words chosen by the Jews of Jaffa (cza z4/41245). A similar statement came from Safed: "The Sephardi community of Safed firmly protests the reports disseminated by the Arab delegation, according to which the Sephardi Jews in the Land of Israel are on its side, and hereby declares openly that it is in total agreement with the rest of the Jews of the Land of Israel in their demand to carry out the promises made to create a Jewish national home in the Land of Israel. There is no difference between its opinions on this subject and those of the rest of the Jews in the Land of Israel and the Exile" (CZA Z4/41245).

One of the signatories was Safed's Chief Rabbi Yishma'el Hakohen, whom we will encounter below. In the meantime, the point is to see, once again, that intra-Jewish differences were dwarfed by the historic opportunity all Jews saw to provide a firm political foundation for themselves in the Holy Land, under British protection.

In the Background: More Distant History

Even if, with good reason, we do not accept the common Muslim claim that Jewish life under Islamic rule was one uninterrupted golden age, Safed was a classic example of how a creative and vibrant Jewish community could develop under Muslim rule. At the encouragement of Sultan Bayezed II, Jewish exiles from Spain settled throughout the Ottoman Empire. In the sixteenth century many Jews settled in Safed, both because the wool industry there offered them a livelihood and because of the city's proximity to the tombs of many Tana'im, the rabbis of the Mishnaic period, among them Rabbi Shimon Bar Yohai. Some of the period's greatest Jewish legal scholars (such as Rabbi Yosef Karo, author of the *Shulkhan Arukh*), liturgical poets (among them Rabbi Shlomo Alkabetz, author of *Lekha Dodi*), and mystics (most notably Rabbi Yitzhak Luria, known as the Ari; Rabbi Moshe Cordovero; and Rabbi Hayyim Vital) lived and worked there. No better proof of the city's Jewish cultural and religious blossoming during the early Ottoman period is needed.

This celebrated period demonstrates that the Muslim rulers of the time did not see Jewish settlement in Palestine in a negative light, and that contemporary Islamic law and practice did not deny Jews the right to purchase land and settle there. In fact, opposition to Jewish settlement in Palestine is largely a modern Muslim phenomenon, the product of the age of colonialism and nationalism. Amnon Raz-Krakotzkin suggested in a seminar at the Van Leer Institute in Jerusalem in 2011 that when the Spanish exiles settled in the Galilee and connected with the tombs of the Sages of the Mishnah, they fashioned a model of Jewish life in Palestine with roots in the period of the Mishnah and Talmud — that is, an era in which the Jewish people lacked political sovereignty. This differed from the Zionist approach of three hundred years later, which saw itself as a direct heir of the Jewish sovereignty of the biblical era. As such, the Jewish settlement in Safed was seen as unthreatening and even desirable, while Zionist settlement was perceived as a menace. Raz-Krakotzkin's claim is debatable — after all, Jewish religious and redemptive activity of the type practiced by Safed's rabbis and mystics also challenges Islam. Belief in Jewish messianic redemption implies that Islam is not the true faith. But religious belief need not focus on rivalry with other creeds. For many years a different conception was prominent, one that focused on what Judaism and Islam shared. In and around Safed this was expressed in a variety of ways. Here is a passage written by a native of Safed, Rabbi Shlomo Meinstral, taken from a letter he wrote at the beginning of the seventeenth century: "They [the non-Jews in Palestine] treat with great sanctity the tombs of the holy Tana'im and the synagogues and they light candles on the tombs of the saints and vow [gifts of] oil to synagogues. In the village of Ein Zeitim and Meron there are, as a result of our abundant sins, ruined and empty synagogues, and within them innumerable Torah scrolls in their arks, the gentiles treat them with great respect, and hold the keys and honor them and light candles before the arks, and no one may approach and touch the Torah scrolls." Natan Shor, who includes this quote in *Toldot Tzfat* (A history of Safed; 1983, 94), warns that Meinstral tended to exaggerate. Shor also attributes the good treatment of the Jews to the firm hand of the authorities, which induced "the Muslim population to act with such a measure of tolerance, despite its natural inclinations" (ibid., 95).

The phrase "natural inclinations" used by Shor is not a product of in-depth analysis or precise historical reportage, if for no other reason than the fact that enmity between Muslims and Jews is not anything like a natural law. Interconfessional violence, or antagonism between any different populations, is generally a result of religious or political power struggles. Its manifestation and intensity are affected by changes in the balance of power between different groups. Islamic moderates like to quote a verse from the Qur'an: "People, We created you all from a single man and a single woman, and made you into races and tribes so that you should recognize one another" (*al-Hujurat*, The Private Rooms 49:13). In other words, the existence of different nations, as well as different genders, is a foundation of human life.

The violence of 1929 does not negate the coexistence that prevailed in Safed during the sixteenth century, but perhaps the later period casts new light on the earlier one. Another book on Safed, by Yasar al-'Askari, a volume in the series *al-Mudun al-Falistiniyya* (The cities of Palestine) published by the Cultural Department of the Palestine Liberation Organization (PLO), addresses the changes that took place under the Mandate.

The PLO's Version

Al-'Askari's *Qussat Madina: Safad* (Story of a City: Safed, 1989) adopts the common Islamic view of Muslim rule as benevolent. The author, himself a refugee from Safed, writes at length about relations between Jews and Arabs in the town. He describes the Sephardi and Ashkenazi communities, explains that the Jews were part of the social fabric, notes that they spoke Arabic, and says that those who frequented Arab villages in the area donned the Palestinian headdress, the *kufiyyeh*. He tells how Jews and Arabs frequented the same cafés and waxes nostalgic about the common Muslim custom (which many Jews from Islamic lands also fondly recall) of bringing cakes, pita bread, and sweets to the Jews on the night when the Pesach holiday ends, and receiving in exchange surplus matzot from the Jews. But the canvas was more intricate than such idyllic scenes suggest: "This tranquil life did not conceal ambiguous attitudes, especially in light of political developments, and in particular the growing Arab rebellion movement and the escalation of the conflict between it and the British, as well as the growth of the Zionist movement and the clarification of its intentions regarding Palestine" (al-'Askari 1989, 67).

So What Happened in 1929?

The skirmishes over the Western Wall and al-Aqsa caused tension and discord in Safed as well. Rumors about events in Jerusalem reached Safed much elaborated, describing a Jewish attack on al-Aqsa and the city's Muslim community. Tempers in Safed flared; the local mufti, Sheikh As'ad Qadura, and others tried to calm them ('Abasi 1999). On Thursday, August 28, a large protest assembly against Jewish attacks in Jerusalem was held in the al-Suq Mosque, located in Safed's marketplace. The commander of the local police, John Faraday, rose to offer reassurances but was unable to pacify the crowd. According to al-'Askari, Faraday confirmed that the Jews had attacked al-Aqsa and that they had forcefully taken control of al-Buraq. He declared, however, that the government was in control of the situation and would punish the offenders. Faraday's speech only exacerbated the fury of the masses.

Faraday spoke in Arabic but was apparently misconstrued by his audience, members of which began calling out "Revenge!" and "If we don't defeat the Jews, they will defeat us!" ('Abadi 1977, 136). Yet what incensed the crowd even more, according to al-'Askari, was a report that reached the protestors while the rally was still in progress. It said that the body of Ahmad Tafish had been found near Safed's Jewish quarter. Tafish was also known as Sheikh al-Shabab, the leader of the youth.

What set off this rumor? It might have been an incident that took place that afternoon, during the rally at the mosque. After addressing the audience, Faraday had set out on horseback for the Jewish quarter. He saw Jews running and calling out "Arabs, Arabs!" He advanced to see what was going on and to calm things down. A Jewish officer, Kalman Cohen, and an Arab officer, Shawkat Mubashir, also arrived. They found a badly wounded man. The victim's dress and looks convinced the police officers that he was an Arab. To prevent a further escalation of tension, they took him into a building off the main road (Commission 1930; 2:1028).

It was only the next day that it was determined that the victim, who had since died, was a Jew. His name was Yitzhak Maman, and like many Sephardi Jews he normally dressed like a *franji* (a Westernized Arab). Yosef Benderly, born in Safed in 1900 and a local member of the Haganah, witnessed the murder, but had no means of saving Maman. The two men had been walking down the street when they were attacked by four Arabs. Benderly was able to get away, but the four assailants began to beat Maman with sticks. The survivor testified in court that he had heard the victim calling out to one of the attackers: "Ahmad, have mercy!" But Benderly was unable to say what happened subsequently. Benzion Borodinsky, a physician at the town's Hadassah clinic, testified that Maman was brought to the clinic with his ribs broken and his lungs punctured. The doctor tried to save him, but the broken body could not hold out and Maman died in surgery. One of the suspects in the murder was Ahmad Tafish. In other words, it was not the leader of the youth who had been murdered during the gathering in the mosque. Instead, Tafish had murdered Maman (Criminal Assize 20/30 Haifa — Ahmad Khalil Tafish, in TNA CO 733/181/4).

Maman's widow, Malka, testified in court that on the operating table, before his death, her husband told her who had attacked him: "He said: 'Ahmad Tafish, Ahmad Ghana'im, and Awad Ghana'im.' He was breathing with difficulty. I stayed with him until the morning. He'd utter a single word and then lose consciousness" (ibid.). The defense attorneys claimed she was lying. She responded: "I swear that he himself and no one else told me the names. May God send me to him if I am lying." The court, however, rejected her testimony (it had good reason to be suspicious of the witnesses — recall that future Supreme Court Justice Zvi Berenzon confessed that he lied at the trial of the Safed murderers). But Tafish did not go free. He was sentenced to fifteen years in prison for the murder of the elderly Khanum Cohen in full view of her son Shmuel, who testified to the crime in court.

Only Fifteen Years for Murder?

The prosecution sought the death penalty for a charge of premeditated murder, but Tafish's lawyer, Hasan Asfur, cited the precedent of Simha Hinkis of

Jaffa, whose story appears in chapter 1. The Muslim assailants had not plotted in advance to murder Jews, Asfur argued. Rather, having heard that Arabs had been killed by inhabitants of the Jewish quarter, angry Muslims set out to take revenge against the Jews and killed some in the heat of the moment. Taking a life under such circumstances, he averred, is not premeditated. In other words, the legal parsing in Hinkis's trial (apparently greased by a bribe) ended up influencing the decisions made in subsequent trials growing out of the riots.

Another Way Jaffa Influenced Safed

We have jumped ahead to the end of the trial, but we are still at the start of the story. Crowds of Arabs exit the mosque. They are angry. They have been told that al-Aqsa was burned and that Tafish had been murdered by Jews. They might have heard something else as well. Binyamin Geiger, who was about five years old at the time, offers this account of the events of that week:

> The riots reached Safed on Thursday, August 29. On the previous Saturday a large demonstration was organized. Crowds of inflamed Arabs entered the alleys of the Jewish quarter. The man leading the procession waved a flag, a drummer striding beside him, and they stirred up the crowd with loud roars: "*Seif al-din Hajj Amin*" [Hajj Amin (al-Hussayni) is the sword of the faith]. The mob smashed windows and ripped off doors. While no one was killed that day, it was a premonition of what was to come. . . . A tense peace prevailed that entire week, until Thursday. That day rioters came out of the large mosque in the heart of the *shuk* [market]. The riots started after provocative speeches, in which the worshipers were told that Jews had killed five Arabs in Jaffa. (Geiger 2011, 163)

It is interesting that Geiger, a respected citizen of Jewish Safed, who commanded its defense in 1948 and then settled there, cites the murder of the 'Awn family in the context of the attack on his city's Jewish quarter. It is hard to see where he got this from. As a Jewish child he obviously was not present in the mosque at the time of the speeches. None of the Arab sources make this connection. And how could the news have reached Safed so quickly when — as part of the British efforts to prevent the spread of unauthorized information — all telephone lines except official ones had been cut and newspapers had been shut down? How is it that Geiger is almost the only source who accurately reports the number of people killed in the attack on the 'Awn home? Nevertheless, it could well be that some shred of a rumor about what had happened in Jaffa had reached the Galilee, and that this, along with the news from Jerusalem, made the blood of Safed's Arabs boil.

Geiger continues: "The inflamed rioters broke into the Jewish quarter, bearing knives (cutlasses), axes, and clubs. At their head strode no other than 'Abd al-Rahman, an Arab laborer who worked at Eisenberg's bakery. He led the crowd, bearing a huge drum on his shoulder, beating it in ecstasy" (ibid.).

Back to Faraday and His Men

This was just after Faraday and his men had spotted the badly wounded man in the street, thought he was an Arab, and hid him in a nearby building until he could be evacuated to the hospital. At the same time the commander ordered his policemen to deploy rapidly in the Jewish quarter and on the boundary between it and the town's Arab neighborhoods. But as he, in the Ashkenazi neighborhood in the upper reaches of the quarter, conveyed orders via mounted policemen and tried to organize his forces, the massacre continued. In a report he authored, Faraday acknowledged his failure: "The police do not appear to have got into close contact with the bands of Moslems in the various parts of the Jewish Quarter; while the police were in the upper part of the Quarter murders were committed in the lower part, and when they proceeded to the lower part attacks were intensified in the upper part" (Commission 1930, 2:1028). At one of the Shaw Commission's sessions, the counsel for the Arab Executive Committee, William Stoker, tried to advance the claim that the riots in Safed began when Jews killed two Arabs there:

> Were not two Arabs killed when these were sitting in houses just opposite to each other? — No. They were not killed by Jews.
> Who were they killed by? — By me.
> By yourself personally? — By me personally.
> With your own hand? — Yes.
> What were they doing? — They were rushing up the street trying to burn the stores belonging to Mr. Klinger. (ibid., 2:175–76)

It was at about this time that a different band of rioters killed Safed's elderly Sephardi chief rabbi, Yishma'el Hakohen.

Rabbi Yishma'el Hakohen

Hakohen was born in the Persian city of Yazd, in or around 1845. At the age of thirteen he set out with his father on the long trip to the Land of Israel. His father never made it. He died in Iraq, where the boy Yishma'el remained in the home of an uncle and studied at a local Jewish academy. In 1868 he completed his journey, arriving in Safed at the age of twenty-three. Eight years later he was appointed a rabbinic judge, and in 1904 he was invited to serve as rabbi of the Turkish city of Tire. He spent fourteen years there, until, after World War I, his longing for Safed overcame him and he returned to serve as presiding judge on the Sephardi religious court (Grayevski 1929, 4).

The French journalist and writer Albert Londres and the illustrator Georges Rouquayrol met Hakohen a short time before he was murdered. The rabbi was already weak and homebound. Londres recounted his visits to Jewish communities in Europe and Palestine in a book in 1930, *Le juif errant est arrivé* (The Wandering Jew has come home; published in Hebrew in 2008). As he wrote there, when he heard about the riots, he rushed back to Palestine. Returning to the house where he had met Hakohen, he recalled that earlier encounter:

> I went again to his house. I climbed the stairs. The door was no longer closed. Bloody rags were strewn over the divan he had sat on when he received me. A pool of coagulated blood stained the tiles, like a broken mirror face down on the floor. His fingerprints are smeared on the wall in blood.
>
> "Mr. chief rabbi," I had said to him then, on this very spot. "Will you permit my friend Rouquayrol to sketch your portrait?"
>
> "My dear guests," he replied, "the faith of Moses forbids it, but Yishma'el Cohen no longer sees well. He will certainly know nothing about it."
>
> He extended me his white hand.
>
> The imprint of his palm, all red, now stands on the wall. (Londres 2008, 175)

Most of the city's dead were Jews from the Islamic world. Thus, in the context of Safed, no claim was made, as it was in Hebron, that the Arabs attacked only recently arrived Jews. In certain cases the murderers and their victims knew each other fairly well. The person who opened the door for the band that murdered Hakohen was a Muslim who served as a *Shabbat goy* in his house, performing for the rabbi actions forbidden to Jews on the Sabbath. There were cases of even more intimate familiarity, such as the case of Rashid Khartabil.

Khartabil and the Afriyat Family

Rashid Khartabil was a dairyman, tending goats and cows at his homestead and selling their milk to Jews and Arabs. He was one of ten defendants tried for breaking into the Afriyat family home and murdering the father and mother. Like the others, he denied involvement in the murder, but he admitted to knowing the family. At his trial he related that one of the Afriyat girls had been his lover and had lived in his home for two years alongside his wife and sisters. He related that he knew that this fact was a source of some discomfort for her Jewish family, but that the affair had in any case ended long ago. His Jewish girlfriend had left him and his home, married, and given birth to children (TNA CO 733/181: 56–57).

Intermarriages were not common during the Mandate period, but neither were they unheard of (Ovadiah 2009). In any case, Khartabil told the court that he had not even gotten close to the area of the disturbances. But many witnesses testified otherwise. The court accepted the prosecution's position and sentenced Khartabil to death, along with Fuad Hijazi and the eight other defendants. Eventually, most of the sentences were commuted, as I will relate below. But we are still in Safed on Thursday afternoon, at the time of the attack on the Sephardi neighborhood. We understand that a shared culture and even close association may well not serve as protection at such a turbulent time. The rioters proceeded from the Sephardi neighborhood up to the Ashkenazi area, where Geiger was playing with his friends.

How Geiger Escaped Death

Geiger relates in his memoirs that he and his playmates suddenly saw their neighbor, Reb Levi Yitzhak, running in panic past the Ha'Ari Synagogue. Pursuing him was an Arab holding an ax in one hand and a club in the other. The children scattered. The Arab began running after Geiger. The boy ran into the yard of the Avrutch Synagogue and, hearing the Arab still running behind him, leapt into the excrement-filled pit in the synagogue's latrine. He spent several minutes in stinking fear, but the Arab did not think of looking into the pit, and so Geiger was saved (Geiger 2011, 164–65).

Rachel Kahana, sixteen years old at the time, sent an account of what happened to members of her family immediately after the riots ended. She related that when the Arabs arrived at her house, only children were there. Her younger brother ran to call their father, who returned home and hid with the rest of the family in the cellar while the house was under attack: "Father was already despairing of our lives, and we were all trembling in fear and alarm. The children fainted and we did not know what to do" (Kahana's letters, BHMA, file "1929 riots"). But a while later a police patrol chased away the assailants. The family emerged from the cellar and tried to figure out what was going on around them:

> We went up to the roof and there it was, woow, the city was in flames and Hebrew boys were running and shouting: Go up, Jews, come up! To Lunz! To the bank! We were barefoot because it was a hot day, so we had been barefoot at home, so each of us put a child on our shoulders and we are running, running in the crowd with our knees buckling, our hearts pounding, pounding like a hammer. The Arab policemen, amusement showing in their faces, urged us on. Oh, those Arab policemen, they are to blame for it all. For all the horrible destruction. . . . Our family held on, one to the other. I was bearing Budik on my back, Levi had Yocheved, Tzvi had Budis, Haya had Simaleh, Father had Mother, Haya had Rivkeleh, Mr. Zilber had Tzipora. . . . With much effort we all got into the yard [of the Saraya, a government building]. The night was dark and overcast and we couldn't see a thing. . . . A deathly horror overcame me when I saw the tragic sight in the yard — imagine for yourself a

Jews of Safed before the funerals, August 1929 (Central Zionist Archives).

throng of 3,000 people lying flat in a yard filthy with the offal of horses and straw and garbage.

As Kahana recounts here, the police gathered up Safed's Jews and herded them into the Saraya. Another survivor, five years old at the time of the riots, described these hours in a testimony he wrote eighty years after the events:

> One day I heard shouts, cries, and screams, and loud beating on sheet metal. I was frightened. I asked my mother who was shouting and why they were shouting. She told me: It's the Arabs, who want to kill us. I asked: Why? She said that they wanted to kill all the Jews. I saw a mob of hundreds of Arabs in the street, screaming and shouting. I was frightened. In the evening Mother took me and my sister Naomi to the house of friends of ours. The Arabs threw hundreds of stones at the house, at the windows and shutters. They beat on the doors and shutters with huge clubs and cast blazing torches through the windows. The house began to burn. The shutters, curtains, and even my mother's and sister's nightgowns began to go up in flames. (Tal's testimony, BHMA, file "1929 riots")

The members of this family also survived, thanks to a group of young Jews who extricated them from their house. They, like the rest of the city's Jews, were evacuated to the Saraya. The witness goes on to provide the rest of his biography. From Safed his family moved to Be'er Tuvia, which had also been at-tacked during the riots, and in 1942 he enlisted in the Jewish Brigade and fought the Germans on the Italian front:

> We returned from the Brigade and joined the Haganah forces, and took an active part in the War of Independence. During the War of Independence I changed my targets in battle. Before, in the Brigade, I shot at Germans and they shot at me. Now I began to shoot at the Arabs with my personal machine gun and I hit them. Each time I fired a volley I added: Take this and take another. It was revenge for spilling the blood of Safed's Jews. I thought that it was my right and duty to ensure that the Arabs paid back the blood of the Jews murdered in the riots. To this day I believe that revenge is a duty and is moral. (ibid.)

The person who tells this is General Yisrael Tal, famous in Israel for being the father of the Merkava tank. He served in the Jewish Brigade under Mordechai Maklef, a survivor of the Motza massacre, whose story I have told above. After World War II, Tal took part in revenge operations against the Germans. In his own words, "with the Germans we went crazy. We shot at Germans. We carried out pogroms against the Germans" (quoted in Ginosar and Bar-On 2010, 22).

Tal was one of the officers in the Israeli Defense Forces for whom 1929 was a seminal experience. Another one, as noted above, was Rehavam Ze'evi, and yet another was Yohai Bin-Nun, who served as commander of Israel's navy. In a detailed testimony for the Haganah History Archives, Bin-Nun relates that his earliest childhood memory was the Arab attack on Jerusalem's Beit HaKerem neighborhood, and that the first dead body he saw in his life was one of the vic-tims in Bayit VeGan in 1929. These experiences led him to resolve to devote his life to military and security affairs (HHA 141/36).

Tal's account in the Hameiri Museum Archive offers an understanding of how such a frame of mind was shaped. At the age of eighty-five, he reported a brief exchange he had had with his mother eighty years previously: "I asked my mother who was shouting and why they were shouting. She told me: It's the Arabs, who want to kill us. I asked: Why? She said that they wanted to kill all the Jews. I saw a mob of hundreds of Arabs in the street, screaming and shouting. I was frightened."

That is the kind of moment that shapes a person's life. A young boy finds himself in mortal danger, along with his mother and sister. They are assailed in their home by hundreds of people (Tal's father was at his job at the electric power station at Naharayim, on the Jordan River). Their neighbors and friends are being slaughtered all around. His mother interprets the world for him: the Arabs want to kill all the Jews. Or at least that is what he remembers her telling him. His mother's explanation became part of the lens through which he viewed the world, irrespective of its accuracy (in fact, not *all* the Arabs wanted to kill Jews, and those who wanted to kill Jews did not necessarily want to kill *all* Jews). As a result of this worldview, he sets out in 1948, so he declares, "to ensure that the Arabs paid back the blood of the Jews murdered in the riots." Note that he says "the Arabs" and not "the murderers." That does not mean that these men, looking through the sights of their rifles, made no distinction between a German soldier and an Arab, between an SS officer and a Palestinian fellah. But if we take Tal at his word, the memory of the riots blinded him, making him forget the fact that not every Arab was a murderer, and that in Safed, too, there were Arabs who in 1929 opposed the attacks on the Jews. Mahmoud Abbas is one example.

Mahmoud Abbas

Mahmoud Abbas belonged to the extended family of his more famous namesake, the president of the Palestinian Authority who also goes by the nom de guerre Abu Mazen. Esther Keizerman, later a member of the Etzel underground, provided the Hameiri archive with an account of her acquaintance with him (BHMA file "1929 riots"). Citing the good relations between the town's Jews and Arabs, she recalls that both Jews and Arabs spoke Arabic, Hebrew, and Yiddish, and that they visited each other's homes. An Arab maid worked in her family's home. She also recalls, however, cases in which Jews were attacked by Arabs, frequent cries of "*idbah al-Yahud*" following Friday prayers in the mosques, and the murder of many Jews by Arabs in such circumstances.

The final claim, like other details she offers, is not accurate. There are no documented instances of Jews being murdered by Arabs in Safed before 1929, certainly not "many." It is hardly surprising that, in bringing up memories of her early childhood, Keizerman mixes up her chronology and provides inaccurate information. The same happens later in her testimony, when she offers an account of gunfire aimed at the Jews taking shelter in the Saraya, at the end of the attack on Thursday evening. It was an incident that further pained and terrorized an already beaten community. According to Keizerman, "about seventy dead, men, women, and children, were gathered up from the yard after that evil attack" (ibid.). But according to the other sources we have, only two Jews were killed in this shooting—Ayala and Rafael Mizrahi. Keizerman's young age and panic most likely multiplied the number of dead in her memory many times over. What requires our attention here, then, is not the ostensible facts she provides but rather her impressions. Here is another of her recollections:

One Thursday evening I was getting ready for bed and there were knocks on the door. Father picked up his loaded pistol and went to open the door after checking to see who was on the other side. Two Arab men came in, whom I knew from visits in our house, and we children played with their children. The older one's name was Mahmoud Abbas and the second was Hajj Ahmad al-Hussayni. They closed and locked the door, sat down, and told Father in a whisper that they had learned that a group of young men had decided to attack him and us, the children. The next day, Friday at dawn, they stationed themselves outside the two doors to the house. Father took out his pistol, loaded it with bullets, hid us under the bed, closed the windows and doors, and the two men with their pistols stood outside at the two entrances to the house. I drowsed off and suddenly I heard horrifying shouts, curses in Arabic, and gunshots. I shook with fear and Elhanan began to cry. I quieted him down and hugged him hard and then I heard a strong voice in Arabic: "You will not enter this house and you will not touch my friend and his family unless you kill me first, and then my family, who are at the ready, will arrive and nothing will remain of you. Leave the house immediately. I am shooting." They fled. (ibid.)

By the way, not only was Abu Mazen's family living in Safed in the mid-1920s. So was Binyamin Netanyahu's grandfather, Natan Milikowsky. He was the principal of the town's Hebrew-language school, but some four years before the riots he moved to the United States and engaged in public relations for the Zionist movement, as did his son Benzion and his grandson Binyamin. The grandfather belonged to the Revisionist movement, Zionism's maximalist faction.

Revisionists in Safed

Milikowsky wasn't the only Revisionist in Safed. The movement was growing rapidly there on the eve of the 1929 riots. Eitan Wijler, who worked in the Hameiri Museum archive, later wrote about this in a master's thesis he authored. Its title speaks for itself: "Kitzonim Tzionim veFalastinim: HaMikreh shel Me'oraot TaRPa"T beTzefat" (Extremist Zionists and Palestinians: the case of the 1929 Riots in Safed). According to Wijler:

Both Hajj Amin, through his men, and the Revisionists, through their people, made great efforts to export the conflict beyond Jerusalem and bring it to the Land of Israel's northernmost city. Those elements were not satisfied with offering Safed's population general news about the conflict, but rather made efforts to persuade them to accept their positions in the dispute. Both Hajj Amin and his people, on the Arab side, and the Revisionists, on the Jewish side, brought to Safed the same policies that they pursued in Jerusalem, on the matter of the Western Wall. Their policies led to growing extremism and the deterioration of the situation. (Wijler 2005, 137)

The claim that the Revisionists bore some responsibility for fanning the flames just prior to the riots — on the national level, not only in Safed — was made also by Ha'aretz (although following the disturbances it blamed the Arabs solely) and by *Sefer Toldot HaHaganah*—more on that in the next chapter. But we should not deduce from that that the absence of extremist Jews in Safed would have prevented the attack on its Jews. On the one side was the example of Hebron, where the city's Arabs attacked its Jews because they viewed them as part of the Zionist collective, even in the absence of Jewish nationalist activity in the city. On the other side was the example of Tiberias, where Jewish and Arab community leaders were able to keep tempers in control and to prevent casualties. The case of Tiberias shows that local leaders can avoid violence, even in times of crisis. That is, they can set their community outside national disputes, or at least avert violent manifestations of such disputes.

And after an Outbreak of Violence

After the massacre, Safed's Jews and Muslims continued to live side by side. The British wanted to evacuate the Jews from Safed, in part because of the sanitation crisis that followed the riots—bodies lay in the streets for several days, and there was fear that an epidemic would break out. But the Zionist leadership sent Yitzhak Sadeh from Haifa and Shlomo Ze'evi from Jerusalem to reorganize the community and clean up the Jewish quarter, thus avoiding the evacuation. The crisis of confidence between the two communities, however, proved difficult to assuage. Many Jews felt betrayed, even though there had been a few cases of Arabs rescuing Jews and despite the fact that a delegation representing Arab families came to the Saraya, bringing food to the Jews as a gesture of reconciliation and goodwill and to symbolize that they had not been involved in the crime (Wijler 2005, 95). Both sides knew that the dead could not be brought back to life.

The police officer Dov Ben Efrayim related, in testimony to the Haganah History Archives that when he was sent to collect testimonies about the massacre, "Many of them, the Jews, were afraid to talk because they had been in Safed for generations, and the Arabs had been their friends at first. They had never imagined that the Arabs were capable of doing such things, because they had lived with them like brothers, and suddenly something like this had happened. They knew that they would have to continue to live there, so they were scared of testifying" (HHA 135/20). The town's Arabs, for their part, had other concerns. More than 250 Arab inhabitants of Safed had been arrested by the British police. Many of them were heads of families, and their absence left their families without their main means of support. On top of this, the local residents had trouble finding the funds to pay their relatives' legal expenses ('Abasi 1999). The Arabs brought their grievances before the Supreme Muslim Council, and on September 4, Mufti Hajj Amin al-Hussayni sent a letter of complaint to the British high commissioner.

The Complaint of Safed's Arabs

In his letter, the mufti laid out the claims of the Arabs: The disturbances had begun because of Jewish aggression: Jews had opened fire on unarmed Arabs on the town's streets. On the sole basis of Jewish accusations, the police had arrested many Arabs, including merchants and other respected citizens known for their integrity and uprightness. After the riots, the Jews looted and set fire to Arab commercial establishments. Arabs, too, had been killed in the riots, and therefore Jews should also be arrested. The man the government sent to Safed to represent it was a Jew who favored the Jews and harassed the Arabs. The mufti's letter is preserved in the Supreme Muslim Council's archive in Abu Dis, and was published, along with other documents relating to the 1929 disturbances, in the journal *Hawliyat al-Quds* (Hammuda 2011).

The mufti dissimulates in his letter. Only two Arabs were killed in Safed, both of them — as noted above — by Police Commander Faraday. Jews caught looting were brought to trial, but other Jews were falsely accused of this crime by supposed witnesses. The charge that Jews had opened fire on Arabs and set off the riots was shown to be untrue.

In the end, eighteen of the Arab detainees were sentenced to prison terms of between three and fifteen years. Fourteen were sentenced to life imprisonment, and another fourteen to death. Of the latter, thirteen had their sentences commuted by the high commissioner. Only one, Fuad Hijazi, went to the gallows, convicted of incitement and involvement in the murders of the Afriyat family and Mazal Cohen.

The End

In the weeks and months following the massacre in Safed, while the murderers were still on trial, a few Jews and Arabs began discussing ways of returning to normal. The idea of a sulha, a reconciliation ceremony, was broached. Yosef Nahmani, a Keren Kayemet functionary and veteran of an early Jewish self-defense organization, HaShomer, met with advocates of reconciliation on both sides. The Zionist leadership supported the idea but preferred that the Arabs, rather than the Sephardi community, take the initiative so that the Jews would not give an appearance of weakness (Nahmani letter to Kisch, May 1930, CZA S25/4429). Another such proposal came from two public figures — Meir 'Abu, scion of a long-standing and well-off Safed Jewish family, and Na'if Subh, Safed's Arab mayor. They tried to set up a local organization called Brit Shalom (unconnected to the movement of the same name centered in Jerusalem). 'Abu received a certain measure of support for this from the United Bureau, a body established by the Zionist Organization and Jewish National Council to handle Jewish-Arab relations in Palestine.

Palestinian Arab leaders, 1930 (Matson Photograph Collection, Library of Congress).

According to Mutstafa 'Abasi (1999), 'Abu and Subh's effort failed. Many Jews and Arabs, it seems, had no interest in a common framework. The town's Jews and Arabs continued to live side by side for lack of an alternative, but the scars left by the riots did not fade. Beyond the unbearable pain felt by individuals, and beyond the different points of view within each community, each group reached a collective consensus. For the Jews, the Arabs were murderers. The Arabs, for their part, felt more strongly than ever that they were facing a large and organized force that wanted to take over their country. Here is Keizerman's account, in her testimony for the Hameiri Museum archive, of how she interrupted a conversation between her father and Abbas, who visited their home a short time after the riots. She told Abbas:

> "Every Friday you go out into the streets shouting *idbah al-Yahud, idbah al-Muskub, din Mohammad bil-seif*, and every passing Jew dies, whether from knives or axes. . . . How can your hatred be explained? Why are you doing this and what do you really want from us?" He [Abbas] was shocked, he patted me and tried to calm me. He said that only bands of undisciplined young people had done such things. You, too, have young people who kill Arabs for revenge. I didn't know about that and his words mollified my anger. I said: "I hope that's true. It's about time that you also feel suffering, pain, and death as we do." After he left I began shouting at my father: "After what they've done to us you sit down with them?" He then seated me and my brother next to him and said: "If you have any complaints, make them to the Patriarch Abraham.

The Arabs are the descendants of Ishmael and Esau and we are the descendants of Isaac and Jacob. This land belongs both to them and to us."(Keizerman testimony, BHMA, file "1929 riots")

The father's ideal of Jewish-Arab friendship did not get carried over to the next generation. The idea that the country belonged to both nations remained the preserve of just a few. The younger Keizermans and their Arab contemporaries did not feel that they belonged to the same urban fabric or that they all belonged in some way to some larger community. They faced off against each other to fight for control of the land, each community convinced that justice was on its side.

Jews and Arabs continued to live together in Safed for another twenty years following the riots, with fluctuating levels of accommodation and animosity. The murderers and their abettors were gradually released from prison and returned to the city streets. Wijler, relying on testimonies in the Hameiri Museum archive, relates that one of the murderers returned to man a stall in the Jewish quarter. When he was asked about his deeds in 1929 he replied: "What can I say, a demon got in me"(Wijler 2005, 93). During the Arab Revolt of 1936–39 tensions increased and did not subside until 1948. In May of that year the Palmach conquered the town in Operation Yiftah. The background to the operation was, writes the historian Anita Shapira, "the traumatic memory of the massacre that the Arabs committed there against the Jews during the 1929 riots, leaving a profound premonition that such a thing could happen again." In her account of the Palmach operation, she writes that "in the process of taking key points in the city, central buildings in the Arab Quarter were shelled, and the bombardment of the Jewish Quarter by the Arabs continued. The bombardments, the falling of commanding points in the city, and the conquest of the village of ʿAkbara led to a huge panic in the Arab Quarter. Mass flight ensued. The way through the ʿAmud channel in the direction of Meron and Saʿsaʿ remained open and the refugees took this path. Yigal [Allon] always made sure that a way was left open for the Arabs to flee. When the Palmach forces entered the Arab Quarter the next day, they found a ghost town" (2007, 197).

But that happened nineteen years later. In the meantime, Jews and Arabs throughout the country had to cope with the bloodshed of August 1929 and what it had produced.

AFTER THE STORM

A Postmortem

In this final chapter we will meet the inmates of death row in Acre Prison. We will delve into the positions taken by Sheikh Ahmad al-Shuqayri and Albert Einstein, and join the freed prisoner Simha Hinkis, now wearing the uniform of the Hapo'el Tel Aviv soccer team. On the way, we'll encounter the author Shmuel Yosef Agnon, whose home in Talpiot was ransacked. We'll also look at how the murderers of 1929 fared in the years that followed. But let's begin with a poem.

On the road to Zion
A lamb lay slain beside the trail
On the road to Zion
A brother's blood cries from the vale.

Cursed be he who does a deal
Cursed the man who absolves my blood
In my flesh the wound's still raw
A Lord Avenger is my God.

The poem, by Yonatan Ratosh, appeared in the newspaper *Ha'am*, edited by Abba Ahimeir, the leader of Brit HaBiryonim, on May 8, 1931. Ratosh wrote it in protest against a sulha conducted by the Arabs of Qalunya and the Jews of Motza. The sulha was arranged with the encouragement of the Zionist Executive as part of a broader effort to allay tensions between Jews and Arabs; similar ceremonies were held in other areas. As part of the ceremony the Jews of Motza dropped their demand for financial compensation, and the two sides committed themselves to living peacefully as good neighbors. (The Maklef family did not take part in the ceremony.) Many felt uncomfortable with the process. Ratosh was furious. Why were the Jews of Motza prepared to make peace with the Qalunyans, as if the latter had not attacked their homes and murdered them mercilessly? How could the Zionist institutions advocate a sulha while spilt blood was still crying out to be avenged? Curse them! His invective was directed not at the Arabs but rather at the Jews who, in reaching a compromise with their enemies, compromised their own dignity.

Ratosh's poem expresses one of the extreme sentiments that the 1929 massacres aroused in the Yishuv—not just terror, but a thirst for revenge. The Jews in Palestine bitterly debated their future relations with the country's Arabs. The intra-Jewish struggle, however, did not turn bloody. It was limited to mutual recrimination, proscriptions, and sometimes fistfights.

Accusations

The main accusation that the Revisionists made against the Zionist leaders was that they were no less than accessories to the murders. The reasoning was that they had not alerted the Yishuv to the approaching danger, and even worse, they had deliberately offered false assurances. So wrote Yehoshua Yevin, one of the most important polemicists of the time. As noted in chapter 2, he, Abba Ahimeir, and Uri Zvi Greenberg founded Brit HaBiryonim in response to the 1929 riots. In the same article Yevin attacked the Zionist leadership for its policy of silence: "Not only was the sacredness of the defiled Western Wall not important to them. Neither was the sullied honor of Jewish women. The murdered pioneer who had no redeemer for his blood was not important to them. All that was important to them was quiet and money" ("Hokhmat haHashtakah haBezuyah" [The wisdom of contemptible silence], *Do'ar Hayom*, May 28, 1930).

The Honor of Jewish Women

Yevin charged that the Zionist institutions had not taken action to defend the honor of Jewish women. As already noted, both before and after the riots there were cases in which young Arab men harassed Jewish women; the Haganah took action in response. Here is another testimony, from Ya'akov Vaksman-Sagi. He remembered such incidents very well: "With regard to that the Haganah carried out a number of actions. I recall that once two girls were sent to walk at the edge of the Jewish neighborhoods, and we (four men) were sent to trail them. Near the Russian Compound, right next to Hadassah, two Arabs started bothering them. We jumped them and beat them senseless. On one clear day two Arabs were killed on the edge of King George Street (by the big quarry). I participated in securing this action" (HHA testimony 37/1).

Given such evidence, it does not seem that the Haganah ignored Arab sexual harassment of Jewish women. In fact, the Haganah took a dim view of intercommunal sexual and romantic relations even if they were consensual or if the favors were paid for. Meir Spector, commander of the Hebrew Police in Tel Aviv, testified that in 1924–25 the Yishuv grappled with the problem of immigrant

Polish Jewish women who "lacked proper morals" (HHA testimony 180/29). These women welcomed rich men from Jaffa into their homes, according to Spector:

> On nice summer evenings the sounds of laughter and wild goings-on would emerge from those apartments, lasting until the small hours of the night. Some fellows from Tel Aviv who heard the neighbors gossiping about the immoral acts taking place in those apartments suspected the owners of fancy cars in Jaffa, that they were playing around with the new tenants at stuff that wasn't so moral, and [the guys] were concerned about the good name of the first Hebrew city. Unable to strike at the owners of the cars, they resolved, at the very least, to take revenge against the fancy cars themselves by slashing the tires and doing other damage.

Since they were officially part of the Mandate police force, the Tel Aviv policemen were not authorized to take action against Jewish-Arab sexual liaisons. But the policemen were also members of the Haganah and thus considered themselves duty bound to fight the phenomenon. Yitzhak Steinberg, another Tel Aviv policeman, offers another account:

> There were a small number of girls who came from good families in Eastern European countries who met with Arabs for the purpose of prostitution. Yehuda resolved to combat this blight with our help and that of Efrayim Dekel and Yitzhak Agadati. The idea was not to take on the Arabs who showed up but to get the girls to desist from this stuff. We'd go around at night, try to persuade them, and sometimes they would be punished severely. For example, when they caught such a girl, they would take her out of the car she was driving in, turn her over head-down, and pour hot pepper into her vagina. Sometimes there were even harsher actions. (HHA 165/38)

The Hebrew police seem to have stretched the concept of prostitution beyond its original meaning. That is, in some cases the victims were engaging in sex for pay, but at other times they were people who had developed friendships that cut across national lines. This can be seen in the testimony of another policeman, Yosef Dekel: "We protected Tel Aviv's purity. We also intervened if, for example, there were girls who insisted on going out with Englishmen or Arabs. We didn't let them. It wasn't that the police didn't let them. There were two or three guys in the police who oversaw the matter with the help of some very good folks who were committed to the idea" (HHA testimony 176/15).

In this regard, there was little difference between the labor movement and the parties and ideological streams of the bourgeois center and the ideological right. Right-wingers might have made a bigger fuss about it, but the Haganah seems to have accomplished more. Whatever the case, they all opposed romantic relations between Jews and Arabs.

Light from the Darkness?

A more significant difference between the Yishuv's left and right wings could be seen in attitudes toward the Arabs who had saved Jews during the riots. As noted in chapter 2, following the massacres, *Davar* ran a column titled *Orot MeOfel* (Light from the darkness), which chronicled the instances in which Jews were rescued by Arabs. Presumably the newspaper's editors understood that Jews and Arabs would continue to live side by side in the country and believed that publicizing these stories could help quell the flames and reduce animosity. The importance of telling such stories in the wake of massacres and murders has recently been suggested in an article published by Ron Dudai (2012), in which he argues that doing so helps promote reconciliation. However, in addition to showing the Jewish interest in reconciliation and gratitude toward the rescuers, the Yishuv leadership wanted to make two political points—that the mufti was not the true representative of the Arab masses, and that Arab opposition to Zionism was confined to a small group. After all, other Arabs had saved Jews.

Yevin was furious at this preoccupation with "the righteous among the nations." In his view, the leaders had lulled the Yishuv to sleep before the riots and was continuing this evil policy afterward. "They have found a new slogan," he griped. "'Not all the Arabs are murderers.' They've begun to look for the 'Hebron saints'—yes, in Hebron, the city of atrocity, mention of which makes the flesh of every Jew crawl and will do so for generations, they have gone to look for saints!" (*Do'ar Hayom*, May 28, 1930). In an editorial he wrote for *Do'ar Hayom*, Greenberg lamented, or scoffed: "They sought light in the dark of the Hebroni race." (December 21, 1930).

The Hebroni Race

Greenberg's use of the word "race" gave *Davar*'s writers the opportunity they had been waiting for. They wrote a response to the "poet of darkness":

> You of course know about those who declare their contempt of the "other race." Their time has come not only on our street in the Land of Israel. The Jews of Berlin now feel on their backs the lash of the German "race" fighters, who have now risen to power, led by their own wolf [ze'ev], called Hitler, who is also a talented man, an excellent orator, who warns against the silence of the newspapers, and against those treasonous labor leaders who for thirteen years have preached "industry and construction" and have not allowed even a single war to break out in Europe. (*Davar*, December 23, 1930)

When You Could Still Make That Comparison

Comparing political rivals to Hitler and accusing them of being in league with Nazism was a common trope in the noxious political discourse of the

Yishuv following the 1929 massacres. The labor movement viewed itself not just as Zionist but also as part of the international antifascist and anti-Hitler camp. As in the quotation above, some of the movement's spokesmen likened Ze'ev Jabotinsky, the leader of the Zionist right, to Hitler. While Ahimeir and his cohort openly referred to themselves as fascists, they accused the labor movement of aiding the *Führer*. The war of words reached its climax with an article that appeared in the Brit HaBiryonim newspaper, *Hazit Ha'am*:

> What impelled this party to kiss the boots of Hitler and Goering. To crawl before Hitler and his henchmen on all fours as Mapai's red diplomat does, because the despicable condition of the Mapai Party, which has sold itself to the champion of Jew haters for lucre, has now reached a peak without precedent in Hebrew history. Nor are there any justification that can explain this shameful and disgraceful sight.
>
> The Jewish public in the Land and overseas will greet the triple Stalin–Ben-Gurion–Hitler pact with contempt and disgust and will not forgive those who for lucre sold their people's honor in full view of the enlightened world to the antisemitic madmen. ("Mister Arlosoroff, haYenuka ha 'Adom" [Mister Arlosoroff, the red boy], June 16, 1933)

Haim Arlosoroff had recently returned from a trip to Germany during which he helped further the Transfer (*Ha'avara*) Agreement between the Zionist leadership and Germany. Hitler, who had just recently come to power, consented to allow German Jews who wished to emigrate to Palestine to take most of their money with them in the form of German-made products. The Revisionists, who had called for an across-the-board boycott of Nazi Germany, vociferously opposed the agreement. In the minds of many of them, Arlosoroff, one of the young leaders of the socialist Mapai Party and thus by implication a stooge of the antisemitic Soviet regime, had now also concluded an alliance with the Jewish people's other great nemesis.

A few hours after the newspaper containing this article hit the stands, Arlosoroff was murdered. The British police connected the dots, and suspected Brit HaBiryonim. Many members of the labor movement also believed that the killing was a political one carried out by the right. Ahimeir was arrested for incitement to murder, and his colleagues Avraham Stavsky and Zvi Rosenblatt were accused of murder. The two latter men shared a jail cell with Yosef Urfali and Simha Hinkis — who, as mentioned in chapter 1, had been convicted of murder. The prisoners grew close. According to one witness in the Arlosoroff murder trial, Urfali was involved in an attempt to bribe Arab prisoners to assume responsibility for the murder (*Davar*, February 20, 1934).

But what interests us here is not who killed Arlosoroff. (The controversy continues to this day. While an official national commission of inquiry appointed by the government of Menachem Begin in 1982 cleared the Revisionists of the crime, its report did not persuade many who were not already of that opinion.) Our subject is the polarization of Yishuv politics following 1929, and the dispute between Jewish political camps about the massacres. The labor movement thought it right and proper to commemorate the Arabs who saved Jews. For Brit HaBiryonim and its sympathizers, to say anything good about Arabs — even Arabs who had saved Jews — was to grovel before them and defile the memory of the dead. Furthermore, Brit HaBiryonim believed, spreading stories about Arabs who had saved Jewish lives was liable to divert the attention of the Jews from reconquering their homeland. But people who are not concerned about such diversions can learn quite a bit from an account of how laborers from the village of Sur Baher saved their Jewish fellow workers.

The Sur Baher Rescue

Four Jewish workers at a quarry just south of Jerusalem were saved by the inhabitants of a nearby village in one of the most striking rescue stories of 1929. Readers of *Ha'aretz* and *Davar* read the story. *Ha'am* and *Do'ar Hayom* did not publish it, for ideological reasons. Here it is, as told by one of the rescued stone breakers, a former member of HaShomer, Zelig Shturman:

> The day the riots broke out found me at the quarry near Bethlehem. I had been taken on there as an assistant to the director of the government quarry, who was an Italian mining engineer. Three other Jews worked there in addition to me, one as chief mechanic and two others as chief excavators. There were about 100–120 Arabs, most of them Christians from Bethlehem and Beit Jala. The Christian Arabs did not like the fact that the management was Jewish, but we had friends and sympathizers among the Muslim Arabs. We were especially friendly with a group of Arabs from the village of Sur Baher, next to [the kibbutz] Ramat Rachel, which was by the way not known to be friendly to the Jews. (HHA 17/48)

It's understandable why the longtime local workers objected to bringing in foreign managers to run their quarry. The stone quarrying industry was, like many other economic sectors in Palestine, a theater of contention between Jews and Arabs, who vied for jobs and, in particular, for management positions. Tension between the two groups thus preceded the riots, but it climaxed on that turbulent Friday. In the afternoon, a group of fifteen Arabs from Hebron arrived at the site, armed with knives and pistols, and demanded that the Jews be handed over to them. The four Jews hid in the explosives shed:

> The four of us decided to blow up the shed with its ton and a half of explosives, killing ourselves and the Arabs together. Things got more and more tense. We lit a cigarette so that we'd be ready to light the fuse . . . but at the very last second, with the attack-

ers approaching and crowding around the shed, we suddenly saw a group of Arabs from Sur Baher, led by one of our friends, Mohammad Jaber, trying to break a way through the crowd. When they reached the leaders of the gang, in the midst of a wild uproar, there were shouts and screams, fierce objections and threats. (ibid.)

This is the critical moment in any rescue attempt, the point at which, if no one acts, blood will be shed. To save lives, a person has to muster the courage to stand up against the assailants. It does not necessarily have to be a frontal confrontation — it can be done by offering momentary shelter. At other times the attackers have to be confronted directly, and the rescuer has to disregard shouts and intimidation and resolutely face weapon-wielding killers. That is what Abu Shaker 'Amru did in Hebron and Ezra Kiryati did in the Bukharan quarter (see below). And it is what Mohammad Jaber did at the quarry, as Shturman relates:

> After a few minutes, we saw, to our total astonishment, that the Hebronites were retreating, and in the end they left the area. Mohammad Jaber knocked on the door and asked to come in. We let only him in, but he asked that we allow three of his friends in as well. The Arabs who entered said that they had come to rescue us from our plight. They produced Arab garments from under their robes and dressed us in them. Mohammad Jaber examined our appearance and made adjustments to the clothing as he saw fit. He did not prevent us from taking a few bombs with us. (ibid.)

Thus armed, the mixed company, Jews and Arabs, set out for Sur Baher. On the way they ran into an armed Arab who suspected that members of the party were Jews and demanded that they be handed over. Mohammad Jaber and his friends seized the Arab's gun, once again proving that they were prepared not only to hide their Jewish friends, but even to enter into a potentially dangerous altercation with an armed man. That is no small thing. Shturman continues:

> At Sur Baher we were put into a yard surrounded by huts belonging to Jaber's clan. . . . At two in the afternoon a gang of thugs broke in and tried to get into the hut we were in. An old Arab woman who stood guard at the doorway did not let them pass and shouted until they went away. Immediately afterward, two Arabs appeared and transferred us to a filthy dark cellar and a guard was placed at the door. . . .
> In the early morning we dressed up as Arabs again. Five Arabs, led by Mohammad Jaber's cousin, known in the village as an adventurer, set out with us in the direction of Talpiot. At the edge of the village dozens of other Arabs joined us, thinking that we were heading out to loot [the Jewish neighborhood]. The leader of our escort held back, gathered these unwanted followers around him, and explained that he was setting out with his group to scout out the situation, and that after it was clear that the place was free of army and police he would signal them and they could come and do as they saw fit.

We entered Talpiot at first light. . . . The sight of Talpiot was horrible. Feathers and ripped pillows filled the air, doors and windows stood open, revealing vacant rooms. Broken furniture, household items, and clothes were scattered all around. The roar of water spurting out of open faucets onto everything added to the scene of destruction and desertion. (ibid.)

Talpiot

We have already encountered airborne feathers and slashed pillows — the iconic visual image of the Eastern European pogrom — in Jerusalem in 1921. The image appears over and over again in 1929. Talpiot, a neighborhood at what was then Jerusalem's southeastern edge, was cut off from the city's other Jewish neighborhoods. It was subject to a concerted attack during the initial days of the riots, as were the adjacent workers' farm and Ramat Rachel. The attackers of the kibbutz killed thirty-three-year-old Pinhas Wolman, who had fought alongside Joseph Trumpeldor, the Zionist military legend and martyr, at the battle of Tel Hai nine years before. The page devoted to Wolman on the Israeli Defense Ministry's memorial website relates that his father, a member of a Jewish self-defense military in the town of Bramcha in Bessarabia, was killed in a pogrom, and Pinhas grew up an orphan. His widow, Tzipora, was killed in the battle of Ramat Rachel in May 1948.

The attackers of Talpiot and Ramat Rachel came from Sur Baher, Hebron, and nearby Bedouin tribes. The author Shmuel Yosef Agnon, a resident of Talpiot, lived through the attack and afterward sent his publisher, Shlomo Zalman Schocken, a detailed account displaying a rare capacity for self-examination at times of both danger and boredom. He ended with a personal political inference: "My attitude toward the Arabs has changed since the riots. My attitude is now this. I do not hate them and I do not love them. What do I ask? Not to see their faces. In my humble opinion we now need to make a large ghetto of half a million Jews in the Land of Israel, for if we do not, we are lost" (Agnon 1976, 399).

At that time such thoughts lay outside the Jewish consensus, but here we find the seeds of the doctrine of separation that became official Israeli policy at the beginning of the twenty-first century. The Arabs also promoted separation following 1929, when the Arab Executive Committee declared a boycott of the Jewish economy, and social contacts between members of the two peoples became ever more rare (Sela 1994).

Agnon, the Land of Israel, and the Arabs

Agnon proposed, as a temporary solution, the establishment of a Jewish ghetto in part of Palestine. But he maintained his belief that the entire Land of

Shmuel Yosef Agnon (Israel Government Press Office, Photography Department).

Israel belonged to the Jews. A year and a half later he put this view into words in a letter he sent to Judah Leon Magnes, a member of Brit Shalom and chancellor of the Hebrew University: "I and the entire Jewish people have not ceased to believe that the Land of Israel is ours and that all the nations residing here are but caretakers that God settled here until the return of the Land of Israel to the Jews" (Agnon 1976, 413). This is the classic religious nationalist view — the Creator granted the Land of Israel to the Jews alone. It denies that the Arabs have any connection to the land and views them as temporary residents without any rights. It is important to realize that this was precisely the view against which the Arabs rose up in 1929. They believed that every single Jew, of every party and belief, held to Agnon's view, deep down if not explicitly. This was the major ideological factor that motivated the attackers and murderers, their justification for indiscriminate attacks on Jewish settlements and communities, no matter what their political and religious affiliations.

But here it is important to make a further distinction between Jews who used this religious belief as the basis for a political program, and those who maintained that the politics should be left to heaven. Agnon belonged to the second camp. Two of his short stories show this clearly: "MeOyev LeOhev" (From enemy to lover; 1953a) and — even more powerfully — "MiTahat La'Etz" (Under the tree; 1953b). It seems that Agnon persuaded himself that the Arabs would slowly come to realize that the Land of Israel had been designated by God for the Jews alone. He thus maintained that the Jews should not resort to force more than necessary and generally sought to quell the flames of the conflict rather than to feed them.

He displayed this approach just before the 1929 riots. In the letter to Magnes quoted from above, Agnon wrote that when tensions began to rise around the issue of the Western Wall, he had tried, unsuccessfully, to calm down Jewish hotheads: "When I attended a meeting of the [Jewish] National Council (the only time in my life) and I saw the burgeoning machismo of the heroic orators, I felt like shouting leave it alone, but by nature I am a shy man and since then I have regretted that I did not stand in the breach" (1976, 414). Two years passed between that public meeting and Agnon's recollection of it, yet he was still plagued by the thought that he might have been able to calm the rising tempers and prevent the subsequent bloodshed.

Rabbi Kook Repented, Too

After the fact, Rabbi Avraham Yitzhak HaCohen Kook regretted his involvement in fanning the flames of the Western Wall controversy. He may also have been remorseful about the interview he gave to *Do'ar Hayom*, quoted above, in which he called for the evacuation of the Maghrebi quarter. He voiced his *mea culpa* during a meeting of the Zionist Executive on November 20, 1929, at which the Western Wall was discussed:

> I am sorry that the question of the Western Wall was overly inflated. The question of ownership is not a matter for negotiation and the resolution is in the hands of heaven. . . . We do not need to make a big first-class religious fuss about a table and chairs and divider. The most important thing is to maintain the principle of the Wall's sanctity for us and our right to pray next to it, and through negotiations with our neighbors we can always obtain the comfort we need. But any concession we make on comfort cannot deprive us entirely of the Wall. With regard to comfort, the government has decided, and we can say that in this matter we trust the government. (CZA S100/10)

So, after waxing enthusiastic over the Jewish mass demonstration at the Wall, which he had termed an "eruption of the holiness" (quoted in "A Conversation with Chief Rabbi Kook," *Do'ar Hayom*, August 18, 1929); after the tears had dried — the ones that had come to his eyes when he was told about the national anthem being sung for the first time in history near the Western Wall; and after

Rabbi Kook (National Photo Company Collection, Library of Congress).

the massacre, Kook reached the conclusion that it would really be better to leave the matter of ownership of the Western Wall to heaven, and decisions about the day-to-day arrangements for Jewish prayer there to the Mandate government. Even if he made a point of blaming the Arab leadership for the outbreak of violence, Kook changed his attitude and preached calm, compromise, and conflict resolution through negotiations with the Jews' neighbors.

Another Rabbi Who Reconsidered

After twenty of his students were murdered, the head of Hebron's Slabodka Yeshiva did not blame mortals. He sought a religious explanation, connected to the place — Hebron — and the establishment of the yeshiva there: "After the catastrophe, the heart of the head of the yeshiva, Rabbi Moshe Mordechai Epstein, was broken. 'The Holy Patriarchs did not want us here,' the rabbi said to his associates" (D. Cohen 2009, 254; see also Salmon and Golan 2003, 238). In retrospect, he concluded that it had been a mistake to locate the yeshiva in Hebron.

And the Admor of Chabad

Recall that the admor of Chabad visited Hebron just prior to the riots, ascending to the Tomb of the Patriarchs together with Eliezer Dan Slonim, who was murdered during the massacre. In a letter he sent to Judge Gad Frumkin in Jerusalem in June 1930, the admor blamed the Zionist Yishuv: "I left the Land last year with my heart pained at the state of the Old Yishuv as a whole and Torah institutions in particular. From the few things that I revealed to you, you presumably discerned my view of the New Yishuv and its consequences. My heart told me a sad sight, I saw bloodstains floating in the air of the Land of Israel, and to the sorrow of all of the Jewish people and my heart, what happened happened, and may God have mercy on his people and his Land" (quoted in Frumkin 1954, 311).

The admor seems to have wanted to convey that he had foreseen the deadly disaster, and that it was connected to the New Yishuv's disregard for Torah institutions. Inasmuch as it puts the blame on the Zionists, that is an important statement, but it is not a personal reckoning.

The Labor Movement

Sefer Toldot HaHaganah also pointed the finger at the Jews—in its case, right-wing provocateurs. It recalled the warning made by Yosef Aharonowitz, a Zionist labor leader, just prior to the riots, that "the hysteria of the rabbinate and the hysteria of Brit Trumpeldor [Betar movement] can lead to bloodshed" (Dinur 1973, vol. 2, 307–8). Among other things Aharonowitz meant the Ninth of Av demonstration at the Wall. "Those participating in the demonstrations must certainly have felt that they did a great deed," according to the book. "But the truth is that at that hour they were nothing—objectively—but helpless puppets in the hands of dogged players who energetically prepared the Arab mutiny" (ibid., 308) That was his analysis of the intra-Jewish arena. But a look at all the actors in the event, he continued, showed that the initiators of the riots were senior pro-Arab British officers and officials who thought that the Balfour Declaration and support for Zionism ran counter to Britain's true interests in the Middle East. They sought to weaken the Yishuv and put it into conflict with the Arabs.

The Palestinian Reckoning

As Jews have a long tradition of writing and documentation, many recorded their responses to the 1929 riots, and much of this material survives today. It offers a broad spectrum of opinions and feelings as voiced by thinkers, rabbis, political activists, and ordinary people from all circles and ideological currents. Only a relatively small number of accounts were produced by Arabs. Nevertheless, we know that Arab society was not monolithic: there was a range of thinking and feeling in the Palestinian community. The main evidence for this is that some Arabs attacked Jews and others saved them. That is by far the most important and meaningful proof. But there were also written and oral responses, immediately following the riots and later on, like that of Mohammad al-Tawil.

Mohammad al-Tawil

Al-Tawil was born in Acre, lived in Tiberias, and served in World War I as an officer in the Ottoman army. At the beginning of the 1920s he got involved in Transjordanian politics. He then returned to Palestine and moved between the political and business worlds. Al-Tawil was one of the only Arab witnesses who criticized his people's leadership before the Shaw Commission. He later published his opinion of the Arab Executive Committee:

> Alas, O Muslims, alas the miserable and the weak, alas the poor workers, alas the fellahin. You have fallen prey to the talons of partisan interests of sinister intent, who toy with you and your country as they wish, leading you astray with their words, and you believe them and do as they wish. And so you find yourselves thrown in prison . . . and your women becoming widows and your children orphans, but they have no pity on you, because they lack conscience and morality, for if they had a conscience it would prevent them from deceiving you. See how they tricked you and spread among you false rumors as if the Jews had slaughtered Muslims and were trying to take over al-Haram al-Sharif and had actually attacked it. (1930a, 42–43)

In a booklet titled *Tariq al-Hayah* (Path of life; 1930c), which came out that same year, al-Tawil maintained that the mufti had failed as a leader and that the path he had chosen would end in the loss of Palestine. In the Acre newspaper *al-Zamar*, al-Tawil published an open letter to Musa Kazem al-Hussayni, chairman of the Arab Executive Committee: "Your negative approach is causing damage to the country and devastates the lives of its inhabitants. . . . The Muslims want to live with the Jews in Palestine. You must improve living conditions in the country, as the Zionists do . . . history will demand that you pay for your actions" (September 16, 1930). Al-Tawil's attack on the political leadership, and the (justified) suspicion that he was receiving financial support from the Zionists, caused many Arabs to view him as a traitor. He received death threats and was compelled to leave the country. But that is no reason to doubt that he felt real pain when he saw the Jews murdered in Safed. He wrote to Chaim Weizmann: "My heart ached at the sight of the dead because I knew that Arabs had attacked them for no reason and without them having committed any provocation (undated letter, CZA J015/31).

Haidar 'Abd al-Shafi

But it was not necessary to be subsidized by the Zionist Executive to be upset about the murder of defenseless people, as demonstrated in the story of Haidar 'Abd al-Shafi. Al-Shafi, who had been born in Gaza in 1919, was a physician and had been a social and political activist from a young age. He served as a member of the Palestine National Council from the time of its establishment in 1964 until 2007, and also as a member of the Executive Committee of the Palestine Liberation Organization (PLO). In 1991 he headed the Palestinian delegation to the Madrid peace talks. He opposed the Oslo agreements because he feared that they would permit Israel to expand its hold on the territories, but he supported reconciliation between Jews and Arabs in Israel-Palestine. Al-Shafi fought for the democratization of Palestinian institutions until his death in 2007.

During the Mandate period, his father, Muhi al-Din al-Shafi, worked as a senior official in the Islamic waqf. In the mid-1920s the family moved to Hebron, where Muhi al-Din had been appointed director of waqf properties. His son recounted that period in a documentary film:

> As part of his duties, my father was responsible for the holy mosque [Machpelah Cave], sacred to the Jews as well. That being the case, Abu Yussef, the Jewish clergyman, would visit our home along with his children. This rabbi was a noble man. I remember that time very well. In Hebron I began attending school and there I began to understand the world. A Jewish family lived in the apartment across from us, and I remember that the Jewish woman would ask me every Sabbath to turn off the light. That was my job [chuckles], to turn off the light on Sabbaths.
>
> These things remained etched in my memory. So when the 1929 uprising broke out as a result of Zionist provocation — we had returned to Gaza by then — I was very sad to hear that the Jewish priest I had known, who was a man of peace, had been killed. These disturbances have affected me deeply since my childhood. I experienced the difference between living in cooperation, love, and peace between peoples and the Zionist propaganda that created animosity and led to the killing of people whom I knew and respected. (Baitar 2006)

The Abu Yussef mentioned by al-Shafi was Rabbi Meir Kastel, who was seventy when he was murdered. Unlike al-Tawil, Haidar al-Shafi accepted the Arab nationalist analysis of the cause of the riots, but he still expressed pain at the death of innocent Jewish acquaintances. Iyad al-Sarraj, a psychiatrist in Gaza, told me that al-Shafi incessantly spoke about the Hebron chapter in his life to his children and friends, each time achingly recalling the death of the Jewish rabbi. It may well be that it was during this period of his childhood that his humanistic worldview began to develop. It was that way of thinking that led him to study medicine (at the American University of Beirut) and to help found the Gaza Strip's heath services. In the 1948 war he was one of Gaza's few physicians. He witnessed the contempt for Palestinian life of an Israeli military detachment when the soldiers prevented him from taking an ambulance into al-Breir, an Arab village that then stood on the site currently occupied by Kibbutz Bror Hayil, a few miles north of the Gaza Strip so that he could treat the wounded there (Abdel Shafi et al. 1998). He seems to have been successful in passing humanism onto his children. His son Salah, who in 2010 was appointed the PLO's ambassador to Germany, has termed the Holocaust the greatest crime ever committed against humanity and has called for it to be taught so that it not be repeated (*Ha'aretz*, July 2, 2012).

Jabotinsky: I Was Right

The Arab nationalists accused the Zionist movement of promoting the tension that led to the 1929 disturbances. The Yishuv blamed the Arab leadership. Within the Yishuv, the Revisionists blamed the Zionist Executive for being feeble. The labor movement, the liberal middle class (as exemplified by *Ha'aretz*), and the Haredim blamed the right. Most of the arrows were aimed at Jabotinsky, *Do'ar Hayom*, and Betar. Jabotinsky, at least, had no regrets. Speaking of the Betar-led procession to the Western Wall on the Ninth of Av and the newspaper's coverage, he wrote in *Do'ar Hayom*: "Had I been with them I would have done as they did" ("Tov" [Good], January 7, 1930). Why? First, national honor. It is a newspaper's duty to speak out against "a national insult that is liable to lower esteem for our nation in the eyes of our neighbors, the government, and the entire world." Second, he said, the demonstration had raised the spirits of Jews in the Diaspora. And third, the gentiles hardly needed a Jewish demonstration as an excuse to riot, "and jokers should not come forward now to tell us that such events are the product of the good or bad behavior of Jews themselves."

The claim that animosity and aggression directed at Jews is not a response to Jewish behavior but is rather a law of nature was quite widespread. In *The Origins of Totalitarianism*, Hannah Arendt writes that it is clear why antisemites endorse this view:

> It gives the best possible alibi for all horrors. If it is true that mankind has insisted on murdering Jews for more than two thousand years, then Jew-killing is a normal, and even human, occupation and Jew-hatred is justified beyond the need of argument.
>
> The more surprising aspect of this explanation, the assumption of an eternal antisemitism, is that it has been adopted by a great many historians and by an even greater number of Jews. It is this odd coincidence that makes the theory so very dangerous and confusing. Its escapist basis is in both instances the same: just as antisemites understandably desire to escape responsibility for their deeds, so Jews, attacked and on the defensive, even more understandably do not wish under any circumstances to discuss their share of responsibility. (1958, 7)

Jabotinsky indeed claims that the Jews bore no responsibility for what happened. But he goes one step further, arguing that the conduct of right-wing groups during the months of tension over the Western Wall was absolutely proper. They acted as they should have not only morally but also in terms of political and military strategy: "There is no greater lesson in all books on strategy: to compel your hater to attack you before he has had time to complete and improve his preparations. This outburst had two notable characteristics: on the one hand it showed all of us that they had been making preparations. On the other it showed that they had not had time to prepare properly" ("Tov," *Do'ar Hayom*, January 7, 1930).

Talpiot and Sur Baher—The End of the Story

Jabotinsky's strategic analysis is not convincing. There is no evidence that the Arabs had begun organizing armed units or purchasing large quantities of arms in preparation for launching a real offensive. The Jews were much better armed and trained, and their military preparedness, as provisional as it was, was much more advanced than that of the Arabs. But let's return to the local level, to Shturman and his three companions who were rescued by men from Sur Baher.

When the four Jews got out of the village, they rushed to report to the Haganah command in Jerusalem. They were immediately sent to guard the Gurji courtyard near the Nablus Gate, where seven Jews had been murdered on Friday afternoon. When they got there, Shturman relates in his testimony, they chased away Arabs who were trying to set fire to the local synagogue.

When their mission there came to an end, a couple of days later, they were summoned to the Public Works Department in Jerusalem, where their savior, Mohammad Jaber, was waiting for them. He told them that the man who had guided them from Sur Baher to Talpiot had been shot dead on his way back to the village, and a man who had been with him had been badly wounded. "The Arab newspaper in Bethlehem had made hay from it," Shturman says in his testimony, "reporting, ostensibly from eyewitnesses, that the English had shot them at our request. The village refuses to believe it, Jaber added, but if it turns out to be true they will take revenge against us . . . he, Jaber himself, didn't believe it. The news was a heavy blow to me" (HHA, 17/48).

Shturman took Jaber to Yitzhak Ben-Zvi, who used his connections to ensure that the British police and army conduct a rapid inquiry to find out what had happened. Shturman continues: "After that we hired a cab and filled it with flour, rice, sugar, and other food supplies to bring the people of Sur Baher as a gesture of gratitude and peace. Despite the danger, the four of us drove to the village. When we reached the edge of the village many youths joined us. Our condolences looked sincere and real to them" (ibid.).

The guide was not the last villager to die. The British arrived in Sur Baher soon afterward and killed more inhabitants. They did the same in Qalunya and other places. In both villages they arrived after the end of an incident, when no one was in danger any longer, and fired indiscriminately, killing women and old people. The leaders of these villages sent detailed reports to Mufti Hajj Amin al-Hussayni and the Supreme Muslim Council (Hammuda 2011). Their letters contain inaccuracies that were meant, among other things, to cover up the actions of inhabitants of the village who took part in attacks on Jews. But there is no disputing one basic fact: British forces went into these villages and shot women and unarmed men. The arbitrary British response was the principal cause of the large number of Arab casualties in Jerusalem and its surrounding villages. Fifty Arabs died as a result.

The Rescuers in the Eyes of the Arabs

The Arab newspapers covered the rescuers of Jews in a very positive way. That was an interesting position for the press to take: on the one hand the newspapers justified the attacks, but on the other hand they celebrated those who rescued Jews. One example, regarding Hebron, comes from *Filastin*: "The Arabs succeeded in saving 350 Jews by hiding them and giving them shelter in private homes and keeping them from any harm. Some of the best-known Arabs saved 30 or 40 Jews, women, children, old and young. One Arab woman even saved 60 Jews" (September 8, 1929). These acts of rescue appear prominently in Palestinian histories to this day.

In contrast, the cases in which Jews saved Arabs received no mention in the Arab press. In fact, they were not cited in the Hebrew press, either, because the Zionist institutions made no mention of Jewish attacks on Arabs (except for reports of trials of Jews accused of this crime). Here is one case I have mentioned only very briefly above: At the same time that the Jewish quarry workers were hiding in Sur Baher, the Haganah militiaman Ezra Kiryati, who also served as a Mandate policeman, went to the Bukharan quarter and saw a crowd besieging the home of an Arab family and trying to lynch them. On-duty policemen stood close by, he related in later testimony, but they did nothing. "It made a very harsh impression on me," he said. "I went in and managed to shock the Jewish mob, I started shouting and extracted the children and put them on horses. It's interesting that the policemen could have shot at the crowd but did not" (HHA 122/24).

Policemen Not Shooting

The same thing happened during the massacres in Hebron and at the Gurji courtyard in Jerusalem. Some of the policemen were not armed, but some had weapons but did not open fire at critical junctures. The Jews tended to see this as a deliberate decision aimed at enabling the slaughter, but it seems more likely that the policemen were confused, inexperienced, and unwilling to take the initiative. The fact that policemen also failed to use their arms when Arabs were in mortal danger strengthens the presumption that they were not pursuing an anti-Jewish policy. Furthermore, during incursions like those in Qalunya and Sur Baher, Mandate police shot innocent Arabs.

Brutality

The prominence the Arab press gave to the number of Arab dead and the Arab acts of rescue was motivated partly by the first statement issued by British High Commissioner John Chancellor when he received word of the massacre. Here is the proclamation he issued on September 1, after returning to Palestine from his vacation:

> I have learned with horror of the atrocious acts committed by bodies of ruthless and bloodthirsty evil-doers, of savage murders perpetrated upon defenseless members of the Jewish population regardless of age or sex, accompanied as at Hebron, by acts of unspeakable savagery, of the burning of farms and houses in town and country and of the looting and destruction of property.
>
> These crimes have brought upon their authors the execration of all civilized peoples throughout the world. (JTA, September 3, 1929)

There were many Arab responses to the statement, one of them from the Arab Executive Committee. Bulus Shehada, owner and editor of *Mir'aat al-Sharq*, could not restrain himself. Not only was there no mention of Jewish murders of Arabs, but neither were the acts of rescue carried out by Arabs given any mention. He knew enough of world and regional history to point out that what stood out in these riots, as opposed to other intercommunal and interethnic outbreaks of violence, was the number of Arabs who risked their lives to save Jews. The banner headline of the first issue of his newspaper following the riots was "Arab Nobility Revealed to All during the Uprising," and the subheading was "The Enlightened World Should Praise the Arabs, Not Condemn Them":

> The moral level of the Arabs and the Jews was revealed in this uprising, which showed people what lies deep in the hearts of each nation toward the other nation. True, the wise did not manage to control the wild mob at times of eruption, when all judgment was lost, because at turbulent times emotions and exploding passion are what control the mob. That happens in the most enlightened of nations and in other nations as well, as can be seen in the atrocities that took place during revolutions in the most advanced countries. But acts of many members of the Arab nation during this uprising are worthy of being engraved in fire on the pages of history, and this nation is worthy of being inscribed in the most honorable book of human fame. We will cite several examples from which one can deduce good characteristics and high moral level and noble manliness, and it would have been fitting for the high commissioner, who is the high commissioner of both the Jews and the Arabs, to relate

these noble deeds, deserving of the blessing of the entire enlightened world, instead of placing an eternal curse on them. (*Mir'aat al-Sharq*, September 1, 1929)

But, like the Yishuv, High Commissioner Chancellor was more angered by the acts of murder than he was impressed by the deeds of rescue. He wrote in horror to his son Christopher: "I do not think that history records many worse horrors in the last few hundred years" (quoted in Segev 2000, 327).

Worse Horrors

Chancellor's horror is understandable but lacking in historical perspective. The Turks had slaughtered the Armenians just a decade previously. The French and Germans had slaughtered natives in their African colonies, such as the massacre of the entire Ouled Rhia tribe at Dahra, Algeria, in 1845. Chancellor also forgot the millions of Indians who starved to death because of the British policy of exporting the wheat produced on the subcontinent during the great drought of 1876–78, and those Indians who died as a result of, among other British atrocities, the Amritsar Massacre of 1919, in which hundreds of Indians were killed by British troops.

Imperialism and Zionism: Another Angle

The brutal face of British world imperialism slowly seeped into the minds of the inhabitants of Palestine, sharpening the debate in the Yishuv over cooperation with the British Empire. But the two sides of the debate were not equally matched. A firm majority in the Yishuv—the center, the labor movement, Weizmann and the Zionist Executive, and Jabotinsky and his supporters—believed that the Jews had to ally themselves with Great Britain. After all, the British had issued the Balfour Declaration just a decade previously and since then had assisted, if with some vacillation, in putting the Yishuv on its feet and granting it limited self-governance. The opponents consisted of two small groups, each with its own reason for opposing the British—the Communists and the Central European intellectuals associated with Brit Shalom. The members of the latter group argued that rather than allying itself with Britain, the Zionists should join hands with colonized and oppressed nations, whose struggle for freedom was just and with whom the future lay. Two years and one month after seeing the body of Khalil al-Dajjani lying by his house, and twenty months after refusing to offer advice to the committee set up by the Zionist Executive on the central place of the Western Wall in Judaism, Gershom Scholem wrote in the Brit Shalom periodical *She'ifoteinu*:

Zionism has taken its stand, whether it likes it or not—and the truth is, it likes it— alongside the declining rather than the rising powers. . . . The force that Zionism has attached itself to in these victories has been the evident, the resolute power. Zionism has forgotten to join with the hidden, oppressed power that will in the future rise and be revealed tomorrow. Can a [national] revival movement stand at their side, or more correctly, shelter in the shadow of the victors in the war? Many of the socialists in our camp do not like such questions, and get very upset when you speak of the imperialism we have wed ourselves to with the ring of the Balfour Declaration. . . . If it is still possible for an entire movement to change direction and try to attach itself to the forces that will determine the next generation, I do not know. But I know that there is no other way but to try. . . . And even if we do not win, once more, and the fire of revolution consumes us, better for us to be standing on the right side of the barricades. (1931, 202–3)

Scholem's associate Hans Kohn also opposed dependence on British bayonets. As one of the first critical scholars of colonialism and nationalism, Kohn was well aware of the suffering that colonial rule had brought to other nations. He associated Zionism with Western imperialism. In an article he published following the riots, he opposed the hard-line policy declared by the high commissioner in the first edict he promulgated following the disturbances. The Yishuv, Kohn charged, was hypocritical:

> We make ourselves out to be innocent victims of attack. It's true that in August the attackers were Arabs. Since they have no army, they cannot observe the rules of the game. They availed themselves of all the barbaric means typical of an anticolonialist rebellion. But we need to look at the deepest sources of the uprising. We have spent twelve years in Palestine without having even once asked the Arabs' consent, without conducting any sort of discussion with the people living in this land. We have trusted solely to British power. We have set ourselves goals that must inevitably lead to conflict. (Lavsky 1990, 204)

Davar quoted Kohn in order to counter his claim (September 22, 1929). *Do'ar Hayom* went one step further and called on Kohn to resign from his position as director of public relations at a central Zionist fundraising organization, Keren HaYesod (United Israel Appeal), on the ground that his opinions lay outside the pale of the broad community of Zionist donors. In the end, Kohn did resign. He left not only his job but also the country, later becoming one of the world's leading scholars of modern nationalism.

Ben-Gurion and the Admor of Munkacz

Founded on a profound sense of justice, Brit Shalom offered its own distinctive analysis of the political and historical situation. David Ben-Gurion's analysis was different, and so was his conception of justice. The great majority of Jews agreed with Ben-Gurion. In his view, without British support, the Yishuv would have been annihilated in a day. He told the Mapai Party Council in February 1931: "If anything shields us from the sword of Ibn Saʿud, that fanatic king half a day distant from Tel Aviv . . . it is not Ibn Saʿud's love for us, but rather British bayonets. In their absence, he would be here tomorrow and wreak devastation. . . . We are defended by a European nation against the savages of the desert" (quoted in Hazan 2009, 199).

Yet the question is unavoidable: what leads the people of the desert to attack? The Satmar Hasidim and other members of the Edah Haredit have an explanation, one they declared then and still hold to now: "And the wise and holy admor, author of *Minhat Eliezer*, may his memory protect us [the admor of Munkacz] cried and shouted in the year 1929, at the time of the pogrom in Hebron, that if [the Zionists] really loved the Jewish people they would immediately halt all the killings if they were to issue [a statement] that they renounce all Balfour's promises that angered the Arabs—but they did not want to have mercy on Jewish blood" (*HaKotel HaShavuy* 2011, 28).

There are two basic claims here. The first is that the Zionists are motivated not by love for the Jewish people but rather by political interests. The second is that the Balfour Declaration and Zionist inflexibility were the source of the Yishuv's and Israel's troubles. A radical faction within the Edah Haredit, Neturei Karta, has a view of history that places an even wider chasm between it and the Zionist state: "The Zionists, whose entire history is nothing but shedding Jewish blood like water, are those who today declare themselves to be 'the saviors of Israel.' But without them none of these troubles would have come upon us. And even now, by annulling their state and submitting to the [gentile] nations, all bloodshed would immediately cease!" (ibid., 31).

More than eighty years have gone by since 1929, and the Zionist movement still depends on the support of the Western powers. Neturei Karta, which still holds fast to an extreme anti-Zionist doctrine that in the past was more widespread in the Haredi community, continues to boycott the Western Wall. Its members refuse to pray there as long as it remains under Zionist control. Scholem's proposal that the Jews ally themselves with the Arab world instead of the West was not accepted, and his prediction that the Zionists and the West would collapse together did not come to pass. But history has not ended yet, and the Israeli public might yet, if the regional power equation changes, have to face the question of whether to ally with the Arab world or the West. We will shortly return to other debates set off by the 1929 riots, but first we need to compare and contrast Jewish anti-Zionism with the Arab rejection of Zionism.

Comparing Positions

At first glance there would seem to be much in common between Neturei Karta's position (and, to a certain degree, that of Brit Shalom) and the most widespread Arab view of Zionism. But there are some important differences worth noting. Ahmad al-'Alami (whose father, Sheikh Sa'd al-Din al-'Alami, served as the Jordan-appointed mufti of Jerusalem from 1953 until his death in 1993), offers a summary of prevailing Arab nationalist historical takes on Zionism: "The European Jews did not arrive in Palestine for the purpose of establishing a national home but rather to achieve British-European goals. The Jewish problem could have been solved in sparsely populated areas such as Africa or even South America. But Europe wanted not only to get rid of its Jews but also to instigate conflict with the inhabitants of Palestine and to injure them, in revenge for the defeat of the crusaders" (2000, D).

According to al-'Alami, imperialism was the major force that impelled Jews to settle in Palestine, and the goal of such settlement was to hurt the Arabs. In contrast, the members of Brit Shalom, the Yishuv's Jewish Communists, and the Edah Haredit all knew, from personal experience, that they had come to Palestine because they felt a profound connection with the Land of Israel and because of the persecution many of them had experienced in Europe. They certainly did not see themselves as emissaries of imperialism. This explains why Arabs who have internalized the Arab national discourse and Jews, even those who are radical opponents of Zionism, still find it hard to find common ground. An article by the philosopher and scientist Yeshayahu Leibowitz, then pursuing physiological research at the University of Cologne, in Germany, puts these differences — not only between Jews and Arabs, but also between different parts of the Jewish opposition camp — in sharp focus.

Yeshayahu Leibowitz

Yeshayahu Leibowitz was twenty-seven years old at the time and a member of Mizrahi, the religious Zionist movement. Decades later he would anger many of his compatriots with his radical critique of Israel's actions in the Occupied Territories and of Israeli politics and society. In an article originally published on October 18, 1929, Leibowitz called on the members of his movement "to place themselves at the vanguard of a movement that will lead Zionism back to its human and Jewish core" (Leibowitz and Leibowitz 2010, 68–69). Lead Zionism back? Leibowitz's appeal implies three claims that distinguish him from both Zionist and non-Zionist thinkers. Unlike Arab nationalists, he maintains that the foundation of Zionism is humanism. Unlike the anti-Zionist Haredim, he maintains that Zionism is consistent with Jewish religion. Unlike the Zionist mainstream, he feels that Zionism has severed itself from its humanist and Jewish foundations:

> We will never question our right to establish the national home of the Jewish people in Palestine, a home in which it can develop in national-cultural and national-economic freedom. This demand, which on its own is the essence of Zionism, we can present with a clear conscience. It is based on our history, on the fact that we exist, and does not impinge on others' just demands. It rejects only chauvinistic Arab nationalism in Palestine—the demand to establish an Arab nation-state . . . to preserve an Arab majority relative to the Jews, etc. We may [rightly] reject such Arab demands if, and only if, we ourselves do not make identical demands for ourselves. We demand for ourselves in the Land only those rights and that status that we are prepared to recognize with regard to the Arabs. (ibid., 68–69)

Leibowitz's formulation is based on parity and equality. The Zionists should not refuse the Arabs in Palestine the same rights that the Zionists demand for the Jews, and Zionism should not demand for the Jews any rights that it is not prepared to grant the Arabs as well. It is a mirror image of Agnon's position. Below we will see what Arabs thought of this and similar interesting ideas.

The Question of the Balfour Declaration

What turned Magnes and his fellow members of Brit Shalom into pariahs in the eyes of many Zionists was their rejection of the Balfour Declaration and of dependence on Great Britain. Magnes voiced this position following World War I and reiterated it after the 1929 riots. In a speech at the start of the 1929–30 academic year he went one step further, declaring: "If we do not succeed in finding ways to achieve peace and understanding, our labor will not be worth doing" (quoted in *Davar*, November 22, 1929). In other words, the Zionist project should be suspended until the Arabs consent to it. The workers' newspaper responded: "There is no justice in this submission and it contradicts our nation's desire for life and creative power. The return of the Jewish people to its land is an absolute value." In its first response to Magnes's speech, *Davar* stressed, in keeping with the Zionist mainstream's view of itself, that the land "is also the land of the Arab community, and no Zionist seeks to expel them or fight them" (November 22, 1929).

American Jewry: Between Self-Righteousness and Anti-Zionism

Davar's position might seem self-righteous or detached from reality—in particular, the claim that no Zionist wanted to expel the Arabs. But the American Jewish Congress's response to Magnes went even further. "The very call by Jews to live in peace with Arabs is a sin," the Congress declared, "because it makes it sound as if the Jews are fomenting war and committing an injustice against the Arabs" (*Davar*, November 25, 1929). The statement demonstrates the blind spot that many Zionists had when it came to the distress the Arabs felt at the prospect of their country turning Jewish and their own community becoming a minority.

But this was not the opinion of all American Jews, who had not yet adopted the stance that they should not level public criticism of the Jewish state in the making. All of the ideological and religious streams in American Jewry mourned the Jews killed in the riots, but American Jews disagreed about who was responsible for the outbreak of the riots and how best to solve the national conflict in Palestine. Like the debate within the Yishuv, some members of the American Jewish community blamed the Revisionists for provoking the crisis, while others blamed Weizmann and the other leaders of the Zionist World Organization for weakness. But among American Jews there was a larger camp—Reform Jews, socialists, and others—that rejected the idea of a Jewish state and even the concept of a Jewish nation (W. Cohen 1988, 91–99).

The attitude toward Magnes—himself a Reform rabbi who had immigrated from the United States—became one of the focal points of debate within American Jewry. Following the riots, Magnes did not limit himself to speaking out about the future of the Yishuv. He also entered the political arena, trying to fashion a peace plan with Palestine's Arabs against the will of Jewish national institutions. His partner in this effort was John Philby—Weizmann called him "a former British official, an adventurer and enemy"—who claimed to speak for the Arabs but apparently lacked any authorization from them to do so. Magnes argued that the Land of Israel or Palestine should not be either a Jewish or an Arab state, but rather the country of two peoples and the three monotheistic faiths. He presented his position to High Commissioner Chancellor, who, Magnes wrote in his diary, responded with great enthusiasm. On November 24, 1929, Magnes and Philby published complementary articles in the *New York Times*. Magnes called for turning Palestine into "a place where all together will create an international enclave, an interreligious and interracial home" (quoted in Kaufman 1998, 4; see also 164–68).

Weizmann, who was at the time battered by charges that he had been too accommodating and negligent in his leadership, found himself on the offensive when it came to Magnes. Weizmann sharply criticized Magnes and his supporters in the American Jewish community, especially condemning the idea that the Jews should consent to remaining a minority in Palestine, at the mercy of the Arabs. In a letter to Albert Einstein, whom he sought to enlist in the fight against Magnes's initiative, Weizmann offered his characterization of both the Arab leadership and Brit Shalom: "The present Arab leaders, murderers and thieves, want but one thing—to drive us into the Mediterranean. . . . Now come the Magnesses, the Bergmanns [Hugo Bergmann, professor of philosophy at the Hebrew University and an associate of Magnes] and break our united front, presenting matters as if *we* [emphasis in the original] do not want peace. That hypocrite, that Tartuffe Magnes, lightly abandons the Balfour Declaration. He did not bleed for it, he only gained by it!" (quoted in ibid, 63).

Weizmann's view of the Arab leadership is quite different from that offered by Jabotinsky in his essay "The Iron Wall" (1923). Rather than portraying the Arabs as merely murderers and thieves, Jabotinsky acknowledged their national aspirations. But he and his followers also opposed Magnes: they had already demanded the establishment of a Jewish state in Palestine. American Revisionists made their views felt as well. In March 1931, at a lecture Magnes gave in New York, young radical Revisionists set off a stink bomb in the auditorium and got into fistfights with members of the audience, preventing Magnes from finishing his talk (*Do'ar Hayom*, March 23, 1931).

And in the Home Court

A year later, Magnes again encountered opposition, this time on his own campus. In February 1932 the Hebrew University held a ceremony to mark the establishment of a chair for the study of international peace. The chair was to be occupied by Norman Bentwich, a Zionist with close ties to Brit Shalom. He has appeared previously in our story in his capacity as attorney general of the British Mandate administration, and later as legal counsel to Keren Kayemet. A group of young nationalists led by Ahimeir disrupted the ceremony. They claimed that the university should have established a chair of Hebrew militarism rather than one of peace studies. The organizers were unable to restore order, and Magnes called in the police. Thirteen of the demonstrators were arrested. The incident set off a media frenzy that lasted for many days.

In 1998 Ben-Zion Netanyahu, then eighty-eight years old, was invited to be the guest of honor and keynote speaker at an event marking the centennial of Ahimeir's birth. Ben-Zion's son, Binyamin, was serving as Israel's prime minister at the time. Ahimeir's son, Yossi, wrote on the Abba Ahimeir Archive's website that Netanyahu had been invited "not only in his capacity as a Zionist thinker, historian of the Jewish people, and his capacity for profound examination of our history, . . . for his superb talents as a speaker and writer" (2010), but also because of his personal acquaintance with Ahimeir and his participation in the demonstration at the university against Magnes and Bentwich. The older Netanyahu's name does not appear on the list of those arrested that was published in *Davar* (February 16, 1932)—apparently he managed to elude the police.

In a Truck, Outside the Camp

The members of Brit Shalom, Magnes included, viewed themselves as Zionists, and some of them held important positions in Zionist organizations. In contrast, the members of the Palestine Communist Party, almost all of whom were Jews at that time, were firmly anti-Zionist. On the first day of the riots members of the party's secretariat gathered for a previously arranged meeting with a special emissary from Moscow. The venue was a safe house in the village of Beit Safafa, to the south of Jerusalem. In the middle of their discussion of party affairs, reports of violence throughout Jerusalem began to arrive. They were not caught entirely by surprise. During the preceding days they had watched tensions rise steadily, and they had pasted up posters calling on Jewish and Arab workers to unite in a struggle against imperialism and not to be swept up into a bloody spiral of mutual hatred. The posters also denounced both the Zionist and the Arab leaders. The participants — a group of Jews in an Arab village — now realized that no one had listened to them. Haganah troops arrived in a truck after hearing that there were Jews stuck in an isolated house in the village. With some hesitation, the leaders of the Palestine Communist Party boarded the truck, which took them to a safe spot in downtown Jerusalem. In their memoirs, these Communists disagree about what happened. Some claim that the party accepted the command of Ben-Zvi and Haganah headquarters in Jerusalem and placed their small store of arms at the disposal of the Jewish force. Others claim that they organized a separate self-defense force that took special care not to hurt innocent people. Both groups stress that, in all their actions before and during the riots, they did all they could to avoid human injury (Zahavi 2005).

But on November 4, 1929, *Davar* published a black list of surveillance targets, prepared by the Jerusalem Police District in August. *Davar*'s reporter concluded from the names on the list that the British were aware that violence was brewing, and that the names on the list were those who had planned the riots. At the top of the list were the mufti and his associates — among them Jamal al-Hussayni, 'Abd al-Qader Muzaffar, and Subhi Bey al-Khadra. Also listed were the leaders of the Palestine Communist Party, including Yitzhak Berger-Barzilai, Yeshayahu Drapel, Haim Auerbach (also known as Danieli), and Meir Kuperman.

This newspaper report, and the demonstrations organized in Jaffa by Hamdi al-Hussayni, who was closely associated with the Communists, led many Jews to believe that the Communists supported the Arab attacks on Jews. It was a time when everyone was searching for traitors in the camp. A magazine called *Yerushalayim* published a ferocious article: "The few Jewish traitors included in the police force's black list along with the heroes of the Arab riots show us the Satanic covenant these extreme improvers of the world made with social and religious reactionaries. Moscow's emissaries bribed the mufti and incited the Arab masses to slaughter Jews who were living in peace, to destroy placid settlements built by workers and watered by the sweat and blood of working people" (Hitzoni 1929, 3).

Sefer Toldot HaHaganah also attacked the Communists. According to it, only two Jewish groups removed themselves from the community at this time of trouble and aligned themselves with the English imperialists and Arab rioters. These were the members of the Bund in Poland and the other European countries, and the Communists throughout the world. This fact should remain etched in the memory of the nation, which was doomed to struggle not only against external enemies, but also against malignant cells in its own body (Dinur 1973, 2:397).

But that picture is not complete. The book was based on Communist publications from outside Palestine, in particular from the United States. But the conduct of the Palestine Communist Party, or at the very least its Jewish members, seems to be better encapsulated in a statement by Berger-Barzilai: "We in the party leadership knew the truth very well: that members of the party played no role, not directly and not indirectly, in the 1929 riots. In no leaflet, in no conversation was there any provocation of violence. Bloodshed was not only against the party line, but was a mortal blow to the development of the party and of the dream that was the basis of the party consciousness of most of the Jewish party members—the dream of full unity and solidarity of all the country's workers, Jewish and Arab together" (quoted in Zahavi 2005: 161).

It turns out that the local Communists did not follow Moscow's lead in this instance. Soon after the riots, the Soviet leadership reversed its previous position and resolved to support the Arab offensive. The Communists in Palestine, especially the Jews, took a more nuanced view of the disturbances. They were cognizant of the motives for the Arab attacks on Jews but opposed the deeds. As they had done in their publications before the riots, they continued to call for Arab-Jewish cooperation after the riots, and they blamed the Arab leadership, British imperialism, and Zionism for the bloodshed (Zahavi 2005, 156–95). The Soviet leaders, acting through the Comintern, had in any case wanted to transfer leadership of the party in Palestine from the Jews to the Arabs. The Arabs, after all, constituted a majority of the country's population and an even larger majority of its working class. Now there was another reason to reconstitute the local leadership—the Soviets no longer had any confidence in the party's Jewish leaders, some of whom had drawn too close to the Zionists.

The riots of 1929, like the Arab Revolt of 1936–39, showed just how hard it was to maintain a consolidated and unified Jewish-Arab political organization during a time of national contention. Nevertheless, the broad framework of a Jewish-Arab Communist Party managed to stay together until 1944, despite disputes, resignations, and splits, and despite the marginal position that the party occupied in Arab society and the venomous opposition to it in the Zionist camp.

The Death Penalty

The dispute about nationalism and Marxism was a theoretical one, as was the debate over the causes of the riots. But there were arguments over practical issues as well. One of the most complex of these was the death sentence that had been imposed on men convicted of murder during the riots. According to figures that the high commissioner provided to the colonial secretary on May 31, 1930 (TNA CO 733/180), following the riots a total of 120 men were charged with murder or abetting murder. Of these, 62 were acquitted, including those accused of killing the Maklef family. The remaining 58 were found guilty, and 26 of these were sentenced to death. The latter sentences were confirmed by courts of appeals. One of these was a Jew, Yosef Urfali, the others Arabs. Of the Arabs, eleven had taken part in the massacre in Hebron and fourteen in the massacre in Safed. They asked for permission to appeal to the British Privy Council, a petition that was denied (except in the case of Urfali, who had not yet been sentenced at that point). The cases of the condemned men were placed before the high commissioner, whose signature was required in order to carry out a death sentence.

Following the Sentences

Even before the sentences were placed on the high commissioner's desk, a few figures in the Zionist establishment began to weigh whether it would not be right to support commutation of the death sentences. That may sound surprising. Why should Jews want to pardon Arabs who had murdered their brethren? One of the first people to broach the subject, in an informal way, was Shlomo Kaplansky, a member of the Jewish National Council and head of the Zionist Executive's Settlement Department. The idea shocked the head of the Zionist Executive in Palestine, Colonel Frederick Kisch, who maintained in a letter to a colleague on the Zionist Executive, Harry Sacher, on November 15, 1929, that any pardon would be perceived as a sign of the authorities' fear and weakness, and would thus exacerbate the security situation. Kisch was also concerned about the coverage of the death sentences in the *Palestine Bulletin*, the predecessor to the *Palestine Post*, which in 1950 became the *Jerusalem Post*. The newspapers' editors were Gershon Agronovsky (later, as Gershon Agron, mayor of Jerusalem), and David Goitein, later Israel's ambassador to South Africa and a Supreme Court justice. On December 6, 1929, Kisch requested the newspaper's editors to restrict their coverage. Items using the words "three more Arabs have been sentenced to death," and "women dressed in black were present in the courtroom," he warned, were eliciting sympathy for men who had coldbloodedly murdered elderly Jews, women, and children (CZA S25/4429).

Toward the Moment of Truth

But the issue of a commutation of the death sentences continued to engage the public. The high commissioner, the colonial secretary, and King George V received a flood of requests for commutation from figures and institutions in the Arab world as a whole and Palestine in particular. Everyone waited for the high commissioner's decision. On April 12, 1930, just before the final decision, *Filastin*'s English edition published a call for the high commissioner to pardon the convicted men. It also made a special appeal to the Hebrew press and Jewish public, calling on them to raise their voices against the death penalty and in doing so to demonstrate the full majesty of the prophetic morality of which the Jews were so proud. This appeal set off a stormy debate in the Jewish leadership, during which it emerged that there was some support for Jewish participation in the effort to have the death penalty commuted.

Jews for Commutation?

Officials at the Yishuv's national institutions discussed the issue of the death sentences in a joint forum of the Jewish Agency Executive and the Jewish National Council that was convened on April 18, 1930. The record of the meeting is not detailed, but the principal arguments can be deduced from it. Ben-Zvi, then chairman of the National Council and a leader of the Histadrut labor union, presented the position of the latter organization. The Histadrut, he said, had always opposed the death penalty, and he declared that it would oppose it in the current cases as well. However, he rejected commuting the death sentences if the death penalty remained in the law books, on the ground that doing so would send the message that convicted murderers in Palestine were liable for the death penalty except in cases in which they massacred Jews. Ben-Zvi added that, were the Zionist institutions to receive an official Arab appeal expressing regret about the massacres and offering securities for the future, there would be reason to discuss support for commutation. Lacking that, such support would be tantamount to permitting the shedding of Jewish blood.

Another speaker was Yosef Meyuhas, who had grown up in the village just south of the Old City walls of Jerusalem that the Jews called Kfar HaShiloah and the Arabs Silwan. The neighborhood's Jewish residents had fled their homes during the riots. Meyuhas had written books on Palestine's Arabs and their traditions and had served both as chairman of the Jerusalem Jewish Committee and as a representative of the Sephardi Jews in the Zionist Organization. As David Yellin's brother-in-law, he had been among the purchasers of Motza's land. Meyuhas believed that the old-time Sephardi community understood the Arabs better than the European Zionists did, and he proposed consulting with the Sephardi leaders regarding the anticipated effects of supporting commutation of the death penalties on Jewish-Arab relations. In the meantime, he recommended opposing any across-the-board commutation of the death sentences, fearing that this would give the impression that the law need not be taken seriously. He also feared that the Arabs, "because of their primitive mentality," would see the pardon only in utilitarian terms. Nonetheless, he also opposed a mass execution, proposing that the death penalty be carried out only on those who had actually themselves killed more than one person. Were the high commissioner to follow this recommendation, Meyuhas thought, it should be publicized that he had done so in consultation with the Jews.

Haim Salomon, deputy to Jerusalem's Mayor Ragheb Nashashibi and a leader of the Jewish National Council, had been born in Nahalat Shiva, the son of that neighborhood's founder Yoel Moshe Salomon and his wife Fruma. He offered his own analysis of the situation: the Arab press wanted pardons for the convicted men not because they valued human life but rather because they and the Arab leadership feared being the brunt of their community's wrath were twenty-six of its members put to death. The Arabs had not yet risen up against their leadership, but they might well do so if the executions went forward—and if they did, they would discover some of what their leaders had concealed from them up to that point. Salomon maintained that it was not reasonable for Jews to request clemency for men who had murdered Jews. But, like some of his colleagues, he would not object to it on condition that the Arabs made a formal appeal to the Zionist institutions expressing their readiness for peace.

Yosef Sprinzak, a prominent figure in the newly established Mapai Party who would later serve as the first speaker of the Knesset, proposed discussing the issue from a political rather than a moral point of view. He presumed that the execution of more than two dozen men would make it difficult to reach an accommodation with the Arabs in the future. A large group of men ascending the gallows would also turn into martyrs and symbols of the battle against Zionism. Yet Sprinzak, like his colleagues, preferred that a pardon come as part of a more comprehensive political move rather than being presented as a humanitarian act.

Maurice Hexter, a non-Zionist representative on the larger Jewish Agency Executive that had been established in 1929, began his remarks by quoting a biblical verse: "For out of Zion will the Torah go out, and the word of God from Jerusalem." Hexter argued that the Jewish Agency should not wait for any outside actor, British or Arab, to prevent the killing of the convicted fellahin. It should fulfill its moral obligation even if it made no difference to the Arab effendis. He also maintained that there was no obligation to attend to the majority opinion in the Yishuv. The role of leaders is to lead, and they were duty bound to oppose the death penalty.

Kisch finalized his position on May 2, and it became the position of all official Zionist institutions. The argument went as follows: there was no longer any justification, eight months after the riots, to execute more than twenty people, because doing so was liable to cause further deterioration in Jewish-Arab relations. The Yishuv should advocate commutation of the sentences, but not those of all the murderers. Kisch proposed recommending the commutation of the death sentences of those who had been incited by others. The relatively educated convicts, however, and those who had coldbloodedly planned and perpetrated the murders, should be executed (CZA S25/4429).

Brit Shalom did not wait for the official decision. It immediately took up *Filastin*'s challenge. On April 22 Brit Shalom sent the high commissioner a petition asking for the commutation of the death sentences:

> We oppose the death penalty on principle, and hope that the day will come when capital punishment will be terminated in the Land of Israel. But even if this moral imperative has not yet been realized, we see it as our duty to ourselves to apply to His Excellency in this matter, because we believe that the murders of August were committed in an atmosphere of incitement and a turbulent and emotional situation, to the point where it is difficult to place all the blame on the murderers.
>
> Our organization believes that a pardon issued by His Excellency to these criminals can help clear the atmosphere so charged with venom and hatred and hasten the establishment of normal relations between Jews and Arabs. In contrast, carrying out the death penalty will exacerbate resentment and tension in relations between the two peoples, at a time when all inhabitants of the land are interested in putting an early end to it. (CZA S25/4429)

The members of Brit Shalom collected signatures on a petition opposing the implementation of the death sentences. The Revisionists immediately responded. *Do'ar Hayom*—playing on the meaning of Brit Shalom's name, "peace covenant"—called the group a "blood covenant." Brit Shalom, the newspaper said, was groveling before the Arabs just as Jews in Poland kissed the lash with which the local lord whipped them (*Do'ar Hayom*, May 8, 1930).

The Decision: Commutation

A few days after Kisch announced his position, High Commissioner Chancellor convened his senior staff to discuss the issue. His advisors agreed with him that a way needed to be found to reduce the number of hangings. The chief justice of the Supreme Court offered the legal justification. An appeals court had overturned the death penalty imposed on Hinkis, who had murdered an entire family, on the ground that the act had not been premeditated. There was similar doubt regarding the premeditation of the murders committed by Arabs. The high commissioner decided that only three or four men should be hanged, those who had committed the most serious crimes (TNA CO 814/26).

This decision was very close to the position taken by Kisch and his staff. It would be difficult to determine the extent to which the Zionist Executive encouraged the high commissioner to reach this determination. In any case, the high commissioner announced that all the death sentences would be commuted to life imprisonment, except for three, those for: 'Ata al-Zir, Mohammad Jamjum, and Fuad Hijazi.

Albert Einstein and his associates thought that these three men should also escape the gallows.

Albert Einstein

When they learned of the high commissioner's decision, Albert Einstein, Oscar Cohen of Bnai Brith's Anti-Defamation League, the German Jewish leader and liberal rabbi Leo Baeck, and the German Jewish playwright Ernst Toller sent the following letter to the high commissioner: "Your Excellency, for purely humane reasons we oppose the death penalty in any form, without exception, no matter how great the crime. Our conscience requires us at this time to speak as human beings and as Jews. We, Zionists and non-Zionists, ask Your Excellency to pardon the three Arabs, which will greatly help achieve the peace between Jews and Arabs that we strive for" (*Davar*, June 18, 1930).

Einstein was not then unaware of what was going on in the Zionist movement at the time and stood by it on central questions. On October 12, 1929, a lengthy piece of his appeared in the *Guardian*, a British newspaper, in which he harshly criticized the British press for making no distinction between the attackers and victims in its reporting on the riots. He declared that the Jews would carry on their labor of building the country for the benefit of both peoples and termed the mufti an adventurer who sought to create animosity between Jews and Arabs. Just two months previously Einstein had sent a telegram of congratulations to the Zionist Congress in Zurich. Along with other prominent Jewish figures such as Herbert Samuel, who had served as the first British high commissioner in Palestine; and Léon Blum, the French socialist leader, he traveled to Zurich that year to attend the ceremony being held in conjunction with the Congress to inaugurate the expanded Jewish Agency.

The Expanded Jewish Agency

The expansion of the Jewish Agency was one of the most important decisions made by the Sixteenth Zionist Congress in Zurich. It was the product of long years of efforts to bring non-Zionists, including American Jews who were not members of Jewish national organizations, into the agency. The hope was that these people would offer economic, moral, and political support for Jewish settlement in Palestine. As Ben-Gurion put it, "everyone who took part in that ceremony felt that a new chapter was opening in the history of the building of the Land. Not a Zionist Organization but rather the entire Jewish people took upon itself to speed the construction [of the national home]" (quoted in Malkin 2007, 527). It was also one more step in the blurring of the boundaries between Jew and Zionist, accomplished at the initiative of the Zionist movement. And it was extensively covered in the Arab press. Arab leaders would later hold it up as a primary cause of the 1929 disturbances.

Einstein, who was involved in these intra-Jewish processes but combined his commitment to Zionism with radical humanism, proclaimed that the three Arabs chosen for death by the high commissioner should not be hung.

'Ata al-Zir

Al-Zir from Hebron was sentenced to death twice. In one trial he was convicted of breaking into the home of Rabbi Kastel (who Haidar al-Shafi knew as Abu Yussef and remembered as a family friend) at the head of a mob, wielding an ax. In another case the court ruled that al-Zir had also attacked the Kapiluto home where he murdered the yeshiva student Avraham Shapira, who died on the spot, and stabbed Eliahu Kapiluto, seriously injuring him (Kapiluto died a year later).

At al-Zir's trial for the stabbing of her husband, Rivka Kapiluto testified that when the Arabs attacked she and her husband fled to the house's backyard, with al-Zir at their heels. She grabbed him with both hands and pleaded that he not kill them, as they were natives of the country, or that he kill her but spare her husband and children. Al-Zir threw her to the floor, she claimed, and with his knife drawn, ran after her husband and stabbed him (*Davar*, May 6, 1930).

Al-Zir was born in about 1900 to a family of butchers and skinners and began to work in the family business as a boy. His height (almost two meters) and his strength (he had once lifted a camel) were legendary, and so was his temper. At the time of the riots he was married to two wives, with whom he had had five children ('Alami 2000, 324). He had proper relations with Hebron's established Jews, and in court he spoke of his personal acquaintance with the Kapiluto family. He denied involvement in the attack on their house. He claimed that he had been suffering from an eye ailment at the time and that he hadn't even been in the city that day, but rather in his vineyards. The court did not believe him, finding Rivka Kapiluto's testimony more reliable.

Mohammad Jamjum

The second Hebronite whose death sentence remained in force, Mohammad Jamjun, had been born in 1910 to a merchant family. His nickname was al-Asmar (Blackie) because of his dark skin. He had received a basic religious education at the school in his neighborhood mosque. Ahmad al-ʿAlami relates that he was devoted to his friends and family. Once Jamjun's father fell ill and, after he recovered a few days later, the first word he uttered was "watermelon." Mohammad immediately set out for Palestine's watermelon capital, Jenin, in northern Samaria, to bring his father the fruit he longed for. Mohammad was crazy about driving, and he managed to save up enough money to buy a car. A short time prior to the riots Jamjum became engaged and began to build a house in anticipation of the wedding, planned for the summer of 1929.

His family insisted that he had not been involved in the massacre in any way. Like al-Zir, he claimed that he had come down with an eye ailment and had spent that Saturday in the vineyards. According to al-ʿAlami, they claimed that a Jewish boy who had hidden in a closet while his father was murdered had testified that the murderer was al-Asmar, and that on this basis the British arrested and charged him.

The court judgments tell a different story. Jamjum and four others were sentenced to death for the premeditated murder of four people in the Abushedid home in Hebron: Eliahu Abushedid and his son Yitzhak, and Yaʾakov Gozlan and his son Moshe. They also had intent "to carry out another offence, namely pillage" (trial court, file 47/29; appeal, file 8/30, both in TNA CO 733/181/4). There were several witnesses to the murder, among them Victoria Gozlan and Venezia and Yosef Abushedid, who identified the assailants and testified that they saw them "striking the deceased with swords or daggers." As noted above, five of the men involved in the murders in this house were sentenced to death. The high commissioner commuted the sentences of four of them, leaving only Jamjum's death penalty standing. Jamjum was also accused of taking part in the killings in the central site of the massacre, Slonim's home. But Jamjun was acquitted of this charge on the ground that the court "was not satisfied with the evidence against the accused."

Jamjum's two brothers, ʿAbdallah and Badawi, moved to Jerusalem. ʿAbdallah, who lived in Silwan, was killed during the 1948 war. Badawi took part in the battle of Qastel in that year but survived the war. He made his living as a cobbler and died in 1984.

The Man from Safed: Fuad Hijazi

David Hacohen of the Haganah, who was dispatched to Safed to help the decimated Jewish community there, described the scene when Shoshana Afriyat encountered her parents' murderer this way: "The wounded and desperate Shoshana Afriyat clutched Fuad Hijazi. She lunged like a leopardess from the automobile with her last strength, leaped on him and sent chills through the street when she recognized the murderer of her father and mother, Fuad Hijazi, who murdered them before her eyes, who also cut her with his knife—he, the one who was sent by the government doctor to evacuate the wounded" (*Davar*, August 14, 1930). Born in 1904, Hijazi was the most educated of the condemned men. He completed secondary school in Safed and enrolled in a Jesuit college in Beirut. When he returned to the city of his birth a few months prior to the riots, he was appointed to a position in the city health department. In that capacity he was assigned to transfer the wounded victims of the riots in Safed to Haifa, just a few days after he had led an armed gang that attacked Jewish homes.

Hijazi was not arrested during the disturbances. He carried on with his work as if nothing had happened and as if he had not been a party to the atrocities. It was Afriyat's screams that led to his arrest. He tried to argue that Afriyat should not be trusted—a wounded and beaten young woman whose parents, Moshe and Frieda, had been murdered before her eyes. But the police arrested him. In court, Hijazi argued that he had not even been in Safed that day—his widowed mother had been staying with her brother in the village of Ras al-Ahmar, and he had gone on horseback to his uncle's house to see her, he claimed. But his alibi was not persuasive and was rejected. The testimony that tipped the scales against him was that of Police Officer Sa'id al-'Askari, who told the court that he had seen Hijazi enter the Afriyat home with the murderers (Haifa Court file 32/29, TNA CO 733/181). The court was persuaded that Hijazi had been one of the assailants and that he had drawn his pistol and ordered his companions to enter and kill the family. "He was a loyal nationalist. He hated the Jews because they had killed the prophets, and because they had come to Palestine to expel its inhabitants," al-'Alami wrote (2000, 330). In other words, political anti-Zionism mixed with Jesuit antisemitism.

Prophet Killers

Jews are seen as prophet killers not only in Christian antisemitic tracts but also in the Qur'an and Islamic literature. The roots of this characterization can be found in the Bible and midrashic literature, but there it appears not as a sweeping indictment or essential trait, but rather as a demand for repentance. Some commentators on the Qur'an, among them Muqatil bin Suliman and Mohammad Ibn Jarir al-Tabari, quote rabbinic tales and Christian traditions, adding John the Baptist and Jesus to the list of prophets killed by the Jews.

Clemency? Eliahu Sasson's Approach

Einstein maintained that the sentences of all the murderers should be commuted because the death penalty was inherently wrong. Eliahu Sasson also called for a complete amnesty. At the beginning of June 1930, when the date of the executions was announced, Sasson called in the pages of *Filastin* for "an absolute amnesty that will include all those sentenced to death in connection with the Av [August] disturbances, [sentencing them instead] to life imprisonment, and to other terms, as a foundation for a new era in the Palestine, an era of forgetting hatred between the Jews and the Arabs, and of a life of cooperation and mutual understanding from this day onward, for the benefit of the common homeland" (quoted in *Davar*, June 8, 1930). Most Jews viewed such a position as much too conciliatory—not just because of the pardon Sasson proposed, but also because of his view that the homeland was common to the two peoples. But *Filastin* viewed Sasson's position as belligerent—Palestine, in the newspaper's view, was not a homeland shared by Jews and Arabs, its editors stated, but a solely Arab land. "If Jews wished to live in peace with the Arabs, they would have to set aside their Zionist aspirations" (quoted in *Davar*, June 9, 1930).

The editors of another newspaper, *al-Aqdam*, did not conceal their astonishment at Sasson's opinion. After all, Sasson was no stranger—he was a man who lives with us, they wrote, a man whose Arab identity preceded his Zionism. He should thus know very well that the Zionists were strangers in the country and that they had no sanction to settle or to speak their foreign language in Palestine. "If the Jews native to the country wash their hands of Zionism, their connections with which are weaker than a spider's web, then these Jews will be reaccepted into the Arab bosom," the editors wrote (quoted in *Davar*, November 17, 1929). The newspaper compared Sasson to Brit Shalom, the position of which had also been rejected by the Arabs (ibid. See also *Davar*, August 3 and September 29, 1930).

A Man whose Arab Identity Preceded his Zionism

Sasson was born in Damascus in 1902 to a family of rabbis and merchants. His father was one of the leaders of the local Jewish community. Eliahu studied at the city's Alliance Française school and then moved on to a Christian Arab high school that enrolled many of the sons of prominent Arab families. Along with his classmates, he joined the Arab national movement, in which he was active during World War I. In 1919 Sasson organized the Jewish community in Damascus to welcome King Faisal ibn Hussayn after his return from the San Remo conference. His parents then decided to move to Palestine. Eliahu joined them a short time later, dividing his time between writing articles for Arab newspapers and working as a manual laborer. In 1933, Moshe Shertok invited him to join the Jewish Agency's Political Department, where he was appointed to head the Arab branch. In this capacity Sasson frequently met with Arab leaders, some of whom he knew from his activity in the national movement. Years later he related that his mother had ordered him to move from Syria to the Land of Israel and to replace his work with the Arab national movement with working for the Zionist movement, and he obeyed. That was what *al-Aqdam* meant when it claimed that Sasson's Arab identity had preceded his Zionism. After Israel was founded, Sasson was Israel's ambassador to several countries. In the 1960s he served as a member of the cabinet. His youth and political activity is recounted in his memoir, *BaDerekh el haShalom* (On the road to peace; 1979).

Red Tuesday

The die was cast. The calls for amnesty from Arabs, Jews, Arab Jews, religious scholars, scientists, pacifists, and others were rejected. On June 2, High Commissioner Chancellor announced his final decision and ruled that the three men on death row would be brought to the gallows on Tuesday, June 17, 1930. In Palestinian historical memory the day came to be called Red Tuesday. The Palestinian press depicted the decision as callous, an indication of Britain's pro-Zionist stance. It also highlighted the fact that the Jewish murderers had been pardoned and claimed that the attacks on Jews were legitimate acts of defense. Legends glorifying the convicts quickly began to spread.

Stories of Heroism

For example, after hearing that the high commissioner had confirmed the sentences, the youngest of the convicts was said to have declared: "If this is the price that must be paid to get rid of the British nightmare and to shock the world, it is worth it." His comrades responded: "We are not sorrowful at our fates. It is an honor that we never thought possible. Tell our friends that no one should ask for a pardon for us" (quoted in 'Alami 2000, 273).

Jamjum and al-Zir praised God for one more thing. "How good is it that we, simple people, are going to the gallows and not leaders whom the homeland needs," they said (quoted in ibid.). They asked that henna be brought to their cells so that they could stain their hands, as was customary at celebrations in Hebron.

Al-'Alami (ibid., 330–31) quotes a letter by Hijazi that had been published in the newspaper *al-Yarmuk* immediately after his execution. He instructed his brothers to behave toward each other with brotherhood and love, pleaded with them not to grieve at his death because his entire life had been directed toward this moment, and asked them to continue to live a life full of happiness. He told his brother Ahmad to work hard at his studies and listen to their mother, and he announced that he forgave all those who had testified against him, including Sa'id al-'Askari, the policeman who had incriminated him. Allah would judge him at the end of days. He asked that his funeral be conducted like a wedding and reminded his family that, as a *shahid* (a Muslim martyr), he should be buried in his clothes. He told his mother not to turn his grave into the focus of her life.

Gallows in Acre

The prison administration announced the order of the hangings:

8 a.m. — Hijazi
9 a.m. — al-Zir
10 a.m. — Jamjum

From early morning on, crowds streamed toward the citadel in Acre so that they could be as close as possible to the execution site. Large numbers of soldiers were deployed to guard the prison, and machine guns were positioned on its roof. The Arabs called a general strike throughout Palestine. In Jerusalem it was only partially observed, but in Hebron, Safed, Haifa, Jaffa, and most of the rest of the country compliance was absolute. In Jaffa hundreds of people massed silently in Clock Square. The same happened in the central squares in Haifa and Nablus. At eight o'clock Hijazi was led to the gallows. "I am ready and willing to water the soil of the homeland with my blood," he cried (ibid., 273).

According to al-'Alami, Hijazi "ascended to the platform, toward his death. Out of the corner of his eye he saw Kalman Cohen, the Safed police officer who was one of those charged with his interrogation. 'Go away,' he shouted. 'I do not want a Jew to be looking at me at the moment of my death, when I am on the verge of the next world'" (2000, 273). We do not know if Cohen left. The noose was placed around Hijazi's neck, the hangman opened the hatch, and Hijazi plunged down. The noose tightened and his neck was broken, killing him instantly. Church bells rang throughout the country. The waiting Muslims recited *Surat al-Fatiha*, the opening verse of the Qur'an.

Racing to Their Deaths

Al-Zir's turn came at nine o'clock, but Jamjum announced that he wanted to die first. As al-'Alami relates, Jamjum "pushed his jailers aside and ran toward the gallows. He asked that his bonds be removed, but the police refused. With a huge effort he managed to smash the chains on his hands, ascending the gallows with determination and courage, a smile on his face" (2000, 273).

Why was Jamjum in such a hurry? Tradition has it that, on the morning of the executions, a rumor reached Acre that the high commissioner intended to pardon the convicts in the middle of the executions. Jamjum did not want to miss the chance to become a martyr. But the rumor turned out to be baseless. At ten o'clock the remaining prisoner, al-Zir, was led to his death. Church bells pealed at the time of each execution. After each one, *Surat al-Fatiha* was recited. The bodies were then handed over to the men's families, and a funeral procession of thousands escorted them to the Acre cemetery. The parade was led by schoolchildren, followed by members of the Muslim-Christian Association and other national organizations. They were followed by religious leaders, after whom came the litters carrying the bodies. Following them were delegations from all over the country and crowds of mourners. High Commissioner Chancellor turned down the families' requests to bury their dead in their cities of birth. All three were buried in Acre.

Sing a Song for the Shahid

Palestinian poets and songwriters competed over who could praise the martyrs more highly. A poem by the Palestinian national poet Ibrahim Tuqan, "Red Tuesday," won a wide audience and praise from the critics. Here is the final verse:

Their bodies in homeland's graves
Their souls in the vaults of heaven
Where no wrongs can be found, no one carps
Only an abundance of forgiveness and atonement.
Clemency is asked only of God
He whose esteem and greatness
And power exceeds that of those who were blinded
By their [British] power on sea and land. (Tuqan 1996, 98)

Another poem, one that was turned into a popular song, was written by a Haifa poet, Noah Ibrahim. Coming from a poor family, he could not enroll in college and had to go to work at a young age. He found a job at a printer's, where he could grow intoxicated with the written word and play with letters. Like many others of his generation, Ibrahim had a potent national sensibility. The poem's refrain begins with the words "Min sijn 'Akka til'at jinaza (From Acre Prison the funeral set out)," and it is sung to this day:

Three men on a race to their deaths
Facing the hangman's verdict
Became a symbol and emblem
In the land, from end to end

From Acre Prison the funeral set out
Mohammad Jamjum and Fuad Hijazi
Mourn, my people, mourn them. ('Alami 2000, 338–39)

Ibrahim himself became a martyr eight years later. In 1936 he joined the Arab Revolt, which lasted for three years throughout Palestine. First he supported the rebellion as a poet, and then he took part as a fighter. He was arrested by the British and, for a time, was incarcerated in Acre Prison. After his release he returned to the ranks, dying in 1938 in a battle against the British army in the Western Galilee (Hajjab 2005).

Should Murderers Be Made into Martyrs?

Following the executions, the Arab leaders in Palestine declared June 17 to be Martyrs' Day, calling for it to be celebrated annually. When the date approached in the following year, only a single voice was raised against the idea. Sheikh As'ad al-Shuqayri declared that murderers should not be made into martyrs (*Davar*, August 26, 1931). A bitter opponent of Hajj Amin al-Hussayni, al-Shuqayri was one of Palestine's leading Muslim clergymen. He served as the mufti of the Ottoman Fourth Army during World War I, and later as mufti of Acre. In 1964, his son Ahmad founded the Palestine Liberation Organization, which he headed until 1967. But we have already seen that in 1929 the son was much more militant than the father. Those who thought the murderers were martyrs carried the day then and continue to do so to this day.

One More Pardon

The Jew on death row, Yosef Urfali, did not have his sentence commuted in May 1930 because his appeal was still before the Privy Council. Only when the appeal was rejected was his sentence final and conveyed to the high commissioner. In August 1930 Chancellor commuted Urfali's death sentence to fifteen years in prison. He was transferred to the prison in Jerusalem's Russian compound, were he was kept alongside Simha Hinkis and dozens of Arab prisoners. To protest the reduction of Urfali's sentence, the Arab Executive Committee declared a general strike for August 23. The Arab Women's Association petitioned the high commissioner. "Out of humane feelings," the petition stated, the association "does not demand the killing of this criminal, who has been sentenced to death twice. The protest is directed at the discrimination in favor of Urfali as an individual, and of the Jews as a whole, which is not for the good of the regime in Palestine" (quoted in *Davar*, August 14, 1930). Notably, the Arab leaders, as an act of humanity, did not demand the hanging of a Jew who had been convicted of murdering Arabs.

Early Release

Ever since the verdicts had been handed down, the Zionist institutions had sought the early release of Hinkis and Urfali, while the Arab national institutions did the same for the Arab prisoners. From time to time some of the Arabs were freed for reasons of health or advanced age. For example, in January 1931 three men from Safed were released from prison after reaching the age of seventy. The three had been convicted of setting fire to the home of Sheyndl Goldzweig, who was burned to death (JTA, January 6, 1931). The campaign to bring about the early release of the two Jews was not successful. The men felt that they had been abandoned. Hinkis sent Ben-Gurion a furious letter about himself and Urfali: "You are responsible for our lives and for our families. They will demand our lives from you. Because we have had enough of suffering." From time to time an article about them appeared in the press, but, not surprisingly, their cases slipped off the public agenda. The only Yishuv leader who made a point of visiting them was Ben-Zvi. So did Rabbi Aryeh Levin, known as the "father of prisoners." The letters and reports written by both prisoners and their visitors can be found in the CZA (s25/4434).

The Mufti

Mufti al-Hussayni visited the Arab prisoners more often than Zionist leaders visited the Jewish prisoners. That is what Ben-Zvi wrote to Arlosoroff following a visit to the prison on the Simhat Torah holiday in October 1932. But the Arab prisoners were also upset. They felt that they had acted in the name of their nation but that the Palestinian leaders were not doing enough to get them released. At the same time, rumors were circulating that the aid funds for Arabs hurt in the disturbances, for whom the Supreme Muslim Fund collected large sums, never reached the needy families. Instead, some people claimed that the money had lined the pockets of several leaders. It is difficult today to determine whether the rumors were accurate, but Mohammad al-Tawil, who worked in the service of the Zionist institutions, helped spread them by including them in a pamphlet in Arabic and Hebrew that he put out right after the riots. The title was *Eikh Hithilu haMe'ora'ot beFalastina* (How the riots in Palestine began; 1930b). These allegations circulated among the Palestinian population throughout this period.

Clemency: Jewish-Arab Cooperation

In December 1934, with King George V's seventieth birthday to be celebrated on the following July 2, efforts to obtain pardons for the prisoners were redoubled. Both Jews and Arabs realized that the coming celebration was an opportunity. Women's organizations, local governments, the Chief Rabbinate, and other institutions—both Jewish and Arab—petitioned the high commissioner, with each organization asking for clemency for its people's prisoners. The Arabs proposed to the Jews that they act jointly. The Haifa-based Arab national leader Rashid Hajj Ibrahim wrote to Tiberias's Jewish mayor, Zaki Alhadif, requesting that the municipal council of Tiberias sign a petition by Palestine's local governments asking that all the prisoners convicted in the 1929 trials be pardoned. I have not been able to locate any documents indicating how Zionist institutions responded to this initiative. In any case, the Arab institutions in the meantime acted unilaterally, calling for an amnesty that would include the two Jewish prisoners. Ben-Zvi informed his colleagues on the Jewish National Council about the Arab initiative in February 1935 (CZA S25/3724). Some six years after the riots — and one year before the Arab Revolt broke out — there was a moment of political partnership between the two warring camps.

When the king's birthday arrived, Arthur Wauchope, then the high commissioner, declared that he hoped that the deadly riots would be expunged from the memories of both the Jews and the Arabs, and he announced the clemency procedure he had decided on. All prisoners who had been sentenced to less than fifteen years in prison would be released immediately. The list included fourteen prisoners, one of them a Jew — Simha Hinkis. The sentences of the remaining twenty prisoners were reduced, and they would be released in August 1936. The only Jew in this category was Yosef Urfali. Three more Arab prisoners whose death sentences had been commuted had their sentences shortened and would be released five years later.

The next day, on July 3, following a brief ceremony at the prison, the first fourteen prisoners were released. The families of the Arab prisoners waited for them outside. A large crowd of Jews greeted Hinkis.

Hinkis's Welcome

When he was released, Hinkis set out with his entourage to meet Rabbi Kook. From there they proceeded to the compound housing the Jewish national institutions, which was not far away. The Jewish National Council staged a festive reception. Hinkis spoke briefly, asking the leadership to help Urfali, who remained in prison. After this Hinkis set out for Tel Aviv in a convoy, accompanied by motorcycles. He was given a hero's welcome in the first Hebrew city. Thousands awaited him and cheered his arrival (HHA, Baumrosen testimony, 7/39). Baruch Hinkis, Simha's brother, related that "afterward we entered the Mugrabi Cinema. They brought us in through the back door and there was a huge crowd there. They turned off the electricity, and written on the screen was 'Hinkis has been released and he is here with us.' Then the electricity was turned on again and everyone cheered" (*Ma'ariv*, March 10, 1988).

Land to Build on, a Job with the City, and Soccer

Following his release, Hinkis met the philanthropist Yitzhak Leib Goldberg, the father of Binyamin, who had died in Hinkis's arms. Goldberg had founded a school in his son's memory, as well as providing scholarships at many other

Celebrating Simha Hinkis' freedom, Jerusalem 1935 (Central Zionist Archives).

educational institutions. Goldberg told Hinkis that he would give him a lot on which he could build himself a house. The Tel Aviv government also resolved to support the freed prisoner, offering him a job. One of the city's soccer teams, HaPo'el Tel Aviv, staged an exhibition game in his honor the following Saturday. The stands were packed, a band played, and Hinkis received a wreath and was honored by being invited to make the opening kick. It was a display of national unity — *Davar* published an account of the game, reporting that even a delegation from HaPo'el's bitter rival, Maccabi Tel Aviv, showed up to commend him (June 9, 1935).

Hapo'el won, three to zero, against a team from Egypt. Hinkis's victims had been of Egyptian extraction, but the Egyptian players almost certainly did not know who Hinkis was.

How to Make a Hero

In the years that followed a haze descended over the story of Hinkis's murder of the 'Awn family. Hinkis was occasionally interviewed by reporters and offered his account of what had happened on August 25, 1929, the day Tel Aviv was attacked. Some thirty years after the incident, when he was appointed to the post of director general of the Israel Sports Association, *Ma'ariv* told the story: "During an exchange of gunfire Hinkis and several other boys noticed that Arabs were ascending and descending from the roof of one of the buildings in the Abu Kabir citrus grove. 'We immediately decided to go there and finish them off," he now recalls. Along with three boys armed with pistols, they advanced in stages through the grove up to the building. They broke in and found seven rioters armed to the teeth. The surprise was total and within a few seconds not a single Arab remained alive" (March 17, 1958).

More than two decades later, on the fiftieth anniversary of the 1929 riots, the children's magazine *Davar Leyeladim* recounted the story to its young readers in "HaShoter HaYehudi sheNidon leMavet" (The Jewish policeman who was sentenced to death; Pines 1979, 1574). This version also stated that all seven people killed by Hinkis had been armed with sticks and pistols.

Hinkis also granted an interview to Gershon Gera, author of a biography of Goldberg, Hinkis's benefactor. This time Hinkis related that, as he approached the 'Awn home he heard voices calling *"Yahud, yahud!"* (Jews! Jews!). In Hinkis's words, "I broke in with two youths after me, and we obliterated the armed gang." Gera, who had researched the incident before the interview, pressed Hinkis, asking about the child and woman who had lost their lives. Hinkis replied: "I shot and wounded an Arab woman, a very fat one, in her backside. Neither she nor the child were killed" (Gera 1984, 215).

From time to time journalists dredge up Hinkis's case from their memories. Or they encounter for the first time the story of the Jewish policeman who was sentenced to death for defending Tel Aviv. They use their journalistic imaginations to embellish it. While Hinkis was still alive, some reporters contacted him and, without bothering to look for other sources, recounted the story uncritically from his point of view. In 1985, when Hinkis was appointed treasurer of Tel Aviv's Association of Haganah Members, Shimon Samet of *Ha'aretz* revived the legend. He offered an even more perfect version—the seven people killed by Hinkis were not only rioters but the very same Arabs who had killed the Haganah men shortly before. All of them were armed. They outnumbered Hinkis and his comrades and were better armed, but the Jews conducted a pitched battle against them, killed seven, and the rest of the Arabs fled (Shimon Samet, *Ha'aretz*, June 25, 1985). Three years later, *Ma'ariv* quoted Hinkis, who had recently died: "I approached the house. I heard the voices of Arabs trading stories from the pogrom. I broke in. They sat on the ground with clubs in their hands, but had no time to move. I shot a few bullets into each one. There were seven of them and I took them out one by one" (March 7, 1988). For obvious reasons, Hinkis and his defense team did not tell such stories in court.

Were Arabic newspapers to offer such stories about their community's murderers, some would term them the products of wild Oriental imagination. But these were Hebrew newspapers, so another explanation is in order. I suggest that the Jewish public wanted to honor Hinkis, who risked his life during the riots and paid for it by spending several years in prison. However, the same public had difficulty accepting the fact that this hero had killed unarmed men and women. The solution was to fashion a heroic story. Once this version came into being, a journalist like Amnon Lord could, covering Hinkis's funeral for *Hadashot*, offer a fantastical version of the events under the headline "Hu Haya Gever" (He was a [real] man; March 7, 1988) without bothering to research the story. A few academic studies grappled with the facts (Haskin 2008), although from within the Zionist discourse and without reference to the Palestinian understanding of the events.

And the Palestinian Murderers?

Palestinian writers are no different. They do not name the Jewish victims of the three Arab martyrs, and they certainly do not mention the fact that their victims had been unarmed and innocent. They, too, offer a simplistic and one-dimensional picture: the Jews were trying to take over the country, and young Arabs gave up their lives and freedom to defend their nation. And since the sense that the Jews were trying to seize control of Palestine did not dissipate, the Arab martyrs were not forgotten. The song memorializing the martyrs, "From Acre Prison the funeral set out," has gained new popularity in recent years and is often played at Arab demonstrations and rallies. In 2005, for the first time in several decades, a memorial ceremony was held in Acre, on the occasion of the seventy-fifth anniversary of their execution. Palestinian-Israeli leaders and public figures took part in the march, which followed the path of the funeral procession from Acre Prison to the city's Muslim cemetery.

Ahmad 'Awda, a member of Acre's city council for Hadash, a Communist-dominated party, spoke at the ceremony. He linked the events of 1929 in Acre directly to the new millennium. The Arabs of Acre now faced the same challenge faced by the Palestinians in 1929, he said: Jewish settlers in the city were trying to squeeze out the Arabs. The problem was not that Jews lived in Acre, he declared, but they should not do so at the expense of the city's Arabs (Bakri 2005).

A writer for the Israeli news website Ynet asked a Hadash member of the Knesset, Issam Makhoul, why his party's leaders treated people who had murdered innocent civilians as if they were freedom fighters. Makhoul replied that the three men had been victims of British colonialism: "They turned the Arabs and the Jews into victims by causing them to fight among themselves rather than to fight together for a better and common future" (Ravad 2005). He made no reference to the actual deeds for which the three men were executed.

So this is how collective memory is shaped. Men and women who gave their lives for the sake of their nation or displayed their willingness to do so are fashioned into symbols for the generations that follow. Their problematic actions are papered over. The pain of compatriots killed by the enemy is lamented in story and song. Horrifying historical stories are made over, and the versions of each side in a conflict grow so different from each other that each side comes to view its version as the only truth. Who now remembers that in 1929, at the height of the bloodshed, there were both Arabs and Jews who opposed this crude view?

And the Israeli New Historians?

In the 1980s some young historians began delving into newly opened archival material on the 1948 war and challenging the versions and interpretations of events expounded by mainstream Zionist historians. These new scholars worked independently, but collectively they came to be called the New Historians, and they are still writing today. They offered differing views of the events of 1929 and their relation to 1948. None of them placed the 1929 riots at the center of their studies, but neither did they ignore those riots. The works they produced demonstrate, however, that they did not seek to understand what happened in 1929. Rather, they used the events of that year as a means of presenting their own views. One of the New Historians, Ilan Pappé, offers an account in which he suggests that Hajj Amin al-Hussayni tried to prevent the eruption of violence in Jerusalem and that his supporters were not involved in the massacre in Hebron:

> Al-Hajj Amin held talks with the leaders of Nablus and Hebron, but failed to pacify them. This was especially true where the Hebronites were concerned, since al-Hajj Amin's standing in that town was shaky and they would not listen to him. There the Nashashibis were better entrenched. . . . They incited the mob against the Jewish community, with the result that sixty-four Hebronite Jews were killed. The same thing happened in Safed, where twenty-six Jews were murdered. The opposite camp, Zionist and British, was no less ruthless. In Jaffa a Jewish mob murdered seven Palestinians, and all in all 133 Jews and 116 Muslims perished during that bloody week. (2011, 244)

The inaccurate figures cited by Pappé result mainly from the disparities in contemporary reports. A more significant error is Pappé's assertion that all the Arab dead were Muslims; in fact, four Christians were killed. These are relatively minor errors. In his analysis, Pappé offers an innovative thesis — that the Nashashibi clan, which led the opposition to the al-Hussayni dominance in Jerusalem and the rest of Palestine, bore the responsibility for the massacre in Hebron. In fact, there is no evidence to support this claim. Even if it is true that the mufti did not instigate the massacre and played no direct role in it, and even if the Nashashibis were relatively strong in Hebron, that creates no link between the murderers and the Nashashibis. This unfounded accusation seems to be a result of Pappé's agenda of clearing the mufti of all guilt. Keep in mind that even if al-Hussayni spoke out publicly against violence, some of his followers thought, with or without cause, that he did not actually mean it. In fact, some of the assailants in Hebron, such as Ibrahim Abu Gharbiyya, were associated with the al-Hussaynis. So was the preacher Taleb Maraqa, who was sentenced to two years in prison for incitement. Recall also the sources who claim that Fakhri Nashashibi tried to halt the violence on Friday in Jerusalem. Furthermore, the men who attacked Hebron's Jews were not necessarily supporters of either political faction.

In addition to factual errors, Pappé uses imprecision to color the events in the imaginations of his readers. For example, "the opposite camp, Zionist and British, was no less ruthless." Is that really the case? If the measure of brutality is the number of innocent, unarmed people killed, then the numbers Pappé gives disprove rather than support this assertion. Furthermore, was the "other side" really composed of Zionists and the British? That is, did those two groups really act in concert? And to what extent does the cruelty of individuals represent all the Jews, all the British, and all the Arabs? What is Pappé's source for his claim that the 'Awn family of Jaffa was killed by a "Jewish mob?" All the evidence shows that it was carried out by a team of Jewish militiamen led by Hinkis.

Until recently, another of the New Historians, Benny Morris, took a different approach. He based his work on careful and meticulous perusal of archival sources. His views about the Zionist-Palestinian conflict differ from Pappé's (Morris identifies himself as a Zionist and supports Zionist actions; Pappé does neither). In a critique of Pappé's work bearing the title "The Liar as Hero," Morris surveys his target's complete *oeuvre* and argues that he is a careless and unprincipled historian. Regarding Pappé's claim about mutual bloodletting in 1929, Morris writes: "Actually, there were no massacres of Arabs by Jews, though a number of Arabs were killed when Jews defended themselves or retaliated after Arab violence" (2011).

In that article and in *Righteous Victims* (1999, 114–15), Morris tends to minimize Jewish violence in 1929. *Righteous Victims* makes no mention at all of Arabs murdered by Jews in lynchings and other attacks (such as the cases of Karkar and al-Dajjani) prior to the outbreak of the riots or during them (the Arabs killed in Bayit VeGan, the case of 'Aisha al-'Atari, and the killings in Haifa). Morris mentions the murder of the 'Awn family only in passing: "In one incident four Haganah men were killed and five wounded. In retaliation a Haganah unit raided an Arab house, killing four people" (1999, 115), without mentioning that this retaliation operation was directed against men and women (five of them, not four) who were unarmed and uninvolved in the attacks. The error seems not to be an accident. Rather, it is the result of a change in Morris, who appears not to check his facts carefully and prefers to offer stock images in extreme form.

This can be seen in a critical article Morris wrote on the Hebrew edition of the book you are now reading, in which he exaggerated the number of Jews killed on the first day of the riots: "Dozens of Jews were murdered in the Gurji courtyard and Meah She'arim and the British repelled the attackers" (2013). In fact, not a single Jew was killed in Meah She'arim, and seven, not dozens, were killed in the nearby Gurji courtyard—I named them above.

Morris, so it seems, is careless and thus no more persuasive than Pappé. To determine whether or not Jews committed massacres in 1929, it is not sufficient to declare that "there were no massacres of Arabs by Jews." You need to offer a definition of the term "massacre" that is generally accepted and then see if what happened in fact conforms to that definition. The murder of the 'Awn family, like that of the Maklefs, can be termed a massacre inasmuch as both accord with some of the existing definitions of the word. According to other standards, of course, they would not be massacres. The choice of what definition to prefer and what terminology to use is thus the historian's choice and depends in large measure on how he seeks to portray the Jews and the Arabs. Pappé wants to show that the Jews were as brutal as the Arabs and thus calls them massacres. Morris disagrees and plays with the numbers to argue that Arabs were killed only in revenge. In doing so he disregards the fact that Karkar and al-Dajjani were murdered in Meah She'arim by Jews at about the same time as—or maybe slightly earlier than—Eliahu Raitan, Ya'akov Ben-Shim'on, and the Rotenberg brothers were murdered by Arabs near the Jaffa Gate. Basing his work on unconfirmed biased assumptions, Morris terms the acts of the Jews revenge and those of the Arabs aggression.

So who is the aggressor and who the defender? In the case of any single event, and when looking at the larger picture, to understand what really happened it is necessary to delve deeply into not only the facts but also the claims made by each side. One person who did this very well was Ben-Gurion (even if he presented his conclusions only in internal discussions). At a meeting of the Jewish Agency Executive Committee in 1937, during the Arab Revolt, Ben-Gurion declared: "We must see the situation for what it is. On the security front we are those attacked and who are on the defensive. But in the political field we are the attackers and the Arabs are those defending themselves. They are living in the country and own the land, the village. We live in the Diaspora and want only to immigrate [to Palestine] and gain possession of (lirkosh) the land from them" (quoted in Morris 2008, 393).

AFTERWORD

The 1929 riots pose difficult questions. What caused Arabs in Hebron and Safed and other places in Palestine to murder their Jewish neighbors? What motivated Jews to lynch Arabs in Jerusalem? What triggered the general Arab offensive against Jews that summer? What leads individual human beings to turn against the tide and save the very people that most members of their own community see as enemies? And at another level, what were the long-range effects of the riots on Jewish-Arab relations and on internal relations within each community?

This book offers a number of insights into the 1929 riots. Some of these touch on the events themselves, and others are more general. Some are not new but here come into sharper focus, while others depart from the common wisdom. The fact that Jews murdered Arabs in 1929 does not change the larger picture, which is that of an Arab attack on Jewish communities. This larger picture does not change the broader historical landscape, in which Jews immigrated to Palestine beginning in the waning days of the Ottoman Empire under European (in particular, British) protection. These Jewish immigrants expressly intended to make the country they called the Land of Israel into a Jewish one. The corollary of that intention was that the Arabs would become a minority in their own land. Over the course of the book I have presented the range of views regarding the question of whether the Zionist project was a just one. Here I will offer my own opinion: the Jews, as a persecuted people whose property and lives were in constant danger, had a right to take refuge in the Land of Israel. But this right did not strip the Arabs of their own rights in Palestine, nor can it justify every action and policy pursued by the Zionist movement to achieve its larger goal.

Granting refuge to refugees does not necessarily run counter to the spirit of Islam, even if the refugees are Jews and the refuge they seek is the Holy Land. Proof of this is the fact that the Ottoman Empire permitted many Jews to settle in Palestine following their exile from Spain at the end of the fifteenth century. But in 1929, following a century or so of waves of Jewish immigration under the protection of foreign powers and almost fifty years of organized Zionist activity, the Jews were no longer merely refugees seeking shelter but settlers taking possession of land and seeking sovereignty. Under Zionist influence, the long-standing Jewish minority in Palestine, which had at first sought equality with the Arab majority, now gradually became enamored of the European Zionist goal of a Jewish nation-state in the Land of Israel. As that happened, the country's Arabs gradually ceased to discern any sharp line that distinguished avowedly Zionist Jews from other Jews who declared themselves anti-Zionists or who did not take an unambiguous stand. Language, however, sometimes lags behind perception. In Arab speech and writing, as well as in daily life, the old vocabulary persisted. *Al-Yahud al-'Arab* (Arab Jews) were considered part and parcel of Middle Eastern culture; the *Siknaj* (Ashkenazi Haredim), who arrived in several waves beginning in the early nineteenth century, were absorbed into the fabric of Palestine's society because they accepted the hegemony of Islamic Arabs. Then there were the Zionists, whom the Arabs called Moskobim (Muscovites), who brought with them foreign habits and mores from Eastern Europe and, even more critically, had national and political aspirations. The terms remained in use, but by the bloody summer of 1929 they no longer meant much. When the Arabs attacked, they made no distinction between Jews of different political views, or between those who came from long-established families and those who were relative newcomers. The clearest proof of this comes from the screams of the Cohen and Afriyat families of Safed, and of the Abushedid and Kapiluto families of Hebron, who in vain beseeched the neighbors who were attacking them, saying that they were natives of the country who had done no harm to the Arabs.

This was the summer that made it clear that the distinctions that meant so much to Jews within their community were virtually meaningless to the Arabs. They saw no appreciable difference between Haredim and secular Jews, between Old Yishuv and New Yishuv, and between the different streams within the Zionist labor movement or between the labor movement and the Revisionists. It was not that Muslims thought that all Jews deserved to die — that is not a Muslim belief — but because by the end of the 1920s they felt very powerfully that all these groups of Jews had much more in common than whatever it was that separated them. All of the groups maintained that the Jews were a nation, all of them believed that the Jews had an inalienable right to immigrate to what they viewed as the land of their fathers, and all of them aspired to establish a Jewish state in Palestine (whether that state would be founded by human action or by the Messiah, and whether it would be a capitalist or socialist state). All of them believed that Jews should be first and foremost loyal to and responsible for each other. All these principles were utterly opposed to the way Palestine's Arabs saw the place of Jews in their society, and thus all Jews now looked the same to them. As the Arabs saw it, in the summer of 1929 they killed not their Jewish neighbors, but rather enemies who were seeking to conquer their land.

The Arabs were conscious of the danger that the Jewish community's consolidation under the Zionist movement posed for them while that process was still embryonic. Paradoxically, their attack accelerated the very process they understood to be so dangerous. Jews of Middle Eastern or other extraction who had lived for generations in Palestine initially had an ambiguous attitude toward the Zionist movement. They had felt rejected by the socialists and the Zionist institutions and some of them aspired to carry on their traditional way of life alongside the Arabs. They felt much more comfortable with their Arab neighbors than with the insolence and debauchery they thought the Zionist pioneers exhibited, and they waited impatiently for the next hit by the superstar Egyptian chanteuse Umm Kulthum. The Haredi Jews kept their distance from politics and preferred to leave the issue of sovereignty in the Holy Land to Heaven. But after the attack they realized that, as Jews, their only political home was with the Zionists. Some started to be actively involved with Zionist institutions, while others viewed them only as shelters when the weather got rough. But they all realized that they had no real political alternative of joining forces with the country's Arabs—the Arabs had no interest in that.

In this sense we can say that the 1929 riots founded the Yishuv. That is, following the riots, the disparate Jewish community in Palestine became the single Yishuv that was the precursor to today's Israeli state, with its hegemonic values and pugnacious defensive spirit. Massacres were committed in places where no Hebrew defense forces were deployed, and where they were deployed, Jewish defenders succeeded in repelling Arab attacks. That was enough to prove to most Jews that only a Jewish army could save the Yishuv from obliteration. Ben-Gurion wrote as much in his diary on September 8, 1929: "The Yishuv's value has risen in the eyes of the people" (BGA, "Yoman"). By "Yishuv" he meant the organized Yishuv—the Zionist institutions, including the Haganah. He knew that these institutions did not have an exclusive claim to represent the Jewish people, but he understood that the fact that the Zionist labor movement had founded the Haganah gave it the right to claim leadership of the Yishuv. As a consequence, the Zionist fighting force attracted the Yishuv's best young talents. Military commanders garnered the adulation of the public, and military service became the natural and accepted steppingstone to political leadership. I have noted above that not a few of the Israel Defense Force's first generation of senior officers, those who fought in the War of Independence in 1948, were men for whom the 1929 riots had been a formative experience.

The events of 1929 also highlight the huge abyss that yawns between the Jewish and Arab reading of history. Many Jews view the riots as a link in the chain of Jewish oppression that began with the Egyptian captivity and continued in European pogroms and the persecution that Jews experienced in some Islamic lands. According to this view, Jews are persecuted simply because they are Jews ("In every generation they rise up to destroy us," as the Passover Haggadah says), and without reference to what they do or do not do, as we saw Ze'ev Jabotinsky say, and as many Israelis and Jews who reject criticism of Israeli actions assert today. They often support their argument by mentioning that the Arabs massacred Jews in Hebron and Safed in 1929, long before the establishment of the Jewish state in 1948 and the occupation of the West Bank and Gaza in 1967.

But that is not how the attackers of 1929 saw it. They — or, more precisely, the ideologues who speak in their name — stress how well Jews were treated in Palestine and other Muslim lands under the Ottoman Empire. They reject any accusation of antisemitism and locate the riots in an entirely different context: that of the struggle of indigenous people against colonialist powers. In their view, the Jews of Palestine — who, with British backing, acted to make Palestine into a Jewish national home — were legitimate targets of attack.

No victim, and certainly not the Jews, can accept that they were legitimately attacked. The year 1929 thus marks the beginning of the greatest Jewish-Arab rivalry of all — the competition over who is the aggressor and who the victim, who the overlord and who the underdog.

The Jews were certainly the obvious victims of the riots, at least in Hebron and Safed. They came to the Land of Israel to live in their native land, to take refuge from pogroms and slaughter, and they found themselves under attack in their own homes or while plowing fields they had bought with good money. But from the Arabs' point of view, the homes the Jews built stood in an Arab land, and the fields they plowed were Arab soil. No matter that the Old Yishuv had no intention of taking control of the country. No matter that the Zionists did not stage an armed invasion of Palestine but rather arrived to settle there in large numbers. They did so under the protection of British bayonets with the goal of transforming the land into a Jewish one. How else could that project be described if not as a colonial offensive? Of course, this account of Zionism utterly disregards the long-standing connection of the Jews to their ancestral land, but as far as the Arabs were concerned that connection was meaningless in political terms, and in no way could justify making Palestine Jewish.

Native peoples have at times committed brutal massacres in uprisings against colonial powers. In *The Wretched of the Earth* (1965), the Afro-French revolutionary and philosopher Frantz Fanon offered an ideological and psychological grounding for such violence. He claimed, in fact, that it was necessary and positive: only by committing massacres, he argued, could the oppressed truly liberate themselves. Furthermore, he declared, colonialists were no less violent and cruel.

The vantage point of the Zionist movement is that of the Eastern European

Jew who sought refuge from antisemitism. Accordingly, Zionists viewed their movement as both a national liberation movement and a humanitarian rescue mission. As such, Zionism from the start rejected, as it continues to do today, its characterization as a colonialist enterprise. This viewpoint has led Zionists to avert their gaze from their own crimes against innocent Arabs in 1929, such as the lynchings Jews staged in Jerusalem and Simha Hinkis's murder of a family in Jaffa.

We saw this clearly at the beginning of our journey. In a conflict between peoples, each side feels the pain of its losses more strongly than it does the pain of the other side. Each side mourns its own dead, not the dead of its enemies. This is not deliberate or malicious disregard—it is natural and understandable. Consequently, each side feels and displays elemental gratitude toward those who risked their lives to defend their compatriots.

Now it is time to offer another insight. These emotions are great forces in the consolidation of each side's historical narrative. There is no need for a guiding hand from above for each side to center the story it tells itself on its own victims, and for it to mythologize as heroes those who risked or gave their lives for the nation. Furthermore, such gratitude shunts aside questions about just who the people those heroes fought were, why they fought them, who they killed, and how they killed them. National narratives are not formed by leaders instructing their people; rather, they are products of the encounters between the perceptions and feelings of the public at large with the structured ideology of the leadership.

So national narratives are born. It is the reason why each side fashions a closed world of its own. Only within a world shut off from the view of the other side can each side mourn its dead and celebrate its heroes. When two nations are at war, one side's heroes, be it Hinkis or 'Ata al-Zir, must necessarily be the other side's villains.

In this book I have endeavored to introduce to my readers the opposing historical stories of each side. Inevitably, the book largely runs counter to the instincts of many Israelis and Palestinians, many Jews and Arabs. I have also augmented these national stories with alternative stories that were offered within each community—there were many voices on each side. That is another conclusion I draw from my study of the events of 1929: these alternative stories, ultimately marginalized by the mainstream narratives, are an important part of the picture and can teach us no less than the central story can. Yes, there is an Arab national story and a Jewish national story about what happened in 1929. But not all Arabs and not all Jews necessarily subscribe to their own community's central story. Neither society is homogeneous, and each society produces more than one story and more than one understanding of the events. Even as the riots raged, the

Arabs of Hebron did not experience them the way Jaffa's Arabs did, and the Jews of Tiberias did not experience them the way Jerusalem's Jews did. Those who opposed bloodshed did not experience the disturbances the way those who advocated violence did; those whose goal was compromise did not experience them as firebrands did. The courage of the rescuers, those Jews who saved Arabs and those Arabs who saved Jews as swords flashed and bullets whistled, shows that the mobilizing force of even the strongest national story has its limits — it cannot shatter a solid moral stand, whether that morality is clearly voiced or instinctive.

Were the killings of 1929 a necessary result of the Arab-Zionist encounter in Palestine? Determinists argue that everything that happened had to happen, that the bloody conflict between the two peoples not just in 1929 but before and after was the inevitable outcome of the fateful Zionist-Arab encounter; of the contradictory national aspirations of the Jews and Arabs; and of the view that if one religion is the true faith, all others must be lies. But there are other possibilities. There are more nuanced theologies, national rivalries that develop into alliances, and more complex and nuanced views of national rights. The decisions made and deeds done by Jews and Arabs prior to and during the riots were those of human beings. At each decision point, at each occasion of spontaneous action, there are a range of possibilities. Need I cite once more the villagers of Sur Baher who saved four Jewish miners; Abu Shaker 'Amru of Hebron; Shimon, the owner of the Bukharan quarter grocery store; and Mina Albert of Meah She'arim to show that at any given moment other actions were possible? That it is possible to behave differently from the majority, against the current of hatred of the Other? Need I cite once more Haidar 'Abd al-Shafi and his pain at the death of innocents, and the members of Brit Shalom who sought to divert the two nations from their collusion course? The marginality of these people in the two national narratives about 1929 shows how difficult it is to adopt a viewpoint that is not in concert with the reigning chauvinistic perspective of each side. Yet their actions prove that under the deep currents of nationalism and religion, below the enmity and extremism and rivalry, something else flows — a sense of human brotherhood, of a common recognition of the fundamental value of human life. That is what makes it possible to declare that the killings of 1929, and other killings by Arabs of Jews and by Jews of Arabs, those before and since and those that still may happen, were not and are not preordained.

Acknowledgments

I want to express my gratitude to many people who, sometimes without their knowledge, contributed to the writing of this book: to friends, colleagues, and lovers of literature who discussed with me ideas over coffee, read chapters of the manuscript, traveled with me to Hebron and other sites, and brought to my attention sources I was unaware of; to readers of drafts who told me how much they appreciated what I was doing, and to readers who were less enthusiastic; to friends and research assistants who went with me (and sometimes without me) to archives to photocopy documents; to historians whose understanding of history helped me to shape my own through agreement or through debates; and of course, to people whose friendship makes my life nicer. The following list does not include all of them, and I hope and believe that my friends whom I do not mention will not take it too hard. So, thank you Ra'anan Alexandrowicz, Noa Bar-Haim, Dina Berdichevsky, Amitai Barouchi-Unna, Sigi B. Be'eri, Hillel Ben Sasson, Efrat Ben Ze'ev, Yigal Bronner, Karam Dana, Assaf David, Ron Dudai, Adva Falk, Yair Kunitz, Jeremy Hodges, Amos Noy, Iyad al-Sarraj, Hagit Ofran, Eli Osheroff, Amnon Paran, Assaf Peled, Amnon Raz-Krakotzkin, Yehuda Shenhav, and Yael Shenker. Special thanks go to Yosef Barnea, who shared documents from his collection with me, and to Avner Wishnitzer. Many thanks to the following archives for granting me permission to use photographs for this book: The Library of Congress; The Central Zionist Archives; and Israel's Government Press Office. I also thank the Karkar family of al-Quds (Jerusalem), who lent me the photograph of the family's grandfather.

The Hebrew University of Jerusalem is my academic home, and it deserves a special thank you. And the Cohen-Bars of Jerusalem — my wife Efrat and my children Aya, Avshalom, and Osnat — deserve even more. Their love and happiness helped me not to fall into despair and depression while delving, day after day, into detailed descriptions of massacres and lynchings.

At the age of fifty-three, I come to realize how much my consciousness was shaped by my parents, Esther and Aharon, who both passed away during the writing of this book. My mother came to Jerusalem from Poland in 1933 at the age of five, and my father came to our city from Afghanistan in 1951 at the age of twenty-six. Both were happy and proud to be part of what they saw as the revival of the Jewish people in their ancestral homeland, and they had no qualms about the right of Jews to establish their national home in Eretz Yisrael, known in Arabic as Palestine. Nevertheless, this did not prevent them from seeing the Palestinian Arabs as equal human beings. Their generation, however, left to the next generations the question of whether it is possible to reconcile Jews' and Arabs' rights in this country. This book is dedicated to their memory, and to the memory of the rescuers, both Jews and Arabs.

Bibliography

Archives

BGA — Ben-Gurion Archive, Sde Boker
BHMA — Beit Hameiri Museum and Archive, Safed
    (Institute for the Study of Jewish Settlement in Safed)
CZA — Central Zionist Archives, Jerusalem
HHA — Haganah History Archives, Tel Aviv
ISA — Israel State Archives, Jerusalem
JTA — Jewish Telegraphic Agency. www.jta.org
NLI — The National Library of Israel, Jerusalem
TNA — The National Archives of the United Kingdom, London

Newspapers — Hebrew

Besheva'
Davar
Do'ar Hayom
Ha'am
Ha'aretz
Hadashot
Hahavatzelet
Hatzefirah
Hatzofeh
Hazit Ha'am
Hed haMizrah
Herut
Ma'ariv
Yediot Aharonot

Newspapers — Arabic

al-Aqdam
al-Yarmuk
al-Zamar
Filastin
Mir'aat al-Sharq
Sawt al-Haqq

Other Items

Abadi, Mahmoud al. 1977. *Safad fi al-Tarikh*. Amman: n.p.
'Alami, Ahmad al. 2000. *Thawrat al-Buraq*. Jerusalem (?): n.p.
'Abasi, Mustafa. 1999. "Tzefat biTekufat haMandat: Hebetim Hevratiyim uPolitiyim."
    PhD diss., University of Haifa.
Abdel Shafi, Haidar, et al. 1998. "Reflections on al-Nakba." *Journal of Palestine Studies*
    28, no. 1: 5–35.
Abu Gharbiyya, Bahjat. 1993. *Fi Khidam al-Nidal al-'Arabi al-Filastini: Mudhakkarat
    al-Munadil Bahjat Abu Gharbiyya*. Beirut: Mu'asasat al-Dirasat al-Filastiniyya.

Abushedid, Yehuda. 2012. "Hebron: Nitsol Tarpat Yehuda Abushedid." Accessed January 12, 2015. https://www.youtube.com/watch?v=Y6NiKDXS1eU.

Adalah. 2007. *Adalah's 2006 Annual Report of Activities*. May. Accessed January 11, 2015. http://www.adalah.org/eng/publications/annualrep2006.pdf.

Agnon, Shmuel Yosef. 1953a. "MeOyev LeOhev." In Shmuel Yosef Agnon, *Elu VaElu*. Tel Aviv: Schocken. 490–82.

———. 1953b. "MiTahat La'Etz." In Shmuel Yosef Agnon *Elu VaElu*. Tel Aviv: Schocken. 461–89.

———. 1976. *Me'Atzmi el 'Atzmi*. Tel Aviv: Schocken.

Ahimeir, Yossi. 2010. "Bein Prof. Netanyahu le-Dr. Ahimeir." Accessed January 13, 2015. http://www.beitaba.com/content.php?id=54.

Amikam, Yisra'el. 1929. *HaHatkafah 'al haYishuv haYehudi beEretz Yisra'el beTaRPa"T*. Haifa: Defus Omanut.

Arce, Agustin. 1979. "Hagbalot 'al Hofesh Tenua'tam shel Yehudei Yerushalayim beShalhei Yemei haMamlukim uveReshit haTekufah ha'Othomanit." In *Perakim beToldot Yerushalayim biYemei haBeinayim*, edited by Ze'ev Kedar and Zvi Baras, 206–20. Jerusalem: Ben-Zvi Institute.

Arendt, Hannah. 1951. *The Origins of Totalitarianism*. New York, Harcourt, Brace.

Arnon, Noam. 2005. "Hitnagdut haMimsad haTziyoni leHidush haYishuv haYehudi beHevron la'ahar Pera'ot TaRPa"T." *Mehkarei Yehudah veShomron* 14:233–46.

'Askari, Yasar al. 1989. *Qussat Madinah: Safad*. Cairo (?): Munazzamat al-Tahrir al-Filastiniyya.

Atkins, S. C. 1929. "Report of Mr. S. C. Atkins, A.D.S.P. Jaffa, 25.8.29." In *Report of the Acting Commandant, Police and Prisons Department, on the Disturbances in Palestine, August, 1929*, enclosure 11 (D). Jerusalem: n.p.

Avisar, Oded, 1970a. "HaHitnakhalut." In *Sefer Hevron: 'Ir haAvot veYishuvah beRe'i haDorot*, edited by Oded Avisar, 482–98. Jerusalem: Keter.

———, ed. 1970b. *Sefer Hevron: 'Ir haAvot veYishuvah beRe'i haDorot*. Jerusalem: Keter.

———. 1970c. "Yishuv SheLo Pasak." In *Sefer Hevron: 'Ir haAvot veYishuvah beRe'i haDorot*, edited by Oded Avisar, 37–76. Jerusalem: Keter.

———. 1973. *Sefer Teveriah: 'Ir Kinarot veYishuvah beRe'i haDorot*. Jerusalem: Keter.

Bakri, Rafiq al-. 2005. "Min Sijn Akka." Hadash, June 20. Accessed January 3, 2015. http://www.aljabha.org/index.asp?i=12770.

Baitar, Said al. 2006. *Al-Hares*. Gaza: Palestine Women's Information & Media Center. Accessed January 3, 2015. https://www.youtube.com/watch?v=-uOVMwefB_c.

Barakat, Rana. 2007. "Thawrat al-Buraq in British Mandate Palestine: Jerusalem, Mass Mobilization and Colonial Politics 1928–1930." PhD diss., University of Chicago.

Bartal, Israel. 1997. "Du-Kiyum Nikhsaf: Eliahu Elyashar 'al Yahasei Yehudim ve'Aravim." Introduction to Eliahu Elyashar, *Lihyot 'im Falastinim*, ix–xx. Jerusalem: Misgav Yerushalayim.

Barzin, A. Z. 1930. *Yizkor 'Am Yisra'el et Kdoshei Av TaRPa"T*. Jerusalem: Defus Merkaz.

Be'er, Haim. 1993. "'Ir Lo Museget." In *Minha liYerushalayim: BiMlot K"H Shanim leIhudah*, edited Eli Shiller, 199–219. Jerusalem: Ariel.

Behar, Moshe. 2007. "Palestine, Arabized Jews and the Elusive Consequences of Jewish and Arab National Formations." *Nationalism and Ethnic Politics* 13, no. 4: 581–611.

Ben Gurion, David. 1970. "Ahota shel Yerushalyim." In *Sefer Hevron: 'Ir haAvot veYishuvah beRe'i haDorot*, edited by Oded Avisar, 15–16. Jerusalem: Keter.

Ben-Hamo, Shlomo. 1979. "HaKri'ah leShalom leOr haHalakhah." In *Leket Ma'amarim: 'Eduyot veTemunot BiMlot Hamishim Shanah leMe'ora'ot TaRPaT beHevron*, edited by Hannah Barnes, 14–25. Kiryat Arba: n.p.

Ben-Zion, Simha. 1970. "BeDamayikh Hayyi." In *Sefer Hevron: 'Ir haAvot veYishuvah beRe'i haDorot*, edited by Oded Avisar, 409–56. Jerusalem: Keter.

Berenzon, Zvi. 2000. "MiYaldut BiTzefat leBagrut Biyerushalayim." In *Sefer Berenzon*, edited by Aharon Barak and Haim Berenzon, 31–81. Jerusalem: Nevo.

Betzalel, Yitzhak. 2007. *Noladetem Tzionim: HaSefaradim beEretz Yisra'el beTzionut ubeTehiyat ha'Ivrit beTekufah haOthomanit.* Jerusalem: Ben-Zvi Institute.

Brenner, Uri. 1980. *HaKibbutz HaMe'uchad baHaganah, 1923–1939.* Tel Aviv: HaKibbutz HaMe'uchad.

Brenner, Yosef Haim. 1911. *MiKan umiKan.* Warsaw: Sifrut.

———. 1962. *Kol Kitvei Y.H. Brenner.* Edited by M. Z. Poznanski. Vol. 2. Tel Aviv: HaKibbutz HaMe'uchad.

———. 1985. *Ktavim.* 4 vols. Tel Aviv: HaKibbutz HaMe'uhad.

Broide, Gideon. 1997. *Yashru ba'Aravah Mesilah: Yeshayahu Broide vehaHanahalah haTzionit.* Jerusalem: published by the author.

Broza, Meir, and Tzari Broza. 1994. *Motza: Sipur Eretz-Yisra'eli.* Jerusalem: Kana.

Cohen, Amnon. 1984. *Jewish Life under Islam: Jerusalem in the Sixteenth Century.* Cambridge, MA: Harvard University Press.

———. 2003. *Yehudim beVeit haMishpat haMuslemi: Hevrah, Kalkalah, veIrgun Kehilati beYerushalayim haOthomanit, baMe'ah haTesha'-Esreh.* Jerusalem: Ben-Zvi Institute.

———, with Elisheva Simon-Pikali and Ovadiah Salameh. 1996. *Yehudim beVeit haMishpat haMuslemi: Hevrah, Kalkalah, veIrgun Kehilati beYerushalayim haOthomanit, baMe'ah haShemonah-'Esreh.* Jerusalem: Ben-Zvi Institute.

Cohen, Dov. 2009. *VaYelchu Sheneihem Yahdav: Na'ar Amerika'i haMuva 'al Yedei Imo leHevron sheLifnei Shmonim Shanah, Mutal leTokh Nisyonot, Pera'ot, Kesha'ei haYomyom uMilhamot haDat beEretz Yisra'el.* Jerusalem: Feldheim.

Cohen, Hillel. 2008. *Army of Shadows: Palestinian Collaboration with Zionism, 1917–1948.* Translated by Haim Watzman. Berkeley: University of California Press.

Cohen, Mark R. 1994. *Under Crescent and Cross: The Jews in the Middle Ages.* Princeton, NJ: Princeton University Press.

Cohen, W. Naomi. 1988. *The Year after the Riots: American Responses to the Palestine Crisis of 1929–1930.* Detroit, MI: Wayne State University Press.

Commission on the Palestine Disturbances of August 1929. 1930. *Report of the Commission on the Palestine Disturbances of August 1929.* 3 vols. London: H. M. Stationery Office.

Curtis, William Elroy. 1903. *Today in Syria and Palestine.* Chicago: Fleming H. Revell.

Dabbagh, Mustafa Murad al. 2002. *Biladuna Filastin.* 10 vols. Kafr Qara': Dar al-Huda.

De Lacretelle, Jean Charles Dominique. 1854. *Napoleon: His Army and His Generals; Their Unexampled Military Career.* New York: Leavitt and Allen.

Dinur, Ben-Zion, chief ed. 1973. *Sefer Toldot HaHaganah.* 3 vols. Tel Aviv: Am Oved.

Doumani, Bishara. 1992. "Rediscovering Ottoman Palestine: Writing Palestinians into History." *Journal of Palestine Studies* 21, no. 2: 5–28.

Dudai, Ron. 2012. "'Rescues for Humanity': Rescuers, Mass Atrocities, and Transitional Justice." *Human Rights Quarterly* 34, no. 1:1–38.

Elkayam, Mordechai. 1990. *Yafo–Neveh Tzedek: Reshitah shel Tel Aviv*. Tel Aviv: Ministry of Defense.

———. 1994. *Arbaʻim Shenot Yishuv Yehudi beʻAzah, Beʼer Shevaʻ, veHakamat Havat Ruhama*. Netzarim: Center for Jewish Heritage in Gaza.

Elyashar, Eliahu. 1997. *Lihyot ʻim Falastinim*. Jerusalem: Misgav Yerushalayim.

Eshel, Tzadok. 1973. *Hativat Karmeli beMilhemet haKomemiyut*. Tel Aviv: Ministry of Defense Publishing House.

Fanon, Frantz. *The Wretched of the Earth*. 1965. Translated by Constance Farrington. New York: Grove.

Far, Mustafa al. 2009. *Madinat al-Lidd: Mawqaʻan wa-Shaharatan waTaʼrikhatan wa-Niḍalan*. Beirut: al-Massa al-ʻArabiyya lal-Darasat wa-al-Nashar.

Fogelman, Shay. 2011. "Port in a Storm." *Haʼaretz Magazine*, June 3. Accessed January 12, 2015. http://www.haaretz.com/weekend/magazine/port-in-a-storm-1.365729.

Frumkin, Gad. 1954. *Derekh Shofet biYerushalayim*. Tel Aviv: Dvir.

Geiger, Binyamin. 2011. *Ahad miZiknei Tzfat*. Givatayim: Dapei Hayyim.

Gera, Gershon. 1984. *HaNadiv HaLo Nodaʼ*. Tel Aviv: Modan.

Ginosar, Pinhas, and Mordechai Bar-On. 2000. "Raʼyonot ʻim Aluf (Mil.) Yisraʼel Tal." *Iyyunim biTekumat Yisraʼel* 10:15–86.

Gottesman, Leo. 1930. *The Martyrs of Hebron: Personal Reminiscences of Some of the Men and Women Who Offered up Their Lives during the Massacre of August 24, 1929 at Hebron, Palestine, and of Some Who Were Spared*. New York: n.p.

Grayevski, Pinhas Ben Zvi. 1929. *Halaley BatʼAmi: Zikaron-Kadosh lehaKedoshim vehaTehorim sheNehergu beEretz Yisraʼel beShavuaʻ haDamim, Yemei haPeraʼot vehaZevaʼot Av HaTaRPaʼT—Shemoteihem veTemunoteihem*. Jerusalem: published by the author.

Greenberg, Uri Zvi. 1990–2013. *Kol Ktavav*. Edited by Dan Meron. 18 vols. Jerusalem: Bialik Institute.

Haetzni, Elyakim. 1999. "Pogrom TaRPaʼT veTismonet Yehudei heHasut ʻAkhshav." *Netiv* 69–70:32–36.

Hajjab, Nimr. 2005. *Al-Shaʼir al-Shaʻabi al-Shahid Nuh Ibrahim*. Amman: al-Yazuri.

HaKotel HaShavuy. 2011. Jerusalem: Neturei Karta (?).

Halperin, Shmuel Elazar. 1980. *Sefer HaTzeʼetzaʼim: Ilan Yuhasin leTzeʼetzei Maran Rabi Shneur Zalman miLiadi*. Jerusalem: n.p.

Hammuda, Samih. 2011. "Habbat al-Buraq 1929." *Hawliyyat al-Quds* 11 (summer): 65–79.

Harusi, Avner. 2009. "Shir Eres LeAvner." In *Hadashot Ben Ezer*, edited by Ehud Ben Ezer. Accessed January 5, 2015. https://library.osu.edu/projects/hebrewlexicon/hbe/hbe00411.php.

Haskin, Gilad. 2008. "Mekomam shel Shikulim Etiʼim–Musariʼim beHafʻalat haKoah viYisumam beFoʻal, meReshit haHityashvut haTzionit beEretz-Yisraʼel veʻAd Hakamat haMedinah, 1882–1948." PhD diss., University of Haifa.

Hazan, Meir. 2009. *Metinut: HaGishah haMetunah beHapo'el Hatza'ir uveMaPA"I, 1905–1945.* Tel Aviv: Am Oved.

Heller, Yosef. 1989. *LeH"i: Ide'ologyah vePolitikah, 1940–1949.* Jerusalem: Shazar Center.

Hinkis, Simha. 1957. "Yafo beTarpat." In *Yafo: Mikra'ah Historit Sifrutit: Perakim beDivrei Yemei ha'Ir MeReshitah ve'Ad Yameinu,* edited by Yosef Aricha, 229–32. Tel Aviv: Tel Aviv–Jaffa Municipality, Department of Education and Culture.

Hitzoni, B. "Brit HaSatan." *Yerushalayim.* November 6, 1929, 3.

Ibn Hanbal, Ahmad. 1978. *Al-Musnad.* 6 vols. Beirut: al-Maktaba al-Islamiyya.

Ja'bari, Tareq al. 1999. "Thawrat 'Am 1929 wa-Majriyyat Ahdathiha fi al-Khalil." Master's thesis, Hebron University.

Jabotinsky, Ze'ev. 1923. "The Iron Wall." Accessed October 25, 2014. http://www .jabotinsky.org/multimedia/upl_doc/doc_191207_49117.pdf.

Jabrah, Taysir. 1995. *Samahat Mufti al-Quds Rais al-Majlis al-Islami al-Shar'i al-Hajj Mohammad Amin al-Hussayni: Dirasah fi Nashatihi al-Dini 1921–1937.* Irbid, Jordan: Dar al-Furqan.

Jacobson, Abigail. 2003. "Sephardim, Ashkenazim and the Arab Question in Pre-First World War Palestine: A Reading of Three Zionist Newspapers." *Middle Eastern Studies* 39, no. 2: 105–30.

Kahane, Meir. 1980. *LeShikim be'Eineichem.* Jerusalem: Institute of the Authentic Jewish Idea.

Kana'na, Sharif, and Nihad Zaitawi. 1987. *Al-Qura al-Falistiniyya al-Mudammara: Dir Yasin.* Bir Zeit: Bir Zeit University.

Karsh, Efraim. 2001. "Nakbat Haifa: Collapse and Dispersion of a Major Palestinian Community." *Middle Eastern Studies* 37, no. 4: 25–70.

Katinka, Baruch. 1961. *Me'Az ve'ad Henah.* Jerusalem: Kiryat Sefer.

Kaufman, Menahem. 1998. *The Magnes-Philby Negotiations, 1929.* Jerusalem: Magnes.

Kayyali, 'Abd al-Wahhab. 1970. *Ta'rikh Filastin al-Ḥadith.* Beirut: al-Mu'asasa al-Arabiyya lil-Dirasat wal-Nashr.

———. 1988. *Watha'iq al-Muqawama al-Filastiniyya Al-Arabiyya 1918–1939.* Beirut: Mu'asasat al-Dirasat al-Filastiniyya.

Khalidi, Rashid. 1997. *Palestinian Identity: The Construction of Modern National Consciousness.* New York: Columbia University Press.

Khalidi, Walid. 2008. "The Fall of Haifa Revisited." *Journal of Palestine Studies* 37, no. 3: 30–58.

Kimmerling, Baruch, and Joel S. Migdal. 1993. *Palestinians: The Making of a People.* New York: Free Press.

Kramer, Gabi. 1998. "Nisyonot Yehudim Lirkosh Nikhsei Waqf leyad haKotel haMa'aravi beShelhei haTekufah ha'Osmanit." *Jama'ah* 2:29–45.

Lampel, Maz. 1954. *Laila Tov.* Tel Aviv: Tsabar.

Landau, Betzalel. 1985. "HaYishuv HaHasidi beHevron." In *Kerem haHasidut,* edited by David Haim Zilbershlag, part 2, 183–257. Jerusalem: Zekher Naftali Institute for the Study of Hasidism.

Lapidot, Yehuda. n.d. "Pra'ot Tarpat." *Daat.* Accessed January 11, 2015. http://www.daat .ac.il/encyclopedia/value.asp?id1=1720.

Lavsky, Hagit. 1990. *BeTerem Por'anut: Darkam veYihudam shel Tzionei Germaniah, 1918–1932*. Jerusalem: Magnes.

Lax, Ofra. 2009. "HaGerush Me'Aza." *BeSheva*, July 23, 24–26.

Leibowitz, Yeshayahu, and Gerta Leibowitz. 2010. *Shaya': Kitvei Shaharut shel Prof Yeshayahu Leibowitz veRa'ayato Gerta leVeit Vinter*. Edited by Henry Wasserman. Jerusalem: Carmel.

Lewis, Bernard. 1984. *The Jews of Islam*. Princeton, NJ: Princeton University Press.

Lockman, Zachary. 1996. *Comrades and Enemies: Arab and Jewish Workers in Palestine, 1906–1948*. Berkeley: University of California Press.

Londres, Albert. 2008. *HaYehudi haNoded Higia': 'Itonai Tzarfathi be'Ikvot haYehudim*. Translated by Michal Ilan. Binyamina: Nahar.

Lussin, Yigal, dir. 2005. *Pillar of Fire: Chapters in the History of Zionism*. Jerusalem: Israel Broadcast Authority.

Ma'ayta, Mohammad al. 1950. "Al-Khalil." *Sawt al-Khalil* 1:11.

Malak, Hanna 'Issa. 1993. *Dhikriyat al-'A'ilat al-Yafiyya: Bayn al-Madi wa-al-Ḥader*. Jerusalem: published by the author.

Malkin, Ahuvia. 2007. *HaAktivist: Sipur Hayav shel Eliyahu Golumb*. Tel Aviv: Am Oved.

Mandel, Jonah. 2011. "Muslim Sectarianism and the Jewish Connection." *Jerusalem Post*, May 31.

Mani, Menasheh. 1963. *Hevron veGiboreha*. Tel Aviv: Yavneh.

———. 1970. "R. Eliahu Mani." In *Sefer Hevron: 'Ir haAvot veYishuvah beRe'i haDorot*, edited by Oded Avisar, 100–107. Jerusalem: Keter.

Manna, Adel. 1995. *A'lam Filastin fi Awakhir al-'Ahd al'Uthmani*. Beirut: Mu'asasat al Dirasat al-Filastiniyya.

Marcus, Itamar, and Nan Jacques Zilberdik. 2011. "PA TV: Western Wall Area To Be Turned into Arab Housing Neighborhood." Palestinian Media Watch, August 17. Accessed January 6, 2015. http://palwatch.org/main.aspx?fi=157&doc_id=5490.

Meiraz, Yair. 2007. "Meir Meiraz (Mizarizki): Yair Kotev 'Al Abba." Accessed January 4, 2015. http://www.gshavit.net/site/wordDocs/Roots/Aba%20Meir%20Mizarizki.htm.

Milikowsky, Natan. 1994. *'Am uMedinah*. Tel Aviv: Yediot Aharonot.

Montefiore, Moses, and Judith Montefiore. 1983. *Diaries of Sir Moses and Lady Montefiore*. Edited by Louis Loewe. 2 vols. London: Jewish Historical Society of England.

Morgenstern, Eliahu. *Meshihiyut veYishuv Eretz Yisra'el baMahatzit haRishonah shel haMeah haY"T*. Jerusalem: Ben-Zvi Institute.

Morris, Benny. 1999. *Righteous Victims: A History of the Zionist-Arab Conflict, 1881–1999*. New York: Alfred A. Knopf.

———. 2008. *1948: A History of the First Arab-Israeli War*. New Haven, CT: Yale University Press.

———. 2011. "The Liar as Hero." *New Republic*. April 7. Accessed October 25, 2014. http://www.newrepublic.com/article/books/magazine/85344/ilan-pappe-sloppydishonest-historian.

———. 2013. "Bikoret Sefer: TaRPa"T: Shenat haEfes biSikhsukh haYehudi-'Aravi." *Midah*, November 22. Accessed January 13, 2015. http://tinyurl.com/ntfc8b4.

Nedivi, Gershon. 1983. *Shorashim BeHevron*. Kiryat Arba: published by the author.

Oliphant, Laurence. 1887. *Haifa, or Life in Modern Palestine*. Edinburgh: William Blackwood and Sons.

Ovadiah, Moshe. 2009. "HaYehudim haMa'aravim beArba' 'Arei haKodesh miMilhemet ha'Olam haRishonah 'ad Tom haShilton haBriti." PhD diss., Bar-Ilan University.

Pappé, Ilan. 2006. *The Ethnic Cleansing of Palestine*. Oxford: Oneworld.

———. 2011. *The Rise and Fall of a Palestinian Dynasty: The Husaynis, 1700–1948.* Berkeley: University of California Press.

Pines, Shimon. "HaShoter HaYehudi sheNidon leMavet." *Davar Leyeladim* 1979, 45: 1572–75.

Porath, Yehoshua. 1974. *The Emergence of the Palestinian-Arab National Movement, 1918–1929*. London: Frank Cass.

———. 1977. *The Palestinian Arab National Movement, 1929–1939: From Riots to Rebellion*. London: Frank Cass.

Rajabi, Shehada al. 2000. *Al-Jaliya al-Yahudiyya fi al-Khalil 1917–1936*. Nablus: Al-Najah University.

Ratner, Yohanan. 1983. *Hayai veAni*. Translated by Rina Kalinov. Jerusalem: Schocken.

Ratosh, Yonathan. 1974. *Shirei Yonatan Ratosh*. Tel Aviv: Hadar.

Ratzabi, Shalom. 1996. "Anti-Tzionut veMetah Meshihi beHaguto shel Rav Shalom Dovber." *Hatzionut* 20:77–101.

Ravad, Ahiya. 2005. "'Akko: Tahalukha leZekher ha'Shahidim' sheRatzhu Yehudim beTaRPaT." Ynet, June 17. Accessed October 22, 2014. http://www.ynet.co.il/articles /0,7340,l-3100396,00.html.

Raz, Avi. 2012. *The Bride and the Dowry: Israel, Jordan and the Palestinians in the Aftermath of the June 1967 War*. New Haven, CT: Yale University Press.

Raz-Krakotzkin, Amnon. 2005. "Ein Elohim aval Hu Natan Lanu et haAretz." *Mita'am* 3:71–76.

Rotenberg, Leon. 1935. *Collection of Judgments of the Courts of Palestine, 1919–1933*. Tel Aviv: Rotenberg.

Rustum, Asad. 1938. *The Royal Archives of Egypt and the Disturbances in Palestine, 1834*. Beirut: American University of Beirut.

Sa'id, Hasan Ibrahim. 2006. *Yafa: Min al-Ghazu al-Naboliyoni ila Hamalat Ibrahim Fasha*. Beirut: Mu'asasat al Didrasat al-Filastiniyya.

Salmon, Yocheved, and Yehudit Golan. 2003. *Elef 'Olamot: Sipuro shel haRav Avraham Yohanan Blumental uMif'al Hayav—Beit haYeladim "Tzion," Shazur beZikhronot Hamisha Dorot biYerushalayim*. Jerusalem: Feldheim.

Samrin, Ghaleb Mohammad. 2003. *Qaryati Qalunya: Al-Ard wa-al-Jadhur, Filastinuna fi Qussat Qariya*. Amman: Dar al-Yara'.

Samuel, Maurice. 1929. *What Happened in Palestine: The Events of August 1929, Their Background and Their Significance*. Boston: Stratford.

Sapir, Yitzhak. 2006. "Tzava'ah sheLo Mul'ah." *Eretz Aheret*, March, 54–56.

Sarugo, Shai. 2010. "MiMifratz Saloniki leMifratz 'Ako: Perek beKoroteihem shel Dayagim 'Ivri'im bein Shetei Milhamot ha'Olam." *Pe'amim*, nos. 122–23: 9–39.

Sasson, Eliahu. 1979. *BaDerekh el haShalom: Igrot veSihot*. Tel Aviv: Yediot Aharonot.

Schneurson, Yehuda Leib. 1980. *Hoy Hevron, Hevron*. Edited by Shabtai Ben-Dov. Tel Aviv: Ya'ir.

Schölch, Alexander. 1993. *Palestine in Transformation, 1856–1882: Studies in Social, Economic, and Political Development*. Translated by William C. Young and Michael C. Gerrity. Washington: Institute for Palestine Studies.

Scholem, Gershom. 1931. "Bemai Ka Mifalgei." *She'ifoteinu*, September, 93–102.

———. 1989. *'Od Davar: Pirkei Morashah veTehiyah*. Tel Aviv: Am Oved.

Schwartz, Yoel ben Aharon. 1994. *Hevron: MiPra'ot TaRPa"T 'ad Me'ora'ot TaShNaD*. Jerusalem: Eretz Hemdah.

Sefer haMishpatim: Din veHeshbon miKol Mishpatei haMe'ora'ot beEretz Yisra'el beAugust 1929. 1930. Tel Aviv: Tel Aviv.

Segev, Tom. 2000. *One Palestine, Complete: Jews and Arabs under the British Mandate*. Translated by Haim Watzman. New York: Metropolitan.

Sehayek, Shaul. 1991. "Demut haYehudi beRe'i ha'Itonut ha'Aravit bein haShanim 1858–1908." PhD diss., Hebrew University.

Sela, Avraham. 1994. "The 'Wailing Wall' Riots (1929) as a Watershed in the Palestine Conflict." *Muslim World* 84, nos. 1–2: 60–94.

Semelin, Jacques. 2007. *Purify and Destroy: The Political Uses of Massacre and Genocide*. Translated by Cynthia Schoch. New York: Columbia University Press.

Shalev, Yitzhak. 1951. *Ohezet 'Anaf Shaked: Shirim*. Tel Aviv: Hebrew Writers Association.

Shapira, Anita. 2007. *Yigal Allon: Native Son*. Translated by Evelyn Abel. Philadelphia: University of Pennsylvania Press.

Shashar, Michael. 1992. *Sihot 'al Rehav'am Gandi-Ze'evi*. Tel Aviv: Yediot Aharonot.

Shenhav, Yehouda. 2006. *The Arab Jews: A Postcolonial Reading of Nationalism, Religion, and Ethnicity*. Stanford, CA: Stanford University Press.

Shina'a, Tal'at. 1993. *Ayyam Zaman: al-Ta'rikh al-Shafawi Lil-Urdun wa-Filastin*. Amman: al-Aahliyya.

Shlush, Aharon. 1991. *MiGalabiyah leKova' Tembel: Sipurah shel Mishpaha*. Tel Aviv: published by the author.

Shlush, Yosef Eliahu. 1931. *Parshat Hayai: 1870–1930*. Tel Aviv: Strod and Sons.

Shor, Natan. 1983. *Toldot Tzfat*. Tel Aviv: Am Oved.

Shuqayri, Ahmad al. 1969. *Arba'un 'Aman fi al-Haya al'Arabiyya wa-al-Dawliyya*. Beirut: Dar al-Nahar.

Slonim, M. S. 1970. "Harav HaShahor." In *Sefer Hevron: 'Ir haAvot veYishuvah beRe'i haDorot*, edited by Oded Avisar, 309. Jerusalem: Keter.

Stanley, Arthur Penrhyn. 1863. *Sermons Preached before His Royal Highness during His Tour of the East*. London: J. Murray.

Sternberg, Yehiel. 2003. "Perakim miToldot Hayav shel haRAVa"D Rabi Yisra'el Ya'akov Fisher ZTz"L. *Yeshurun* 13:363–478.

Supreme Muslim Council. 1925. *A Brief Guide to al-Haram al-Sharif*. Jerusalem: Supreme Muslim Council.

Tamari, Salim. 2008. *Mountain against the Sea: Essays on Palestinian Society and Culture*. Berkeley: University of California Press.

Tawil, Mohammad al. 1930a. *Al-Haqa'iq al-Majhula: Idatrabat Filastin al-Akhira*. Jerusalem: Malul.

———. 1930b. *Eikh Hithilu haMeòra'ot beFalastina*. Tel Aviv: Hashahar.

———. 1930c. *Tariq al-Hayah*. Haifa: Farafatiq.

Tawil, Raymonda. 1979. *Ma'atzar Bayit: Sipurah shel Ishah Falastina'it*. Translated from the Arabic by Naomi Gal. Jerusalem: Adam.

Tazi, 'Abd al-Hadi al. 1984. "*Awqaf al-Masgharbe fil-Quds al-Sharif*." In *Dirasat fi Ta'rikh wa-Aathar Filastin*, edited by Shawki Sha'ath, 193–247. Aleppo, Syria: University of Aleppo.

Tikochinsky, Shlomo. 2009. "Yeshivot haMusar miLita leEretz Yisra'el: Yeshivat Slabodkah veShitatah haHinukhit, 'Aliyatah veHitbasesutah beEretz Yisra'el haMandatorit." PhD. diss., Hebrew University.

Tzfania, Shmuel. 2011. "Me'ora'ot Tarpa"t im Tsilumei ha-Nitsolim veha-Korbanot." Accessed January 11, 2015. https://www.youtube.com/watch?v=-0-wDGrETXk.

Tubasi, Isma'il. 1979. *Kifah al-Sha'ab al-Filastini 1908–1965*. Amman: n.p.

Tuqan, Ibrahim. 1966. *Al-Diwan*. Beirut: Dar al-Adab.

Von Weisel, Niva. n.d. "BeKifley HaHistoria." Accessed January 11, 2015. http://tinyurl.com/k5r8aez.

Weinshal, Ya'akov. 1956. *HaDam asher baSaf: Toldot Hayav uMoto shel Avraham ben Mordechai Stern*. Tel Aviv: Hamatmid.

Wijler, Eithan. 2005. "Kitzonim Tzionim uFalastinim: HaMikreh shel Me'oraot TaRPa"T beTzefat." MA thesis, University of Haifa.

Wikalah al-Yahudiyyah, al. 1931. *Al-Ṣuhyoniyyah wa-al-Amakin al-Islamiyyah al-Muqddasah fi Filastin*. Jerusalem: Beit al-Maqdis.

Yaari, Avraham. 1943. *Igrot Eretz Yisra'el: SheKatvu haYehudim haYoshvim baAretz leAheihem shebaGolah miYemei Galut Bavel ve'ad Shivat Tzion shebeYameinu*. Ramat Gan: Masada.

———. 1960. "'Aliyat haHasidim haHamonit leEretz Yisra'el." *Mahanayim* 46, no. 1: 136–45.

Yana'it Ben-Zvi, Rachel, Yitzhak Avrahami, and Yerah Etzion. 1973. *HaHaganah biYerushalayim: 'Eduyot veZichronot mePi Haverim*. Jerusalem: Kiryat Sefer.

Ye'or, Bat. 1985. *The Dhimmi: Jews and Christians under Islam*. Translated by David Maisel, Paul Fenton, and David Littman. Rev. and enl. ed. London: Associated University Presses.

Zahavi, Leon. 2005. *Lehud o Beyahad: Yehudim ve'Aravim beFalastina (E"Y), 'al-pi Mismekhei haKomintern (1919–1943)*. Jerusalem: Keter.

Zaki, Ahmad. 1930. *Taṣḥiḥ al-Aglaṭ al-Waridah fi Difa' al-Ustadh Yellin al-Muḥami 'an al-Yahud*. Jerusalem: Dar al-Aytam.

Index

Page numbers in *italics* indicate photos or tables. Surnames beginning with article "al-" are alphabetized by the name that follows the article.

favoring Zionists, 186; civil servants'
conflicting pressures, 30–31; on
clemency for prisoners, 247–48; on
colonialism, 16–20, 191, 251, 258; colonialism as impetus to sectarianism,
13; and executed Arabs as martyrs,
246; grouping of all Jews into Zionist
movement, 55, 107, 134, 139–41, 158–59,
256–57; al-Haram al-Sharif (Temple
Mount), 59–63, 83; Hebron massacre,
124–25, 128–29, 132–35, 139–43, 149,
156–61, 162; historical memory, 251–52,
257–58; Jaffa violence, 1–2, 7–8, 20,
57–58; Jewish land purchases as
dispossession, 170–71, 173–74; Jews
as prophet killers, 241; merging of
Zionists with all Jews, 55, 107, 134,
139–41, 158–59, 256–57; moral high
ground claim, 172–73, 178, 189–90;
Motza massacre, 166–67, 168–69,
173–77; nationalism, 56–57, 69–70, 74,
82–83, 180, 190, 215, 221; on ownership
of history in Holy Land, 34–35, 76;
ownership of holy sites, 67; Palestinian
leaders, *205*; peaceful and prosperous
relations with local Jews, 15, 158–59,
258; police loyalty dilemma, 30–31;
post-riot legacy, 218–22; pre-1920s
sympathy for persecuted Jews, 4;
Safed, 203–4, 205; sovereignty issue, 8,
18, 48, 191–92; summary of casualties,
xxi; suppression and whitewashing of
crimes, xiv, 251–52; suspicion of Jewish
intention to take over Jerusalem,
72–73; true religion belief and
discrimination against Jews, 150–53;
victimhood claim in Jerusalem, 87; on
Zionism, 3, 8, 81, 172–73, 227–33, 228;
Zionist disrespect for Arab culture,
48, 50
Arab Revolt (1936–39), 89, 167, 169,
176–77, 206, 233
Arafat, Yasir, 72
Arce, Agustin, 64
Arendt, Hannah, 221

Aricha, Yosef, 10–12
Arlosoroff, Haim, 77–78, 211–12
Arman, Yosef, 185
Armoni, Gedalia, 113–14
Asfur, Hasan, 194–95
Ashkenazi (European) Jews, 49–56, 122,
136. *See also* Haredi Jews; Moscobim;
Zionist movement
Ashkenazi shamash at Western Wall,
101–2
al-'Askari, Yasar, 192–93
al-'Atari, 'Aisha, 87–88
Atkins, S. C., 21
Auadis, Yitzhak, 45–47
Avigur, Shaul, 9
Avisar, Oded, 131
Avrahami, Levi, 168
'Awda, Ahmad, 251
'Awn, Sheikh 'Abd al-Ghani, 29
'Awn, 'Ali, 29
'Awn, Ibrahim Khalil, 29
'Awn family, murder of, 2, 9–10, 25–26,
28–30, 253. *See also* Hinkis, Simha
Azra, Azyumardi, 13

Baeck, Leo, 238
Bahalul, 'Abd al-Gani 'Ali, 29
Bahalul, Halima, 29
Bahalul, Maryam, 29
Bajayo, Hakham Haim, 165
Balfour, Arthur, 44
Balfour Declaration, 190, 229
Barakat, Husni, 175
Barakat, Rana, 93
Bartal, Israel, 50
Barzin, A., 123–24
Basta, Halim, 30–31
Bayit VeGan neighborhood, 113–14, 200
Bedouin tribes, 41–42, 214
Be'er, Haim, 112
Be'er Tuvia (Jewish village), 28
Beisan, casualties in, *xxi*
Beit Alfa kibbutz, 41–42
Beit HaKerem neighborhood, 127, 200
Ben-Avi, Itamar, 97

al-Haram al-Sharif. *See* Temple Mount

Harari-Bloomberg, Moshe, 27

Haredi Jews: Edah Haredit, 112, 113, 227; as non-Zionist, 52, 132, 257; Rabbi A. Fisher and Alperstein, 112–16, 149; relationship to Zionism, 139–43; on right-wing in Yishuv as riot instigators, 221; on Zionists as riot instigators, 227. *See also* Chabad sect of Hasidim; Slabodka Yeshiva

Haritonov, Shalom, 41

Hartuv farming settlement, xviii, 27

Harusi, Emmanuel, 39–41, 42–44, 114

Hasan, 'Ali 'Abdallah, 90

Hasan Beq Mosque, 10, *11*, 20, 25, 44

Hasidic Judaism, 41, 68. *See also* Chabad sect of Hasidim

HaTzadik, Shimon, 94

Hatzofeh (religious Zionist newspaper), 91

havlaga, 36

Hawa, Habib, 54

Hazit Ha'am (right-wing Jewish newspaper), 211

Hebron: Arab perspectives on Jews and massacre, 124–25, 128–29, 132–35, 139–43, 149, 156–61, 162; British perspective, 132, 161–62, 163–64; casualty numbers, *xxi*, 160–61; Chabad relationship to Zionism, 137–39, 142–43; as climax of riots, 2; fathoming the why question, 123, 143–44; Haredi relationship to Zionism, 137–43, 148–49; Jewish Old Cemetery, *164*; Jewish perspectives on massacre, 124–32, 133–35; legal consequences for Arabs, 161; long-term disposition of Jewish community in, 131–32, 164–65; massacre descriptions, 123, 127, 130–31, 159–60; Mussar movement and Jewish settlement in, 135; peaceful and prosperous Arab-Jewish relations, 144–46, 147–48, 150; police action (delayed) against attackers, 163–64; prelude to massacre, 122–23; rape charges,

123–24; rescue of Jews by Arabs, 128, 145, 161, 162–63; sectarian transformation of, 135–37; *Sefer Hevron* memorial and power of historical memory, 131; Slabodka Yeshiva, 122, 134, 139, 141–43, 148–49, 152, 156, 164–65; Tomb of the Patriarchs, 149–55, 161

Hecht, Yosef, 116, 117

Heichal, Eliahu-Dov, 125

Heichal, Yisrael-Aryeh, 125

Herzl, Theodor, 138, 174

Hexter, Maurice, 236

Hijazi, Fuad, 198, 204, 240–41, 243–44

Hijazi, Hajj Hussein, 45

Hinkis, Simha: appeal of conviction, 37–39, 44; on British investigation, 28–29; celebration of release from prison, *249*; commutation of death sentence, 37, 194–95, 237; conviction and sentencing of, 35–37; description of incident leading to 'Awn family murders, 25–26; early release mission for, 246, 248; Harusi's song for, 39–40; indictment of, 29–30; legend creation for, 249–51; post-prison life, 248–49; Schiff's testimony, 31; *Sefer Toldot* as source for, 9; and Stavsky and Rosenblatt, 211; trial of, 33

historical memory: contribution to 1929 riots, 2; focus on victimhood, 87, 125, 126, 253, 259; inclusive vs. exclusive history, xii–xiv; Jewish vs. Arab, 257–58; knowledge gaps between participants/observers and later perspective, 6–7; late 20th-century perspective, 252–53; massacres, comparison challenges, 125–28; nationalism bias, 20, 132–33, 259–60; ownership of Holy Land's history, 75–76; *Sefer Hevron* memorial, 131; worldview as filter for, 128; on Zionism, 228

Hitler, Adolf, 210, 211

Hittin, 181

Holy City. *See* Jerusalem

homeland status, Jewish vs. Arab justifications for, 8. *See also* Land of Israel

Hovevei Zion, 49

Hurva Synagogue, 80

Hussayn, Faisal ibn, 85

Hussayni, Hamdi, 23–24

al-Hussayni, 'Abd al-Qader, 179, 219, 223

al-Hussayni, Ahmad Rasem, 170

al-Hussayni, Mufti Hajj Amin, 23, 53–54, 67, *86*, 86–87, 92–95, 203–4, 246, 247, 252–53

al-Hussayni, Su'ad, 174

Ibrahim, Noah, 245–46

Ibrahimi Mosque. *See* Tomb of the Patriarchs

ideology's trumping of historical details, 129, 259

Ikar, Avraham, 147

inclusive vs. exclusive history, xii–xiv

intermarriage, 197–98

Islam. *See* religion

Islamic rule, and independence of Arabs, 82–83. *See also* Ottoman Empire

al-Israa (the night journey), 60

Israel Defense Force (IDF), 126, 154, 163, 177, 179, 200, 257. *See also* 1948 Arab-Israeli War

al-Ja'bari, Mohammad 'Ali, 165

al-Ja'bari, Tareq, 132–33, 152

Jaber, Mohammad, 213, 222–23

Jabotinsky, Ze'ev, 88, 99, 100, 211, 221–22, 231

Jaffa: 'Abd al-Qader al-Muzaffar, 24–25; Arab perspective, 1–2, 7–8, 20, 57–58; 'Awn family's murder, 2, 9–10, 25–26, 28–30, 253; Baruch Rozin, 20; British perspective, 21–23, 44; context for riots in, 2, 6, 12–13; Hamdi Hussayni, 23–24; immigrants in, 35; influence on Safed, 194–96; Isma'il Tubasi, 22–23, 25, 44; knowledge gaps, 6–7; Mizrahim's tensions with Zionists vs.

Arabs, 48–56; Napoleon's massacre, 12–13; prostitution in Tel Aviv, 209; summary of casualties, xxi; Yitzhak Auadis, 45–47; Yosef Urfali, 44–45, 57, 211, 246, 248; Zionist narrative, 9–10. *See also* Hinkis, Simha; Tel Aviv

Jaffa Gate events, 96–97

Jaffa Road events, 97–100

Jamjum, Mohammad, 239–40, 243, 244–45

Sheikh Jarrah neighborhood, 94

Jerusalem: Alperstein legend, 111–16; Arab suspicion of Jewish intentions, 72–73; ascertaining start of riots, 2, 87–92, 95, 120–21; British policing perspective, 91, 97, 106, 118; Bukharan quarter, 89–92, 107–9, 138–39, 173, 213, 223; Gurji courtyard, 102–3, 106, 167, 173, 254; impact of riots on Motza massacre, 166; initial attempts to quell violence, 90–91; Islamic rule and relations with Jews and Christians, 63–65; Jaffa Gate events, 96–97; Jaffa Road events, 97–100; Jewish independence in Palestine, 82; and Jewish motivation to own holy sites, 76–84; lack of mention in sacred texts, 61–62; Maghrebi quarter, 68–70, 75–76, 106–7; Meah She'arim, 98, 107–14, 118–21, 254; messianic redemption theme, 79–82, 83–84; Nabi 'Ukkasha desecration, 116–18, *117*; Nablus Gate events, *xxi*, 102–6; Peasants' Revolt of 1834, 14; press's role in reporting violent events, 87–90; Rabbi Kook on riots, 74–75, 91; as sacred to Muslims and Jews, 60–63; summary of casualties, *xxi*; Talpiot, 27, 214, 222–23; victimhood claim from both sides, 87; Zionism and initial confrontations in, 90–91. *See also* Temple Mount

Jewish Agency, 126, 235–38, 238–39

Jewish-Arab Communist Party, 233–34

Jewish immigration, 16–17, 48–49, 70, 169–74, 190, 255–56

of in Yishuv, 51–52; relations with
Arabs in Acre, 53–54; relation to
Zionist movement, 46–56, 257; role in
Jerusalem riots, 89; Safed's violence as
focused on, 197
Mizritzki, Meir, 114–15
Mizritzki-Meiraz, Yair, 114–15
Mohammad (Prophet), 60–63, 73
money lending, 144–46
Montagna, Rabbi Yosef da, 15
Montefiore, Moses, 70, 152–53
moral issues: and Jewish real estate
deals in Palestine, 171–72; Jewish vs.
Arab claiming of moral high ground,
172–73, 178, 189–90; for mass actions,
17
Morris, Benny, 253–54
Morton, Geoffrey, 32
Moscobim, 48, 49, 161. See also Ashkenazi
(European) Jews
Moshenson, Nelly, 45–47
Motza: British perspective, 180–81,
185–87; and Jerusalem riots, 59;
Jewish perspective, 169, 175–76; land
purchases and Jewish immigration,
169–74; Maklef family massacre,
174–87; Ratosh's poem, 207–8;
Samrin's perspective, 166–67, 168–69,
173–77; survivors of massacre, 178–79;
trial for Maklef family massacre,
180–87; and Y. Landberg, 167–68
Motza: Sipur Eretz-Yisra'eli (Motza:
A story of the Land of Israel) (Broza
and Broza), 169
Mubashir, Shawkat, 194
Munkacz, admor of, 227
Muslim-Christian Association, 156–57
Muslim perspectives. *See* Arab Muslim
perspectives; religion
Mussar movement, 135
al-Muzaffar, Sheikh 'Abd al-Qader, 22,
24–25, 94

Nabi 'Ukkasha desecration, 116–18, *117*
Nablus Gate events, *xxi*, 102–6

Nadav, Tzvi, 42–44
Nahalat Shiva neighborhood, 98, 99, 173
Nahmani, Yosef, 204
Nakba, xi. *See also* 1948 Arab-Israeli War
Napoleon Bonaparte, 12–13
Nashashibi, Fakhri, 96, 253
Nashashibi, Ragheb, 236
Nashashibi clan, 252
nationalism: and Arab grouping of all
Jews into Zionist threat, 139–41; and
Balfour Declaration, 56; and bias in
historical writing about massacres,
20, 132–33, 259–60; Brit HaBiryonim,
71; dividing of Mizrahi Jews from
Arab neighbors, 52, 55; as driver for
both Jews and Muslims, 57, 74, 82–83
190, 180, 191, 215, 221; and existential
religious dispute over Holy Land,
65, 66, 69, 73–74, 84–85, 86–87; and
Kohn's opposition to dependence
on Britain, 226; press promotion of,
88; sovereignty concept, 8, 18, 27, 48,
191–92; Zionist influence on Arab
Muslim, 56–57; in Zionist movement,
18–19, 47, 56–57
Natour, Qadi Ahmad, 117
Nazareth, casualties in, *xxi*
Nazi Germany: Arab alliance with, and
opposition to, 25, 93; comparing
Zionist parties to, by Jewish rivals,
210–11
Nedivi, Gershon, 161
Netanyahu, Ben-Zion, 231
Netanyahu, Binyamin, 202
Neturei Karta, 227, 228
Neveh Shalom neighborhood, 45–46
New Historians, 252–53
1921 riots, 2–5, 87–92, 95–96, 120–21
1929 riots: and anti-Zionism/non-
Zionism among Jews, 225–34,
237; British Mandate's post-riot
relationship with Jews, 223–30; death
penalty debate and commutation,
234–46; as determined destiny vs.
free choice, 260; post-riot legacy for

Samrin, Ghaleb, 59, 63, 65–66, 76–77, 166–67, 168–69, 173–78, 182–83

Samrin, Mohammad (al-Badawi), 175, 176–77, 178, 181–83

Samuel, Herbert, 79–80, *81*, 85

Samuel, Maurice, 19–20

Sapir Yitzhak, 141, 147

Saraya of Safed, 199–200

al-Sarraj, Iyad, 220

Sasson, Eliahu, 103, 241–43

Satmar Hasidim, 227

Saunders, Police Commandant, 106

Savlani, Menahem, 103

al-Sayyed, Khamis Salem, 107–9

Schiff, Shlomo, 31–32

Schlesinger, Rabbi Akiva, 141

Schneurson, Shalom Ber, 137

Schneurson, Yehuda Leib, 145, 146, 147–48, 156

Schneurson, Rabbi Yosef Yitzhak, 152, 217–18

Scholem, Gershom, 109–11, 225–26, 227

Second Aliyah, 2, 47, 48–49

secular Zionism, 84, 139–40

Sefer Hevron (The Hebron book) (Avisar), 131, 160

Sefer Toldot HaHaganah (The Haganah history book) (Dinur), 9–10, 67, 92–93, 148, 218, 233

Segev, Tom, 67, 90

Sehayek, Shaul, 4

Semelin, Jacques, 129, 134

Sephardi Jews: on death penalty debate, 235–36; in Hebron, 122, 136, 137, 142, 158–59; initial settlement during Ottoman Empire, 47, 191; socialist Zionism's marginalization of, 49; Zionist mission to get support from, 47, 190–91

Sephardi shamash at Western Wall, 101–2

Sephardi Synagogue, Hebron, *136*

seventh step at Tomb of the Patriarchs, 152–55

Shach, Rabbi Zalman, 175

al-Shafi, Muhi al-Din, 220

Shalev, Yitzhak, 85

Shami, Yitzhak, 142

Shammas, Mikhail, 110–11

Shapira, Anita, 206

Shapira, Avraham, 239

Shapira, Tzvi, 181

Sharon, Gilad, 56

Sharvit, Meir, 106

Shaw Commission: ascertaining the start of the riots, 118–21; al-Hussayni's testimony, 92–93, 94–95; interest in Jewish participation in Zionism in Hebron, 142–43; Luke on atmosphere at Wall prior to riots, 72–73; photo, *119*; Porath's accusation of Arab bias in, 67; and rape allegations in Hebron, 124; Saunders on lack of order to stop Muslim attackers, 106; von Weisel's testimony, 100; White's deposition for Jaffa Gate events, 96; Y. Broide's testimony, 90–91

Sheetrit, Bechor Shalom, 109, 180–81

Shehada, Bulus, 224–25

Sher, Avraham, 3

Shertok, Moshe, 242

Shlush, Aharon, 51

Shlush, Yosef Eliahu, 49–50

Shor, Natan, 192

Shturman, Zelig, 212–14, 222–23

al-Shuqayri, Ahmad, 54, 246

al-Shuqayri, Sheikh As'ad, 53–54, 246

Shvili family, 103–6

Sigrist, Sgt. Alan, 97–99

Siknaj (Ashkenazi Haredim), 256. *See also* Haredi Jews

Silley, Reginald, 143

Sirkis, Miriam, 175

Six-Day War (1967), 75

Slabodka Yeshiva, 122, 134, 139, 141–43, 148–49, 152, 156, 164–65, 217

Slonim, Eliezer Dan, 130–31, 135, 136, 142, 146, 147–48, 152, 157

Slonim, Malka, 163

Slonim, Menuha Rachel, 137

influence on, 57; question of justness of cause, 255–56; on reconciling Safed's Jews and Arabs, 204; religious basis of, 56–57, 84–85, 139–41; as responsible for 1929 riots, 217–18; secular Zionism, 84, 139–40; socialist Zionism, 2–3, 36, 49–50, 78–79; sovereignty issue, 27, 48, 191–92; al-Tawil's connection to, 219; Western Wall, 1, 58, 66, 70–72, 221. *See also* anti-Zionism/non-Zionism among Jews

al-Zir, 'Ata, 239, 243, 244–45
al-Zir, Salih, 183–84
Zu'bi, Salah, 181